C000173348

# Power Maths

# Year 4A

## A Guide to Teaching for Mastery

Series Editor: Tony Staneff

# Contents

# Introduction

## Foreword by the series editor and author, Tony Staneff

For far too long in the UK, maths has been feared by learners – and by many teachers, too. As a result, most learners consistently underachieve. More crucially, negative beliefs about ability, aptitude and the nature of maths are entrenched in children's thinking from an early age.

Yet, as someone who has loved maths all my life, I've always believed that every child has the capacity to succeed in maths. I've also had the great pleasure of leading teams and departments who share that belief and passion. Teaching for mastery, as practised in China and other South-East Asian jurisdictions since the 1980s, has confirmed my conviction that maths really is for everyone and not just those who have a special talent. In recent years, my team and I at Trinity Academy, Halifax, have had the privilege of researching with and working alongside some of the finest mastery practitioners from the UK and beyond, whose impact on learners' confidence, achievement and attitude is an inspiration.

The mastery approach recognises the value of developing the power to think rather than just do. It also recognises the value of making a coherent journey in which whole-class groups tackle concepts in very small steps, one by one. You cannot build securely on loose foundations – and it is just the same with maths: by creating a solid foundation of deep understanding, our children's skills and confidence will be strong and secure. What's more, the mindset of learner and teacher alike is fundamental: everyone can do maths … EVERYONE CAN!

I am proud to have been part of the extensive team responsible for turning the best of the world's practice, research, insights, and shared experiences into *Power Maths*, a unique teaching and learning resource developed especially for UK classrooms. *Power Maths* embodies our vision to help and support primary maths teachers to transform every child's mathematical and personal development. 'Everyone can!' has become our mantra and our passion, and we hope it will be yours, too.

Now, explore and enjoy all the resources you need to teach for mastery, and please get back to us with your *Power Maths* experiences and stories!

# What is *Power Maths*?

Created especially for UK primary schools, and aligned with the new National Curriculum, *Power Maths* is a whole-class, textbook-based mastery resource that empowers every child to understand and succeed. *Power Maths* rejects the notion that some people simply 'can't do' maths. Instead, it develops growth mindsets and encourages hard work, practice and a willingness to see mistakes as learning tools.

Best practice consistently shows that mastery of small, cumulative steps builds a solid foundation of deep mathematical understanding. *Power Maths* combines interactive teaching tools, high-quality textbooks and continuing professional development (CPD) to help you equip children with a deep and long lasting understanding. Based on extensive evidence, and developed in partnership with practising teachers, *Power Maths* ensures that it meets the needs of children in the UK.

## *Power Maths* and Mastery

*Power Maths* makes mastery practical and achievable by providing the structures, pathways, content, tools and support you need to make it happen in your classroom.

To develop mastery in maths children need to be enabled to acquire a deep understanding of maths concepts, structures and procedures, step by step. Complex mathematical concepts are built on simpler conceptual components and when children understand every step in the learning sequence, maths becomes transparent and makes logical sense. Interactive lessons establish deep understanding in small steps, as well as effortless fluency in key facts such as tables and number bonds. The whole class works on the same content and no child is left behind.

## *Power Maths*

- Builds every concept in small, progressive steps.
- Is built with interactive, whole-class teaching in mind.
- Provides the tools you need to develop growth mindsets.
- Helps you check understanding and ensure that every child is keeping up.
- Establishes core elements such as intelligent practice and reflection.

## The *Power Maths* approach

### Everyone can!

Founded on the conviction that every child can achieve, *Power Maths* enables children to build number fluency, confidence and understanding, step by step.

### Child-centred learning

Children master concepts one step at a time in lessons that embrace a Concrete-Pictorial-Abstract (C-P-A) approach, avoid overload, build on prior learning and help them see patterns and connections. Same-day intervention ensures sustained progress.

### Continuing professional development

Embedded teacher support and development offer every teacher the opportunity to continually improve their subject knowledge and manage whole-class teaching for mastery.

### Whole-class teaching

An interactive, whole-class teaching model encourages thinking and precise mathematical language and allows children to deepen their understanding as far as they can.

# Introduction to the author team

*Power Maths* arises from the work of maths mastery experts who are committed to proving that, given the right mastery mindset and approach, **everyone can do maths**. Based on robust research and best practice from around the world, *Power Maths* was developed in partnership with a group of UK teachers to make sure that it not only meets our children's wide-ranging needs but also aligns with the National Curriculum in England.

### Tony Staneff, Series Editor and author

Vice Principal at Trinity Academy, Halifax, Tony also leads a team of mastery experts who help schools across the UK to develop teaching for mastery via nationally recognised CPD courses, problem-solving and reasoning resources, schemes of work, assessment materials and other tools.

## ✚ A team of experienced authors, including:

- ⚡ **Josh Lury** – a specialist maths teacher, author and maths consultant with a passion for innovative and effective maths education

- ⚡ **Trinity Academy, Halifax** (Michael Gosling CEO, Tony Staneff, Emily Fox, Kate Henshall, Rebecca Holland, Stephanie Kirk, Stephen Monaghan and Rachel Webster)

- ⚡ **David Board, Belle Cottingham, Jonathan East, Tim Handley, Derek Huby, Neil Jarrett, Stephen Monaghan, Beth Smith, Tim Weal, Paul Wrangles** – skilled maths teachers and mastery experts

- ⚡ **Cherri Moseley** – a maths author, former teacher and professional development provider

## ✚ Professors Liu Jian and Zhang Dan, Series Consultants and authors, and their team of mastery expert authors:

- ⚡ **Wei Huinv, Huang Lihua, Zhu Dejiang, Zhu Yuhong, Hou Huiying, Yin Lili, Zhang Jing, Zhou Da and Liu Qimeng**

Used by over 20 million children, Professor Liu Jian's textbook programme is one of the most popular in China. He and his author team are highly experienced in intelligent practice and in embedding key maths concepts using a C-P-A approach.

## ✚ A group of I5 teachers and maths co-ordinators

We have consulted our teacher group throughout the development of *Power Maths* to ensure we are meeting their real needs in the classroom.

# Your *Power Maths* resources

To help you teach for mastery, *Power Maths* comprises a variety of high-quality resources.

## Pupil Textbooks

Discover, Share, and Think together sections promote discussion and introduce mathematical ideas logically, so that children understand more easily.

Using a Concrete-Pictorial-Abstract approach, clear mathematical models help children to make connections and grasp concepts.

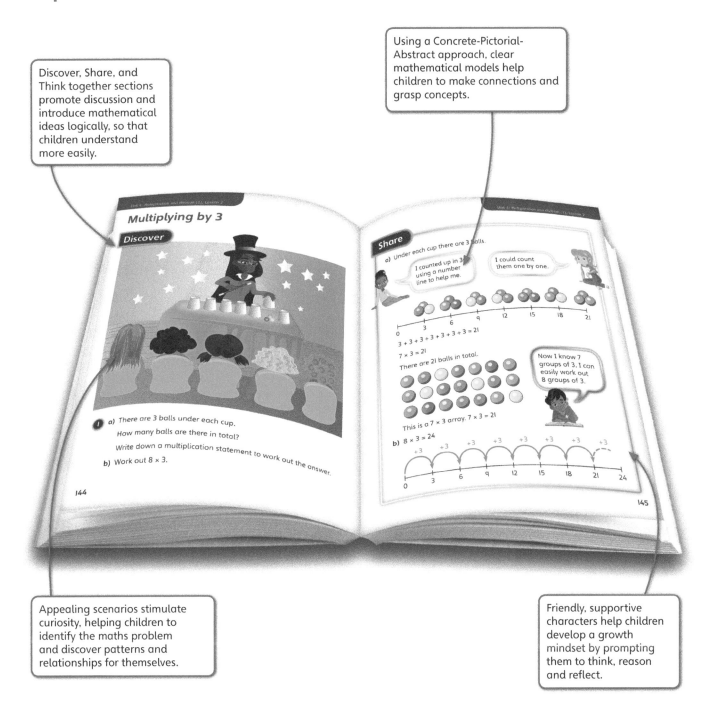

Appealing scenarios stimulate curiosity, helping children to identify the maths problem and discover patterns and relationships for themselves.

Friendly, supportive characters help children develop a growth mindset by prompting them to think, reason and reflect.

The coherent *Power Maths* lesson structure carries through into the vibrant, high-quality textbooks. Setting out the core learning objectives for each class, the lesson structure follows a carefully mapped journey through the curriculum and supports children on their journey to deeper understanding.

# Pupil Practice Books

The Practice Books offer just the right amount of intelligent practice for children to complete independently in the final section of each lesson.

The practice questions are for everyone – each question varies one small element to move children on in their thinking. Look at the different parts in question 1!

Calculations are connected so that children think about the underlying concept. In question 3, children have to write out the calculation to find the answer. Concepts are presented differently again in question 4 to challenge children.

Practice questions are finely tuned to move children forward in their thinking and to reveal misconceptions.

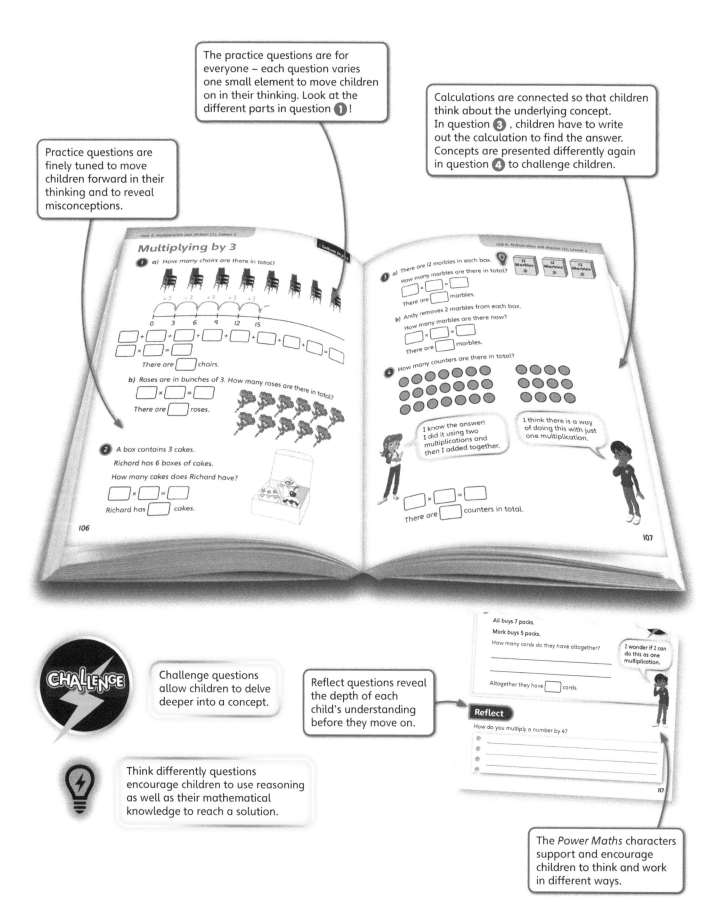

Challenge questions allow children to delve deeper into a concept.

Reflect questions reveal the depth of each child's understanding before they move on.

Think differently questions encourage children to use reasoning as well as their mathematical knowledge to reach a solution.

The Power Maths characters support and encourage children to think and work in different ways.

## Online subscriptions

The online subscription will give you access to additional resources.

### eTextbooks

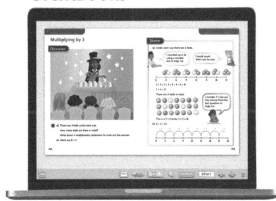

Digital versions of *Power Maths* Textbooks allow class groups to share and discuss questions, solutions and strategies. They allow you to project key structures and representations at the front of the class, to ensure all children are focusing on the same concept.

### Teaching tools

Here you will find interactive versions of key *Power Maths* structures and representations.

## Power Ups

Use this series of daily activities to promote and check number fluency.

## Online versions of Teacher Guide pages

PDF pages give support at both unit and lesson levels. You will also find help with key strategies and templates for tracking progress.

## Unit videos

Watch the professional development videos at the start of each unit to help you teach with confidence. The videos explore common misconceptions in the unit, and include intervention suggestions as well as suggestions on what to look out for when assessing mastery in your children.

## End of unit Strengthen and Deepen materials

Each Strengthen activity at the end of every unit addresses a key misconception and can be used to support children who need it. The Deepen activities are designed to be 'Low Threshold High Ceiling' and will challenge those children who can understand more deeply. These resources will help you ensure that every child understands and will help you keep the class moving forward together. These printable activities provide an optional resource bank for use after the assessment stage.

Underpinning all of these resources, *Power Maths* is infused throughout with continual professional development, supporting you at every step.

# The *Power Maths* teaching model

At the heart of *Power Maths* is a clearly structured teaching and learning process that helps you make certain that every child masters each maths concept securely and deeply. For each year group, the curriculum is broken down into core concepts, taught in units. A unit divides into smaller learning steps – lessons. Step by step, strong foundations of cumulative knowledge and understanding are built.

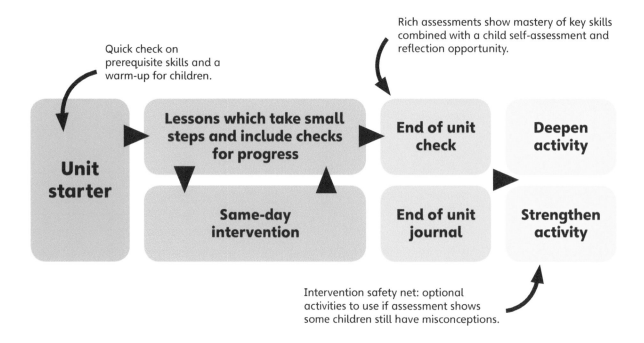

Quick check on prerequisite skills and a warm-up for children.

Rich assessments show mastery of key skills combined with a child self-assessment and reflection opportunity.

Intervention safety net: optional activities to use if assessment shows some children still have misconceptions.

## Unit starter

Each unit begins with a unit starter, which introduces the learning context along with key mathematical vocabulary, structures and representations.

- The Textbooks include a check on readiness and a warm-up task for children to complete.

- Your Teacher Guide gives support right from the start on important structures and representations, mathematical language, common misconceptions and intervention strategies.

- Unit-specific videos develop your subject knowledge and insights so you feel confident and fully equipped to teach each new unit. These are available via the online subscription.

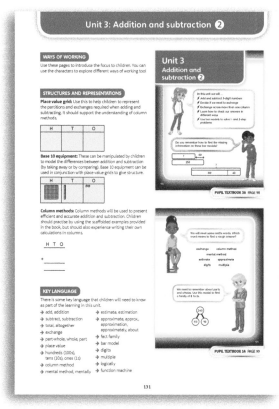

## Lesson

Once a unit has been introduced, it is time to start teaching the series of lessons.

- Each lesson is scaffolded with Textbook and Practice Book activities and always begins with a Power Up activity (available via online subscription).
- *Power Maths* identifies lesson by lesson what concepts are to be taught.
- Your Teacher Guide offers lots of support for you to get the most from every child in every lesson. As well as highlighting key points, tricky areas and how to handle them, you will also find question prompts to check on understanding and clarification on why particular activities and questions are used.

## Same-day intervention

Same-day interventions are vital in order to keep the class progressing together. Therefore, *Power Maths* provides plenty of support throughout the journey.

- Intervention is focused on keeping up now, not catching up later, so interventions should happen as soon as they are needed.
- Practice questions are designed to bring misconceptions to the surface, allowing you to identify these easily as you circulate during independent practice time.
- Child-friendly assessment questions in the Teacher Guide help you identify easily which children need to strengthen their understanding.

## End of unit check and journal

At the end of a unit, summative assessment tasks reveal essential information on each child's understanding. An End of unit check in the Pupil Textbook lets you see which children have mastered the key concepts, which children have not and where their misconceptions lie. The Practice Book includes an End of unit journal in which children can reflect on what they have learnt. Each unit also offers Strengthen and Deepen activities, available via the online subscription.

> The End of unit check presents six to nine multiple-choice questions. These questions are designed to reveal misconceptions and help you target areas that need strengthening.

> The Teacher Guide offers support with handling misconceptions.

> The End of unit journal is an opportunity for children to test out their learning and reflect on how they feel about it. Tackling the 'journal' problem reveals whether a child understands the concept deeply enough to move on to the next unit.

> In KS2, the End of unit assessment will also include one SATs-style question.

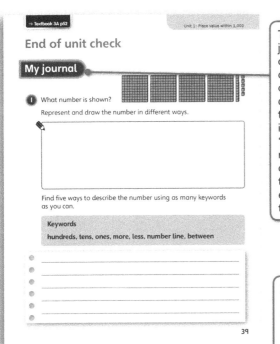

# The *Power Maths* lesson sequence

At the heart of *Power Maths* is a unique lesson sequence designed to empower children to understand core concepts and grow in confidence. Embracing the National Centre for Excellence in the Teaching of Mathematics' (NCETM's) definition of mastery, the sequence guides and shapes every *Power Maths* lesson you teach.

Flexibility is built into the *Power Maths* programme so there is no one-to-one mapping of lessons and concepts meaning you can pace your teaching according to your class. While some children will need to spend longer on a particular concept (through interventions or additional lessons), others will reach deeper levels of understanding. However, it is important that the class moves forward together through the termly schedules.

## Power Up 🕑 5 minutes

Each lesson begins with a Power Up activity (available via the online subscription) which supports fluency in key number facts.

The whole-class approach depends on fluency, so the Power Up is a powerful and essential activity.

**TOP TIP**
If the class is struggling with the task, revisit it later and check understanding.

Power Ups reinforce key skills such as times-tables, number bonds and working with place value.

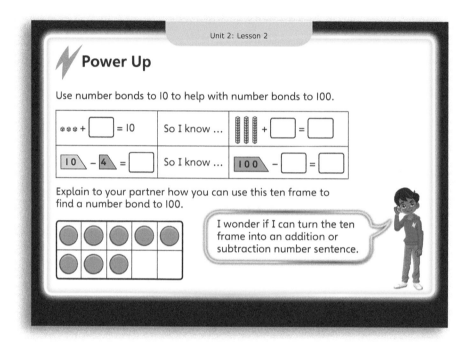

## Discover 🕑 10 minutes

A practical, real-life problem arouses curiosity. Children find the maths through story-telling.

A real-life scenario is provided for the Discover section but feel free to build upon these with your own examples that are more relevant to your class.

**TOP TIP**
Discover works best when run at tables, in pairs with concrete objects.

Question ❶ a) tackles the key concept and question ❶ b) digs a little deeper. Children have time to explore, play and discuss possible strategies.

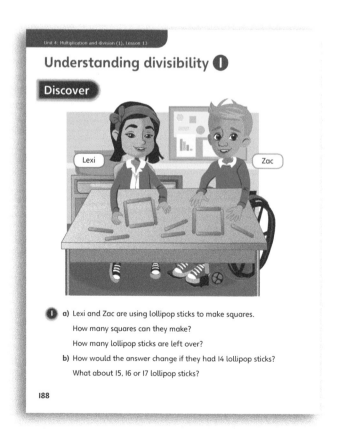

## Share 🕑 10 minutes

Teacher-led, this interactive section follows the Discover activity and highlights the variety of methods that can be used to solve a single problem.

**TOP TIP**
Bring children to the front (or onto the carpet if you have this area) to discuss their methods. Pairs sharing a textbook is a great format for this!

Your Teacher Guide gives target questions for children. The online toolkit provides interactive structures and representations to link concrete and pictorial to abstract concepts.

**TOP TIP**
Bring children to the front to share and celebrate their solutions and strategies.

## Think together

🕑 10 minutes

Children work in groups on the carpet or at tables, using their textbooks or eBooks.

**TOP TIP**
Make sure children have mini whiteboards or pads to write on if they are not at their tables.

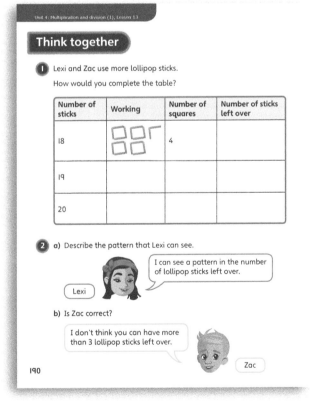

Using the Teacher Guide, model question ① for your class.

Question ② is less structured. Children will need to think together in their groups, then discuss their methods and solutions as a class.

In questions ③ and ④ children try working out the answer independently. The openness of the challenge question helps to check depth of understanding.

## Practice ⏱ 15 minutes

Using their Practice Books, children work independently while you circulate and check on progress.

Questions follow small steps of progression to deepen learning.

**TOP TIP**
Some children could work separately with a teacher or assistant.

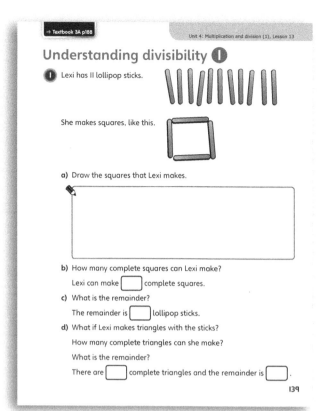

### Understanding divisibility ❶

① Lexi has 11 lollipop sticks.

She makes squares, like this.

a) Draw the squares that Lexi makes.

b) How many complete squares can Lexi make?

Lexi can make ☐ complete squares.

c) What is the remainder?

The remainder is ☐ lollipop sticks.

d) What if Lexi makes triangles with the sticks?

How many complete triangles can she make?

What is the remainder?

There are ☐ complete triangles and the remainder is ☐ .

139

Are some children struggling? If so, work with them as a group, using mathematical structures and representations to support understanding as necessary.

There are no set routines: for real understanding, children need to think about the problem in different ways.

## Reflect ⏱ 5 minutes

'Spot the mistake' questions are great for checking misconceptions.

The Reflect section is your opportunity to check how deeply children understand the target concept.

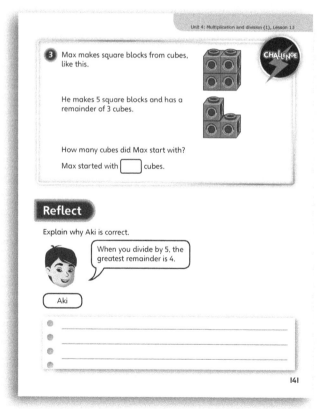

③ Max makes square blocks from cubes, like this.

**CHALLENGE**

He makes 5 square blocks and has a remainder of 3 cubes.

How many cubes did Max start with?

Max started with ☐ cubes.

### Reflect

Explain why Aki is correct.

When you divide by 5, the greatest remainder is 4.

Aki

141

The Practice Books use various approaches to check that children have fully understood each concept.

Looking like they understand is not enough! It is essential that children can show they have grasped the concept.

# Using the *Power Maths* Teacher Guide

Think of your Teacher Guides as *Power Maths* handbooks that will guide, support and inspire your day-to-day teaching. Clear and concise, and illustrated with helpful examples, your Teacher Guides will help you make the best possible use of every individual lesson. They also provide wrap-around professional development, enhancing your own subject knowledge and helping you to grow in confidence about moving your children forward together.

There is a Teacher Guide per year group for every term with unit and lesson level guidance and support.

Tips and advice on key elements such as C-P-A approaches, misconceptions, language, modelling growth mindsets and same-day intervention.

Annotations for every Pupil Textbook and Practice Book page, providing prompts for key questions to ask to expose understanding and explanations as to why key questions have been chosen.

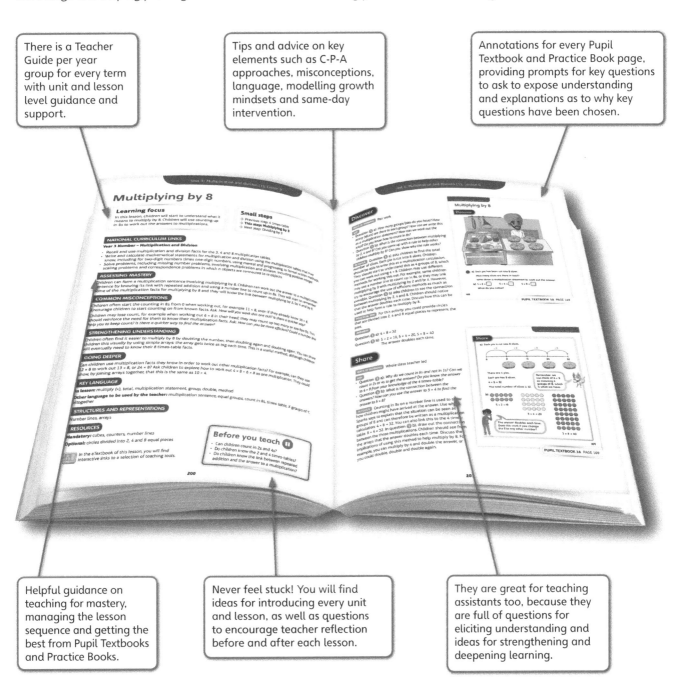

Helpful guidance on teaching for mastery, managing the lesson sequence and getting the best from Pupil Textbooks and Practice Books.

Never feel stuck! You will find ideas for introducing every unit and lesson, as well as questions to encourage teacher reflection before and after each lesson.

They are great for teaching assistants too, because they are full of questions for eliciting understanding and ideas for strengthening and deepening learning.

At the end of each unit, your Teacher Guide helps you identify who has fully grasped the concept, who has not and how to move every child forward. This is covered later in the Assessment strategies section.

# Power Maths Year 4, yearly overview

| Textbook | Strand | Unit | | Number of Lessons |
|---|---|---|---|---|
| Textbook A / Practice Book A (Term 1) | Number – number and place value | 1 | Place value – 4-digit numbers (1) | 9 |
| | Number – number and place value | 2 | Place value – 4-digit numbers (2) | 9 |
| | Number – addition and subtraction | 3 | Addition and subtraction | 15 |
| | Measurement | 4 | Measure – perimeter | 5 |
| | Number – multiplication and division | 5 | Multiplication and division (1) | 11 |
| Textbook B / Practice Book B (Term 2) | Number – multiplication and division | 6 | Multiplication and division (2) | 15 |
| | Measurement | 7 | Measure – area | 5 |
| | Number – fractions (including decimals) | 8 | Fractions (1) | 7 |
| | Number – fractions (including decimals) | 9 | Fractions (2) | 8 |
| | Number – fractions (including decimals) | 10 | Decimals (1) | 10 |
| Textbook C / Practice Book C (Term 3) | Number – fractions (including decimals) | 11 | Decimals (2) | 7 |
| | Measurement | 12 | Money | 9 |
| | Measurement | 13 | Time | 5 |
| | Statistics | 14 | Statistics | 5 |
| | Geometry – properties of shapes | 15 | Geometry – angles and 2D shapes | 10 |
| | Geometry – position and direction | 16 | Geometry – position and direction | 6 |

## Power Maths Year 4, Textbook 4A (Term I) Overview

| Strand 1 | Strand 2 | Unit | | Lesson number | Lesson title | NC Objective 1 | NC Objective 2 | NC Objective 3 |
|---|---|---|---|---|---|---|---|---|
| Number – number and place value | | Unit 1 | Place value – 4-digit numbers (1) | 1 | Numbers to 1,000 | Recognise the place value of each digit in a four-digit number (thousands, hundreds, tens, and ones) | | |
| Number – number and place value | | Unit 1 | Place value – 4-digit numbers (1) | 2 | Rounding to the nearest 10 | Round any number to the nearest 10, 100 or 1,000 | | |
| Number – number and place value | | Unit 1 | Place value – 4-digit numbers (1) | 3 | Rounding to the nearest 100 | Round any number to the nearest 10, 100 or 1,000 | | |
| Number – number and place value | | Unit 1 | Place value – 4-digit numbers (1) | 4 | Counting in 1,000s | Count in multiples of 6, 7, 9, 25 and 1,000 | Identify, represent and estimate numbers using different representations | |
| Number – number and place value | | Unit 1 | Place value – 4-digit numbers (1) | 5 | Representing 4-digit numbers | Identify, represent and estimate numbers using different representations | Recognise the place value of each digit in a four-digit number (thousands, hundreds, tens, and ones) | |
| Number – number and place value | | Unit 1 | Place value – 4-digit numbers (1) | 6 | 1,000s, 100s, 10s and 1s | Recognise the place value of each digit in a four-digit number (thousands, hundreds, tens, and ones) | Identify, represent and estimate numbers using different representations | |
| Number – number and place value | | Unit 1 | Place value – 4-digit numbers (1) | 7 | The number line to 10,000 (1) | Identify, represent and estimate numbers using different representations | Recognise the place value of each digit in a four-digit number (thousands, hundreds, tens, and ones) | |

| Strand 1 | Strand 2 | Unit | | Lesson number | Lesson title | NC Objective 1 | NC Objective 2 | NC Objective 3 |
|---|---|---|---|---|---|---|---|---|
| Number – number and place value | | Unit 1 | Place value – 4-digit numbers (1) | 8 | The number line to 10,000 (2) | Order and compare numbers beyond 1,000 | Identify, represent and estimate numbers using different representations | Recognise the place value of each digit in a four-digit number (thousands, hundreds, tens, and ones) |
| Number – number and place value | | Unit 1 | Place value – 4-digit numbers (1) | 9 | Roman numerals to 100 | Read roman numerals to 100 (i to c) and know that over time, the numeral system changed to include the concept of zero and place value | | |
| Number – number and place value | | Unit 2 | Place value – 4-digit numbers (2) | 1 | Finding 1,000 more or less | Find 1,000 more or less than a given number | | |
| Number – number and place value | | Unit 2 | Place value – 4-digit numbers (2) | 2 | Comparing 4-digit numbers (1) | Order and compare numbers beyond 1,000 | Identify, represent and estimate numbers using different representations | |
| Number – number and place value | | Unit 2 | Place value – 4-digit numbers (2) | 3 | Comparing 4-digit numbers (2) | Order and compare numbers beyond 1,000 | Identify, represent and estimate numbers using different representations | |
| Number – number and place value | | Unit 2 | Place value – 4-digit numbers (2) | 4 | Ordering numbers to 10,000 | Order and compare numbers beyond 1,000 | Identify, represent and estimate numbers using different representations | |
| Number – number and place value | | Unit 2 | Place value – 4-digit numbers (2) | 5 | Rounding to the nearest 1,000 | Round any number to the nearest 10, 100 or 1,000 | | |
| Number – number and place value | | Unit 2 | Place value – 4-digit numbers (2) | 6 | Solving problems using rounding | Solve number and practical problems that involve all of the above and with increasingly large positive numbers | | |
| Number – number and place value | | Unit 2 | Place value – 4-digit numbers (2) | 7 | Counting in 25s | Count in multiples of 6, 7, 9, 25 and 1,000 | | |
| Number – number and place value | Year 5 Number – number and place value | Unit 2 | Place value – 4-digit numbers (2) | 8 | Negative numbers (1) | Count backwards through zero to include negative numbers | Interpret negative numbers in context, count forwards and backwards with positive and negative whole numbers, including through zero | |
| Number – number and place value | Year 5 Number – number and place value | Unit 2 | Place value – 4-digit numbers (2) | 9 | Negative numbers (2) | Count backwards through zero to include negative numbers | Interpret negative numbers in context, count forwards and backwards with positive and negative whole numbers, including through zero | |
| Number – addition and subtraction | Number – number and place value | Unit 3 | Addition and subtraction | 1 | Adding and subtracting 1s, 10s, 100s, 1,000s | Add and subtract numbers with up to 4 digits using the formal written methods of columnar addition and subtraction where appropriate | Solve number and practical problems that involve all of the above and with increasingly large positive numbers | |
| Number – addition and subtraction | | Unit 3 | Addition and subtraction | 2 | Adding two 4-digit numbers (1) | Add and subtract numbers with up to 4 digits using the formal written methods of columnar addition and subtraction where appropriate | | |
| Number – addition and subtraction | | Unit 3 | Addition and subtraction | 3 | Adding two 4-digit numbers (2) | Add and subtract numbers with up to 4 digits using the formal written methods of columnar addition and subtraction where appropriate | | |

| Strand 1 | Strand 2 | Unit | | Lesson number | Lesson title | NC Objective 1 | NC Objective 2 | NC Objective 3 |
|---|---|---|---|---|---|---|---|---|
| Number – addition and subtraction | | Unit 3 | Addition and subtraction | 4 | Adding two 4-digit numbers (3) | Add and subtract numbers with up to 4 digits using the formal written methods of columnar addition and subtraction where appropriate | | |
| Number – addition and subtraction | | Unit 3 | Addition and subtraction | 5 | Subtracting two 4-digit numbers (1) | Add and subtract numbers with up to 4 digits using the formal written methods of columnar addition and subtraction where appropriate | | |
| Number – addition and subtraction | | Unit 3 | Addition and subtraction | 6 | Subtracting two 4-digit numbers (2) | Add and subtract numbers with up to 4 digits using the formal written methods of columnar addition and subtraction where appropriate | | |
| Number – addition and subtraction | | Unit 3 | Addition and subtraction | 7 | Subtracting two 4-digit numbers (3) | Add and subtract numbers with up to 4 digits using the formal written methods of columnar addition and subtraction where appropriate | | |
| Number – addition and subtraction | | Unit 3 | Addition and subtraction | 8 | Subtracting two 4-digit numbers (4) | Add and subtract numbers with up to 4 digits using the formal written methods of columnar addition and subtraction where appropriate | | |
| Number – addition and subtraction | Number – number and place value | Unit 3 | Addition and subtraction | 9 | Equivalent difference | Estimate and use inverse operations to check answers to a calculation | Round any number to the nearest 10, 100 or 1,000 | |
| Number – addition and subtraction | Number – number and place value | Unit 3 | Addition and subtraction | 10 | Estimating answers to additions and subtractions | Estimate and use inverse operations to check answers to a calculation | Round any number to the nearest 10, 100 or 1,000 | |
| Number – addition and subtraction | | Unit 3 | Addition and subtraction | 11 | Checking strategies | Estimate and use inverse operations to check answers to a calculation | | |
| Number – addition and subtraction | | Unit 3 | Addition and subtraction | 12 | Problem solving – addition and subtraction (1) | Solve addition and subtraction two-step problems in contexts, deciding which operations and methods to use and why | | |
| Number – addition and subtraction | | Unit 3 | Addition and subtraction | 13 | Problem solving – addition and subtraction (2) | Solve addition and subtraction two-step problems in contexts, deciding which operations and methods to use and why | | |
| Number – addition and subtraction | | Unit 3 | Addition and subtraction | 14 | Problem solving – addition and subtraction (3) | Solve addition and subtraction two-step problems in contexts, deciding which operations and methods to use and why | | |
| Number – addition and subtraction | | Unit 3 | Addition and subtraction | 15 | Problem solving – addition and subtraction (4) | Solve addition and subtraction two-step problems in contexts, deciding which operations and methods to use and why | | |
| Measurement | | Unit 4 | Measure – perimeter | 1 | Kilometres | Convert between different units of measure [for example, kilometre to metre; hour to minute] | | |
| Measurement | | Unit 4 | Measure – perimeter | 2 | Perimeter of a rectangle (1) | Measure and calculate the perimeter of a rectilinear figure (including squares) in centimetres and metres | | |

| Strand 1 | Strand 2 | Unit | | Lesson number | Lesson title | NC Objective 1 | NC Objective 2 | NC Objective 3 |
|---|---|---|---|---|---|---|---|---|
| Measurement | | Unit 4 | Measure – perimeter | 3 | Perimeter of a rectangle (2) | Measure and calculate the perimeter of a rectilinear figure (including squares) in centimetres and metres | | |
| Measurement | | Unit 4 | Measure – perimeter | 4 | Perimeter of rectilinear shapes (1) | Measure and calculate the perimeter of a rectilinear figure (including squares) in centimetres and metres | | |
| Measurement | | Unit 4 | Measure – perimeter | 5 | Perimeter of rectilinear shapes (2) | Measure and calculate the perimeter of a rectilinear figure (including squares) in centimetres and metres | | |
| Number – multiplication and division | | Unit 5 | Multiplication and division (1) | 1 | Multiplying by multiples of 10 and 100 | Recall multiplication and division facts for multiplication tables up to 12 × 12 | Use place value, known and derived facts to multiply and divide mentally, including: multiplying by 0 and 1; dividing by 1; multiplying together three numbers | |
| Number – multiplication and division | | Unit 5 | Multiplication and division (1) | 2 | Dividing by multiples of 10 and 100 | Recall multiplication and division facts for multiplication tables up to 12 × 12 | Use place value, known and derived facts to multiply and divide mentally, including: multiplying by 0 and 1; dividing by 1; multiplying together three numbers | |
| Number – multiplication and division | | Unit 5 | Multiplication and division (1) | 3 | Multiplying by 0 and 1 | Use place value, known and derived facts to multiply and divide mentally, including: multiplying by 0 and 1; dividing by 1; multiplying together three numbers | | |
| Number – multiplication and division | | Unit 5 | Multiplication and division (1) | 4 | Dividing by 1 | Use place value, known and derived facts to multiply and divide mentally, including: multiplying by 0 and 1; dividing by 1; multiplying together three numbers | | |
| Number – multiplication and division | | Unit 5 | Multiplication and division (1) | 5 | Multiplying and dividing by 6 | Recall multiplication and division facts for multiplication tables up to 12 × 12 | | |
| Number – multiplication and division | | Unit 5 | Multiplication and division (1) | 6 | 6 times-table | Recall multiplication and division facts for multiplication tables up to 12 × 12 | | |
| Number – multiplication and division | | Unit 5 | Multiplication and division (1) | 7 | Multiplying and dividing by 9 | Recall multiplication and division facts for multiplication tables up to 12 × 12 | | |
| Number – multiplication and division | | Unit 5 | Multiplication and division (1) | 8 | 9 times-table | Recall multiplication and division facts for multiplication tables up to 12 × 12 | | |
| Number – multiplication and division | Measurement | Unit 5 | Multiplication and division (1) | 9 | Multiplying and dividing by 7 | Recall multiplication and division facts for multiplication tables up to 12 × 12 | Solve problems involving converting from hours to minutes; minutes to seconds; years to months; weeks to days. | |
| Number – multiplication and division | | Unit 5 | Multiplication and division (1) | 10 | 7 times-table | Recall multiplication and division facts for multiplication tables up to 12 × 12 | | |
| Number – multiplication and division | | Unit 5 | Multiplication and division (1) | 11 | 11 and 12 times-tables | Recall multiplication and division facts for multiplication tables up to 12 × 12 | | |

# Mindset: an introduction

Global research and best practice deliver the same message: learning is greatly affected by what learners perceive they can or cannot do. What is more, it is also shaped by what their parents, carers and teachers perceive they can do. Mindset – the thinking that determines our beliefs and behaviours – therefore has a fundamental impact on teaching and learning.

## Everyone can!

*Power Maths* and mastery methods focus on the distinction between 'fixed' and 'growth' mindsets (Dweck, 2007).[1] Those with a fixed mindset believe that their basic qualities (for example, intelligence, talent and ability to learn) are pre-wired or fixed: 'If you have a talent for maths, you will succeed at it. If not, too bad!' By contrast, those with a growth mindset believe that hard work, effort and commitment drive success and that 'smart' is not something you are or are not, but something you become. In short, everyone can do maths!

## Key mindset strategies

A growth mindset needs to be actively nurtured and developed. *Power Maths* offers some key strategies for fostering healthy growth mindsets in your classroom.

### It is okay to get it wrong

Mistakes are valuable opportunities to re-think and understand more deeply. Learning is richer when children and teachers alike focus on spotting and sharing mistakes as well as solutions.

### Praise hard work

Praise is a great motivator, and by focusing on praising effort and learning rather than success, children will be more willing to try harder, take risks and persist for longer.

### Mind your language!

The language we use around learners has a profound effect on their mindsets. Make a habit of using growth phrases, such as, 'Everyone can!', 'Mistakes can help you learn' and 'Just try for a little longer'. The king of them all is one little word, 'yet ... I cannot solve this ... yet!' Encourage parents and carers to use the right language too.

### Build in opportunities for success

The step-by-small-step approach enables children to enjoy the experience of success. In addition, avoid ability grouping and encourage every child to answer questions and explain or demonstrate their methods to others.

[1]Dweck, C (2007) *The New Psychology of Success*, Ballantine Books: New York

# The *Power Maths* characters

The *Power Maths* characters model the traits of growth mindset learners and encourage resilience by prompting and questioning children as they work. Appearing frequently in the Textbooks and Practice Books, they are your allies in teaching and discussion, helping to model methods, alternatives and misconceptions, and to pose questions. They encourage and support your children, too: they are all hardworking, enthusiastic and unafraid of making and talking about mistakes.

## Meet the team!

**Creative Flo** is open-minded and sometimes indecisive. She likes to think differently and come up with a variety of methods or ideas.

**Determined Dexter** is resolute, resilient and systematic. He concentrates hard, always tries his best and he'll never give up – even though he doesn't always choose the most efficient methods!

'Let's try again.'

'Mistakes are cool!'

'Have I found all of the solutions?'

'Let's try it this way …'

'Can we do it differently?'

'I've got another way of doing this!'

'I'm going to try this!'

'I know how to do that!'

'Want to share my ideas?'

**Curious Ash** is eager, interested and inquisitive, and he loves solving puzzles and problems. Ash asks lots of questions but sometimes gets distracted.

'What if we tried this …?'

'I wonder …'

'Is there a pattern here?'

**Miaow!**

Sparks the Cat

**Brave Astrid** is confident, willing to take risks and unafraid of failure. She is never scared to jump straight into a problem or question, and although she often makes simple mistakes she is happy to talk them through with others.

# Mathematical language

Traditionally, we in the UK have tended to try simplifying mathematical language to make it easier for young children to understand. By contrast, evidence and experience show that by diluting the correct language, we actually mask concepts and meanings for children. We then wonder why they are confused by new and different terminology later down the line! *Power Maths* is not afraid of 'hard' words and avoids placing any barriers between children and their understanding of mathematical concepts. As a result, we need to be planned, precise and thorough in building every child's understanding of the language of maths. Throughout the Teacher Guides you will find support and guidance on how to deliver this, as well as individual explanations throughout the Pupil Textbooks.

Use the following key strategies to build children's mathematical vocabulary, understanding and confidence.

## Precise and consistent

Everyone in the classroom should use the correct mathematical terms in full, every time. For example, refer to 'equal parts', not 'parts'. Used consistently, precise maths language will be a familiar and non-threatening part of children's everyday experience.

## Full sentences

Teachers and children alike need to use full sentences to explain or respond. When children use complete sentences, it both reveals their understanding and embeds their knowledge.

## Stem sentences

These important sentences help children express mathematical concepts accurately, and are used throughout the *Power Maths* books. Encourage children to repeat them frequently, whether working independently or with others. Examples of stem sentences are:

'4 is a part, 5 is a part, 9 is the whole.'

'There are … groups. There are … in each group.'

## Key vocabulary

The unit starters highlight essential vocabulary for every lesson. In the Pupil Textbooks, characters flag new terminology and the Teacher Guide lists important mathematical language for every unit and lesson. New terms are never introduced without a clear explanation.

## Mathematical signs

Mathematical signs are used early on so that children quickly become familiar with them and their meaning. Often, the *Power Maths* characters will highlight the connection between language and particular signs.

# The role of talk and discussion

When children learn to talk purposefully together about maths, barriers of fear and anxiety are broken down and they grow in confidence, skills and understanding. Building a healthy culture of 'maths talk' empowers their learning from day one.

Explanation and discussion are integral to the *Power Maths* structure, so by simply following the books your lessons will stimulate structured talk. The following key 'maths talk' strategies will help you strengthen that culture and ensure that every child is included.

### Sentences, not words

Encourage children to use full sentences when reasoning, explaining or discussing maths. This helps both speaker and listeners to clarify their own understanding. It also reveals whether or not the speaker truly understands, enabling you to address misconceptions as they arise.

### Working together

Working with others in pairs, groups or as a whole class is a great way to support maths talk and discussion. Use different group structures to add variety and challenge. For example, children could take timed turns for talking, work independently alongside a 'discussion buddy', or perhaps play different *Power Maths* character roles within their group.

### Think first – then talk

Provide clear opportunities within each lesson for children to think and reflect, so that their talk is purposeful, relevant and focused.

### Give every child a voice

Where the 'hands up' model allows only the more confident child to shine, *Power Maths* involves everyone. Make sure that no child dominates and that even the shyest child is encouraged to contribute – and is praised when they do.

### Power play or Power puzzle

Each unit ends with either a Power play or a Power puzzle. This is an activity, puzzle or game that allows children to use their new knowledge in a fun, informal way. In Key Stage 2 we have also included a deeper level to each game to help challenge those children who have grasped a concept quickly.

### How to use diagnostic questions

The diagnostic questions provided in *Power Maths* Textbooks are carefully structured to identify both understanding and misconceptions (if children answer in a particular way, you will know why). The simple procedure below may be helpful:

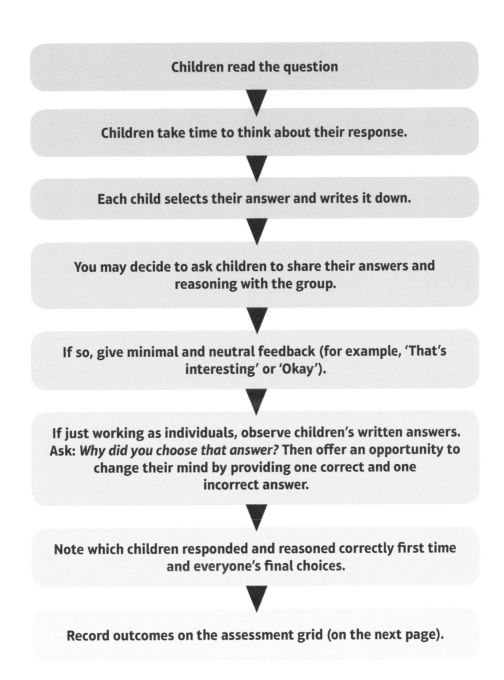

**Children read the question**

▼

**Children take time to think about their response.**

▼

**Each child selects their answer and writes it down.**

▼

**You may decide to ask children to share their answers and reasoning with the group.**

▼

**If so, give minimal and neutral feedback (for example, 'That's interesting' or 'Okay').**

▼

**If just working as individuals, observe children's written answers. Ask: *Why did you choose that answer?* Then offer an opportunity to change their mind by providing one correct and one incorrect answer.**

▼

**Note which children responded and reasoned correctly first time and everyone's final choices.**

▼

**Record outcomes on the assessment grid (on the next page).**

# *Power Maths* unit assessment grid

Year ___          Unit ___ _____

Record only as much information as you judge appropriate for your assessment of each child's mastery of the unit and any steps needed for intervention.

| Name | Diagnostic questions | SATs-style question | My journal | Power check | Power play/puzzle | Mastery | Intervention/ Strengthen |
|------|------|------|------|------|------|------|------|
|      |      |      |      |      |      |      |      |
|      |      |      |      |      |      |      |      |
|      |      |      |      |      |      |      |      |
|      |      |      |      |      |      |      |      |
|      |      |      |      |      |      |      |      |
|      |      |      |      |      |      |      |      |
|      |      |      |      |      |      |      |      |
|      |      |      |      |      |      |      |      |
|      |      |      |      |      |      |      |      |
|      |      |      |      |      |      |      |      |
|      |      |      |      |      |      |      |      |
|      |      |      |      |      |      |      |      |
|      |      |      |      |      |      |      |      |
|      |      |      |      |      |      |      |      |

# Keeping the class together

Traditionally, children who learn quickly have been accelerated through the curriculum. As a consequence, their learning may be superficial and will lack the many benefits of enabling children to learn with and from each other.

By contrast, *Power Maths'* mastery approach values real understanding and richer, deeper learning above speed. It sees all children learning the same concept in small, cumulative steps, each finding and mastering challenge at their own level. Remember that when you teach for mastery, EVERYONE can do maths! Those who grasp a concept easily have time to explore and understand that concept at a deeper level. The whole class therefore moves through the curriculum at broadly the same pace via individual learning journeys.

For some teachers, the idea that a whole class can move forward together is revolutionary and challenging. However, the evidence of global good practice clearly shows that this approach drives engagement, confidence, motivation and success for all learners, and not just the high flyers. The strategies below will help you keep your class together on their maths journey.

### Mix it up

Do not stick to set groups at each table. Every child should be working on the same concept, and mixing up the groupings widens children's opportunities for exploring, discussing and sharing their understanding with others.

### Recycling questions

Reuse the Pupil Textbook and Practice Book questions with concrete materials to allow children to explore concepts and relationships and deepen their understanding. This strategy is especially useful for reinforcing learning in same-day interventions.

### Strengthen at every opportunity

The next lesson in a *Power Maths* sequence always revises and builds on the previous step to help embed learning. These activities provide golden opportunities for individual children to strengthen their learning with the support of teaching assistants.

### Prepare to be surprised!

Children may grasp a concept quickly or more slowly. The 'fast graspers' won't always be the same individuals, nor does the speed at which a child understands a concept predict their success in maths. Are they struggling or just working more slowly?

# Depth and breadth

Just as prescribed in the National Curriculum, the goal of *Power Maths* is never to accelerate through a topic but rather to gain a clear, deep and broad understanding.

*"Pupils who grasp concepts rapidly should be challenged through being offered rich and sophisticated problems before any acceleration through new content. Those who are not sufficiently fluent with earlier material should consolidate their understanding, including through additional practice, before moving on."*

**National Curriculum: Mathematics programmes of study: KS1 & 2, 2013**

The lesson sequence offers many opportunities for you to deepen and broaden children's learning, some of which are suggested below.

### Discover

As well as using the questions in the Teacher Guide, check that children are really delving into why something is true. It is not enough to simply recite facts, such as '6 + 3 = 9'. They need to be able to see why, explain it, and to demonstrate the solution in several ways.

### Share

Make sure that every child is given chances to offer answers and expand their knowledge and not just those with the greatest confidence.

### Think together

Encourage children to think about how they found the solution and explain it to their partner. Be sure to make concrete materials available on group tables throughout the lesson to support and reinforce learning.

### Practice

Avoid any temptation to select questions according to your assessment of ability: practice questions are presented in a logical sequence and it is important that each child works through every question.

### Reflect

Open-ended questions allow children to deepen their understanding as far as they can by discovering new ways of finding answers. For example, *Give me another way of working out how high the wall is … And another way?*

### Online materials

For each unit you will find additional strengthening activities to support those children who need it and to deepen the understanding of those who need the additional challenge.

# Same-day intervention

Since maths competence depends on mastering concepts one-by-one in a logical progression, it is important that no gaps in understanding are ever left unfilled. Same-day interventions – either within or after a lesson – are a crucial safety net for any child who has not fully made the small step covered that day. In other words, intervention is always about keeping up, not catching up, so that every child has the skills and understanding they need to tackle the next lesson. That means presenting the same problems used in the lesson, with a variety of concrete materials to help children model their solutions.

We offer two intervention strategies below, but you should feel free to choose others if they work better for your class.

### Within-lesson intervention

The Think together activity will reveal those who are struggling, so when it is time for Practice, bring these children together to work with you on the first Practice questions. Observe these children carefully, ask questions, encourage them to use concrete models and check that they reach and can demonstrate their understanding.

### After-lesson intervention

You might like to use Think together before an assembly, giving you or teaching assistants time to recap and expand with slow graspers during assembly time. Teaching assistants could also work with strugglers at other convenient points in the school day.

# The role of practice

Practice plays a pivotal role in the *Power Maths* approach. It takes place in class groups, smaller groups, pairs and independently, so that children always have the opportunities for thinking as well as the models and support they need to practise meaningfully and with understanding.

## Intelligent practice

In *Power Maths*, practice never equates to the simple repetition of a process. Instead we embrace the concept of intelligent practice, in which all children become fluent in maths through varied, frequent and thoughtful practice that deepens and embeds conceptual understanding in a logical, planned sequence. To see the difference, take a look at the following examples.

### Traditional practice

- Repetition can be rote – no need for a child to think hard about what they are doing.

- Praise may be misplaced.

- Does this prove understanding?

### Intelligent practice

- Varied methods – concrete, pictorial and abstract.

- Calculations expressed in different ways, requiring thought and understanding.

- Constructive feedback.

All practice questions are designed to move children on and reveal misconceptions.

Simple, logical steps build onto earlier learning.

C-P-A runs throughout – different ways of modelling and understanding the same concept.

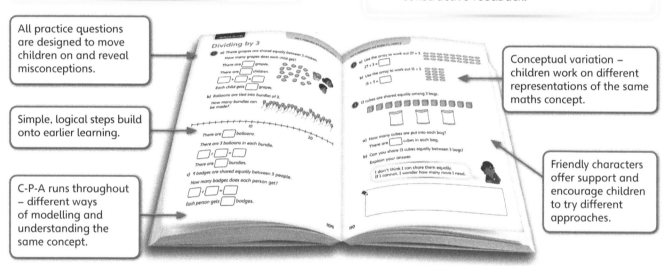

Conceptual variation – children work on different representations of the same maths concept.

Friendly characters offer support and encourage children to try different approaches.

## A carefully designed progression

The Practice Books provide just the right amount of intelligent practice for children to complete independently in the final sections of each lesson. It is really important that all children are exposed to the Practice questions, and that children are not directed to complete different sections. That is because each question is different and has been designed to challenge children to think about the maths they are doing. The questions become more challenging so children grasping concepts more quickly will start to slow down as they progress. Meanwhile, you have the chance to circulate and spot any misconceptions before they become barriers to further learning.

## Homework and the role of carers

While *Power Maths* does not prescribe any particular homework structure, we acknowledge the potential value of practice at home. For example, practising fluency in key facts, such as number bonds and times-tables, is an ideal homework task, and carers could work through uncompleted Practice Book questions with children at either primary stage.

However, it is important to recognise that many parents and carers may themselves lack confidence in maths, and few, if any, will be familiar with mastery methods. A Parents' and Carers' Evening that helps them understand the basics of mindsets, mastery and mathematical language is a great way to ensure that children benefit from their homework. It could be a fun opportunity for children to teach their families that everyone can do maths!

# Assessment strategies

Teaching for mastery demands that you are confident about what each child knows and where their misconceptions lie: therefore, practical and effective assessment is vitally important.

**Formative assessment within lessons**

The Think together section will often reveal any confusions or insecurities: try ironing these out by doing the first Think together question as a class. For children who continue to struggle, you or your teaching assistant should provide support and enable them to move on.

Performance in Practice can be very revealing: check Practice Books and listen out both during and after practice to identify misconceptions.

The Reflect section is designed to check on the all-important depth of understanding. Be sure to review how children performed in this final stage before you teach the next lesson.

**End of unit check – Textbook**

Each unit concludes with a summative check to help you assess quickly and clearly each child's understanding, fluency, reasoning and problem-solving skills. In KS2 this check also contains a SATs-style question to help children become familiar with answering this type of question.

In KS2 we would suggest the End of unit check is completed independently in children's exercise books, but you can adapt this to suit the needs of your class.

**End of unit check – Practice Book**

The Practice Book contains further opportunities for assessment, and can be completed by children independently whilst you are carrying out diagnostic assessment with small groups. Your Teacher Guide will advise you on what to do if children struggle to articulate an explanation – or perhaps encourage you to write down something they have explained well. It will also offer insights into children's answers and their implications for the next learning steps. It is split into three main sections, outlined below.

**My journal**

My journal is designed to allow children to show their depth of understanding of the unit. It can also serve as a way of checking that children have grasped key mathematical vocabulary. Children should have some time to think about how they want to answer the question, and you could ask them to talk to a partner about their ideas. Then children should write their answer in their Practice Book.

**Power check**

The Power check allows children to self-assess their level of confidence on the topic by colouring in different smiley faces. You may want to introduce the faces as follows:

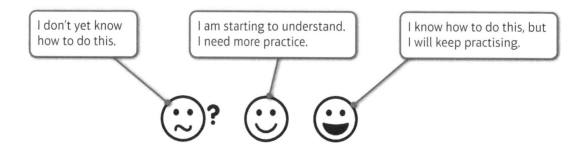

I don't yet know how to do this.

I am starting to understand. I need more practice.

I know how to do this, but I will keep practising.

# Structures and representations

Unlike most other subjects, maths comprises a wide array of abstract concepts – and that is why children and adults so often find it difficult. By taking a Concrete-Pictorial-Abstract (C-P-A) approach, *Power Maths* allows children to tackle concepts in a tangible and more comfortable way.

**Non-linear stages**

## Concrete

Replacing the traditional approach of a teacher working through a problem in front of the class, the concrete stage introduces real objects that children can use to 'do' the maths – any familiar object that a child can manipulate and move to help bring the maths to life. It is important to appreciate, however, that children must always understand the link between models and the objects they represent. For example, children need to first understand that three cakes could be represented by three pretend cakes, and then by three counters or bricks. Frequent practice helps consolidate this essential insight. Although they can be used at any time, good concrete models are an essential first step in understanding.

## Pictorial

This stage uses pictorial representations of objects to let children 'see' what particular maths problems look like. It helps them make connections between the concrete and pictorial representations and the abstract maths concept. Children can also create or view a pictorial representation together, enabling discussion and comparisons. The *Power Maths* teaching tools are fantastic for this learning stage, and bar modelling is invaluable for problem solving throughout the primary curriculum.

## Abstract

Our ultimate goal is for children to understand abstract mathematical concepts, signs and notation and, of course, some children will reach this stage far more quickly than others. To work with abstract concepts, a child needs to be comfortable with the meaning of, and relationships between, concrete, pictorial and abstract models and representations. The C-P-A approach is not linear, and children may need different types of models at different times. However, when a child demonstrates with concrete models and pictorial representations that they have grasped a concept, we can be confident that they are ready to explore or model it with abstract signs such as numbers and notation.

**Use at any time and with any age to support understanding.**

# Practical aspects of *Power Maths*

One of the key underlying elements of *Power Maths* is its practical approach, allowing you to make maths real and relevant to your children, no matter their age.

Manipulatives are essential resources for both key stages and *Power Maths* encourages teachers to use these at every opportunity, and to continue the Concrete-Pictorial-Abstract approach right through to Year 6.

The Textbooks and Teacher Guides include lots of opportunities for teaching in a practical way to show children what maths means in real life.

## Discover and Share

The Discover and Share sections of the Textbook give you scope to turn a real-life scenario into a practical and hands-on section of the lesson. Use these sections as inspiration to get active in the classroom. Where appropriate, use the Discover contexts as a springboard for your own examples that have particular resonance for your children – and allow them to get their hands dirty trying out the mathematics for themselves.

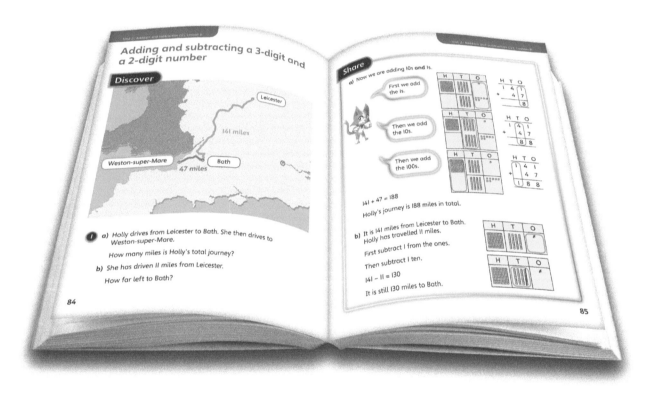

## Unit videos

Every unit has a video which incorporates real-life classroom sequences.

These videos show you how the reasoning behind mathematics can be carried out in a practical manner by showing real children using various concrete and pictorial methods to come to the solution. You can see how using these practical models, such as part-whole and bar models, helps them to find and articulate their answer.

## Mastery tips

Mastery Experts give anecdotal advice on where they have used hands-on and real-life elements to inspire their children.

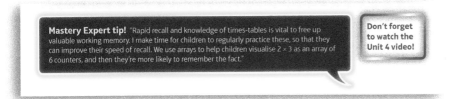

**Mastery Expert tip!** "Rapid recall and knowledge of times-tables is vital to free up valuable working memory. I make time for children to regularly practice these, so that they can improve their speed of recall. We use arrays to help children visualise 2 × 3 as an array of 6 counters, and then they're more likely to remember the fact."

Don't forget to watch the Unit 4 video!

## Concrete-Pictorial-Abstract (C-P-A) approach

Each Share section uses various methods to explain an answer, helping children to access abstract concepts by using concrete tools, such as counters. Remember this isn't a linear process, so even children who appear confident using the more abstract method can deepen their knowledge by exploring the concrete representations. Encourage children to use all three methods to really solidify their understanding of a concept.

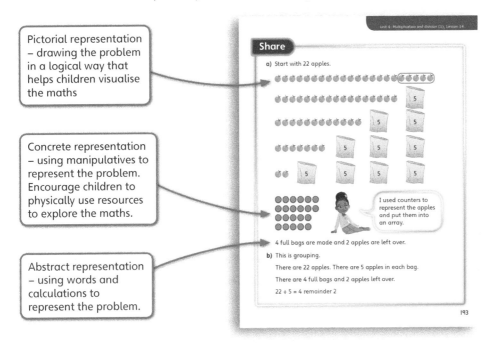

Pictorial representation – drawing the problem in a logical way that helps children visualise the maths

Concrete representation – using manipulatives to represent the problem. Encourage children to physically use resources to explore the maths.

Abstract representation – using words and calculations to represent the problem.

## Practical tips

Every lesson suggests how to draw out the practical side of the Discover context.

You'll find these in the Discover section of the Teacher Guide for each lesson.

> **PRACTICAL TIPS** You could use balls, counters or cubes under plastic cups to re-enact the artwork and help children get a feel for this activity.

## Resources

Every lesson lists the practical resources you will need or might want to use. There is also a summary of all of the resources used throughout the term on page 34 to help you be prepared.

**RESOURCES**

**Mandatory:** cubes, counters, number lines

**Optional:** balls, plastic cups

# List of practical resources

**Year 4A Mandatory resources**

| Resource | Lesson |
|---|---|
| Base 10 equipment | **Unit 1** lessons 1, 4, 5<br>**Unit 2** lessons 1, 2, 5, 6<br>**Unit 3** lessons 1, 2, 3, 4, 5, 6, 7, 8<br>**Unit 5** lessons 1, 2, 7, 9, 10, 11 |
| Cubes | **Unit 5** lesson 11 |
| Number lines | **Unit 1** lessons 1, 2, 3, 7, 8<br>**Unit 2** lessons 5, 7, 8, 9 |
| Part-whole models | **Unit 1** lesson 5 |
| Place value counters | **Unit 1** lessons 1, 6<br>**Unit 2** lessons 1, 2, 5, 6<br>**Unit 3** lessons 1, 2, 3, 4, 5, 6, 7, 8<br>**Unit 5** lessons 2, 3, 4, 5, 6, 7, 8, 9, 10 |
| Place value grids | **Unit 1** lessons 1, 6<br>**Unit 2** lessons 3, 4 |
| Squared paper | **Unit 4** lessons 4, 5 |

**Year 4A Optional resources**

| Resource | Lesson |
|---|---|
| Base 10 equipment | **Unit 1** lessons 2, 7, 8, 9<br>**Unit 2** lessons 3, 4, 7<br>**Unit 5** lessons 3, 4, 5, 6, 8 |
| Cardboard squares and rectangles | **Unit 4** lesson 4 |
| Cardboard strips | **Unit 4** lesson 5 |
| Chalk | **Unit 4** lesson 3 |
| Coloured pencils | **Unit 4** lesson 2 |
| Counters (plain) | **Unit 2** lesson 2 |
| Dice to generate numbers | **Unit 1** lesson 3 |
| Distance tables | **Unit 4** lesson 1 |
| Floor/carpet tiles | **Unit 4** lesson 2 |
| Metre sticks | **Unit 4** lesson 1 |
| Multiplication squares | **Unit 5** lessons 1, 2 |
| Number lines | **Unit 1** lessons 3, 4<br>**Unit 2** lessons 2, 3, 6, 7<br>**Unit 3** lesson 9 |
| Paper clips | **Unit 4** lesson 3 |
| Paper strips | **Unit 3** lesson 12<br>**Unit 4** lessons 3, 4, 5 |
| Part-whole models | **Unit 1** lesson 9 |
| Place value cards | **Unit 1** lessons 1, 2 |
| Place value counters | **Unit 1** lesson 2, 4, 5, 7, 8<br>**Unit 2** lesson 2, 3, 4, 7<br>**Unit 5** lesson 1, 2, 11 |
| Place value grids | **Unit 2** lesson 1, 2, 6 |
| Rulers | **Unit 4** lesson 3 |
| Squared paper | **Unit 4** lesson 2 |
| Sticks | **Unit 4** lesson 5 |
| Straws | **Unit 4** lesson 5 |
| String | **Unit 3** lesson 6<br>**Unit 4** lessons 2, 3 |

# Variation helps visualisation

Children find it much easier to visualise and grasp concepts if they see them presented in a number of ways, so be prepared to offer and encourage many different representations.

For example, the number six could be represented in various ways:

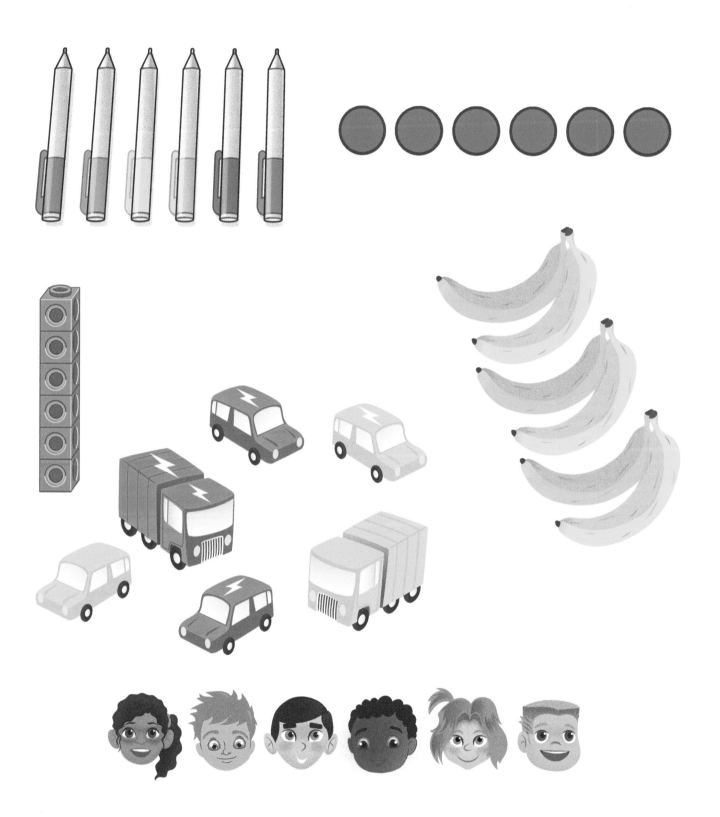

# Getting started with *Power Maths*

As you prepare to put *Power Maths* into action, you might find the tips and advice below helpful.

## STEP 1: Train up!

A practical, up-front, full-day professional development course will give you and your team a brilliant head-start as you begin your *Power Maths* journey. You will learn more about the ethos, how it works and why.

## STEP 2: Check out the progression

Take a look at the yearly and termly overviews. Next take a look at the unit overview for the unit you are about to teach in your Teacher Guide, remembering that you can match your lessons and pacing to your class.

## STEP 3: Explore the context

Take a little time to look at the context for this unit: what are the implications for the unit ahead? (Think about key language, common misunderstandings and intervention strategies, for example.) If you have the online subscription, don't forget to watch the corresponding unit video.

## STEP 4: Prepare for your first lesson

Familiarise yourself with the objectives, essential questions to ask and the resources you will need. The Teacher Guide offers tips, ideas and guidance on individual lessons to help you anticipate children's misconceptions and challenge those who are ready to think more deeply.

## STEP 5: Teach and reflect

Deliver your lesson – and enjoy!

Afterwards, reflect on how it went ... Did you cover all five stages?
Does the lesson need more time? How could you improve it?
What percentage of your class do you think mastered the concept?
How can you help those that didn't?

# Unit 1
## Place value – 4-digit numbers ①

**Mastery Expert tip!** "When I taught this unit I made sure that children had a firm understanding of place value within 1,000, so that I knew they could use and apply this knowledge to the unit. Children need to know how to represent 3-digit numbers confidently and know how to partition them. If children are confident with working within 1,000 they will feel confident when applying their knowledge to numbers within 10,000."

**Don't forget to watch the Unit 1 video!**

## WHY THIS UNIT IS IMPORTANT

This is a pivotal unit because a solid understanding of place value using 4-digit numbers is fundamental to success in other areas of learning, particularly the four operations of addition, subtraction, multiplication and division.

Equally, children who struggle to represent, round and count with 4-digit numbers may struggle when they are asked to apply these skills in future learning. It is important to ensure that enough time is spent on this unit of work so that children have a solid understanding of place value both now and for the future.

## WHERE THIS UNIT FITS

→ **Unit 1: Place value – 4-digit numbers (1)**

→ Unit 2: Place value – 4-digit numbers (2)

This unit builds on previous learning in Year 3 about place value within 1,000. This previous learning introduced children to the concept of counting in 10s, comparing numbers, ordering numbers and using a number line to 1,000. Children will continue to use these previously learnt skills and apply them when working with 4-digit numbers.

Before they start this unit, it is expected that children:
- have a solid understanding of place value within 1,000 from Year 3
- understand how to count in 10s and 100s
- can order and compare numbers to 1,000.

## ASSESSING MASTERY

Children who have mastered this unit will be able to represent 4-digit numbers using a variety of concrete apparatus. They can confidently use a number line to order and compare a variety of 4-digit numbers and are able to round to the nearest 10, 100 and 1,000. Children can read Roman numerals to 100 and have an understanding of how our numeral system has changed to accommodate the concept of zero and place value.

| COMMON MISCONCEPTIONS | STRENGTHENING UNDERSTANDING | GOING DEEPER |
|---|---|---|
| Children may incorrectly round numbers (to the incorrect 10, 100 or 1,000). | Ensure children have access to a number line so that they can see which 10, 100 or 1,000 their number is closest to and round to that. | Children can try to find any patterns or rules to use when rounding. Children can order and compare a set of numbers to deepen learning. |
| When finding 1,000 more or less than a number and comparing numbers children may compare using the incorrect column. | Allow children to physically build the number using concrete apparatus so that they can physically see the digits. In addition to this, present the number in a place value grid so that children can see which place value column is the important one. | |

# Unit I: Place value – 4-digit numbers

## WAYS OF WORKING

Introduce this unit of work using teacher-led discussion. Allow children time to discuss questions in pairs or small groups and share ideas as a whole class. Children should be encouraged to use concrete apparatus so that they can see the numbers they will be working with.

## STRUCTURES AND REPRESENTATIONS

**Number line:** The number line will allow children to see which numbers a number sits between. It also allows children to see how increments can be used to view numbers.

**Place value grid, including using base 10 equipment, place value counters and blank counters:** This model will help children organise 4-digit numbers into 1,000s, 100s, 10s and 1s, with both concrete representations and abstract numbers.

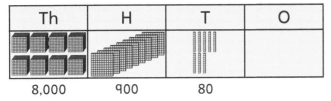

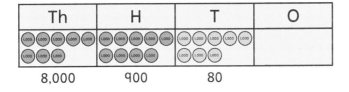

## KEY LANGUAGE

There is some key language that children will need to know as part of the learning in this unit:

→ tens (10s), hundreds (100s), thousands (1,000s)

→ rounding, counting, represent, compare, order

→ more than (>), less than (<)

→ partition, recombine

→ numerals

→ nearest, distance

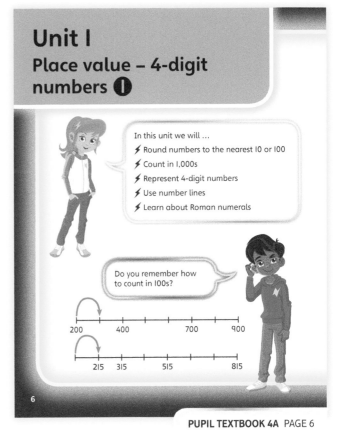

**PUPIL TEXTBOOK 4A** PAGE 6

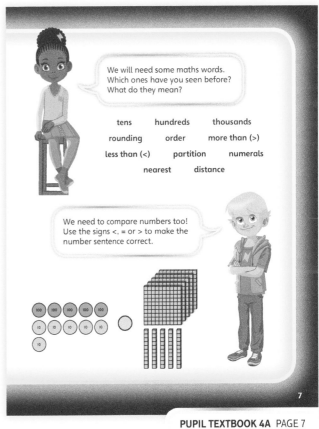

**PUPIL TEXTBOOK 4A** PAGE 7

# Numbers to 1,000

## Learning focus

In this lesson, children will recap their understanding of numbers to 1,000. They will represent numbers using different equipment, and partition numbers.

## Small steps

→ **This step: Numbers to 1,000**
→ Next step: Rounding to the nearest 10

## NATIONAL CURRICULUM LINKS

**Year 4 Number – Number and place value**

Recognise the place value of each digit in a 4-digit number (1,000s, 100s, 10s, and 1s).

## ASSESSING MASTERY

Children can partition a 3-digit number and describe it using the language: 100s, 10s and 1s. They can represent the numbers using different equipment and discuss how the representations are the same and how they are different.

## COMMON MISCONCEPTIONS

It may be that children don't understand the place values of the digits. Ask:
• *Can we make the number using base 10 equipment? How many 1s are equal to a 10? How many 10s are equal to a 100? Can we say the number aloud? Does this help us to work out the values of the digits?*

## STRENGTHENING UNDERSTANDING

To strengthen understanding, encourage children to use base 10 equipment on a place value grid to represent the numbers, as this shows the difference in the values of the columns. Use the place value grid to structure the numbers and help children to see how this can support writing the numbers in numerals and partitioning the numbers into 100s, 10s and 1s.

## GOING DEEPER

To deepen children's understanding, encourage them to think of more than one way to partition by exchanging between columns. They will see that a number made of 3 hundreds, 2 tens and 3 ones is equal to a number made of 2 hundreds, 12 tens and 3 ones.

## KEY LANGUAGE

**In lesson:** hundreds (100s), tens (10s), ones (1s),
**Other language to be used by teacher:** partition

## STRUCTURES AND REPRESENTATIONS

number line, place value counters, base 10 equipment, place value cards

## RESOURCES

**Mandatory:** place value counters, base 10 equipment, number line, place value grid

**Optional:** place value cards

 In the eTextbook of this lesson, you will find interactive links to a selection of teaching tools.

## Before you teach

• Can children partition a 2-digit number?
• Can children describe a 2-digit number as 10s and 1s?
• Can children count up to 1,000?

## Discover

Pair work

**ASK**

- Question ① a): *What equipment has Amelia used to represent her number?*
- Question ① a): *Which piece represents the 100s, 10s or 1s?*
- Question ① b): *What number has each child made? How many 100s, 10s and 1s are there in each child's number?*

**IN FOCUS** Question ① b) allows children to think about what is the same about 542 and 524 and what is different. It encourages them to think about the importance of the order of the digits.

**PRACTICAL TIPS** Give children access to a range of different equipment and ask them to represent the numbers Amelia, Isla and Lee have made. If children use a place value grid it should be very clear which numbers are the same and which are different.

**ANSWERS**

Question ① a): Amelia's number has 5 hundreds, 4 tens and 2 ones.

Question ① b): Amelia and Lee have both made the same number: 542. Isla has made a different number: 524.

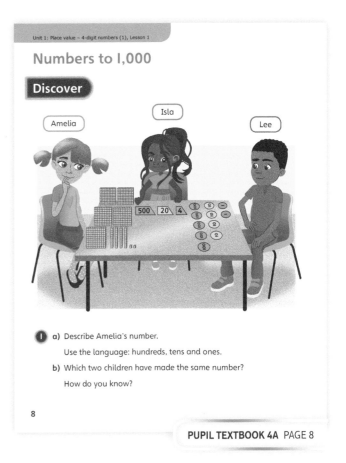

### Numbers to 1,000

**Discover**

Amelia    Isla    Lee

500  20  4

① a) Describe Amelia's number.
   Use the language: hundreds, tens and ones.
 b) Which two children have made the same number?
   How do you know?

8

**PUPIL TEXTBOOK 4A** PAGE 8

## Share

Whole class teacher led

**ASK**

- Question ① a): *How does a place value grid help you to write numbers?*
- Question ① a): *Why is 542 in a different place on different number lines?*
- Question ① b): *Can you describe each of the numbers using 100s, 10s and 1s?*

**IN FOCUS** Question ① a) introduces making a 3-digit number using different equipment. The **Share** section looks at using number lines with different start and end numbers and how this affects the position of the number.

Question ① b) focuses on the distinction between different numbers made with the same digits, showing the importance of place value.

**STRENGTHEN** Encourage children to think about and discuss the equipment they have used to represent numbers. Prompt them with questions, such as: *What is the equipment called? Why do you think it is called that? What number did you make? How do you know? How did you organise your numbers?* Explain that using a place value grid will help them to organise their work.

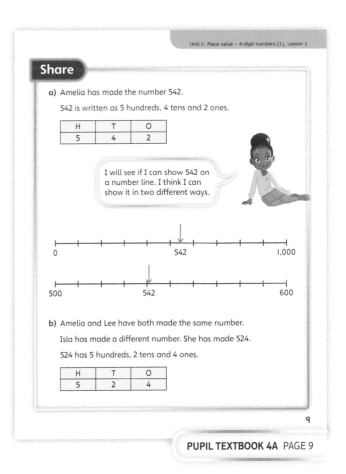

**Share**

a) Amelia has made the number 542.

542 is written as 5 hundreds, 4 tens and 2 ones.

| H | T | O |
|---|---|---|
| 5 | 4 | 2 |

I will see if I can show 542 on a number line. I think I can show it in two different ways.

0 ———— 542 ———— 1,000

500 ———— 542 ———— 600

b) Amelia and Lee have both made the same number.

Isla has made a different number. She has made 524.

524 has 5 hundreds, 2 tens and 4 ones.

| H | T | O |
|---|---|---|
| 5 | 2 | 4 |

9

**PUPIL TEXTBOOK 4A** PAGE 9

# Think together

Whole class teacher led (I do, We do, You do)

**ASK**

- Question ❶ b): *What do we do if there are no tens in a number? What do we do to represent this? Is this the same for other columns?*
- Question ❷: *How does saying a number aloud help us to partition it? Does this help with three hundred and fifteen? Why?*
- Question ❸: *What number has been made with the place value cards?*

**IN FOCUS** Questions ❶ and ❷ are designed to ensure that children are able to partition 3-digit numbers (this is a recap of previous learning). Children should be able to write using the language hundreds, tens and ones as well as number sentences, for example: 3 hundreds, 6 tens and 3 ones and 363 = 300 + 60 + 3. Children should be able to write numbers in words and numerals and to identify numbers regardless of the position of the 100s, 10s and 1s.

**STRENGTHEN** Use base 10 equipment with children. Organise their work on a place value grid and ask them to explain what each piece of base 10 equipment is, and why it is called that. Ask children to read the parts of their numbers aloud.

**DEEPEN** Check whether children can partition numbers in other ways. Do they know that 30 + 600 + 5 = 635 or do they see this as 365?

**ASSESSMENT CHECKPOINT** In questions ❶ and ❷, check that children can use different equipment to represent numbers and can partition 3-digit numbers into 100s, 10s and 1s. Also, check children can use 0 as a place holder.

**ANSWERS**

Question ❶ a): 432 has 4 hundreds, 3 tens and 2 ones.

Question ❶ b): 607 has 6 hundreds, 0 tens and 7 ones.

Question ❷ a): 580 has 5 hundreds, 8 tens and 0 ones.

Question ❷ b): 621 has 6 hundreds, 2 tens and 1 one.

Question ❷ c): Three hundred and fifteen has 3 hundreds, 1 ten and 5 ones.

Question ❸ a): D. The place value cards do not show 303. They represent 33.

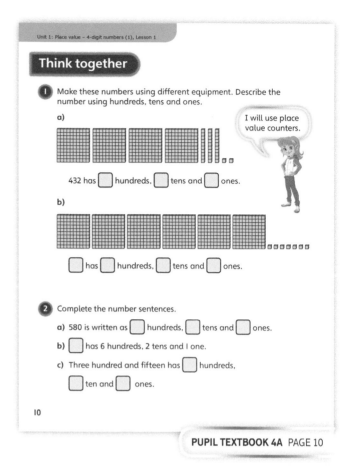

PUPIL TEXTBOOK 4A PAGE 10

PUPIL TEXTBOOK 4A PAGE 11

# Practice

**WAYS OF WORKING** Independent thinking

**IN FOCUS** Question ❶ demonstrates whether children can write numbers presented as base 10 equipment and place value counters or cards in words and numerals.

Question ❷ requires children to partition numbers, writing them as 100s, 10s and 1s.

Question ❸ links the previous two questions together and demonstrates whether children can draw representations of 3-digit numbers.

**STRENGTHEN** Ensure children have a range of equipment, such as base 10 equipment and place value counters, and encourage them to organise their work on a place value grid.

**DEEPEN** Question ❺ demonstrates flexible partitioning. Deepen understanding by asking children to partition different 3-digit numbers in as many ways as they can using 100s, 10s and 1s.

**THINK DIFFERENTLY** In question ❹, children will need to think about the number as a whole and work out that they need to do an exchange rather than just counting the number of 100, 10 and 1 blocks to find the number represented.

**ASSESSMENT CHECKPOINT** Children should be confident when partitioning a 3-digit number and be able to describe what they are doing using the correct language. They should be able to recognise different equipment and explain how they represent the numbers.

**ANSWERS** Answers for the **Practice** part of the lesson appear in the separate **Practice and Reflect answer guide.**

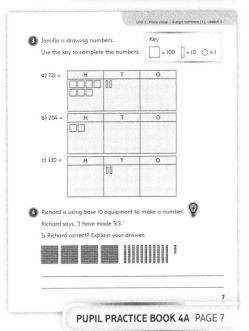

PUPIL PRACTICE BOOK 4A PAGE 6

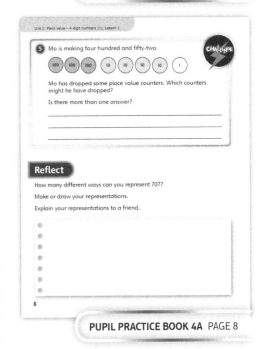

PUPIL PRACTICE BOOK 4A PAGE 7

# Reflect

**WAYS OF WORKING** Independent thinking

**IN FOCUS** The **Reflect** question brings the lesson together by assessing the different representations children can make of a given 3-digit number.

**ASSESSMENT CHECKPOINT** Look for children being able to represent the number in multiple ways using different equipment. Also, be aware of children writing the number in different ways. Do children know what to do with 0 in one of the columns on a place value grid?

**ANSWERS** Answers for the **Reflect** part of the lesson appear in the separate **Practice and Reflect answer guide**.

PUPIL PRACTICE BOOK 4A PAGE 8

## After the lesson ⏸

- Were children able to represent numbers less than 1,000 in different ways?
- Could children write numbers as 100s, 10s and 1s?
- Were children able to organise their work on a place value grid?

# Rounding to the nearest 10

## Learning focus

In this lesson, children will be introduced to rounding to the nearest 10.

## Small steps

→ Previous step: Numbers to 1,000
→ **This step: Rounding to the nearest 10**
→ Next step: Rounding to the nearest 100

## NATIONAL CURRICULUM LINKS

**Year 4 Number – Number and place value**

Round any number to the nearest 10, 100 or 1,000.

## ASSESSING MASTERY

Children can round any 2-digit or 3-digit number to the nearest 10 and understand the multiples of 10 above and below a specific number. Children understand when rounding to the nearest 10 that they need to look at the number of 1s to decide whether to round up or down.

## COMMON MISCONCEPTIONS

Children may not be able to work out which multiples of 10 are above and below a number. Ask:
- *What is the same about multiples of 10?* (They all end in a 0.)
- *Can you represent the number on a number line? Count up and down to find the closest multiples of 10.*

Children may have difficulty deciding whether to round a number up or down. Ask:
- *Which multiple of 10 is your number closest to?*
- *If your number ends in 5 ones, do we round it up or down?*

## STRENGTHENING UNDERSTANDING

To strengthen understanding, make sure children are representing the numbers on number lines and can see that with the majority of numbers we round to the nearest 10 because it is closest on the number line. This will help children to uncover which numbers round up and which numbers round down, by looking at the 1s. To reinforce this learning, ask children to explicitly find the difference. For example, 21 – 20 = 1 and 30 – 21 = 9, so 21 is closer to 20 than 30. It will also help children to see that a number with 5 ones is a special case.

## GOING DEEPER

Children can explore how place value columns change if they round a number to the nearest 10. Ask: *Do the 1s change? What about the 10s?* Can children give an example of a number where the 100s change?

## KEY LANGUAGE

**In lesson:** nearest, rounding, hundreds (100s), tens (10s), ones (1s), round up, round down

**Other language to be used by teacher:** multiple of 10

## STRUCTURES AND REPRESENTATIONS

number line, place value counters, base 10 equipment

## RESOURCES

**Optional:** place value counters, base 10 equipment, place value cards

 In the eTextbook of this lesson, you will find interactive links to a selection of teaching tools.

## Before you teach

- Do children know what multiples of 10 are?
- Can children count up and down in 1s up to 1,000?
- Can children describe a number as 100s, 10s and 1s?

## Discover

**WAYS OF WORKING** Pair work

**ASK**

- Question ① a): *What do we mean by the nearest 10?*
- Question ① a): *Which 2 tens does 48 lie between?*
- Question ① b): *If 60 is the nearest 10, what could the number of snakes be?*

**IN FOCUS** Question ① b) allows children to find a variety of answers, and to think about all the possibilities.

**PRACTICAL TIPS** Encourage children to make the number using maths equipment, such as base 10 or counters. Prompt children with questions, such as: *How many 10s does your number have? What will you do to round to the nearest 10? What is a good way of showing this?* Ask children to identify the 10s either side of the number and to draw a number line to reflect this. Can they see which 10 the number is closer to?

**ANSWERS**

Question ① a): 48 lizards rounds to 50. 131 fish rounds to 130. 25 monkeys rounds to 30.

Question ① b): There could be 55, 56, 57, 58, 59, 60, 61, 62, 63 or 64 snakes.

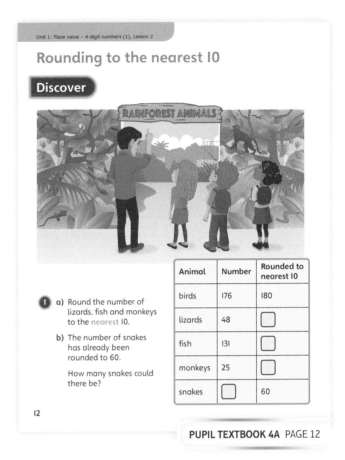

**PUPIL TEXTBOOK 4A** PAGE 12

## Share

**WAYS OF WORKING** Whole class teacher led

**ASK**

- Question ① a): *How does a number line help us to round?*
- Question ① a): *Is it easier or harder to round the number of fish than the number of monkeys? Why?*
- Question ① a): *Does a number line help us to round the number of monkeys? Why?*

**IN FOCUS** Question ① a) introduces the idea of rounding to the nearest 10 using the number line as a clear structure and support. After looking at a few examples, explain that we look at the ones column and depending on the digit we round up or down. Building on this in question ① b), children see all the possible numbers that round to one multiple of 10.

**STRENGTHEN** Discuss how the number line helps us to see which 10 the number is closer to, and encourage children to prove this by working out the subtractions to check their answers. First discuss with children how they can find the 10s that the number lies between. Point out the number of 10s in the number and help them to work out the 10s above and below this.

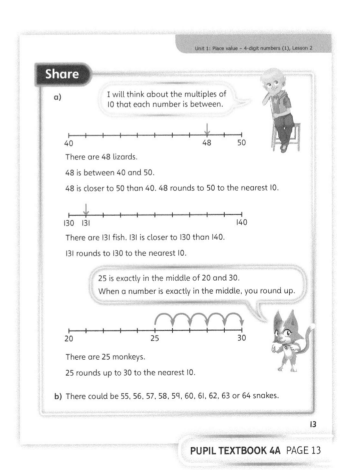

**PUPIL TEXTBOOK 4A** PAGE 13

# Think together

Whole class teacher led (I do, We do, You do)

**ASK**

- Question **1**: *What will the tens be either side of the number?*
- Question **2**: *Can we place these numbers on a number line?*
- Question **3** c): *Does the number round up or down? How is this question different?*

**IN FOCUS** In question **3** c) help children to see that the ten the number rounds to is a multiple of a hundred.

**STRENGTHEN** Continue to use the number line throughout to strengthen the children's understanding of the multiples of 10 either side of a number and how close the number is to a multiple of 10. Also, encourage children to carry out the simple subtractions to check their answers. Some children may look at patterns, such as: 21 – 20 = **1**; 22 – 20 = **2**; 23 – 20 = **3**, alongside 30 – 21 = **9**; 30 – 22 = **8**; 30 – 23 = **7**.

**DEEPEN** Question **4** allows children to deepen their understanding of which digits round up or down. Make all possible numbers with the three digit cards and encourage children to think about which numbers fit the rules given. With the numbers left over, ask: *What would these numbers be, rounded to the nearest 10?* Can children write numbers where all the digits will change when they round to the nearest 10? (For example, 297 rounding to 300.)

**ASSESSMENT CHECKPOINT** In question **1**, assess whether children can find the 10s above and below a given number. For some children, this is a difficult task. Help them to focus on the 1s digit. In question **4**, look for children who are moving towards more abstract rounding (without the support of equipment or number lines) and check they understand which digits round up and which round down.

**ANSWERS**

Question **1**: 434 is between 430 and 440.
434 is closer to 430 than 440.
434 rounds to 430 to the nearest 10.

Question **2** a): 21 + 9 = 30    21 – 1 = 20

Question **2** b): 22 + 8 = 30    22 – 2 = 20

Question **2** c): 23 + 7 = 30    23 – 3 = 20

Question **2** d): 24 + 6 = 30    24 – 4 = 20

Question **2** e): 25 + 5 = 30    25 – 5 = 20

Question **2** f): 26 + 4 = 30    26 – 6 = 20

Question **2** g): 27 + 3 =30    27 – 7 = 20

Question **2** h): 28 + 2 = 30    28 – 8 = 20

Question **2** i): 29 + 1 = 30    29 – 9 = 20
21, 22, 23 and 24 are closer to 20.
26, 27, 28 and 29 are closer to 30.
25 is exactly in the middle of 20 and 30.

Question **3** a): 57 rounds to 60 to the nearest 10.

Question **3** b): 323 rounds to 320 to the nearest 10.

Question **3** c): 195 rounds to 200 to the nearest 10.

Question **4** a): 17 and 18 round to 20 to the nearest 10.

Question **4** b): 78 and 81 round to 80 to the nearest 10.

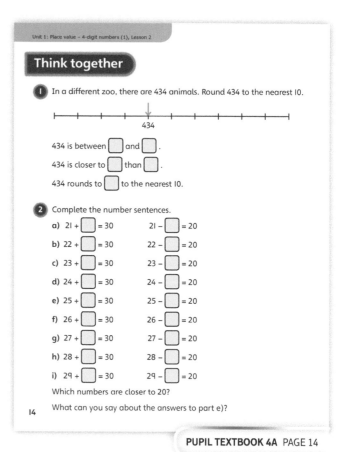

**Think together**

**1** In a different zoo, there are 434 animals. Round 434 to the nearest 10.

434 is between ☐ and ☐.
434 is closer to ☐ than ☐.
434 rounds to ☐ to the nearest 10.

**2** Complete the number sentences.

a) 21 + ☐ = 30    21 – ☐ = 20
b) 22 + ☐ = 30    22 – ☐ = 20
c) 23 + ☐ = 30    23 – ☐ = 20
d) 24 + ☐ = 30    24 – ☐ = 20
e) 25 + ☐ = 30    25 – ☐ = 20
f) 26 + ☐ = 30    26 – ☐ = 20
g) 27 + ☐ = 30    27 – ☐ = 20
h) 28 + ☐ = 30    28 – ☐ = 20
i) 29 + ☐ = 30    29 – ☐ = 20

Which numbers are closer to 20?
What can you say about the answers to part e)?

14

**PUPIL TEXTBOOK 4A** PAGE 14

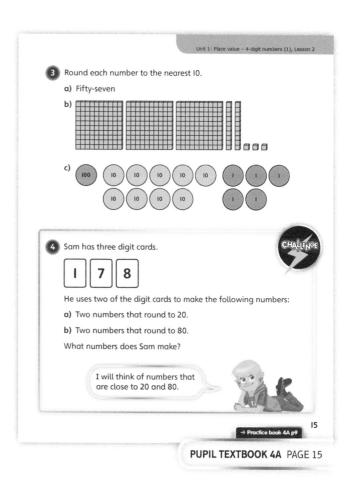

**3** Round each number to the nearest 10.
a) Fifty-seven
b)
c)

**4** Sam has three digit cards.

| 1 | 7 | 8 |

He uses two of the digit cards to make the following numbers:
a) Two numbers that round to 20.
b) Two numbers that round to 80.
What numbers does Sam make?

*I will think of numbers that are close to 20 and 80.*

→ Practice book 4A p9

15

**PUPIL TEXTBOOK 4A** PAGE 15

# Practice

**WAYS OF WORKING** Independent thinking

**IN FOCUS** In question ①, children are focusing on the 1s digits and the idea of which digits round up or down. Question ② checks children's independent use of the number line before moving towards more abstract rounding through questions ③ and ④.

**STRENGTHEN** Give children blank number lines with intervals, to encourage them to continue to position the numbers. Also, give children base 10 equipment, so they can clearly see the number of 10s in each number, and the closest 10 either side. Encourage children to do the simple subtractions that will reinforce which 10 the number is closer to.

**DEEPEN** In question ⑥ challenge children to find all the possible answers. Use Dexter's comment as a prompt to encourage children to work systematically, finding all numbers that round to 50 to the nearest 10 and then look at which pair together makes 99.

**ASSESSMENT CHECKPOINT** In question ②, assess whether children are focusing on the 1s digits in order to decide whether to round up or down. Ensure that children are able to recognise the 10s either side of a given number. In question ④, check that children can round a 2-digit number and a 3-digit number to the nearest 10.

**ANSWERS** Answers for the **Practice** part of the lesson appear in the separate **Practice and Reflect answer guide.**

# Reflect

**WAYS OF WORKING** Independent thinking

**IN FOCUS** Children use their understanding of the importance of the 1s digit when rounding to the nearest 10. Ask children to give examples to justify their answer.

**ASSESSMENT CHECKPOINT** Children should be able to explain that Hannah doesn't know whether to round the number up or down as she can't see the 1s digit. They can give examples of what the number could be to show that it could round up or down.

**ANSWERS** Answers for the **Reflect** part of the lesson appear in the separate **Practice and Reflect answer guide**.

## After the lesson

- Did children rely on the number line in order to find the nearest multiples of 10 and then round to the nearest 10?
- Were children able to understand the importance of the 1s digit when rounding to the nearest 10 and understand that the 1s digit determines whether to round up or down?

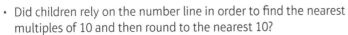

PUPIL PRACTICE BOOK 4A PAGE 9

PUPIL PRACTICE BOOK 4A PAGE 10

PUPIL PRACTICE BOOK 4A PAGE 11

# Rounding to the nearest 100

## Learning focus

In this lesson, children will use their knowledge of place value and rounding to the nearest 10 to develop an understanding of how to round to the nearest 100.

## Small steps

→ Previous step: Rounding to the nearest 10
→ **This step: Rounding to the nearest 100**
→ Next step: Counting in 1,000s

## NATIONAL CURRICULUM LINKS

**Year 4 Number – Number and place value**

Round any number to the nearest 10, 100 or 1,000.

## ASSESSING MASTERY

Children can identify the 100 either side of a given number. They can successfully round to the nearest 100 and identify which place value column will help them to do this.

## COMMON MISCONCEPTIONS

Children may struggle with rounding numbers to the nearest 100 when the answers are 0 and 1,000 (for example with numbers such as 34 or 984). Ask:
• *What are the 100s either side of 34? Try drawing this on a number line. What happens to the place value of the digits in 984 when you round to the nearest 100?*

Children need to be aware that when rounding to the nearest 100 it is important to look at the tens column, rather than the ones column. Encourage children to make numbers on a place value grid and ask:
• *Which column do we need to look at, in order to round to the nearest hundred?*

## STRENGTHENING UNDERSTANDING

To strengthen understanding, clearly represent the number in base 10 equipment and ask children to identify the hundred either side by counting in 100s. Provide children with a clearly marked number line and place a variety of numbers on it so that children can see which 100 a number should be rounded up or down to. Ask: *What is the difference between 249 and 251 when rounding?*

## GOING DEEPER

Ask children to give examples of when they would need to round to the nearest 100. Ask: *What number should 550 be rounded to? Explain why.*

## KEY LANGUAGE

**In lesson:** rounding, hundreds (100s)

**Other language to be used by teacher:** round up, round down, nearest, thousands (1,000s), tens (10s), number line

## STRUCTURES AND REPRESENTATIONS

number lines

## RESOURCES

**Mandatory:** blank number lines

**Optional:** dice to generate numbers, specifically numbered number lines

 In the eTextbook of this lesson, you will find interactive links to a selection of teaching tools.

## Before you teach

• What contexts can children relate to so that their understanding of this concept is deepened?
• Based on previous lessons taught in this unit, are there any additional misconceptions you need to consider?

## Discover

Pair work

**ASK**

- Question ❶ a): *What is Danny's number? What 100s are either side of this number?*
- Question ❶ a): *Which 100 is Danny's number nearer to? How do you know?*
- Question ❶ b): *How far away is Alex's number from the 100s either side of it? How does this help you to round?*

**IN FOCUS** Question ❶ a) encourages children to find the 100 either side of a given number and to explore through counting and subtraction which 100 the number is closer to. Ensure children understand that they are using the dice scores as three digits, not adding them together.

Question ❶ b) reintroduces the vocabulary of 'rounding' and builds on question ❶ a). This will inform the teacher whether children understand the term 'rounding' and whether they can round to the nearest 100.

**PRACTICAL TIPS** Allow children to use a number line so that they can visualise the numbers.

**ANSWERS**

Question ❶ a): 600 is the nearest 100 to 568.

Question ❶ b): 856 rounded to the nearest 100 is 900.

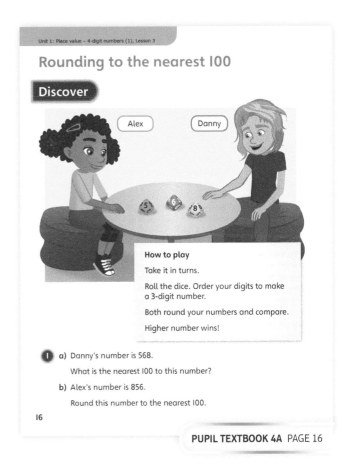

**PUPIL TEXTBOOK 4A** PAGE 16

## Share

Whole class teacher led

**ASK**

- Question ❶ a): *Which 100s does 568 lie between? How do you know?*
- Question ❶ a): *Which hundred is 568 closest to? How does subtracting 568 from 600 help you?*
- Question ❶ b): *How could you round 856 to the nearest 100 without drawing a number line? Which digit would you need to look at?*

**IN FOCUS** Question ❶ a) addresses rounding without stating that we are asking the children to round. The use of number lines to see which hundred the number is closer to, as well as carrying out subtractions, is reinforced from the previous lesson. In part b) children consider each digit and are introduced to the idea that a number with 5 tens is rounded up.

**STRENGTHEN** Look at Flo's statement in question ❶ b). Ask: *How will looking at the tens digit help?* Can children discuss this and share their understanding of place value?

**DEEPEN** Encourage children to discuss what is the same and what is different about rounding to the nearest 10 versus rounding to the nearest 100.

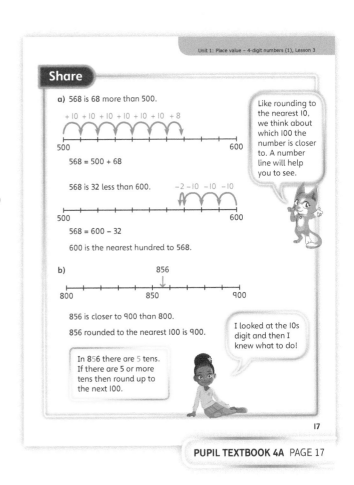

**PUPIL TEXTBOOK 4A** PAGE 17

# Think together

WAYS OF WORKING Whole class teacher led (I do, We do, You do)

**ASK**

- Question **1**: *What number is shown? What other numbers could you make?*
- Question **1**: *Which 100 is the number closer to? How do you know?*
- Question **2**: *Where will you place the number on the number line? How will this help you to round?*

**IN FOCUS** Questions **1** and **2** provide children with a structure that builds on from the **Share** section. It is an opportunity for children to discuss how they know which hundred to round to. In question **2** children revisit what happens when they are presented with a number that has 5 tens.

**STRENGTHEN** Use number lines to support children in identifying which 100s are either side of a given number, and reiterate that this is the starting point when thinking about which is the nearest 100. Encourage children to do the relevant subtractions to work out the difference between the number and each hundred.

**DEEPEN** In question **3** children are required to use Max's digit cards to make numbers that round to a given 100. Give children some other digits to work with and a multiple of 100 to round to. How many numbers can they make that round to the given 100? Can they represent this on a number line?

**ASSESSMENT CHECKPOINT** In question **1** assess whether children understand how to work out the 100s either side of the given numbers. In question **2** check that children are looking at the 10s digit in a number when rounding to the nearest 100. In question **3** assess whether children are able to write a number that rounds to a given 100.

**ANSWERS**

Question **1**: 742 is 42 more than 700. 742 is 58 less than 800.
742 is 700 rounded to the nearest 100.

Question **2**: 850 rounded to the nearest 100 is 900.

Question **3**: Max could have made three numbers.
The numbers are: 453, 534, 543.

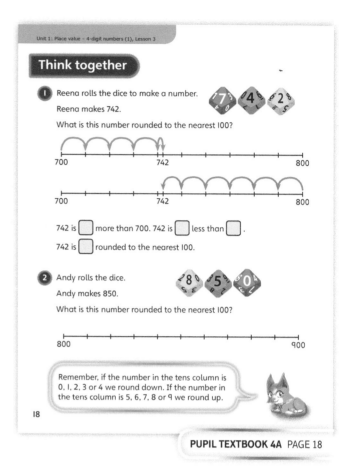

PUPIL TEXTBOOK 4A PAGE 18

PUPIL TEXTBOOK 4A PAGE 19

## Practice

**WAYS OF WORKING** Independent thinking

**IN FOCUS** Questions ❶ and ❷ reinforce the use of number lines to help with assessing which 100 a given number is closest to. Question ❸ becomes more abstract, requiring children to look at the 10s digit to help them round to the nearest 100.

**STRENGTHEN** Ask children to justify how they know which digit to round up or down and why. Is there a real-life context where they would need to round to the nearest 100?

**DEEPEN** Explore rounding to the nearest 100 when 0 or 1,000 is the answer. Ask children: *What does 987 round to? Which digits change? What is 34 rounded to the nearest 100? What is different about your answer?*

**ASSESSMENT CHECKPOINT** Questions ❶ and ❷ should allow you to assess whether children can use a number line to round numbers to the nearest 100. The rest of the questions should allow you to see if children can work in a more abstract way to round a number to the nearest 100. Check that children are able to identify the 100s either side of the given number and that they are looking at the 10s digit to round up or down.

**ANSWERS** Answers for the **Practice** part of the lesson appear in the separate **Practice and Reflect answer guide**.

## Reflect

**WAYS OF WORKING** Pair work

**IN FOCUS** This question requires children to demonstrate their approach to rounding a number to the nearest 100, and should show what they have understood from the lesson. Do they use a number line, subtractions or look at the 10s digit?

**ASSESSMENT CHECKPOINT** The **Reflect** question should show you the methods that children are using for rounding. Children should be moving towards looking at the 10s digit in order to round to the nearest 100.

**ANSWERS** Answers for the **Reflect** part of the lesson appear in the separate **Practice and Reflect answer guide**.

## After the lesson ⏸

- Were children confident using a number line?
- Can children use a number line to round numbers to the nearest 100?
- Are children able to round numbers to the nearest 100 without a number line?

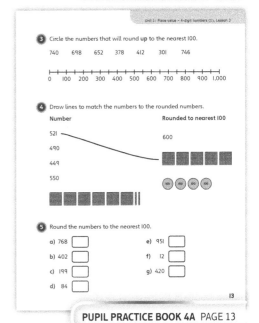

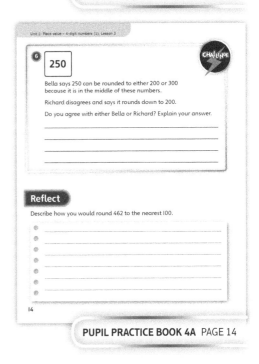

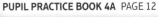

# Counting in 1,000s

## Learning focus

In this lesson, children will count in 1,000s from 0 to 10,000, forwards and backwards.

## Small steps

→ Previous step: Rounding to the nearest 100
→ **This step: Counting in 1,000s**
→ Next step: Representing 4-digit numbers

### NATIONAL CURRICULUM LINKS

**Year 4 Number – number and place value**
- Count in multiples of 6, 7, 9, 25 and 1,000.
- Identify, represent and estimate numbers using different representations.

### ASSESSING MASTERY

Children can count in 1,000s from 0 to 10,000, forwards and backwards. Children should recognise what 1,000 looks like and be able to write numbers in words and numerals.

### COMMON MISCONCEPTIONS

Children may struggle to start counting mid-sequence (for example, starting at 5,000 rather than at 0).

Encourage children to point to a representation of each 1,000 as they say it. Ask:
- *Can you point to the number as you count?*
- *Can you count backwards in 1,000s?*

### STRENGTHENING UNDERSTANDING

To strengthen understanding, ask children to count in 1,000s using base 10 equipment. Use the base 10 equipment to support children's ability to visualise 1,000. Discuss how the 1,000 block is made up of 10 hundreds.

### GOING DEEPER

Ask children to count both forwards and backwards in 1,000s.

Ask them to count in 1,000s above 10,000. Ask: *What number comes next? How do you know?*

### KEY LANGUAGE

**In lesson:** thousands (1,000s), represent, number sequences

**Other language to be used by teacher:** numeral, hundreds (100s), tens (10s), number line

### STRUCTURES AND REPRESENTATIONS

number tracks

### RESOURCES

**Mandatory:** base 10 equipment

**Optional:** place value counters, specifically numbered number lines

 In the eTextbook of this lesson, you will find interactive links to a selection of teaching tools.

## Before you teach

- Can children count in 10s?
- Can children count in 100s?
- Can children use a comma correctly when writing numbers in 1,000s?

## Discover

**WAYS OF WORKING** Pair work

**ASK**

- Question ❶ a): *How many boxes of lemon sweets are there?*
- Question ❶ a): *How many sweets are there in each box?*
- Question ❶ a): *Should we count in 10s, 100s or 1,000s? Why?*

**IN FOCUS** Questions ❶ a) and b) stress the importance of counting from 0 in 1,000s to see how many sweets there are. It is important that children count in 1,000s at this stage, rather than just saying the answer, so encourage them to point to the boxes of sweets as they count.

**PRACTICAL TIPS** Introduce children to the 1,000 block in base 10 equipment and encourage them to use these blocks to represent the boxes of sweets as they count.

**ANSWERS**

Question ❶ a): There are 4,000 lemon sweets.

Question ❶ b): There are 6,000 strawberry sweets.

### Counting in 1,000s

**Discover**

❶ a) How many lemon sweets are there on the pallet?
   b) How many strawberry sweets are there on the pallet?

20

**PUPIL TEXTBOOK 4A** PAGE 20

## Share

**WAYS OF WORKING** Whole class teacher led

**ASK**

- Question ❶ a): *How many sweets does each box represent? How can you use this information to find the total number of sweets?*
- Question ❶ b): *How can you work out part b) using your answer to part a)?*

**IN FOCUS** In question ❶ b) children may see that they can start the count from 4,000, based on the answer to part a). This is a useful discussion point. Ask: *Do we always need to start the count at 0?*

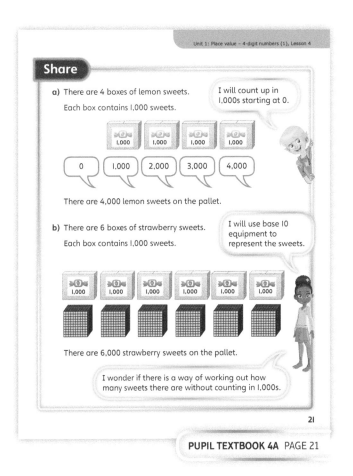

**Share**

a) There are 4 boxes of lemon sweets.
   Each box contains 1,000 sweets.

> I will count up in 1,000s starting at 0.

0 | 1,000 | 2,000 | 3,000 | 4,000

There are 4,000 lemon sweets on the pallet.

b) There are 6 boxes of strawberry sweets.
   Each box contains 1,000 sweets.

> I will use base 10 equipment to represent the sweets.

There are 6,000 strawberry sweets on the pallet.

> I wonder if there is a way of working out how many sweets there are without counting in 1,000s.

21

**PUPIL TEXTBOOK 4A** PAGE 21

# Think together

**WAYS OF WORKING** Whole class teacher led (I do, We do, You do)

**ASK**

Question **1**: *How many boxes of strawberry and lemon sweets are there? How many sweets are in each box?*

Question **2**: *How can the numbers shown help us?*

Question **4**: *Do you know how to make the number using base 10 equipment?*

**IN FOCUS** Question **2** encourages children to apply their knowledge from the beginning of the lesson to working out the missing numbers in a sequence or number track. Question **4** introduces 10,000 as 10 × 1,000 and should strengthen children's understanding of the base 10 system.

**STRENGTHEN** Encourage children to represent numbers using base 10 equipment and to point to the 1,000s as they count.

**DEEPEN** Question **4** could lead to other questions, such as: *How many 100s make 1,000? How many 10s make 1,000? How many 1s make 1,000? Can you see a pattern?*

**ASSESSMENT CHECKPOINT** Questions **1** and **2** will allow you to see whether children can count in 1,000s and what strategies they use. Can children use a number track effectively to find the missing numbers? Do children need equipment to help them with this?

**ANSWERS**

Question **1**: There are 3,000 strawberry sweets.
There are 7,000 lemon sweets.
In total there are 10,000 sweets.

Question **2** a): 3,000, 4,000, 6,000

Question **2** b): 7,000, 5,000, 4,000

Question **2** c): 0, 2,000, 4,000

Question **2** d): 7,000, 9,000, 10,000

Question **3**: Seven thousand, 7,000

Question **4**: 10 thousands make 10,000.

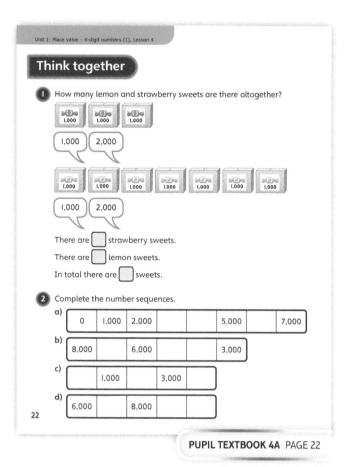

**PUPIL TEXTBOOK 4A** PAGE 22

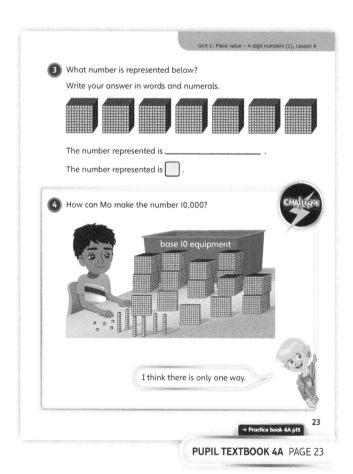

**PUPIL TEXTBOOK 4A** PAGE 23

## Practice

**WAYS OF WORKING** Independent thinking

**IN FOCUS** Question **1** further supports and develops children's ability to count in 1,000s.

Question **2** allows children to use their previous learning of number tracks to count in 1,000s.

Questions **3** and **4** encourage children to use concrete equipment to recognise and count in 1,000s.

**STRENGTHEN** If children struggle to count in 1,000s, allow them to count in 100s to begin with, and then build on this understanding. Children can also use concrete resources to build 100s and count in 100s, then replicate this with 1,000s. Ensure that children are clearly linking the resources to counting, and count aloud with them.

**DEEPEN** Question **6** challenges children to use their reasoning skills and state how and why they know the answer. Look at how children record their answers. Encourage children to work in pairs to prove their answers.

**ASSESSMENT CHECKPOINT** Questions **1** and **2** will allow you to assess whether children can count in 1,000s, forwards and backwards, and whether they can continue a counting sequence regardless of the start point (i.e. not always starting from 0). The rest of the **Practice** section should allow you to see if children can link their understanding to concrete equipment.

**ANSWERS** Answers for the **Practice** part of the lesson appear in the separate **Practice and Reflect answer guide**.

## Reflect

**WAYS OF WORKING** Pair work

**IN FOCUS** This activity requires children to show what they have understood about counting in 1,000s. They should arrive at the answer by counting the number of red and blue pencils, and then counting the remaining boxes to see how many are green.

**ASSESSMENT CHECKPOINT** Look for children counting forwards or backwards in 1,000s to assess their understanding of the lesson. Children should not see this as an addition or subtraction problem.

**ANSWERS** Answers for the **Reflect** part of the lesson appear in the separate **Practice and Reflect answer guide**.

### After the lesson ⏸

- Were children confident counting in 1,000s?
- Are children able to count from any multiple of 1,000, forwards and backwards in 1,000s?
- Can children use concrete equipment, such as base 10, to count in 1,000s?

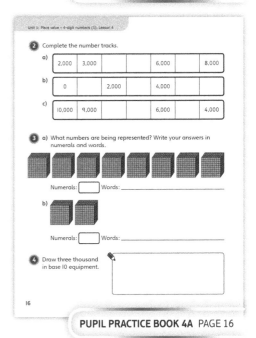

**PUPIL PRACTICE BOOK 4A** PAGE 15

**PUPIL PRACTICE BOOK 4A** PAGE 16

**PUPIL PRACTICE BOOK 4A** PAGE 17

# Representing 4-digit numbers

## Learning focus

In this lesson, children will represent 4-digit numbers using base 10 equipment and part-whole models.

## Small steps

→ Previous step: Counting in 1,000s
→ **This step: Representing 4-digit numbers**
→ Next step: 1,000s, 100s, 10s and 1s

### NATIONAL CURRICULUM LINKS

**Year 4 Number – Number and place value**
- Identify, represent and estimate numbers using different representations.
- Recognise the place value of each digit in a 4-digit number (thousands, hundreds, tens and ones).

### ASSESSING MASTERY

Children can make any 4-digit number using base 10 equipment and then represent this on a part-whole model. Children can partition the number into 1,000s, 100s, 10s and 1s, as well as write 4-digit numbers in digits and in words.

### COMMON MISCONCEPTIONS

Children may initially struggle to make a 4-digit number. To support their first attempts, ask:
- *Let's place the number we are making in a place value grid. How many 1,000s do we need? How many 100s? 10s? 1s?*

If children struggle with the idea of using 0 as a place holder, ask:
- *If there is nothing in one of your four columns, what do you need to do? How could you represent it? If you didn't use 0 as a place holder, what would happen? Would your number be correct?*

Children may not recognise the importance of placing 4-digit numbers in the correct place value order, for example, some children may think that 5 hundreds, 2 thousands, 7 tens and 3 ones make 5,273. To challenge this, ask:
- *What has the largest value; 1,000s, 100s, 10s or 1s? Which value should come first?*

### STRENGTHENING UNDERSTANDING

Get children to represent 4-digit numbers using base 10 equipment, then ask them to say the number aloud whilst pointing to the 1,000s, 100s, 10s and 1s. This will strengthen their understanding of place value and of how to write the number in words and digits. This will also develop children's understanding of the comma as showing where the 1,000s end and the 100s, 10s and 1s begin.

### GOING DEEPER

Children build on their prior knowledge that 10 ones are equal to 1 ten, and 10 tens are equal to 1 hundred, to deepen understanding that 10 hundreds are equal to 1 thousand. They see that this exchange can now be used to represent 4-digit numbers in different ways. Extend this understanding by challenging children to order numbers delivered to them out of their place value order, for example, ask: *What is this number: it has 3 tens, 9 ones, 5 thousands and 2 hundreds?* Take every opportunity to reinforce the importance of ordering digits so that that the largest place value comes first.

### KEY LANGUAGE

**In lesson:** thousands (1,000s), hundreds (100s), tens (10s), ones (1s), representation, digits

**Other language to be used by teacher:** exchange, numerals, altogether

### STRUCTURES AND REPRESENTATIONS

base 10 equipment, part-whole model, place value counters

### RESOURCES

**Mandatory:** base 10 equipment, blank part-whole models

**Optional:** place value counters

 In the eTextbook of this lesson, you will find interactive links to a selection of teaching tools.

## Before you teach

- Can children represent 2- and 3-digit numbers using base 10 equipment?
- Can children count in thousands?
- Can children write 2- and 3-digit numbers in digits and in words?

## Discover

**WAYS OF WORKING** Pair work

**ASK**

- Question **1** a): *How many legs are on each alien? What place values do you think the aliens represent?*
- Question **1** a): *How many of each alien are there?*
- Question **1** b): *Can we exchange some of our 1,000s for 100s, or 10s for 1s to make 7,420 in different ways?*

**IN FOCUS** Question **1** a) focuses on representing numbers up to 10,000. Children focus on the difference between the aliens and therefore the difference in the value of each digit in a 4-digit number.

Question **1** b) looks at making a number in a variety of different ways, allowing children to explore what the possibilities could be.

**PRACTICAL TIPS** To support understanding in question **1** b), remind children of their learning in Year 3 when they looked at place value to 100 and the fact that 10 tens make 1 hundred. Use base 10 equipment in a place value grid to physically represent the number and value of the aliens and their legs.

**ANSWERS**

Question **1** a): There are 4,531 legs altogether.

Question **1** b): There are 7 Thods, 4 Hods and 2 Tods.

> There is more than one answer.
> For example:
> 7 Thods, 4 Hods and 20 Ods
> 6 Thods, 14 Hods and 2 Tods.

## Share

**WAYS OF WORKING** Whole class teacher led

**ASK**

- Question **1** a): *How can you count the total? What would you count first? Why?*
- Question **1** a): *How many ones are in a thousand block? How does this link to the number of legs on a Thod?*
- Question **1** b): *Why can we have different numbers of aliens for 7,420 legs? How does exchanging help us find more answers?*

**IN FOCUS** Question **1** a) focuses on partitioning a number using base 10 equipment. Start by linking each of the aliens to the base 10 blocks and instead of counting the aliens, count the blocks. If necessary, prompt children to start with the highest place value.

Question **1** b) explores flexible partitioning and encourages children to draw on previous learning about exchange. As a class, discuss different ways of partitioning the same number.

**STRENGTHEN** Use base 10 equipment and a part-whole model to reinforce understanding of exchange. For example, how many ways can 7,000 be represented in a part-whole model when 7,000 is the whole? This will help reinforce children's understanding of partitioning.

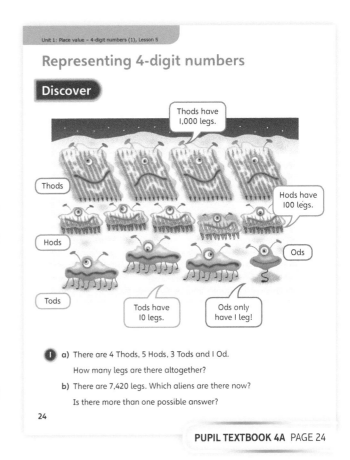

**PUPIL TEXTBOOK 4A** PAGE 24

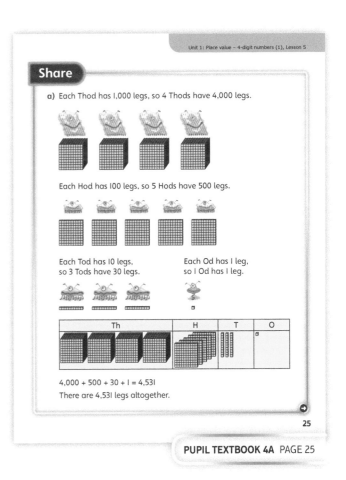

**PUPIL TEXTBOOK 4A** PAGE 25

## Think together

**WAYS OF WORKING** Whole class teacher led (I do, We do, You do)

**ASK**

- Question ❶: *How many thousand blocks do I need? How many 100s, 10s and 1s? What happens if there are 0 hundreds? How could you deal with this?*
- Question ❶: *How can saying the number aloud help you to write it in words?*
- Question ❷: *How does the base 10 equipment match to the part-whole model? Which part do you focus on first?*

**IN FOCUS** In question ❶, children look at what happens when there are 0 hundreds. Discuss with the class that they will need to include the 0 hundred as a place holder, to avoid ending up with a 3-digit number. Use base 10 equipment to link each alien with a block and encourage children to work with a blank place value grid to help them order their base 10 'aliens'. Link this back to the children's work in earlier year groups.

In question ❷, it is important to focus on the difference between part a and part b. Part b only has three parts to complete, even though it is a 4-digit number, as it has 0 as a place holder.

**STRENGTHEN** Children should make the numbers with base 10 equipment throughout this section to build their understanding of how to make 4-digit numbers. Use place value grids as necessary to support children when ordering their numbers.

**DEEPEN** Question ❸ allows children to look carefully at what is the same and what is different. It requires children to understand the difference between the values of 100 and 1,000. It also reintroduces the idea of exchanging 10 hundreds for 1 thousand.

**ASSESSMENT CHECKPOINT** In question ❶, check whether children can write the 4-digit numbers in digits and in words. In question ❸, look for children who understand the exchange between 1 thousand and 10 hundreds.

**ANSWERS**

Question ❶: There are 2,054 legs. There are two thousand and fifty-four legs.

Question ❷ a): Children complete the part-whole model with parts 5,000, 300, 50 and 2. (They may complete it differently and exchange across columns.)

Question ❷ b): Children complete the part-whole model with 1,000, 300 and 7. (They may complete it differently and exchange across columns.)

Question ❸: The base 10 equipment with 2 hundreds and 5 ones does not match the other representations as the other representations show 2,005, whereas this shows 205.

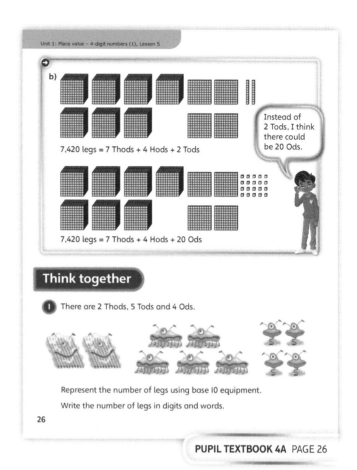

b)

7,420 legs = 7 Thods + 4 Hods + 2 Tods

*Instead of 2 Tods, I think there could be 20 Ods.*

7,420 legs = 7 Thods + 4 Hods + 20 Ods

**Think together**

❶ There are 2 Thods, 5 Tods and 4 Ods.

Represent the number of legs using base 10 equipment.

Write the number of legs in digits and words.

26

**PUPIL TEXTBOOK 4A** PAGE 26

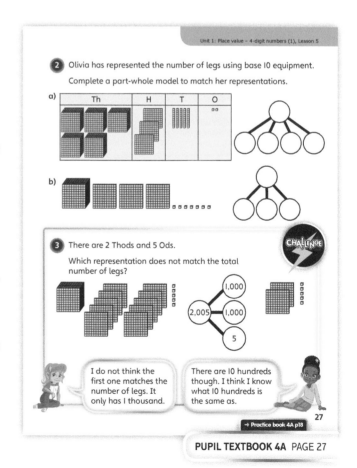

❷ Olivia has represented the number of legs using base 10 equipment.

Complete a part-whole model to match her representations.

a)

| Th | H | T | O |
| --- | --- | --- | --- |

b)

❸ There are 2 Thods and 5 Ods.

Which representation does not match the total number of legs?

CHALLENGE

1,000

2,005 — 1,000

5

*I do not think the first one matches the number of legs. It only has 1 thousand.*

*There are 10 hundreds though. I think I know what 10 hundreds is the same as.*

→ Practice book 4A p18

27

**PUPIL TEXTBOOK 4A** PAGE 27

# Practice

**WAYS OF WORKING** Independent thinking

**IN FOCUS** In question **1**, children use their knowledge of writing numbers in digits and words.

Questions **2** and **3** build on children's understanding and reinforce children's independent use of base 10 equipment and the part-whole model, demonstrating the link between them.

In questions **3**, **4** and **5**, children use their understanding of partitioning to reason, make connections between different models and find the odd one out as well as explain a mistake. They begin to record numbers as a given number of 1,000s, 100s, 10s and 1s. They also link this to a part-whole model.

**STRENGTHEN** Continue to support children with base 10 equipment to encourage them to make the numbers they are working with. Place base 10 equipment into part-whole models to reinforce number values and support the partitioning and exchange of large numbers.

**DEEPEN** Encourage children to justify their understanding in questions **4** and **5** by explaining the odd one out and explaining the mistake. Ensure children are using the correct language and full sentences to explain themselves clearly.

**ASSESSMENT CHECKPOINT** In question **1**, assess whether children can write numbers in words and digits.

In questions **2** and **3**, look at children's understanding of exchanging between columns to make numbers in different ways. Can children represent a number in base 10 equipment and use a part-whole model to organise their work and demonstrate their understanding of partitioning?

**ANSWERS** Answers for the **Practice** part of the lesson appear in the separate **Practice and Reflect answer guide**.

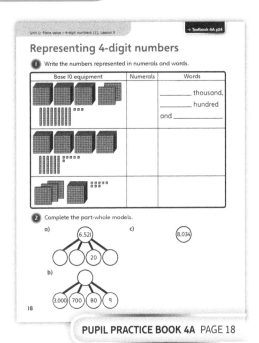

PUPIL PRACTICE BOOK 4A PAGE 18

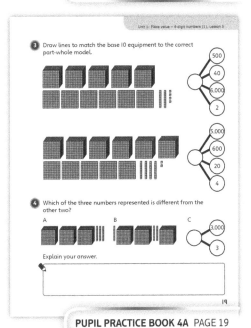

PUPIL PRACTICE BOOK 4A PAGE 19

# Reflect

**WAYS OF WORKING** Independent thinking

**IN FOCUS** Children use base 10 equipment and part-whole models to make a variety of 4-digit numbers.
Encourage children to represent an empty column with a digit of 0. Ask: *What does this mean?*

**ASSESSMENT CHECKPOINT** Children should now be able to make any 4-digit number using base 10 equipment. To reinforce learning, encourage children to make some of the numbers in more than one way.

**ANSWERS** Answers for the **Reflect** part of the lesson appear in the separate **Practice and Reflect answer guide**.

## After the lesson ⏸

- Did children need to use base 10 equipment to make every number?
- Could children represent 4-digit numbers in more than one way?
- Are children confident using a place holder 0 to make 4-digit numbers?

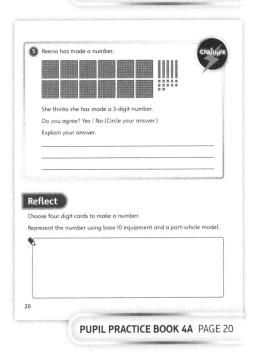

PUPIL PRACTICE BOOK 4A PAGE 20

# 1,000s, 100s, 10s and 1s

## Learning focus

In this lesson, children will represent 4-digit numbers using place value counters. They will use place value grids to help them correctly order and write their numbers in numerals.

## Small steps

→ Previous step: Representing 4-digit numbers
→ **This step: 1,000s, 100s, 10s and 1s**
→ Next step: The number line to 10,000 (1)

### NATIONAL CURRICULUM LINKS

**Year 4 Number – Number and place value**
- Recognise the place value of each digit in a four-digit number (thousands, hundreds, tens, and ones).
- Identify, represent and estimate numbers using different representations.

### ASSESSING MASTERY

Children can make any 4-digit number using place value counters. They can split the number into 1,000s, 100s, 10s and 1s, and write the number in digits and in words.

### COMMON MISCONCEPTIONS

If children are struggling to make a number, ask:
- *Let's place the number you are making in a place value grid. How many 1,000s do you need? How many 100s? How many 10s? How many 1s?*

If children are struggling to make numbers using 0 as a place holder, ask:
- *If there is nothing in one of your four columns, what do you need to do? How could you represent it? If you didn't use 0 as a place holder, what would happen? Would your number be correct?*

### STRENGTHENING UNDERSTANDING

To strengthen understanding, make sure children are representing the 4-digit numbers using place value counters and linking these with base 10 equipment. When children are writing a number in words, encourage them to say the number aloud to help them master the structure of how to write numbers in words. This can then be linked to writing the number in digits and using the comma after the 1,000s to clearly signpost where the 1,000s end and the 100s, 10s and 1s begin.

### GOING DEEPER

Challenge children to make 4-digit numbers using a given number of place value counters. Demonstrate how important place value order is by giving children calculations with a 0 value place holder, or calculations out of their place value order, for example, ask: *What is 200 + 7,000 + 30 + 5?*

It shows a deeper understanding if children realise that they have to tackle the 1,000s first, then 100s, then 10s and then 1s.

### KEY LANGUAGE

**In lesson:** thousands (1,000s), hundreds (100s), tens (10s), ones (1s), different, same, represent

**Other language to be used by teacher:** exchange

### STRUCTURES AND REPRESENTATIONS

base 10 equipment, place value counters

### RESOURCES

**Mandatory:** place value counters, base 10 equipment, blank place value grids

 In the eTextbook of this lesson, you will find interactive links to a selection of teaching tools.

## Before you teach

- Can children represent 4-digit numbers using base 10 equipment?
- Can children count in 1,000s?
- Do children understand how to make 4-digit numbers in a part-whole model?

## Discover

Pair work

ASK

- Question ❶ a): *Can you make the number Aki has made? Use the place value grid to help you.*
- Question ❶ a): *What is the difference between numbered counters and blank ones? (The latter can be used in any column.)*
- Question ❶ b): *How will changing the position of the counters on our place value grid make different 4-digit numbers?*

IN FOCUS  Question ❶ b) allows children to think more creatively to find a variety of answers. Ensure children understand that the value of the counter is now dictated by which column of the place value grid they put it into.

PRACTICAL TIPS  To support question ❶ a), use a place value grid and seven place value counters to physically demonstrate the number that Aki has made, and to compare and link the place value counters to the base 10 equipment. In question ❶ b), use seven blank counters in a place value grid to make as many numbers as possible. Move the counters around to see how the value of the counters changes depending on which column they are placed into on the grid. It is important that children see and understand the difference between the place value counters and the blank counters in this section.

ANSWERS

Question ❶ a): Aki has made 2,311.

Question ❶ b): Children work systematically to find all the different numbers they can make with seven counters: for example: 1,600, 2,410, 7,000.

## Share

Whole class teacher led

ASK

- Question ❶ a): *How do the counters and place value grid help you to partition the number? How does the place value grid help you organise your work? How does it help you see how many 1,000s? Why do we put the columns in this order?*
- Question ❶ b): *How many different answers are there around the classroom using seven counters?*
- Question ❶ b): *How do you partition each of your numbers and write it in digits and in words?*

IN FOCUS  Question ❶ breaks down a single number into 1,000s, 100s, 10s and 1s, using place value counters and a place value grid to scaffold understanding. To support this further, link the value of the counters back to the more familiar base 10 equipment and part-whole model. Can children represent Aki's number using all three models?

Question ❶ b) gives children the opportunity to think about different 4-digit numbers, including numbers that have a 0 value in some columns. Model for children a systematic way of moving the seven counters on a place value grid to make as many 4-digit numbers as possible.

### 1,000s, 100s, 10s and 1s

**Discover**

How many different 4-digit numbers can you make using 7 place value counters?

Aki

❶ a) What number has Aki made using 7 place value counters?

Represent the number using base 10 equipment.

b) Make a different number using 7 plain counters on a place value grid.

28

PUPIL TEXTBOOK 4A  PAGE 28

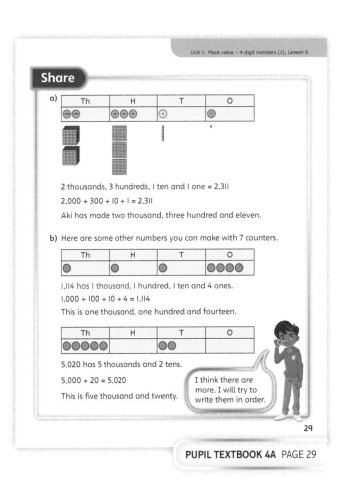

**Share**

a)

| Th | H | T | O |
|---|---|---|---|

2 thousands, 3 hundreds, 1 ten and 1 one = 2,311

2,000 + 300 + 10 + 1 = 2,311

Aki has made two thousand, three hundred and eleven.

b) Here are some other numbers you can make with 7 counters.

| Th | H | T | O |
|---|---|---|---|

1,114 has 1 thousand, 1 hundred, 1 ten and 4 ones.

1,000 + 100 + 10 + 4 = 1,114

This is one thousand, one hundred and fourteen.

| Th | H | T | O |
|---|---|---|---|

5,020 has 5 thousands and 2 tens.

5,000 + 20 = 5,020

This is five thousand and twenty.

I think there are more. I will try to write them in order.

29

PUPIL TEXTBOOK 4A  PAGE 29

# Think together

**WAYS OF WORKING** Whole class teacher led (I do, We do, You do)

**ASK**

- Question **1**: *What is the difference between making a number with blank counters and making it with place value counters on the place value grid? Which is clearer?*
- Question **2**: *How can saying the number aloud help you to write it in words?*
- Question **3**: *Can you make both numbers yourself? Can you exchange any of your counters?*

**IN FOCUS** Question **1** gives children the opportunity to practise making numbers using place value counters on a place value grid, reinforcing their understanding of the place values of different digits in a 4-digit number.

In question **2**, children use their knowledge of place value counters to complete number sentences, writing 4-digit numbers in numerals. Look out for children working on question **2** b) – how do they deal with a 0 value?

Question **3** encourages children to see how the same number can be made in different ways using exchange. What is their initial reaction to this question? Now refer to what Dexter and Ash are saying to encourage broader thinking.

**STRENGTHEN** In question **2**, encourage children to recreate each number using counters on a place value grid. To further support understanding, children can use base 10 equipment to represent the numbers in the questions. Demonstrate how each base 10 block is represented by its corresponding place value counter, to ensure the children's understanding is secure.

**DEEPEN** Question **3** extends learning by allowing children to look carefully at what is the same and what is different. Even though a number is made differently, it may still represent the same value altogether. Discuss the term 'exchange' and ask children which values can be exchanged in this question. It may be helpful to use a 1,000 block and ten 100 blocks to physically demonstrate this exchange.

**ASSESSMENT CHECKPOINT** In question **3**, look for children who understand the exchange between 1,000 and 10 hundreds.

**ANSWERS**

Question **1** a): 3,462

Question **1** b): 4,023

Question **1** c): 5,492

Question **2** a): 2,542 = 2 thousands, 5 hundreds, 4 tens and 2 ones.

Question **2** b): 5,702 = 5 thousands, 7 hundreds, 0 tens and 2 ones.

Question **3**: Kate and Isla have both made 3,232, so Kate is correct. Isla has used 10 hundreds to make one of her 1,000s.

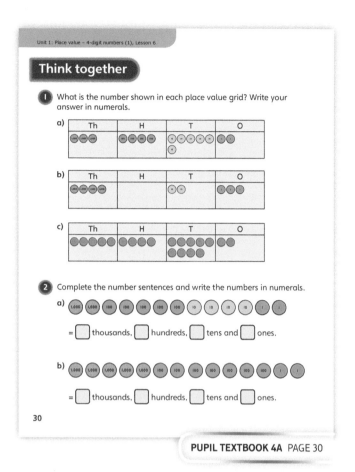

**PUPIL TEXTBOOK 4A** PAGE 30

**PUPIL TEXTBOOK 4A** PAGE 31

## Practice

**WAYS OF WORKING** Independent thinking

**IN FOCUS** Question ❸ gives children further opportunity to write 4-digit numbers in numerals and in digits, reinforcing the links between how numbers are made and represented in digits and in written form.

Question ❺ challenges children to follow a set of rules to make a 4-digit number.

**STRENGTHEN** Continue to support children by giving them access to counters and blank place value grids to encourage them to make the numbers in the questions.

**DEEPEN** In question ❺, encourage children to check their thinking by making the numbers before they draw them. Extend learning by asking: *How many different numbers can you make? Is there a system you can use to help you make the most possible numbers?*

**THINK DIFFERENTLY** In question ❹ children draw on what they have learnt in this lesson to interpret different representations of, and ways of writing, a 4-digit number. They need to notice when the place values are not listed in order.

**ASSESSMENT CHECKPOINT** Assess whether children can write numbers in words and digits. Review children's understanding of exchanging between columns to make numbers in different ways.

**ANSWERS** Answers for the **Practice** part of the lesson appear in the separate **Practice and Reflect answer guide**.

## Reflect

**WAYS OF WORKING** Independent thinking

**IN FOCUS** Children consolidate their understanding that 1 thousand is the same as 10 hundreds. Hence they deduce that 2,300 is the same as 23 hundreds.

**ASSESSMENT CHECKPOINT** Do children understand the principles of place value, including the significance of empty columns and the need to use 0? Can they use their knowledge of exchange between columns to represent numbers in different ways?

**ANSWERS** Answers for the **Reflect** part of the lesson appear in the separate **Practice and Reflect answer guide**.

### After the lesson ⏸

- Can children write any 4-digit number in digits and in words?
- Can children represent 4-digit numbers in more than one way?
- Do children recognise when values can be exchanged to represent numbers in a different way?

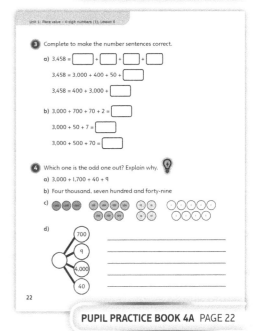

**PUPIL PRACTICE BOOK 4A** PAGE 21

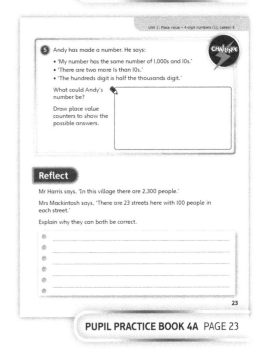

**PUPIL PRACTICE BOOK 4A** PAGE 22

**PUPIL PRACTICE BOOK 4A** PAGE 23

# The number line to 10,000 ①

## Learning focus

In this lesson, children will use their knowledge of counting in 10s, 100s and 1,000s to identify numbers, and fill in intervals, on number lines up to 10,000.

## Small steps

→ Previous step: 1,000s, 100s, 10s, 1s
→ **This step: The number line to 10,000 (1)**
→ Next step: The number line to 10,000 (2)

### NATIONAL CURRICULUM LINKS

**Year 4 Number – Number and place value**
• Identify, represent and estimate numbers using different representations.
• Recognise the place value of each digit in a four-digit number (thousands, hundreds, tens, and ones).

### ASSESSING MASTERY

Children can successfully place the correct numbers on markers of a number line to 10,000. Children can identify and explain mistakes on number lines.

### COMMON MISCONCEPTIONS

Children may find identifying intervals on a number line confusing, and not be sure whether they are counting in 1s, 10s, 100s or 1,000s. It is important that children take note of the numbers at either end of the number line and then count the intervals in between to work out what each one represents. Ask:
• *Where does the number line start? Where does it end? How can we check if the number line is going up in 10s, 100s or 1,000s?*

### STRENGTHENING UNDERSTANDING

To support understanding, make it explicit to children that they need to count in regular intervals to find the numbers that are missing. Can they see a pattern? Check that children can confidently count in 1s, 10s and 100s before starting this unit.

### GOING DEEPER

Can children place 7,000 on an open number line between 0 and 10,000? Children should begin by thinking about the location of the 7,000 in relation to the end point. Encourage more confident learners to put this number on other number lines. For example, where would they place 7,000 on a number line with 5,000 and 10,000 at either end?

### KEY LANGUAGE

**In lesson:** check, counting stick, equal intervals, ones (1s), tens (10s), hundreds (100s), thousands (1,000s), ten thousands (10,000s), end numbers

**Other language to be used by the teacher:** missing, groups, counting up

### STRUCTURES AND REPRESENTATIONS

number lines

### RESOURCES

**Mandatory:** blank number lines

**Optional:** place value counters, base 10 equipment

 In the eTextbook of this lesson, you will find interactive links to a selection of teaching tools.

## Before you teach

• Can children count in 100s?
• Can children count in 1,000s?
• Can children label a number line?

## Discover

**WAYS OF WORKING** Pair work

**ASK**

- Question ① a) or b): *What numbers can you see on the counting stick?*
- Question ① a) or b): *What are the numbers at the ends of the line? What do you think the numbers in between might be?*
- Question ① a) or b): *How many intervals are there? How could you check? Let's count aloud together.*

**IN FOCUS** Question ① b) requires children to think about whether this number line is also going up in 1,000s. Encourage children to discuss the difference between the two lines in the question. Children should count aloud in pairs to check the missing values.

**PRACTICAL TIPS** Make blank number lines and counting sticks available for children to use in this lesson. Work together to produce a class number line that you can display in the classroom to further scaffold and embed learning here.

**ANSWERS**

Question ① a): 1,000, 2,000, 3,000, 4,000, 5,000, 6,000, 7,000, 8,000, 9,000.

Question ① b): 1,100, 1,200, 1,300, 1,400, 1,500, 1,600, 1,700, 1,800, 1,900.

### The number line to 10,000 ①

**Discover**

① a) What numbers are missing from Counting Stick A?

b) What numbers are missing from Counting Stick B?

32

**PUPIL TEXTBOOK 4A** PAGE 32

## Share

**WAYS OF WORKING** Whole class teacher led

**ASK**

- Question ① a) and b): *How did you work out what intervals the number line went up in? How could you check?*
- Question ① a) and b): *Do these number lines go up by the same amount? How do you know? How can you check if you are right?*

**IN FOCUS** Discuss the methods that children have used to work out their answers. Look at how they worked out the answers and explore any wrong answers. For example, if a child says that the first counting stick goes up in 100s, ask questions to unpick their thinking. Encourage children to check their answer by counting up in 100s and realising that this does not produce an end number of 10,000. For question ① a) link the counting stick with the previous lesson's work on counting in 1,000s. Can children see the connection?

Discuss Ash's comment. Children may find out what each line goes up in through pattern spotting or trial and error. Count aloud as a class. Count forwards and backwards too.

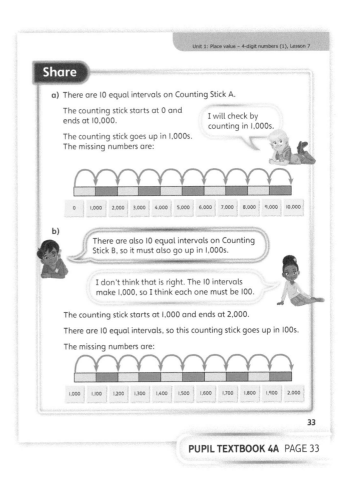

**Share**

a) There are 10 equal intervals on Counting Stick A.

The counting stick starts at 0 and ends at 10,000.

I will check by counting in 1,000s.

The counting stick goes up in 1,000s. The missing numbers are:

| 0 | 1,000 | 2,000 | 3,000 | 4,000 | 5,000 | 6,000 | 7,000 | 8,000 | 9,000 | 10,000 |

b)

There are also 10 equal intervals on Counting Stick B, so it must also go up in 1,000s.

I don't think that is right. The 10 intervals make 1,000, so I think each one must be 100.

The counting stick starts at 1,000 and ends at 2,000.

There are 10 equal intervals, so this counting stick goes up in 100s.

The missing numbers are:

| 1,000 | 1,100 | 1,200 | 1,300 | 1,400 | 1,500 | 1,600 | 1,700 | 1,800 | 1,900 | 2,000 |

33

**PUPIL TEXTBOOK 4A** PAGE 33

# Think together

Whole class teacher led (I do, We do, You do)

**ASK**

Question ❶: *Where does the number line start and end? What does it go up in? How can you check?*

Question ❷: *How do the numbers at the start and the end of this number line help you to fill in the missing numbers? Can you count them aloud?*

Questions ❸ and ❹: *Can you make the start and end numbers on the number lines with base 10 equipment? Now think about what the intervals in between the two points might be.*

**IN FOCUS** Question ❸ presents a different type of number line that goes up in 200s. Many children will use trial and error and realise that it does not go up in 10s, 100s or 1,000s. Discuss how they can use the end point of the number line to help them.

Question ❹ investigates a common mistake that children might make when completing a number line and asks them to explain the mistake. Refer them to what Dexter is saying to help support their thinking.

**STRENGTHEN** Support children in this section by practising counting in 1,000s aloud as a class. Reinforce this by pointing to the 1,000s on a number line at the same time as you count up.

Consider the end points of the number lines together as a class. Ask: *What intervals could this number line be going up in? Let's check.*

Use base 10 equipment to make the end points of the number lines, helping to expose what each interval could be. For example, if the number line ends with a 1,000 block, this should encourage children to investigate whether the number line goes up in 100s.

**DEEPEN** To extend learning in this section, look at number lines that do not go up in 1s, 10s, 100s or 1,000s. For example, ask children to work out intervals on number lines that go up in 200s, 20s or 50s.

**ASSESSMENT CHECKPOINT** In questions ❶, ❷ and ❸, can children recognise when a line goes up in 1s, 10s, 100s and 1,000s? Children should be able to write the numbers on these open number lines by considering the start and end points.

**ANSWERS**

Question ❶: 3,520, 3,530, 3,540, 3,550, 3,570, 3,590

Question ❷: 4,566

Question ❸: 3,200, 3,400, 3,600, 3,800, 4,000, 4,200, 4,400, 4,600, 4,800

Question ❹: Max is incorrect because he is counting in 1s rather than in 10s.

If there were 20 intervals, each jump would be 5.

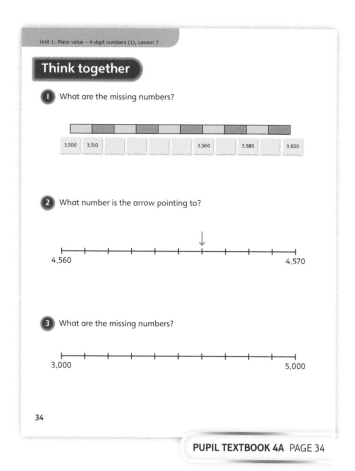

PUPIL TEXTBOOK 4A PAGE 34

PUPIL TEXTBOOK 4A PAGE 35

## Practice

**WAYS OF WORKING** Independent thinking

**IN FOCUS** Question ③ encourages children to use their understanding of number lines and previous counting strategies to identify the position of a number on a number line.

Question ④ challenges children to use their understanding of number lines and to realise that they need to find the value of the intervals in order to find the values of A and B.

**STRENGTHEN** If children struggle with the concept of counting in 1,000s, link the use of a number line back to counting in 1,000s. Allow children to practise this skill first, ensuring they are confident with it before moving on to the questions in the workbook.

**ASSESSMENT CHECKPOINT** Questions ① and ② reveal whether children can identify numbers on a number line and whether they can complete a number line with blank intervals.

Questions ③ and ④ allow children to demonstrate that they can use previous knowledge to identify the position of a number on a number line.

**ANSWERS** Answers for the **Practice** part of the lesson appear in the separate **Practice and Reflect answer guide**.

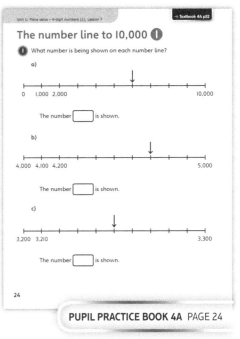

PUPIL PRACTICE BOOK 4A PAGE 24

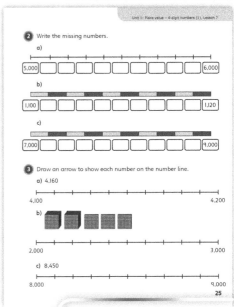

PUPIL PRACTICE BOOK 4A PAGE 25

## Reflect

**WAYS OF WORKING** Pair work

**IN FOCUS** This activity allows children to show what they have understood and to explain what they know about intervals.

**ASSESSMENT CHECKPOINT** This **Reflect** activity should help you to assess whether children can use start and end points to correctly identify missing numbers on a number line. Children's explanations will reveal their thinking and direct you to any remaining misconceptions that may still need to be addressed.

**ANSWERS** Answers for the **Reflect** part of the lesson appear in the separate **Practice and Reflect answer guide**.

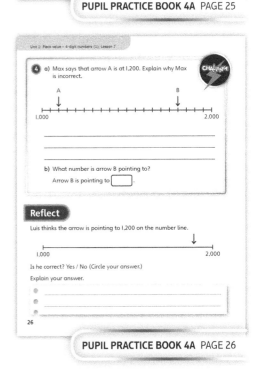

PUPIL PRACTICE BOOK 4A PAGE 26

### After the lesson ⏸

- Can children count in 10s, 100s and 1,000s?
- Can children identify numbers on a 1s, 10s, 100s and 1,000s number line?
- Can children complete number lines with different intervals, such as 200s, 20s and 50s?

# The number line to 10,000 ②

## Learning focus

In this lesson, children will place numbers on a number line and read off values. They will write down numbers between two given numbers on a number line.

## Small steps

→ Previous step: The number line to 10,000 (1)
→ **This step: The number line to 10,000 (2)**
→ Next step: Roman numerals to 100

### NATIONAL CURRICULUM LINKS

**Year 4 Number – Number and place value**
- Order and compare numbers beyond 1,000.
- Identify, represent and estimate numbers using different representations.
- Recognise the place value of each digit in a four-digit number (thousands, hundreds, tens, and ones).

### ASSESSING MASTERY

Children can place numbers on a number line up to 10,000 and are able to fill in gaps in number lines between two given numbers. Children can reason what the intervals between a start and an end number on a number line will be.

### COMMON MISCONCEPTIONS

Children may incorrectly place numbers on a number line because they have not worked out or cannot work out the value of each interval on it. Ask children to use trial and error to come up with sensible conjectures. Ask:
- *Is the number line going up in 10s, 100s or 1,000s? How do you know?*

Advise children to look at what the start and end points are. Ask them to check whether their answer is right. For example, when placing 999 on a number line from 0 to 10,000, many will place it just before the 10,000, even though, when they think about it, they know this is not correct. Encourage children to take a step back and always double check their answer. Read the question aloud and ask them if their answer makes sense.

### STRENGTHENING UNDERSTANDING

To support children in this lesson always encourage them to look at the end points of the number lines they are working on first. Then, to help scaffold their understanding and their ability to work towards the right answers, ask them to write on any intermediate values, as they did in the previous lesson.

### GOING DEEPER

Ask children to locate numbers on a number line between two given end points by considering the width of each interval. Children could also find an end point or start number when they are given just some numbers that lie on the line.

### KEY LANGUAGE

**In lesson:** halfway, half-way between, number line, greater than, how far, **distance**

**Other language to be used by the teacher:** thousands (1,000s), hundreds (100s), tens (10s), intervals, estimate

### STRUCTURES AND REPRESENTATIONS

number lines

### RESOURCES

**Mandatory:** blank number lines

**Optional:** place value counters, base 10 equipment

 In the eTextbook of this lesson, you will find interactive links to a selection of teaching tools.

## Before you teach

- Can children count up to 10,000?
- Can children label a number line?
- Can children place a number on a number line?

## Discover

WAYS OF WORKING Pair work

**ASK**

- Question ① a): *Can you see how this image is a number line? What does it measure? What does it show?*
- Question ① a): *What is the scale on the number line? What units is it measured in? How do you know?*
- Question ① b): *How did you work out where to put 1,950 m on the number line? What numbers does it lie between? What numbers does it lie half-way between?*

**IN FOCUS** Question ① b) asks children to locate 1,950 on the number line. Ask them to explain the reasons for their choice. For example, should the marker lie between 1,900 and 2,000? Where between these two numbers is it? There will be lots of different answers to this question. Ask children to explain the reason for their answer; this will help you explore their thinking and work together to correct any mistakes.

**PRACTICAL TIPS** Ask children to find different scales that they might see at school or at home, such as a measuring jug or a set of scales. Encourage them to think about how this could be used as a number line. What scale does it use? Can children work out any of the numbers that are unmarked?

**ANSWERS**

Question ① a): Sofia has run about 1,070 metres.

Question ① b):

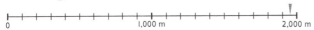

### The number line to 10,000 ②

#### Discover

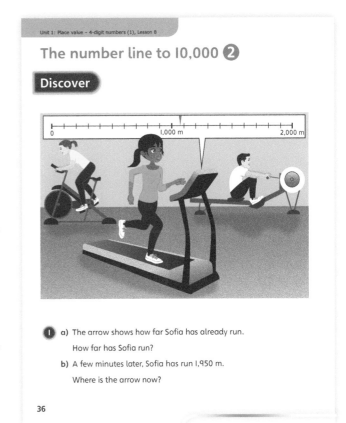

① a) The arrow shows how far Sofia has already run.
   How far has Sofia run?

 b) A few minutes later, Sofia has run 1,950 m.
   Where is the arrow now?

36

## Share

WAYS OF WORKING Whole class teacher led

**ASK**

- Question ① a): *Can you remember the scale used on this number line? What units is it measuring?*
- Question ① a): *What is the half-way point between 1,000 and 1,100? Has Sofia run more than this? How much more?*
- Question ① b): *Can you find the 1,900 mark on the number line? How far between 1,900 and the 2,000 end marker is 1,950?*

**IN FOCUS** Questions ① a) and ① b) demonstrate how number lines are used in the context of everyday life. Encourage children to discuss where they have seen number lines: for example, on dials in kitchens and in cars, on timelines and on measuring equipment. Ask children to think about and discuss what these are used for.

**STRENGTHEN** Support children in working out what each interval on the number line is worth. Encourage them to count aloud to check as Astrid did. For question ① a) prompt children to notice that the arrow is pointing between 1,000 and 1,100 and is over half-way between these two points, but just less than three-quarters towards the 1,100 mark. Explore children's reasoning and eliminate wrong answers in the process of working towards the correct one.

#### Share

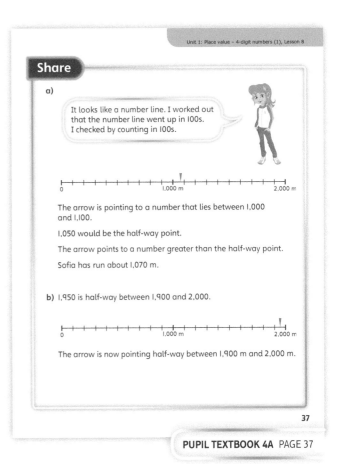

a)

> It looks like a number line. I worked out that the number line went up in 100s. I checked by counting in 100s.

The arrow is pointing to a number that lies between 1,000 and 1,100.

1,050 would be the half-way point.

The arrow points to a number greater than the half-way point.

Sofia has run about 1,070 m.

b) 1,950 is half-way between 1,900 and 2,000.

The arrow is now pointing half-way between 1,900 m and 2,000 m.

37

# Think together

WAYS OF WORKING Whole class teacher led (I do, We do, You do)

**ASK**

- Question **1**: *What does the dial go up in? How do you know? How can you work it out? How can you check?*
- Question **2**: *Look at the scales on the number lines. What is the same about them? What is different?*
- Question **3** c): *How can you find the missing end point? Is there a smallest/largest value it could be? Does it depend on where the other numbers go?*

**IN FOCUS** In question **1** children explore strategies to find missing values. Discuss how this is similar to the **Discover** question and how it is different. Ask children where the number line starts and ends this time.

Question **3** requires children to think about which numbers do and don't lie on a number line. In questions **3** a) and **3** b) they are given a start and an end point. In question **3** c) they must work out the end point. To support children in question **3** c) refer them to what Dexter and Ash are saying.

**STRENGTHEN** To support children when working out the intervals, encourage them to first look at the start and end values, then look at the difference between these values. Discuss how many intervals there are and then ask children to check whether they are right by counting aloud from the starting number. Does their counting match with the end number? If children find it difficult to place a number on a number line ask them what the number lies between. Ask them to mark all the values on the number line, and when they have done this ask them to reason whether the markings are right. For example, 1,050 is half-way between 1,000 and 1,100, and 1,070 is over halfway.

**DEEPEN** Extend children's thinking on from question **2** by discussing why the same number may appear in different places on different number lines. How does the scale of each line affect the values?

**ASSESSMENT CHECKPOINT** Check that children can work out what a scale increases by and where a given number should be placed. Can they work out the value of a given number on a number line?

**ANSWERS**

Question **1**: Sofia has cycled about 3,200 metres.

Question **2**: Arrow just before final interval on first number line.

Arrow just before end point on second number line.

Arrow just before mark between 8,000 and 10,000 on third number line.

Question **3** a): 1,135, 1,650 and 1,001 can be placed on the number line because these numbers are between 1,000 and 2,000.

Question **3** b): 9,300 and 2,330 cannot be placed on the number line.

Question **3** c): Accept all sensible answers, such as 5,500 or 6,000, depending on scale used.

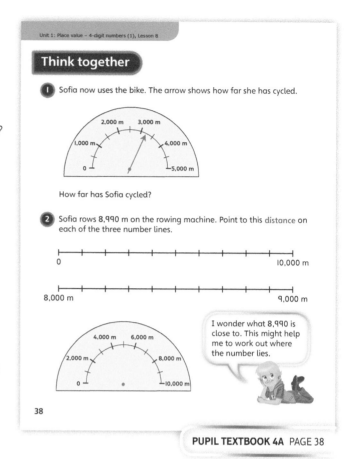

PUPIL TEXTBOOK 4A PAGE 38

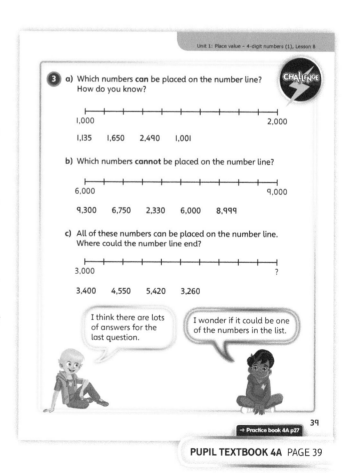

PUPIL TEXTBOOK 4A PAGE 39

## Practice

**WAYS OF WORKING** Independent thinking

**IN FOCUS** Question ① further supports and develops children's ability to locate numbers on number lines with differing increments.

Question ② reinforces that the same number can appear on different number lines in locations that look different.

Question ③ encourages children to develop their understanding by writing down three numbers that could appear on the number lines provided. Children must look at the start and end values and work out which numbers could lie in between.

**STRENGTHEN** In question ③ children may find it useful to make the start and end values on the number lines using base 10 equipment. This should support them to work out the size of the numbers that could go in between the start and end values, as it will give them a sense of the size of the numbers.

**DEEPEN** In question ④ children are given a fully open number line, and through estimation they have to work out the values of three different points on it. They must decide how to divide their line up so that they can start to work out the values. Some children may halve it and halve it again to start working out values. Others may split it up into 10 equal increments (perhaps using a ruler for more accuracy). Children may find it useful to discuss their strategies with a partner.

**ASSESSMENT CHECKPOINT** Questions ① and ② allow you to check that children can place numbers on number lines with differing intervals. Questions ③ and ④ enable children to demonstrate that they can place multiple numbers on number lines with a variety of intervals and ranges.

**ANSWERS** Answers for the **Practice** part of the lesson appear in the separate **Practice and Reflect answer guide**.

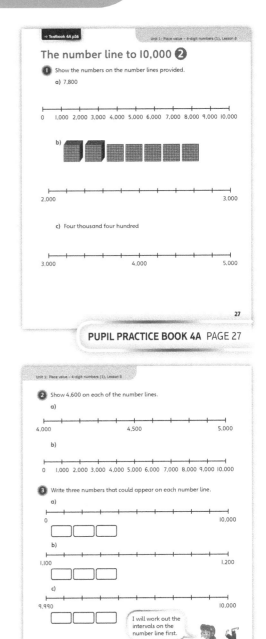

PUPIL PRACTICE BOOK 4A PAGE 27

PUPIL PRACTICE BOOK 4A PAGE 28

## Reflect

**WAYS OF WORKING** Pair work

**IN FOCUS** This activity should alert you to any misconceptions children have about this lesson. Children will need to demonstrate an understanding of the location of numbers on a number line and how the end points determine the relative positions of the numbers.

**ASSESSMENT CHECKPOINT** What can children reason about the end and start points? How many different answers can they place on the number line? Encourage them to discuss which answers are more reasonable than others.

**ANSWERS** Answers for the **Reflect** part of the lesson appear in the separate **Practice and Reflect answer guide**.

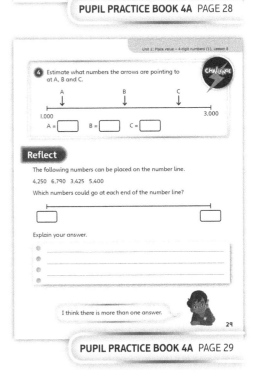

PUPIL PRACTICE BOOK 4A PAGE 29

## After the lesson ⏸

- Can children work out the intervals to correctly place a number on a number line?
- Can children work out numbers between two given numbers on a number line?
- Do children understand that number lines can be used in everyday contexts to measure values?

# Roman numerals to 100

## Learning focus

In this lesson, children learn the Roman numerals for 1, 5, 10, 50 and 100 and use this knowledge to convert between modern-day numerals and Roman numerals.

## Small steps

→ Previous step: The number line to 10,000 (2)
→ **This step: Roman numerals to 100**
→ Next step: Finding 1,000 more or less

### NATIONAL CURRICULUM LINKS

**Year 4 Number – Number and place value**

Read Roman numerals to 100 (I to C) and know that, over time, the numeral system changed to include the concept of 0 and place value.

### ASSESSING MASTERY

Children can identify Roman numerals and convert between them and numbers that they see in everyday life. Children can solve a range of problems that involve Roman numerals.

### COMMON MISCONCEPTIONS

Children may struggle with numbers such as IV and IX and XL as these are where I or X are written in front of numbers 5 or 10 times greater, meaning that children must subtract them from the larger number. For example, XL means '10 before 50, or 40'. Ask:
• *What do you have to do when a smaller number comes in front of a larger number? What number is IV, IX or XL?*

When comparing or ordering numbers in Roman numerals, children may think the greater the number of letters, the greater the number. This is not the case. Children should first work out what each number is before trying to order them.

### STRENGTHENING UNDERSTANDING

To try and help children understand that IV is 4 ask them what I is and what V represents. Next, explain that because the smaller number comes before the greater number this could be read as '1 before 5, which is 4'. VI is '1 after 5, which is 6'. So, IX could be seen as 1 before 10, or 9, and XL could be seen as 10 before 50, or 40.

### GOING DEEPER

To extend learning in this lesson, ask children questions that involve working out problems, for example:
XV + XLII = ___ or C – X = ___ or XXV + ___ = L.

### KEY LANGUAGE

**In lesson:** I, V, X, L and C, numerals, greater than (>), less than (<), order, partitioning

### STRUCTURES AND REPRESENTATIONS

part-whole models

### RESOURCES

**Optional:** base 10 equipment, blank part-whole models

 In the eTextbook of this lesson, you will find interactive links to a selection of teaching tools.

## Before you teach

• Can children tell the time to o'clock and half past the hour?
• Can children find 1 and 10 more or less than a number less than 100?
• Can they compare and order numbers less than 100?

## Discover

**WAYS OF WORKING** Pair work

**ASK**

- Question ① a): *Can you spot any patterns in the Roman numerals? Why isn't 4 written as IIII? Why do you think it is written as IV? Why do you think 6 is written as VI? Can you see the connection?*
- Question ① b): *What number is shown on the coin? Why? Why is the number 34 and not 36?*

**IN FOCUS** In question ① a) the majority of the numbers from 1 to 20 are given and children should look carefully at the numbers to see if they can spot any patterns. They may struggle with numbers such as IV, which is 4 (1 before 5). When a number with lesser value comes in front, this leads to a subtraction. Observe whether children can spot these numbers. Can children continue above 20 to demonstrate that they understand the pattern? Question ① b) provides an opportunity to attempt this.

**PRACTICAL TIPS** This lesson has potential to link with a topic on the Romans. Children could make the numbers out of string and straws to help them spot patterns.

**ANSWERS**

Question ① a): 13, 14, XVI, XX.

Question ① b): 34.

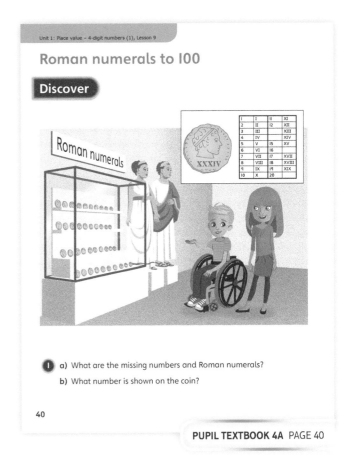

### Roman numerals to 100

**Discover**

a) What are the missing numbers and Roman numerals?

b) What number is shown on the coin?

40

**PUPIL TEXTBOOK 4A** PAGE 40

## Share

**WAYS OF WORKING** Whole class teacher led

**ASK**

- Question ① a): *Can you see how the numbers are formed? Can you continue the pattern beyond 20?*
- Question ① b): *Why does the part-whole model help? What would you do next?*

**IN FOCUS** Question ① b) uses a part-whole model to show how the number 34 is made up: XXX (30) and IV (4). Discuss with children that the part-whole model is a good way to show how a number can be partitioned.

**STRENGTHEN** Listen to children discuss their methods for finding the missing numbers. Discuss going beyond 20, and ask children what they think 21 might look like. Support children by talking them through the two examples given and the fact box and explanation that Sparks provides to explain how you should read Roman numerals. If there is a smaller number in front of a larger number then you subtract the smaller number from the larger one.

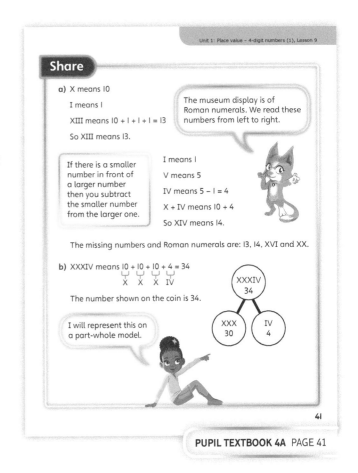

**PUPIL TEXTBOOK 4A** PAGE 41

# Think together

Whole class teacher led (I do, We do, You do)

**ASK**

- Question **1**: *Where do you see Roman numerals in real life?*
- Question **2**: *How do you read a clock? What happens if the big hand is pointing to XII? What is the time if the minute hand is pointing to VI? Do all clocks have IV for 4?*
- Question **3**: *Can you work out these numbers? Can you make your own numbers using these digits?*
- Question **4**: *Are you going to convert to numerals we use today? What is the first step? Can you work out any of Mrs Dean's questions without converting?*

**IN FOCUS** Question **2** provides children with practice reading clock faces marked in Roman numerals. They should be able to read the times o'clock and half past.

Question **3** introduces the symbols for 50 (L) and 100 (C) and asks children to convert between Roman numerals and the numbers used today. Pay special attention to questions where a smaller number precedes a greater one.

Question **4** provides four questions students have met in Year 2, but in this unit they involve using Roman numerals. Children are likely to approach this by converting, but discuss whether this is essential. Some children may think the more letters, the greater the number.

**STRENGTHEN** Try to find concrete examples of Roman numerals, such as volume numbers on old books, to consolidate children's understanding. Sit with children and go through the pattern that is made. Ask them to try and continue it. A part-whole model will help with larger numbers; use it to partition the number into 10s and 1s.

**DEEPEN** Ask children to try to write all the numbers from 1 to 100 in Roman numerals. This will help them with pattern spotting.

**ASSESSMENT CHECKPOINT** Questions **1** and **2** assess whether children understand the meaning of the Roman digits, are learning how they are combined, and recognise the sequence of numbers up to XII. Question **3** assesses understanding of subtractive combinations. Question **4** tests overall understanding.

**ANSWERS**

Question **1** a): 22

Question **1** b): 36

Question **2** a): 7 o'clock

Question **2** b): Half past 2

Question **3** a): 60

Question **3** b): 69

Question **3** c): 94

Question **3** d): LXXII

Question **3** e): XLV

Question **3** f): XC

Question **4**: a) XXXII, b) XXV, XXXIII, LXII, XC, c) XXI and d) LXIV

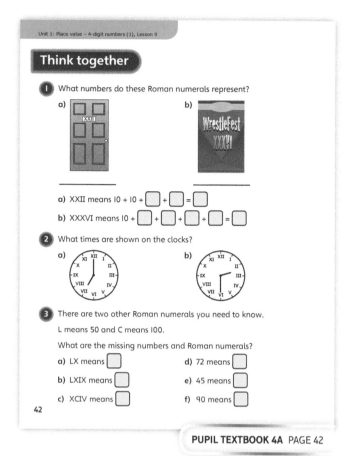

PUPIL TEXTBOOK 4A PAGE 42

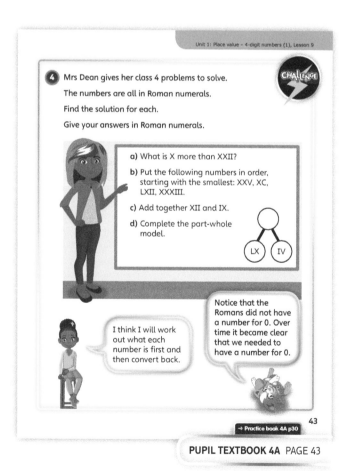

PUPIL TEXTBOOK 4A PAGE 43

## Practice

**WAYS OF WORKING** Independent work and pair work

**IN FOCUS** Questions ❶, ❷ and ❸ focus on converting Roman numerals. This is important because these are situations that children may come across in everyday life.

**STRENGTHEN** For question ❶ sit with children and go through the pattern that is made. Ask them to try and continue the pattern. Focus particular attention on numbers such as IV, where the smaller number comes before the greater. Ask what Roman numerals they can see in the pictures.

**DEEPEN** Question ❺ is a challenge as children need to find unknowns, working with Roman numerals. Look at different ways of working these out. In some questions, children won't need to convert first. Extend children's thinking by asking: *What methods have you used? Did you have to convert first? Were any questions easier than others? Why? Now make up your own problem for a partner.*

**THINK DIFFERENTLY** In Question ❹, children work with Roman numerals to complete comparison statements. Some children may be able to solve the problems without converting; most will need to convert first.

**ASSESSMENT CHECKPOINT** Questions ❶ and ❷ assess whether children can convert Roman numerals to modern numbers and whether they can apply their knowledge to solve problems in a variety of contexts, including telling the time.

**ANSWERS** Answers for the **Practice** part of the lesson appear in the separate **Practice and Reflect answer guide**.

## Reflect

**WAYS OF WORKING**

**IN FOCUS** In this question children have to try and identify numbers less than, greater than or equal to 50. Can they recognise when I, X or C comes before or after a larger numeral and therefore has to be subtracted or added? Understanding the significance of what comes before L or after L will be a key element of their reasoning.

**ASSESSMENT CHECKPOINT** Check that children can convert between Roman numerals and standard numbers that they see on a day-to-day basis. Do children know when a number is less than another number by looking at whether I or X comes before a larger numeral?

**ANSWERS** Answers for the **Reflect** part of the lesson appear in the separate **Practice and Reflect answer guide**.

## After the lesson ⏸

- Do children know the Roman numerals for 1, 5, 10, 50 and 100?
- Can children use these to work out the Roman numerals for other numbers and convert between them?
- Can children solve a range of problems involving Roman numerals, such as telling the time and solving addition and subtraction problems?

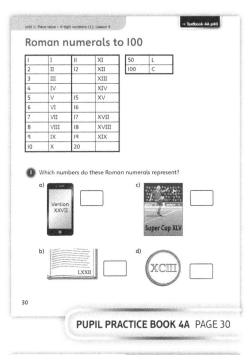

PUPIL PRACTICE BOOK 4A PAGE 30

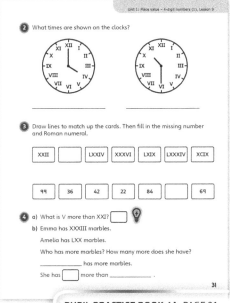

PUPIL PRACTICE BOOK 4A PAGE 31

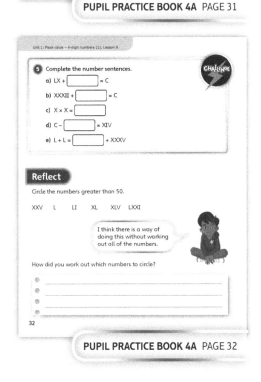

PUPIL PRACTICE BOOK 4A PAGE 32

# End of unit check

Don't forget the *Power Maths* unit assessment grid on p26.

**WAYS OF WORKING** Group work adult led

**IN FOCUS** Questions **1**, **4** and **5** check that children can identify a 4-digit number using different representations. In questions **1** and **4** children demonstrate that they know how a number can be partitioned in different ways.

- Question **2** assesses whether children can round a number.
- Question **3** checks that children can use a Roman numeral clock face to tell the time.
- Question **6** is a SATs-style question and shows understanding of the number line.

**ANSWERS AND COMMENTARY**

Children who have mastered this unit are able to represent 4-digit numbers using a variety of concrete apparatus. They can confidently order and compare a variety of 4-digit numbers and are able to round to the nearest 10, 100 and 1,000. As well as this, children are able to confidently use a number line, and use Roman numerals up to 100.

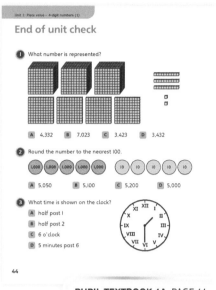

**PUPIL TEXTBOOK 4A** PAGE 44

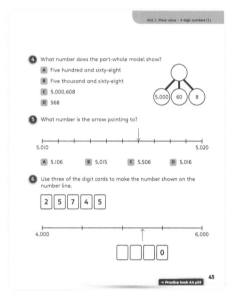

**PUPIL TEXTBOOK 4A** PAGE 45

| Q | A | WRONG ANSWERS AND MISCONCEPTIONS | STRENGTHENING UNDERSTANDING |
|---|---|---|---|
| 1 | D | Choosing A suggests that children have confused the 1,000s and the 100s representation. | Allow children to build the number using base 10 equipment. |
| 2 | B | D suggests that children have mistakenly rounded to the nearest 1,000 and forgotten that 50 rounds up to 100. | Allow children to place the number on a number line or place value grid to see how 5,050 relates to 5,000. |
| 3 | A | C suggests children have only looked at where the long hand is pointing; D suggests they have mixed up the long and short hands. | Provide children with extra practice reading Roman numerals to 100. Use a range of practice activities, including calculations and real-life contexts. |
| 4 | B | A and C suggest children are not remembering that a place value digit may be 0. They have written the non-zero digits sequentially without inserting 0 for the empty place value. | Provide children with a blank place value grid so they can see where each component belongs. |
| 5 | D | A and C suggest children have only looked at the final digit and counted six intervals. B suggests miscounting. | Support children here by counting the increments aloud to help them check their answers. |
| 6 | 5,250 | Children who do not start with 5 have not spotted that 5,000 is the midpoint. Other mistakes indicate they have not found half-way between 5,000 and 5,500. | Support children by counting the increments aloud with them. |

## My journal

**WAYS OF WORKING** Independent thinking

**ANSWERS AND COMMENTARY**

The number shown is 4,563. Children will describe the number using key terms from the unit, including 1,000s, 100s, 10s and 1s.

If children are finding it difficult to put the digits in the correct order, ask: *What number does each piece of base 10 equipment represent? How many 1,000s, 100s, 10s and 1s are there? Which of these comes first?* Encourage them to use a place value grid and put base 10 equipment in the correct columns.

## Power check

**WAYS OF WORKING** Independent thinking

**ASK**

- *How do you feel about place value in 4-digit numbers?*
- *How confident do you feel rounding 4-digit numbers to the nearest 1,000, 100 and 10?*
- *How confident do you feel placing 4-digit numbers in the correct order?*
- *What do you need to improve?*

## Power play

**WAYS OF WORKING** Pair work or small groups

**IN FOCUS** Use this activity to assess whether children can develop a strategy to find out how many 4-digit numbers they can make. Ask what difference it makes to use 6 or 7 counters.

**ANSWERS AND COMMENTARY** There are many possible answers for this question:

For example, here are the 10 answers that do not use a 0 digit: 1,113, 1,131, 1,311, 3,111, 1,122, 1,212, 1,221, 2,112, 2,121, 2,211.

6 of these round down to 1,000 (also, 3 of them round down to 2,000, and 1 rounds down to 3,000).

If you add an extra counter (7) there are twice as many combinations (20).

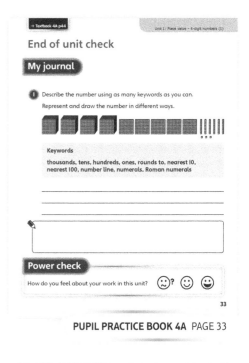

PUPIL PRACTICE BOOK 4A PAGE 33

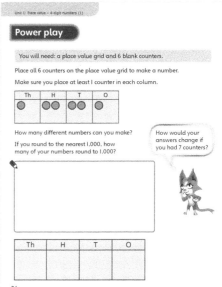

PUPIL PRACTICE BOOK 4A PAGE 34

## After the unit ⏸

- How confident are children with 4-digit numbers?
- Can children round and order 4-digit numbers confidently?

**Strengthen** and **Deepen** activities for this unit can be found in the *Power Maths* online subscription.

# Unit 2
## Place value – 4-digit numbers ②

**Mastery Expert tip!** "Children's understanding of 4-digit numbers will underpin the majority of the work for the year. It is therefore important that children are confident in representing 4-digit numbers in a variety of ways, including using base 10 equipment, place value counters and number lines."

**Don't forget to watch the Unit 2 video!**

## WHY THIS UNIT IS IMPORTANT

This unit is important as it is the first time children are introduced to negative numbers. Consolidating learning from the previous unit, children recap that 4-digit numbers are made up of 1,000s, 100s, 10s and 1s; they will be able to represent these numbers in many different ways. Children will look at 4-digit numbers on a number line up to 10,000 and use their understanding of the number line to help compare and order numbers as well as round numbers to the nearest 10, 100 and 1,000. Children will learn to confidently count forwards and backwards on number lines, including backwards through zero and into negative numbers. The skills and knowledge that children develop in this unit are fundamental to the rest of their learning within Year 4.

## WHERE THIS UNIT FITS

→ Unit 1: Place value – 4-digit numbers (1)
→ **Unit 2: Place value – 4-digit numbers (2)**
→ Unit 3: Addition and subtraction

This unit builds on the previous unit, which introduced 4-digit numbers, emphasising the importance of place value. In the previous unit, children learnt to represent 4-digit numbers and count in 1,000s. In this unit, they will move on to comparing 4-digit numbers and ordering numbers to 10,000. This prepares them for tackling addition and subtraction of 4-digit numbers in the next unit, including numbers where exchanges are needed in more than one column.

Before they start this unit, it is expected that children:

• know that a 4-digit number is made up of 1000s, 100s, 10s and 1s
• can represent 4-digit numbers in different ways, such as with base 10 equipment, place value grids and counters, part-whole models and number lines
• can compare and order 4-digit numbers
• know where a 4-digit number lies on a number line.

## ASSESSING MASTERY

Children who have mastered this unit will know that a number is made up of 1,000s, 100s, 10s and 1s and will be able to represent numbers in multiple ways. They will be able to compare and order 4-digit numbers by looking at the digits in each place value column. Children will understand the number line to 10,000 and start to know where numbers lie on the number line. They will extend this knowledge to look at negative numbers below 0 on the number line. Children will be able to round numbers to the nearest 10, 100 and 1,000.

| COMMON MISCONCEPTIONS | STRENGTHENING UNDERSTANDING | GOING DEEPER |
|---|---|---|
| Children may think that 3 tens + 2 thousands + 5 hundreds + 7 ones is 3,257 as opposed to 2,537. | Use base 10 equipment and place value counters to secure understanding of 4-digit numbers. | Ask children to partition numbers in different ways. For example, 1,223 is 1 × 1000, 1 × 100, 12 × 10 and 3 × 1. |
| Children may compare a 4-digit and a 3-digit number by looking at the first digit rather than the value of the digit. | Use base 10 equipment or place value counters in a place value grid to emphasise that you must compare numbers that have the same place value. | Challenge children to make as many numbers as possible using six counters in a ThHTO place value grid. Ask them to order their numbers on a number line. |

## WAYS OF WORKING

Use these pages to introduce the unit focus to children. You can use the characters to explore different ways of working too!

## STRUCTURES AND REPRESENTATIONS

**Place value grid, including using base 10 equipment, place value counters and blank counters:** This model will help children organise 4-digit numbers into 1,000s, 100s, 10s and 1s, with both concrete representations and abstract numbers.

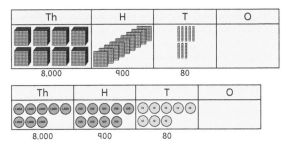

**Number line to 10,000:** This model will help children to visualise the order of numbers, and can help them to compare numbers. It can also help children to round numbers to the nearest 10, 100 and 1,000 and can be used to reinforce understanding of negative numbers.

```
 0   1,000 2,000 3,000 4,000 5,000 6,000 7,000 8,000 9,000 10,000
```

## KEY LANGUAGE

There is some key language that children will need to know as part of the learning in this unit.

→ thousands (1,000s), hundreds (100s), tens (10s), ones (1s)

→ place value

→ more, less

→ greater than (>), less than (<), equal to (=)

→ order, compare

→ round to, nearest

→ negative, positive

→ step

→ ascending, descending

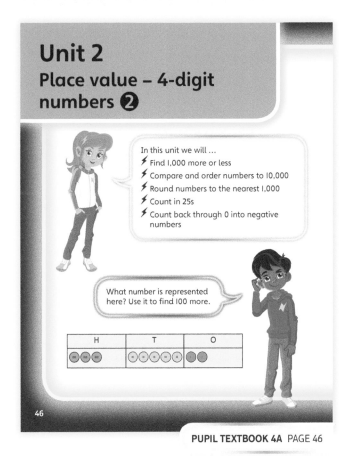

**PUPIL TEXTBOOK 4A** PAGE 46

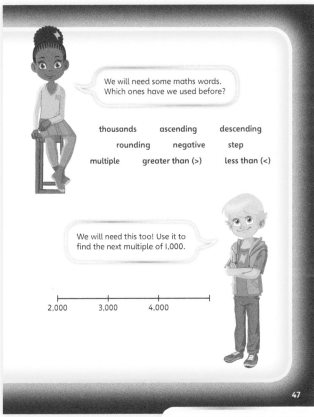

**PUPIL TEXTBOOK 4A** PAGE 47

# Finding 1,000 more or less

## Learning focus

In this lesson, children will find 1,000 more or less than a given number, using their knowledge of place value to help them. Children will also recap their learning on 10 and 100 more.

## Small steps

→ Previous step: Roman numerals to 100
→ **This step: Finding 1,000 more or less**
→ Next step: Comparing 4-digit numbers (1)

### NATIONAL CURRICULUM LINKS

**Year 4 Number – Number and Place Value**

Find 1,000 more or less than a given number.

### ASSESSING MASTERY

Children can successfully find 1,000 more or less than a given number in a range of contexts and identify which place value column will help them to do this. Children can use a variety of concrete apparatus to demonstrate their understanding.

### COMMON MISCONCEPTIONS

When presented with an abstract number, children may incorrectly find 10 or 100 more or less than the number rather than 1,000 more or less than the number. To reinforce children's place value understanding, and to help you address any misconceptions, ask:
• *Can you check your answer using base 10 equipment and a place value grid?*

### STRENGTHENING UNDERSTANDING

Provide children with opportunities to find 10 and 100 more or less than different numbers, using concrete equipment, such as base 10 equipment, to support them. Next, progress to 1,000 more or less than a number. Ensure children's understanding of how to use base 10 equipment, and what each cube represents, is secure. For example, give children a number such as 3,264 and ask them to say out loud how many thousands, hundreds, tens and ones make up this number. Use a place value grid to further support understanding, asking children to complete a grid for each 4-digit number you discuss. Can they find 10, 100 or 1,000 more or less than each number, using the place value grid to support them?

### GOING DEEPER

Can children find 10 or 100 more than a given number that might involve using an exchange? For example, can children work out 10 less than 2,003 or 100 less than 6,004? Encourage children to explore and think deeply about which digits change if they find 10, 100 or 1,000 more or less than a given number. Ask:
• *When you are finding 10 more or less, can the 1,000s digit change? Give an example of when this might happen.*

### KEY LANGUAGE

**In lesson:** less than, more than, subtract, exchange, place value, 10, 100, 1,000, function machine, **step**

**Other language to be used by the teacher:** more, less, greater, smaller, greatest, smallest, least, base 10 equipment, place value counters, place value grids

### STRUCTURES AND REPRESENTATIONS

base 10 equipment, place value counters

### RESOURCES

**Mandatory:** base 10 equipment, place value counters

**Optional:** number lines, place value grids

 In the eTextbook of this lesson, you will find interactive links to a selection of teaching tools.

## Before you teach

• Can children find 10 more or less than a number?
• Can children find 100 more or less than a number?
• Can children represent numbers using concrete equipment?

## Discover

**WAYS OF WORKING** Pair work

**ASK**

- Question ① a): *What does the word 'attendance' mean? How many people attended the game?*
- Question ① a): *What does each digit in the attendance number represent? Which digit will change when you find 1,000 less? Is this the only digit that will change?*
- Question ① b): *Which place value column changes when you have 100 more? Do any other columns change? Why?*

**IN FOCUS** Question ① a) builds on children's understanding of place value. Children recognise that to find 1,000 less they must focus on the thousands column. Encourage children to make the number using base 10 equipment to support their thinking. You could also link this question to subtraction, using the language 'finding 1,000 less than'.

Question ① b) consolidates and extends work children have done in previous years, though they are now dealing with 4-digit numbers. Children should now focus on the hundreds column and look at how this changes when 100 is added.

**PRACTICAL TIPS** Allow children to use concrete equipment or a number line to help them visualise the numbers they are working with.

**ANSWERS**

Question ① a): The attendance last week was 7,980.

Question ① b): The attendance next week will be 9,080.

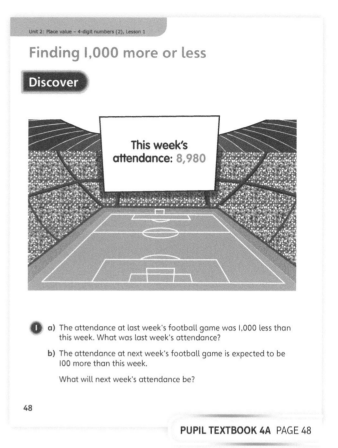

### Finding 1,000 more or less

**Discover**

① a) The attendance at last week's football game was 1,000 less than this week. What was last week's attendance?

b) The attendance at next week's football game is expected to be 100 more than this week.

What will next week's attendance be?

48

**PUPIL TEXTBOOK 4A** PAGE 48

## Share

**WAYS OF WORKING** Whole class teacher led

**ASK**

- Question ① a): *How can you represent the number? What does each digit represent? How does this link to the base 10 equipment? How might a place value grid help here?*
- Question ① a): *What happens when you are finding 1,000 less? How is this similar to subtraction?*
- Question ① b): *When finding 100 more, which piece of base 10 equipment do you need to add? What do you need to do with the 10 hundred cubes/counters? What do you need to exchange here?*

**IN FOCUS** In question ① a), children must find 1,000 less than a given number. It is important to support this abstract subtraction with concrete equipment and pictorial representations to help children visualise how '1,000 less' affects the original 4-digit number of 8,980. Using base 10 equipment or place value counters and a place value grid will support this, making it clear that children must focus on the thousands column when finding 1,000 less than a given number.

In question ① b) the focus is on adding 100, which involves making an exchange of 10 hundreds for 1 thousand. Encourage children to read Flo's comment. Had they already noticed that they needed to exchange? How many digits in the original number of 8,980 need to change?

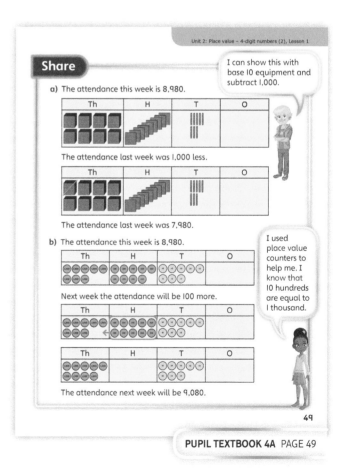

**PUPIL TEXTBOOK 4A** PAGE 49

# Think together

**ASK**

Question **1**: *What was the attendance for the first game? What was different about the attendance for the last game?*

Question **1**: *When representing 100 less than 7,892 on a place value grid, which place value column will change?*

Question **2** b): *What is 10 and what is 100 more than 5,000? If there are 0 tens, what do you need to do to help you find 10 less?*

Question **3** c): *Which number do you need to work out here? What are some ways you could work out this number?*

**IN FOCUS** Question **2** b) is an example that involves making two exchanges. Some children may know that the answer is 4,990. However, children may think that it is 4,090, which is a common misconception. To support children here, make the numbers using place value counters and a place value grid and model making the necessary exchanges. Question **3** consolidates learning on finding 10, 100 and 1,000 more or less than a given number using a fun function machine. Question **3** c) requires children to think a little differently.

**STRENGTHEN** To support children in adding and subtracting 10, 100 and 1,000 to/from a 4-digit number, encourage them to make the number with base 10 equipment on a place value grid, and then add or remove the relevant pieces of equipment to ensure they clearly understand what is happening.

**DEEPEN** Ask children to think deeply about place value with questions such as: *Which columns can change when finding 10, 100 and 1,000 more than a given number?*

Question **3** c) explores that 10 more is the opposite of 10 less, reinforced by 100/1,000 more or less.

**ASSESSMENT CHECKPOINT** Assess children's mastery of 1,000 more or less by asking them to find 1,000 more or less than a variety of 4-digit numbers, including some that will involve exchange. Look for fluency and consistency; are there children who would benefit from further support using concrete equipment and pictorial models to help embed understanding?

**ANSWERS**

Question **1**: The attendance for the final game was 7,792.

Question **2** a): 1,000 more than 5,800 is 6,800.

Question **2** b): 10 less than 5,000 is 4,990.

Question **3** a): 6,785

Question **3** b): 8,103

Question **3** c): 6,540

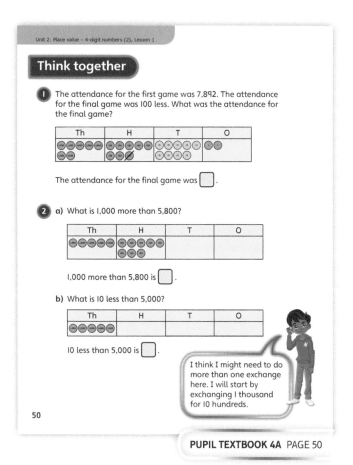

**PUPIL TEXTBOOK 4A** PAGE 50

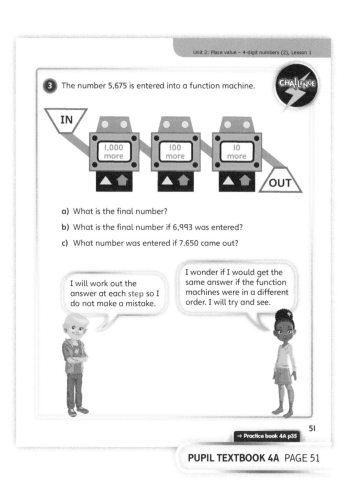

**PUPIL TEXTBOOK 4A** PAGE 51

## Practice

**WAYS OF WORKING** Independent thinking

**IN FOCUS** Question ❶ gives children further practice finding 10, 100 and 1,000 more or less than a number, using pictorial models to support them. Children may want to use concrete equipment to further support their work in this question.

Question ❷ focuses on children's understanding of a variety of pictorial representations. Use this question to look for any misconceptions in children's understanding of these models.

Questions ❸ and ❹ ask children to find the missing numbers to complete some number sentences. The questions slowly build in difficulty and key digits have been kept the same to encourage children to spot patterns as they work through their answers.

**STRENGTHEN** Reinforce place value understanding by reading the numbers aloud and asking children to build each digit of each number using base 10 equipment. Then ask them to add or take away the relevant amount. Ask: *What is the new number? Which digits have changed?*

**DEEPEN** Ask children to think creatively and explore examples of numbers in which, when they find 100 more than the number, a column other than the hundreds column also changes. For example, *What is 100 more than 4,982?* Similarly, can they find examples of numbers in which, when they find 1,000 more than the number, a column other than the thousands column also changes?

**ASSESSMENT CHECKPOINT** Question ❺ provides children with an opportunity to show that they can find 10, 100 and 1,000 more or less than a number, and apply the logic that they must work backwards from a given output number to find the original input number. You could use this question as a model to work through with the class, looking for and discussing any misconceptions as you do so.

**ANSWERS** Answers for the **Practice** part of the lesson appear in the separate **Practice and Reflect answer guide**.

## Reflect

**WAYS OF WORKING** Pair work

**IN FOCUS** Children should recognise that it is the 1,000s digit that changes when finding 1,000 more or less and that the other digits stay the same. Explore finding 100 more or less with children, using examples to establish the fact that the 1,000s digit may also change.

**ASSESSMENT CHECKPOINT** This question assesses whether children can find 10, 100 and 1,000 more or less than a number. Do children know which numbers to focus on and which digits can change?

**ANSWERS** Answers for the **Reflect** part of the lesson appear in the separate **Practice and Reflect answer guide**.

### After the lesson ⏸

- Can children use concrete equipment to explain what happens when finding 1,000 more or less than a given number?
- Can children find 10 and 100 more or less than a given 4-digit number?
- Can children explain which place value columns change when finding 1,000 more or less, and why?

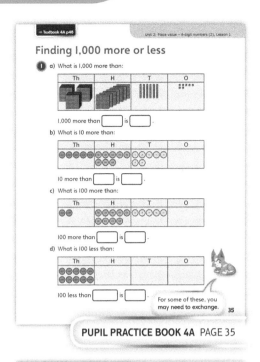

**PUPIL PRACTICE BOOK 4A** PAGE 35

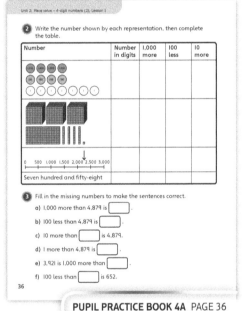

**PUPIL PRACTICE BOOK 4A** PAGE 36

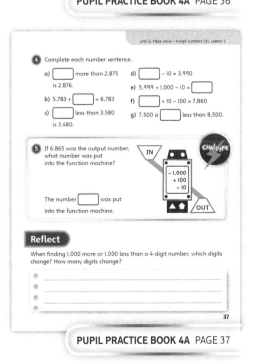

**PUPIL PRACTICE BOOK 4A** PAGE 37

# Comparing 4-digit numbers ❶

## Learning focus

In this lesson children compare 4-digit numbers using concrete equipment and pictorial representations.

## Small steps

→ Previous step: Finding 1,000 more or less
→ **This step: Comparing 4-digit numbers (1)**
→ Next step: Comparing 4-digit numbers (2)

### NATIONAL CURRICULUM LINKS

**Year 4 Number – Number and Place Value**
• Order and compare numbers beyond 1,000.
• Identify, represent and estimate numbers using different representations.

### ASSESSING MASTERY

Children can compare 4-digit numbers using <, > and =. Children recognise 4-digit numbers represented using a variety of concrete and pictorial representations.

### COMMON MISCONCEPTIONS

Children may find it confusing when comparing two numbers with a different number of digits, for example when comparing the numbers 4,569 and 582. Children may compare the 4 with the 5 because they are the initial digits, and they may then go on to reason that 582 is the bigger number. Ask:
• *How many digits does each number have? What is the value of each digit?*

Use concrete equipment, such as base 10 on a place value grid, to visually reinforce place value here.

Children may also assume that the more counters or base 10 equipment used to physically represent a number, the greater the number. For example, children may think that 5,000 is less than 4,923 because you need more counters to represent the number 4,923. To help children visualise amounts you could exchange one of the 1,000s for 10 hundreds. Ask:
• *What is the value of each digit in these numbers?*

### STRENGTHENING UNDERSTANDING

Encourage children to use base 10 equipment to build and then compare the numbers they are working with. Placing the base 10 equipment into a place value grid, one number above the other, will visually support children's understanding of why one number is bigger, smaller or equal to another number.

### GOING DEEPER

Encourage children to compare two numbers where the numbers are made with more than 10 tens or 10 hundreds. For example, can children see that a number made of 3 hundreds, 2 tens and 3 ones is equal to a number made of 2 hundreds, 12 tens and 3 ones, even though the numbers may at first look different?

### KEY LANGUAGE

**In lesson:** how many, more than (>), less than (<), equal to, compare, thousands (1,000s), hundreds (100s), tens (10s), ones (1s)

**Other language used by the teacher:** exchange, larger, smaller, greater

### STRUCTURES AND REPRESENTATIONS

place value counters, base 10 equipment, plain counters

### RESOURCES

**Mandatory:** place value counters, base 10 equipment

**Optional:** plain counters, number lines, place value grids

 In the eTextbook of this lesson, you will find interactive links to a selection of teaching tools.

## Before you teach

• Can children partition a 4-digit number?
• Can children use the <, > and = signs?
• Can children use the language 'greater than' and 'less than'?

## Discover

WAYS OF WORKING Pair work

**ASK**

- Question **1** a): *How many pieces are in each bag? How many bags are in each set? How do you know?*
- Question **1** a): *What base 10 equipment are each of these sets worth? Can you build each amount?*
- Question **1** b): *Why do you start your comparison by looking at the largest sized bags? What happens if each set has the same number of 1,000 bags? What do you do then?*

**IN FOCUS** In question **1** b), the focus is on comparing the two amounts and children should be prompted to do this by comparing the largest place value first. Children should first compare the 1,000 digits of each number and realise they have the same number of 1,000 bags. Prompt children to think for themselves about what they should compare next.

**PRACTICAL TIPS** Children could make the numbers using base 10 equipment to help them visually compare the two numbers. Placing the base 10 equipment onto a place value grid will further support understanding of place value here. Encourage children to make the link between the base 10 blocks and the value of each of the bags in the word problem.

**ANSWERS**

Question **1** a): The treasure island set has 3,543 pieces.

The pirate ship set has 3,456 pieces.

Question **1** b): 3,543 is greater than 3,456. The treasure island set has more pieces.

## Share

WAYS OF WORKING Whole class teacher led

**ASK** Question **1** a): *How does the base 10 equipment help you work out how many pieces each set has?*

Question **1** b): *How do the place value grid and the counters help you read the numbers? What do you need to do if the digits are the same when comparing? Can you use a number line to help you compare?*

**IN FOCUS** Question **1** a) allows children to recap their understanding of writing 4-digit numbers. Ensure children can see the link between the base 10 equipment and each of the different sized bags. Question **1** b) gives children the opportunity to apply their understanding of the language of comparison to 4-digit numbers.

**DEEPEN** Tease out deeper thinking by asking children why they need to compare the largest value first. What happens if the two numbers you are comparing have the same number of 1,000s and the same number of 100s? Explore different ways of comparing values, using words, signs, models and concrete representations.

## Comparing 4-digit numbers **1**

### Discover

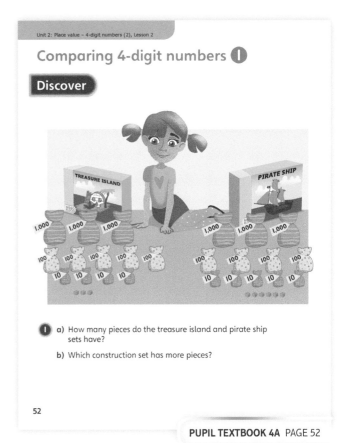

**1** a) How many pieces do the treasure island and pirate ship sets have?

b) Which construction set has more pieces?

52

### Share

a) The treasure island has:

3 thousands + 5 hundreds + 4 tens + 3 ones = 3,543

3,000 + 500 + 40 + 3 = 3,543 pieces

The pirate ship has:

3 thousands + 4 hundreds + 5 tens + 6 ones = 3,456

3,000 + 400 + 50 + 6 = 3,456 pieces

b)

| Th | H | T | O |
|----|---|---|---|
| | | | |

| Th | H | T | O |
|----|---|---|---|
| | | | |

The sets have the same number of 1,000s.
The treasure island set has 5 hundreds.
The pirate ship set has 4 hundreds.
3,543 is greater than 3,456.
The treasure island set has more pieces.

> I will start by comparing the 1,000s, then the 100s, 10s and 1s.

53

# Think together

Whole class teacher led (I do, We do, You do)

**ASK**

- Question ❶: *Which words can you use to complete these questions? Make a list of possible words you can use to compare numbers.*
- Question ❷: *What is the value of the place value counters and the base 10 equipment? How are they the same? How are they different?*
- Question ❸: *What could the missing number be? If you need to use the same number of counters, is there a limit to the number of answers you can give?*

**IN FOCUS** Question ❶ provides a structure for children to compare two 4-digit numbers and gives opportunities to practise the language of comparison and link this language to the key comparison signs <, > and =. Children need to use their knowledge of 4-digit numbers to work out what numbers are represented by the bags. Children may find it useful to represent the amounts physically using base 10 equipment.

Question ❷ gives children the opportunity to compare two numbers that have been represented using different equipment: place value counters and base 10 equipment. The place value grids provide a link between these two distinct representations, allowing children to see how two numbers can be represented differently but compared in the same way.

**STRENGTHEN** Continue to use the place value grid and concrete equipment throughout to support children in comparing numbers. In question ❷, some children may benefit from building both numbers using the same concrete equipment (for example, using base 10 equipment to make both numbers) to enable a more explicit comparison.

**DEEPEN** Question ❸ encourages children to think deeply to find more than one answer, but also to think about the restrictions on the number due to the number of counters being used.

**ASSESSMENT CHECKPOINT** In questions ❶ and ❷, check whether children can use the correct mathematical language and link this language to the comparison signs <, > and =. Assess whether children use a systematic approach in question ❸ to find as many different numbers as possible to complete the number comparison.

**ANSWERS**

Question ❶ a): The castle set is made up of 1,324 pieces.

The dragon set is made up of 1,317 pieces.

Question ❶ b): 1,324 > 1,317

The castle set has more pieces.

Question ❷: 274 < 2,074 or 2,074 > 274

Question ❸: Any number with a digit total of 6 that is more than 2,130.

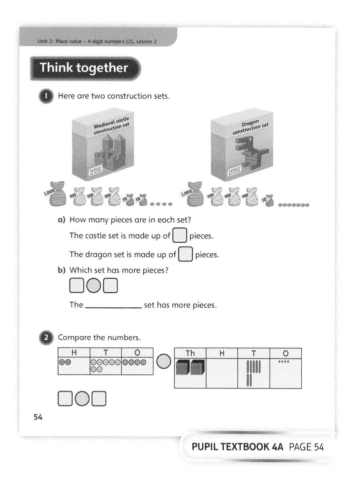

PUPIL TEXTBOOK 4A PAGE 54

PUPIL TEXTBOOK 4A PAGE 55

## Practice

**WAYS OF WORKING** Independent thinking

**IN FOCUS** In question ❶, children focus on practising their use of the mathematical language of comparison. Encourage the use of concrete equipment and place value grids to support learning as necessary.

**STRENGTHEN** Continue to encourage children to make the numbers they are comparing using base 10 equipment or place value counters, setting them on a place value grid to help children compare the numbers more efficiently. Children could stack or line up the equipment to physically compare which number is greater or smaller.

**DEEPEN** Use question ❸ to deepen thinking in this lesson. Ask children to consider how many different answers there are to this question. What happens if they can only use 15 counters in total?

**ASSESSMENT CHECKPOINT** Assess whether children use mathematical language and signs to accurately compare numbers. Can they use their understanding of the signs to complete missing number questions and spot mistakes?

**ANSWERS** Answers for the **Practice** part of the lesson appear in the separate **Practice and Reflect answer guide**.

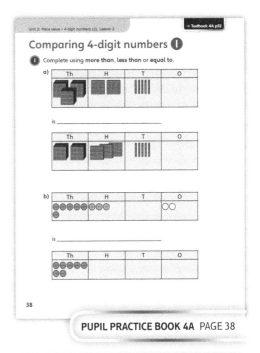

PUPIL PRACTICE BOOK 4A PAGE 38

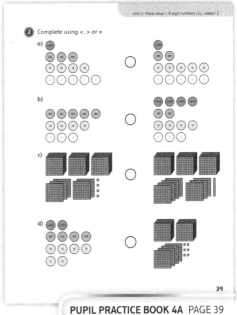

PUPIL PRACTICE BOOK 4A PAGE 39

## Reflect

**WAYS OF WORKING** Independent thinking

**IN FOCUS** The focus of this question is to look at whether children can identify two numbers represented using different manipulatives and then compare these numbers. Some children may be able to do this immediately. Others may need to build both numbers using the same manipulatives.

**ASSESSMENT CHECKPOINT** Can children demonstrate that they understand that two numbers can be compared in more than one way and that if one number can be described as larger than another, then the other number can be described as smaller than the first number? Check whether children compare the 1,000s first, then the 100s, then the 10s and finally the 1s.

**ANSWERS** Answers for the **Reflect** part of the lesson appear in the separate **Practice and Reflect answer guide**.

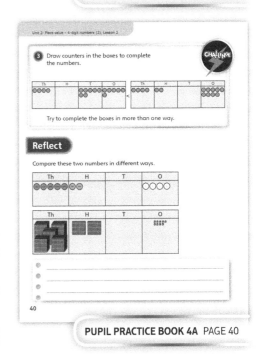

PUPIL PRACTICE BOOK 4A PAGE 40

## After the lesson ⏸

- Do children rely on manipulatives to compare 4-digit numbers?
- How confident are children at making numbers to complete a comparison?
- How many different ways can children compare two 4-digit numbers?

# Comparing 4-digit numbers ❷

## Learning focus

In this lesson children compare 4-digit numbers, focusing on the value of each digit. The reliance on concrete equipment is reduced compared with previous lessons.

## Small steps

→ Previous step: Comparing 4-digit numbers (1)
→ **This step: Comparing 4-digit numbers (2)**
→ Next step: Ordering numbers to 10,000

## NATIONAL CURRICULUM LINKS

**Year 4 Number – Number and Place Value**
• Order and compare numbers beyond 1,000.
• Identify, represent and estimate numbers using different representations.

## ASSESSING MASTERY

Children can compare 4-digit numbers using the mathematical signs <, > and =. Children can compare numbers by focusing on the value of the digits, using a place value grid to support them.

## COMMON MISCONCEPTIONS

Children may make incorrect comparisons when they are comparing a 4-digit number with a 3-digit number, and compare the first digits rather than checking the value of each digit first. For example, when comparing the numbers 4,178 and 542, children might think that 542 is greater because the first digit is a 5 compared to the 4 in 4,178. Ask:
• *What does each digit in each number represent? Which value is greater, 4,000 or 500?*

## STRENGTHENING UNDERSTANDING

Encourage children to use manipulatives to build the numbers they are working with, helping to demonstrate the clear difference between the value of the digits. Read the numbers aloud to children to ensure they see why one number is greater than, or less than, another number. For example, *This number has 5 thousands, and this number has 4 thousands. 5 is greater than 4.* Reinforce this further by writing 5,000 > 4,000 on the whiteboard, modelling for children both the written and spoken language to compare 4-digit numbers.

## GOING DEEPER

Opportunities to extend thinking in this lesson include asking children to find all the possible missing digits for comparisons. For example, can children identify all the possible single digits that could fit into this calculation: 5,___42 < 5,34___? Discuss as a class the various strategies used to answer this.

## KEY LANGUAGE

**In lesson:** how many, more than, less than, higher, highest, greater, smaller, compare, comparison, mass, thousands (1,000s), hundreds (100s)

**Other language used by the teacher:** exchange, larger, place value, tens (10s), ones (1s)

## STRUCTURES AND REPRESENTATIONS

place value grids

## RESOURCES

**Mandatory:** place value grids

**Optional:** number lines, place value counters, base 10 equipment

 In the eTextbook of this lesson, you will find interactive links to a selection of teaching tools.

## Before you teach

• Can children partition a 4-digit number?
• Can children use the <, > and = signs?
• Can children compare numbers using concrete equipment such as base 10 to support them?

## Discover

Pair work

**ASK**

- Question ① a): *What is the mass of each dinosaur? If you are looking at which mass is greater, are you looking for the greater or smaller number?*
- Question ① b): *Which digits should you look at first? Would a place value grid help you to compare the numbers? Which number is higher?*

**IN FOCUS** Question ① a) extends learning from the previous lesson by looking at abstract numbers without the support of concrete representations. Encourage children to link this question back to what they learnt about place value in the previous lesson by writing the number into a place value grid.

Question ① b) allows children to focus on the key misconception of comparing digits without thinking about the value of the digits. Can children articulate that one of the digits is in the 1,000s and the other is in the 100s, and that 1,000s are greater than 100s?

**PRACTICAL TIPS** Children could make the numbers using place value counters or plain counters in a place value grid to support their understanding of which number is greater.

**ANSWERS**

Question ① a): 6,350 kg > 6,040 kg

The Triceratops has a greater mass than the Ankylosaurus.

Question ① b): 907 has no 1,000s. It is smaller than 8,160.

Andy is incorrect.

## Share

**WAYS OF WORKING** Whole class teacher led

**ASK**

- Question ① a): *How can you compare the mass of these dinosaurs? What could you use to help you? How can you be sure which one has the greater mass?*
- Question ① a): *Can you compare the numbers without making them using concrete equipment?*
- Question ① a): *How did you compare the numbers? What did you look at first? What happens if there are the same number of 1,000s – what do you compare next?*
- Question ① a): *Why do you not start by comparing the 1s?*

**IN FOCUS** The focus in question ① a) is on consolidating children's understanding of the place value of 4-digit numbers from the previous lesson. Refer to what Sparks is saying to support children with comparing these two abstract numbers.

Question ① b) specifically addresses the misconception that the higher number is the number with the larger first digit. Consolidate earlier learning by explaining that this is only the case if the digits have the same place value. For example, 8,160 > 907 because the first number has 8 thousands and the second number has 0 thousands.

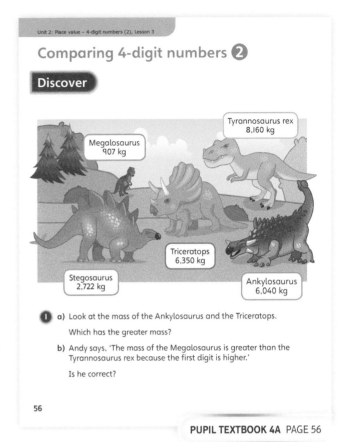

### Comparing 4-digit numbers ②

**Discover**

① a) Look at the mass of the Ankylosaurus and the Triceratops.

Which has the greater mass?

b) Andy says, 'The mass of the Megalosaurus is greater than the Tyrannosaurus rex because the first digit is higher.'

Is he correct?

56

**PUPIL TEXTBOOK 4A** PAGE 56

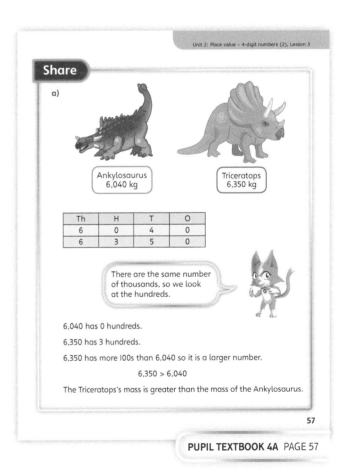

**Share**

a)

6,040 has 0 hundreds.

6,350 has 3 hundreds.

6,350 has more 100s than 6,040 so it is a larger number.

6,350 > 6,040

The Triceratops's mass is greater than the mass of the Ankylosaurus.

57

**PUPIL TEXTBOOK 4A** PAGE 57

# Think together

WAYS OF WORKING Whole class teacher led (I do, We do, You do)

**ASK**

- Question **1**: *Which words can you use to complete the sentence? Make a list of possible words.*
- Question **1**: *Which sign will complete the number sentence? Will putting the numbers into a place value grid help you to compare them?*
- Question **2**: *Which digits should you look at first when making a comparison? How many comparisons do you need to make? When you have compared the 1,000s, do you need to compare any more digits?*

**IN FOCUS** Question **1** builds on learning in the **Discover** section, comparing the digits one at a time to carefully consolidate understanding. Agree with children that, once they have compared the 1,000s, they do not need to continue the comparison because one number has more 1,000s than the other.

In question **2** children must go beyond comparing the first digit of each number. Prompt discussion by asking what is the same and what is different about this question compared to the first question. Children should realise that the 1,000s are the same and so they need to compare the 100s.

Question **3** requires children to reason about the numbers the missing digits could possibly be. Start by modelling some possible answers using trial and error and then move on to discuss how and why you might choose certain digits to fill the missing number boxes.

**STRENGTHEN** Continue to link the place value of 4-digit numbers to concrete representations if this helps to support understanding in this section. As much as possible, encourage children to think about the value of each digit in each number, with a gradual, decreasing reliance on concrete representations and place value grids.

**DEEPEN** Question **3** encourages children to think about the different digits that could complete the comparison. Deepen thinking by asking children to reason and justify their answers to a partner. Prompt discussion by referring to what Astrid and Flo are saying.

**ASSESSMENT CHECKPOINT** In questions **1** and **2**, check that children can use the correct language and link this language to the comparison signs <, > and =.

**ANSWERS**

Question **1**: The Stegosaurus's mass is less than the Ankylosaurus's.

2,722 kg < 6,040 kg

Question **2**: 8,624 is greater than 8,426

8,624 > 8,426

Question **3**: If the second missing digit is completed as an 8, the first missing digit must be 7, 8 or 9.

If the second missing digit is completed as a digit lower than an 8, the first missing digit can be any digit from 0–9.

Th | H | T | O
---|---|---|---
 | 9 | 0 | 7
8 | 1 | 6 | 0

907 has no 1,000s. It is smaller than 8,160.
Andy is incorrect.

I compared the thousands first.

## Think together

**1** The Stegosaurus's mass is 2,722 kg. The Ankylosaurus's mass is 6,040 kg.
Compare the masses of the dinosaurs.
The Stegosaurus's mass is _____ than the Ankylosaurus.
2,722 kg ◯ 6,040 kg

58

**PUPIL TEXTBOOK 4A** PAGE 58

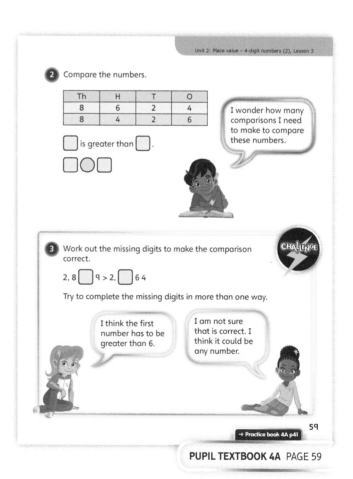

**2** Compare the numbers.

Th | H | T | O
---|---|---|---
8 | 6 | 2 | 4
8 | 4 | 2 | 6

☐ is greater than ☐.

☐ ◯ ☐

I wonder how many comparisons I need to make to compare these numbers.

**3** Work out the missing digits to make the comparison correct.

2, 8 ☐ 9 > 2, ☐ 6 4

Try to complete the missing digits in more than one way.

I think the first number has to be greater than 6.

I am not sure that is correct. I think it could be any number.

59

→ Practice book 4A p41

**PUPIL TEXTBOOK 4A** PAGE 59

## Practice

**WAYS OF WORKING** Independent thinking

**IN FOCUS** Questions ① to ③ gradually build and practise children's understanding of place value in 4-digit numbers. As the questions progress, scaffolds are taken away and children are expected to use more reasoning and demonstrate deeper understanding of the lesson's objectives.

Question ④ assesses whether children are secure in their understanding of how 4-digit numbers can be represented across a variety of pictorial representations, and then can apply this knowledge, along with their place value understanding, to tick the suitable answers.

**STRENGTHEN** To support children in working out answers to the missing box statements in question ③, suggest that they first use a trial and error approach, guessing a number and then checking if their guessed number works. Encourage discussion around the numbers they have guessed to support their reasoning about whether their guess works or not. If it doesn't work, why not? Take opportunities to say the numbers out loud with children, saying, for example, *5 thousands are greater than 4 thousands.*

**DEEPEN** Question ⑤ requires children to successfully identify increments on a number line and to then take this a step further by identifying 6 possible numbers that could be positioned between two markers.

To extend question ⑥, provide children with examples where there is more than one digit missing, and the size of that digit depends on another digit in the number. For example, in the statement: 3___52 < 325___, the first missing digit could be a 2, provided that the last digit on the second number is greater than 2.

**ASSESSMENT CHECKPOINT** Assess whether children are using comparison language accurately and appropriately when comparing two numbers. Check if they can use reasoning skills to help them complete and explain missing digit and number questions.

**ANSWERS** Answers for the **Practice** part of the lesson appear in the separate **Practice and Reflect answer guide**.

## Reflect

**WAYS OF WORKING** Independent thinking

**IN FOCUS** Children use their knowledge of comparing numbers to complete an explanation of how to compare two numbers. Encourage children to check their explanations by comparing any two numbers, following the steps they have written in order to check that their steps work.

**ASSESSMENT CHECKPOINT** Use this activity to assess whether children can show that they can compare two abstract numbers without using concrete equipment or a place value grid.

**ANSWERS** Answers for the **Reflect** part of the lesson appear in the separate **Practice and Reflect answer guide**.

## After the lesson ⏸

- Can children compare numbers without using concrete equipment and place value grids?
- Can children explain how to compare numbers and use mathematical vocabulary when making number comparisons?

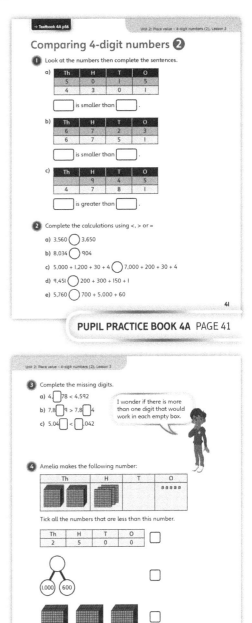

PUPIL PRACTICE BOOK 4A PAGE 41

PUPIL PRACTICE BOOK 4A PAGE 42

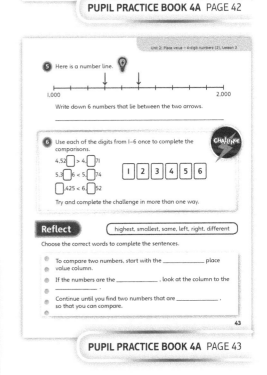

PUPIL PRACTICE BOOK 4A PAGE 43

# Ordering numbers to 10,000

## Learning focus

In this lesson children will order 4-digit numbers, focusing on the value of the digits and using a place value grid to support understanding.

## Small steps

→ Previous step: Comparing 4-digit numbers (2)
→ **This step: Ordering numbers to 10,000**
→ Next step: Rounding to the nearest 1,000

### NATIONAL CURRICULUM LINKS

**Year 4 Number – Number and Place Value**
• Order and compare numbers beyond 1,000.
• Identify, represent and estimate numbers using different representations.

### ASSESSING MASTERY

Children can order numbers by focusing on the values of the digits, using a place value grid to support them. Children can confidently use language such as 'greatest', 'smallest', 'descending' and 'ascending' to order numbers efficiently.

### COMMON MISCONCEPTIONS

Children may need reminding about the order in which we compare numbers. To prompt their thinking, ask:
• *Which digits should you compare first? Why? Are the first digits of each number of the same value? How do you know? If the 1,000s are the same, what do you look at next?*

### STRENGTHENING UNDERSTANDING

Encourage children to use concrete equipment such as base 10 equipment to build the numbers they are working with. This will show the distinctions between the values of each digit in a number. Placing the concrete equipment into a place value grid, and saying out loud what each digit is worth, will further reinforce understanding of place value and order.

### GOING DEEPER

To prompt deep engagement in this lesson, encourage children to complete the missing digit questions by reasoning about the order of the numbers. Challenge children by asking if they can exhaust all possible solutions in each question.

### KEY LANGUAGE

**In lesson:** fewest, order, smallest, greatest, thousands (1,000s), hundreds, tens, ones, highest, lowest, **ascending**, **descending**

**Other language to be used by teacher:** furthest, shortest

### STRUCTURES AND REPRESENTATIONS

place value grids

### RESOURCES

**Mandatory:** place value grids

**Optional:** base 10 equipment, place value counters

 In the eTextbook of this lesson, you will find interactive links to a selection of teaching tools.

## Before you teach

• Can children partition a 4-digit number?
• Can children use the <, > and = signs?
• Can children compare two 4-digit numbers?

## Discover

Unit 2: Place value – 4-digit numbers (2), Lesson 4

**WAYS OF WORKING** Pair work

**ASK**

- Question **1** a): *What are the children's scores? If you are looking for who scored the fewest points, are you looking for the greatest or smallest number?*
- Question **1** b): *Who has the most points? Is the greatest number 1st? Is this always true?*

**IN FOCUS** Question **1** a) encourages children to think about the link between the least/fewest of something being the smallest number of something. Children will build on their learning from the previous lesson by comparing digits abstractly.

**PRACTICAL TIPS** Children can make the numbers using place value counters or plain counters on a place value grid to help them order the numbers more efficiently. Encourage children to present the numbers one above another on the same grid to aid direct comparison. It is vital that children are confident with the place values of 4-digit numbers and comparing two numbers before moving on to ordering numbers.

**ANSWERS**

Question **1** a): Mo has scored the fewest points.

Question **1** b): 8,645 > 8,632 > 8,052

Jamie came 1st. Olivia came 2nd. Amelia came 3rd.

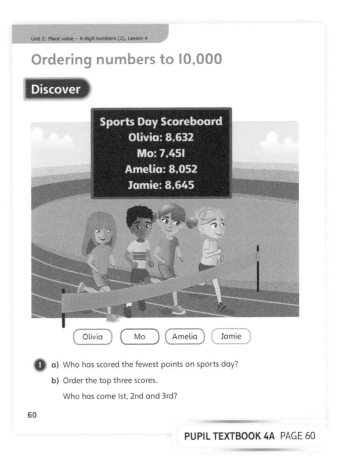

## Ordering numbers to 10,000

### Discover

**Sports Day Scoreboard**
Olivia: 8,632
Mo: 7,451
Amelia: 8,052
Jamie: 8,645

| Olivia | Mo | Amelia | Jamie |

**1** a) Who has scored the fewest points on sports day?

b) Order the top three scores.
Who has come 1st, 2nd and 3rd?

60

**PUPIL TEXTBOOK 4A** PAGE 60

## Share

**WAYS OF WORKING** Whole class teacher led

**ASK**

Question **1** a): *Does putting the numbers in the same grid help you find the smallest number? How did you decide which is the smallest number?*

Question **1** b): *How can you find the greatest number? What do you need to compare first? What challenge do you notice? What do you have to do next?*

**IN FOCUS** Question **1** a) has been designed to show how presenting numbers in the same table makes comparison easier, and that comparing the thousands first is not only the correct way, but also the most efficient way to compare these four numbers. One number should stand out as being of less value than the others. Ensure that children are using the key vocabulary of place value, and that you model the use of key comparison vocabulary such as 'least', 'less than', 'more', 'more than', and so on.

**STRENGTHEN** Displaying each number using counters or base 10 equipment to help children see why one number is more or less than another number will help to secure understanding in this section.

**DEEPEN** Can children use the comparison signs >, < and = to compare the numbers in question **1** b)?

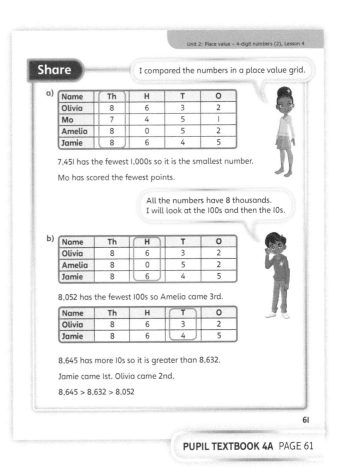

Unit 2: Place value – 4-digit numbers (2), Lesson 4

### Share

*I compared the numbers in a place value grid.*

a)

| Name | Th | H | T | O |
|------|----|----|----|----|
| Olivia | 8 | 6 | 3 | 2 |
| Mo | 7 | 4 | 5 | 1 |
| Amelia | 8 | 0 | 5 | 2 |
| Jamie | 8 | 6 | 4 | 5 |

7,451 has the fewest 1,000s so it is the smallest number.

Mo has scored the fewest points.

*All the numbers have 8 thousands. I will look at the 100s and then the 10s.*

b)

| Name | Th | H | T | O |
|------|----|----|----|----|
| Olivia | 8 | 6 | 3 | 2 |
| Amelia | 8 | 0 | 5 | 2 |
| Jamie | 8 | 6 | 4 | 5 |

8,052 has the fewest 100s so Amelia came 3rd.

| Name | Th | H | T | O |
|------|----|----|----|----|
| Olivia | 8 | 6 | 3 | 2 |
| Jamie | 8 | 6 | 4 | 5 |

8,645 has more 10s so it is greater than 8,632.

Jamie came 1st. Olivia came 2nd.

8,645 > 8,632 > 8,052

61

**PUPIL TEXTBOOK 4A** PAGE 61

# Think together

**WAYS OF WORKING** Whole class teacher led (I do, We do, You do)

**ASK**

- Question **1**: *Which digit do you look at first? Why?*
- Question **1**: *If you are writing the numbers in descending order, will the lowest or highest number be at the beginning? What is the opposite of descending?*
- Question **2**: *Will putting the numbers in a place value grid help you to compare them? How?*
- Question **2**: *What word do you use to describe the order that you have put the scores in?*
- Question **4**: *Which numbers have the same number of 1,000s and 1s? How does this clue help you work out two of the missing digits in the missing number? Which numbers have the same number of 10s? What do the 100s digits added together equal? How can you use this total to help you work out the last missing digit?*

**IN FOCUS** Questions **1** to **3** build on learning from the **Discover** task, requiring children to practise the principles they applied in **Discover**. Check that children are secure using the signs of comparison. Can children answer the questions without using a place grid to support them? In question **1**, refer children to what Sparks is saying and encourage them to repeat out loud the new vocabulary 'descending' and 'ascending'.

Question **4** challenges children to use an efficient strategy to work out the answer. Refer children to what Astrid and Dexter are saying to give them some pointers if necessary.

**STRENGTHEN** Reinforce understanding of effective strategies for ordering numbers by reading the questions aloud. Read aloud as a class each number to be compared and model comparing the 1,000s first, then the 100s, and so on. This activity will help children build the procedural memory that is required to accurately order large numbers.

**DEEPEN** Challenge children by setting problems where they have to reason what a missing digit might be, based on other numbers in a sequence. For example: 3,___26 < ___,52___ < 3,5___8. How many different answers can they find? What sort of reasoning are they using to help them find the missing digits? If the first missing digit is a 5, how does this limit what the other missing digits can be?

**ASSESSMENT CHECKPOINT** In Questions **1**, **3**, and **4** check children understand the new language of 'ascending' and 'descending'.

**ANSWERS**

Question **1** a): 6,490 is the highest score.
Question **1** b): 749 is the lowest score.
Question **1** c): The scores in descending order are: 6,490, 6,485, 6,332 and 749.

Question **2** a): 5,409 is the greatest number.
Question **2** b): 4,905 is the smallest number.
Question **2** c): 5,404 is greater than 4,905 **or** 4,954 but less than 5,409.
Question **2** d): 4,905 < 4,954 < 5,404 < 5,409

Question **3**: 1,250, 1,220, 1,028, 240.

Question **4**: 9,332

---

## Think together

**1** Here are four more scores from sports day.

| Th | H | T | O |
|----|----|----|----|
| 6 | 3 | 3 | 2 |
| 6 | 4 | 9 | 0 |
| 6 | 4 | 8 | 5 |
| 7 | 4 | 9 |  |

When you list numbers from the highest to the lowest, they are in descending order. If you put them from the lowest to the highest, they are in ascending order.

a) Which is the highest score?

b) Which is the lowest score?

c) What are the scores in descending order?

**2** Complete the sentences about the number cards.

| 5,409 | 4,954 | 4,905 | 5,404 |

a) ☐ is the greatest number.

b) ☐ is the smallest number.

c) 5,404 is greater than ☐ but less than ☐.

d) ☐ < ☐ < ☐ < ☐

62

**PUPIL TEXTBOOK 4A** PAGE 62

---

**3** Place the numbers in descending order.

| 240 | 1,250 | 1,220 | 1,028 |

**4** Here are some numbers in ascending order.

8,934, ☐, 9,432, 9,472

Solve the clues to work out the missing number.

Three of the numbers have the same number of 1,000s and 1s.

Three of the numbers have the same number of 10s.

All the 100s digits added together equal 20.

I am going to make each number using maths equipment.

I am going to work through each clue, one at a time.

→ Practice book 4A p44

63

**PUPIL TEXTBOOK 4A** PAGE 63

# Practice

**WAYS OF WORKING** Independent thinking

**IN FOCUS** Question ① requires children to practise the main principles of the lesson and order the numbers.

Question ② revisits learning from earlier lessons, testing children's understanding of pictorial representations of 4-digit numbers.

In question ③ children need to think about whether they should order numbers differently if a unit of measurement such as kg or m is included with the number. Ask: *Does this affect the order?*

Question ④ consolidates learning of key comparison and number ordering vocabulary, including 'furthest', '2nd' and 'shortest'.

In questions ⑤ and ⑥ children must reason what the missing digits or numbers are. It is important that children do not just look at the next number in the list, but instead look at all the numbers to help them make informed decisions about what the missing digits or numbers could be (and therefore what they can't be).

**STRENGTHEN** Continue to encourage children to write numbers in a place value grid to help them compare the numbers. If children find the missing digit questions difficult, encourage them to say the numbers out loud and reason with a partner about what the missing digits can and cannot be. For example, in question ⑤ a), ask: *If the number is more than 3,246 but less than 3,312, what could the 100s digit be? Now look at the 10s and the 1s. How does this help you choose which 100s digit is the missing digit?*

**DEEPEN** Explore children's thinking in question ⑥. What strategies do they use to find out what the missing numbers might be? How do they work out which 4-digit numbers have digit totals of 15 and then apply this to answering the question?

**ASSESSMENT CHECKPOINT** Assess whether children can order numbers in ascending and descending order. Are children able to find missing digits for numbers that are given in order?

**ANSWERS** Answers for the **Practice** part of the lesson appear in the separate **Practice and Reflect answer guide**.

# Reflect

**WAYS OF WORKING** Independent thinking

**IN FOCUS** Children use their knowledge of making 4-digit numbers to make and then compare numbers with the same digits in different orders. Look for children who can order their numbers quickly and those that need additional support.

**ASSESSMENT CHECKPOINT** Assess whether children can explain how they ordered their numbers.

**ANSWERS** Answers for the **Reflect** part of the lesson appear in the separate **Practice and Reflect answer guide**.

## After the lesson

- Do children rely on the place value grid to help them order numbers?
- How confident are children at reasoning to help them work out missing digits?
- Can children explain how they know that they have ordered them correctly?

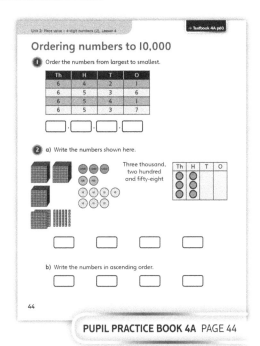

**PUPIL PRACTICE BOOK 4A** PAGE 44

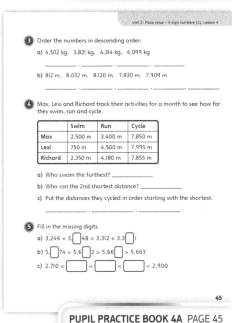

**PUPIL PRACTICE BOOK 4A** PAGE 45

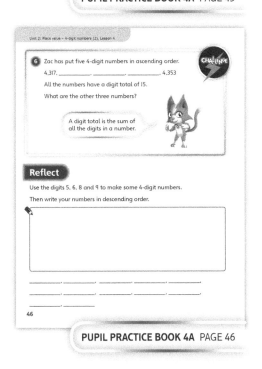

**PUPIL PRACTICE BOOK 4A** PAGE 46

# Rounding to the nearest 1,000

## Learning focus

In this lesson children will use their knowledge of place value and rounding to the nearest 10 and 100 to develop an understanding of how to round to the nearest 1,000.

## Small steps

→ Previous step: Ordering numbers to 10,000
→ **This step: Rounding to the nearest 1,000**
→ Next step: Solving problems using rounding

## NATIONAL CURRICULUM LINKS

**Year 4 Number – Number and Place Value**

Round any number to the nearest 10, 100 or 1,000.

## ASSESSING MASTERY

Children can successfully round to the nearest 1,000 in a range of contexts and identify which place value column will help them to do this. Children can round a 4-digit number to the nearest 10, 100 or 1,000 and can use a variety of concrete equipment to demonstrate their understanding.

## COMMON MISCONCEPTIONS

When presented with an abstract number, children may round to the nearest 10 or 100 rather than the nearest 1,000. Children may also incorrectly round up or down to the wrong 1,000. If rounding to the nearest 1,000, ask:
• *Which two 1,000s does the number lie between? Can you place the number on a number line?*

Children may not round to the correct degree of accuracy. Encourage children to read each question carefully and work out which place value column to consider. Ask:
• *Can you tell me the value of each digit in this number?*

## STRENGTHENING UNDERSTANDING

To support understanding in this lesson, ask children to mark the number they are rounding on a number line and work out the 1,000 either side.

You could ask children what number is halfway to help them work out if the given number is greater or less than half-way between the two 1,000 numbers identified.

Model how to work out the difference between the number and the 1,000 above and the 1,000 below and ask children which is the smaller difference. This is the number it rounds to, to the nearest 1,000.

## GOING DEEPER

Ask children to give examples of when they might need to round to the nearest 1,000. How many examples can they think of?

## KEY LANGUAGE

**In lesson:** nearest, between, closer, closest, round, how many, column

**Other language to be used by the teacher:** round up, round down, difference

## STRUCTURES AND REPRESENTATIONS

number line, base 10 equipment, place value grid

## RESOURCES

**Mandatory:** number lines, base 10 equipment, place value counters

 In the eTextbook of this lesson, you will find interactive links to a selection of teaching tools.

## Before you teach

• Can children round to the nearest 10?
• Can children round to the nearest 100?
• Are there any additional misconceptions you need to consider? Do children know the place value of each digit in a 4-digit number?

## Discover

**WAYS OF WORKING** Pair work

**ASK**

- Question **1**: *How many visitors visited each destination? What does rounding to the nearest 1,000 mean?*

**IN FOCUS** Question **1** a) introduces the term 'to the nearest' rather than 'rounding' so that children become familiar with a variety of mathematical language.

Question **1** b) addresses the key misconception of how to round numbers that are exactly half-way between two 1,000s. Discuss the link to rounding to the nearest 100 or 10 that was covered in previous learning, and what you do with numbers that are half-way between.

Explore together how to find the difference between the number children are rounding and the 1,000 either side to help inform their decision about which 1,000 is closer.

**PRACTICAL TIPS** Allow children to use concrete equipment to represent the numbers, helping to support their decision about whether they need to round up or down.

**ANSWERS**

Question **1** a): 9,000 people visited Paris per week.

Question **1** b): 4,000 people visited New York per week.

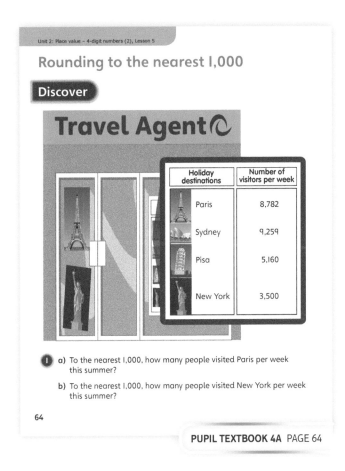

PUPIL TEXTBOOK 4A PAGE 64

## Share

**WAYS OF WORKING** Whole class teacher led

**ASK**

- Question **1** a): *What two 1,000 numbers does 8,782 appear between?*
- *Where does the number 8,782 appear on a number line between 8,000 and 9,000?*
- Question **1** b): *Why is rounding 3,500 different to rounding the other numbers of visitors? How did you round numbers half-way between two numbers when rounding to the nearest 100 and the nearest 10?*

**IN FOCUS** Question **1** a) addresses rounding without using the vocabulary of rounding. When you are rounding to the nearest 1,000 and looking at a number line, the distance from the number to each end of the number line can help you to decide which number to choose. This also links to children's previous knowledge of place value.

**STRENGTHEN** Support children's understanding in this section by reminding them that when rounding to the nearest 1,000, you have to look at the 100s digit. If it is 5 or more, you round up and if it is 4 or less, you round down. Explore as a class which digit to consider when rounding to the nearest 100 or 10 – this will help children recognise that they have to look at the digit one below the number they are rounding to. Making the number with concrete equipment in a place value grid will reinforce this concept.

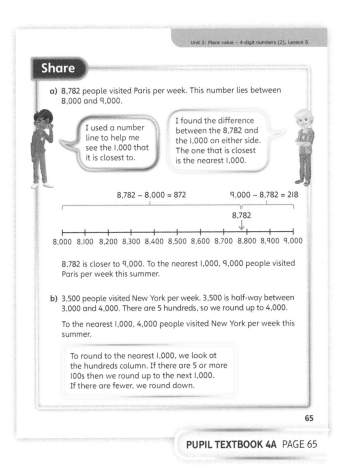

PUPIL TEXTBOOK 4A PAGE 65

# Think together

Whole class teacher led (I do, We do, You do)

**ASK**

- Questions **1** to **2**: *What two 1,000 numbers does _____ appear between? Where does the number _____ appear on a number line between _____ and _____? Which digit is important in this number? Which place value column will change?*

**IN FOCUS** Question **1** provides opportunities for children to practise rounding numbers. Encourage children to work out the 1,000 on either side of the number first, and then to work out where to place this on a number line.

Question **2** focuses on rounding without the visual aid of the number line. Children will now need to look at the 100s digit in order to round this number accurately. The place value counters and grid continue to support understanding here.

Question **3** requires children to think about which values are important when rounding to the nearest 1,000. Ask: *Does it make a difference which digit Isla uses? How about the digits that Zac and Aki use?*

**STRENGTHEN** If children struggle with the concept of finding the nearest 1,000, allow them to find the nearest 10 and 100 and build on this. Children can incorporate place value counters, base 10 equipment and number lines into their reasoning to visually represent the numbers in each question.

**DEEPEN** Challenge children to work in pairs and devise a grid similar to the one in question **3** for their partner. Ask children to write three 4-digit numbers that round to 6,000 in their grids. They can then cover one digit in each number with a plain counter. Can their partners list what each covered digit could be, bearing in mind that each number must round to 6,000?

**ASSESSMENT CHECKPOINT** Questions **1** and **2** allow you to check that children can round to the nearest 100 and 1,000. Question **3** checks that children understand which values it is important to consider when rounding to the nearest 1,000.

**ANSWERS**

Question **1** a): To the nearest 1,000, 5,000 people visited Pisa per week.

Question **1** b): To the nearest 100, 5,200 people visited Pisa per week.

Question **2**: 10,000

You look at the hundreds column to help you.

Question **3**: Isla: any digit from 0 to 9.

Zac: any digit from 5 to 9.

Aki: digit must be 5.

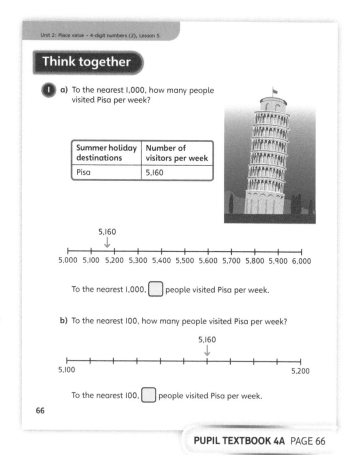

**PUPIL TEXTBOOK 4A** PAGE 66

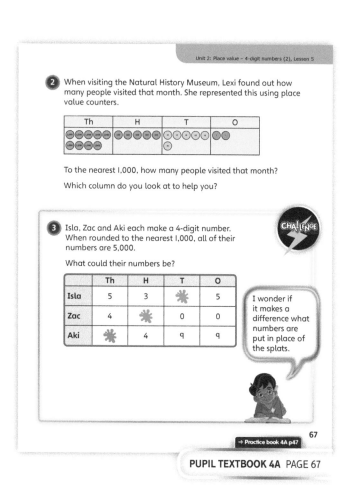

**PUPIL TEXTBOOK 4A** PAGE 67

## Practice

**WAYS OF WORKING** Independent thinking

**IN FOCUS** Questions ❸ to ❹ require children to round numbers to the nearest 100 and 1,000 without the support of a number line. Children must now read the questions carefully and consider which digit it is important to focus on depending on what they are rounding to.

**STRENGTHEN** Now that the number lines have been removed as a support, children may struggle to visualise the questions and answers. Place value grids and concrete equipment such as base 10 or place value counters can be used to visually represent the numbers. If necessary, support children with scaffolded questions such as those modelled in the **Think Together**, **Ask** commentary on the previous page of this **Teacher Guide**.

**DEEPEN** In question ❻ children have to find a number that fits certain criteria for rounding. Challenge children to find as many possible answers as they can. Encourage children to think creatively by writing their own set of criteria for a number to challenge a partner with.

**ASSESSMENT CHECKPOINT** Assess whether children can round to the nearest 1,000. Can they also round a 4-digit number to the nearest 10 and to the nearest 100?

**ANSWERS** Answers for the **Practice** part of the lesson appear in the separate **Practice and Reflect answer guide**.

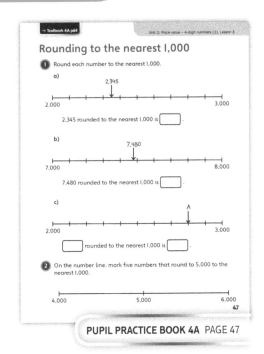

PUPIL PRACTICE BOOK 4A PAGE 47

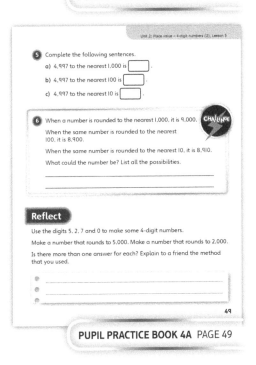

PUPIL PRACTICE BOOK 4A PAGE 48

## Reflect

**WAYS OF WORKING** Pair work

**IN FOCUS** Children make numbers that must round to a particular number. To do this they must first identify which place value column is important to consider. When they have identified this, children can begin to place the digits. Ask children to check their work with a partner. Do they have the same answers, or different answers? Encourage children to work together to find more possible answers to each problem.

**ASSESSMENT CHECKPOINT** Assess whether children can suggest numbers that round to a specific 1,000.

**ANSWERS** Answers for the **Reflect** part of the lesson appear in the separate **Practice and Reflect answer guide**.

### After the lesson

- Can children round a 4-digit number to the nearest 1,000?
- Can children round a 4-digit number to the nearest 10 and the nearest 100?
- Can children identify numbers that round to a given degree of accuracy?

PUPIL PRACTICE BOOK 4A PAGE 49

# Solving problems using rounding

## Learning focus

In this lesson, children will solve problems that involve rounding to the nearest 10, 100 and 1,000.

## Small steps

→ Previous step: Rounding to the nearest 1,000
→ **This step: Solving problems using rounding**
→ Next step: Counting in 25s

### NATIONAL CURRICULUM LINKS

**Year 4 Number – Number and Place Value**
- Round any number to the nearest 10, 100 or 1,000
- Solve number and practical problems that involve all of the above and with increasingly large positive numbers

### ASSESSING MASTERY

Children can successfully use their previous learning of rounding to the nearest 10, 100 and 1,000 to answer a variety of problems, including problems where they must generate numbers that round to a particular degree of accuracy.

### COMMON MISCONCEPTIONS

Children may not realise that a number can round either up or down, depending on the degree of accuracy. For example 7,189 could round up to 7,190 (to the nearest 10) or to 7,200 (to the nearest 100), but also down to 7,000 (to the nearest 1,000). Show a suitable number line and discuss the position of the number on it (for example, the position of 7,189 on a number line from 7,000 to 7,200).

### STRENGTHENING UNDERSTANDING

Children may need further practice rounding numbers that are (or are within a few increments of) half-way between two numbers. Ensure that children have access to concrete equipment and a place value grid and ask questions such as:
- *What is the difference between 6,499 and 6,501 when rounding? How do you know? What place value digits is it important to consider here? What does 6,500 round to, to the nearest 1,000?*

Model the answers as you go, if necessary, to consolidate understanding.

### GOING DEEPER

To prompt deeper thinking in this lesson, ask a series of structured questions such as:
- *A number rounded to the nearest 1,000/100/10 is 3,000. What could the number be? How many numbers can you find? What is the greatest number? What is the smallest number?*

To extend thinking further, ask:
- *A number rounded to the nearest 1,000 is 3,000. The same number rounded to the nearest 100 is 3,100. What could the number be? How many numbers can you find?*

Children who are confident and secure answering these questions could make their own questions to challenge each other.

### KEY LANGUAGE

**In lesson:** rounds to, nearest, number line, closer to, greatest, smallest, hundreds (100s)
**Other language to be used by the teacher:** round up, round down

### STRUCTURES AND REPRESENTATIONS

base 10 equipment, counters, number lines, place value grids

### RESOURCES

**Mandatory:** base 10 equipment, counters
**Optional:** number lines, place value grid

 In the eTextbook of this lesson, you will find interactive links to a selection of teaching tools.

## Before you teach

- Can children round to the nearest 10?
- Can children round to the nearest 100?
- Can children round to the nearest 1,000?

# Discover

**WAYS OF WORKING** Pair work

**ASK**

- Question **1** a): *What number has Danny made? How do you know? What number should Danny's number round to?*
- Question **1** a): *Which place value column do you need to look at? Is the thousands column important? Which column is important after the thousands?*

**IN FOCUS** Question **1** a) focuses on helping children understand what it is important to look at when rounding to the nearest 1,000. Children should first consider the four counters in the thousands column. Some children may think that this means the number cannot round to 5,000. Encourage children to look at the number of counters in the hundreds column. Do they realise that because there are eight counters in this column the number rounds up to 5,000?

Question **1** b) has multiple possible answers and children should be encouraged to think carefully before they move the counters. Ask children which columns it is important to consider when rounding to the nearest 1,000 and which columns are not important. To help children find various possibilities, you could ask them to use a number line, marking on it the smallest number and the greatest number that round to 5,000.

**PRACTICAL TIPS** Allow children to use concrete equipment such as number lines, place value counters and a place value grid so that they can physically represent the question on their classroom tables.

**ANSWERS**

Question **1** a): 4,832 rounded to the nearest 1,000 is 5,000. Danny is correct.

Question **1** b): Accept any answer that rounds to 5,000.

# Share

**WAYS OF WORKING** Whole class teacher led

**ASK**

- Question **1** b): *How many counters can there be in the thousands column? How does this affect how many counters can be in the hundreds column?*

**IN FOCUS** For question **1** b), have children share their thoughts and their methods. Discuss the strategy of drawing on a number line and working out which 1,000 the number is closest to. Discuss the strategy of moving the counters in the thousands and hundreds columns to physically represent the problem. Refer to what Sparks says – which counters could Danny not have moved? Look for clear explanations and share these with the class.

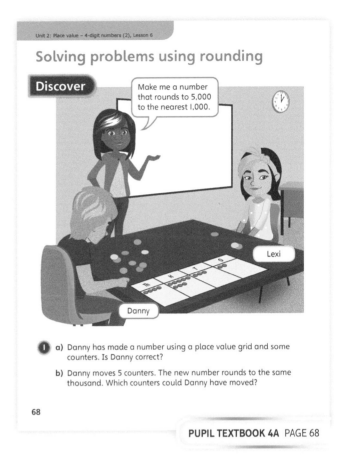

## Solving problems using rounding

**Discover**

**1** a) Danny has made a number using a place value grid and some counters. Is Danny correct?

b) Danny moves 5 counters. The new number rounds to the same thousand. Which counters could Danny have moved?

68

**PUPIL TEXTBOOK 4A** PAGE 68

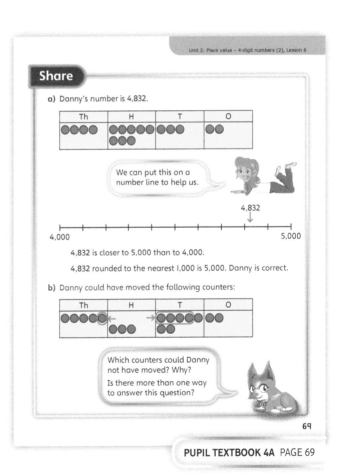

**Share**

a) Danny's number is 4,832.

We can put this on a number line to help us.

4,832 is closer to 5,000 than to 4,000.

4,832 rounded to the nearest 1,000 is 5,000. Danny is correct.

b) Danny could have moved the following counters:

Which counters could Danny not have moved? Why?

Is there more than one way to answer this question?

69

**PUPIL TEXTBOOK 4A** PAGE 69

# Think together

WAYS OF WORKING Whole class teacher led (I do, We do, You do)

**ASK**

- Question **1**: *What number is shown? What is the number to the nearest 1,000? How do you know? Can you round it without a number line? How did you do that?*
- Question **2**: *What can you say about the number of 1,000s in each of the numbers that Danny and Lexi make? How do you know? What other numbers could they make?*
- Question **3**: *What information do you know? Can you use counters to help you? How many 1,000s do there need to be? How do you know? Can you explain your method?*

**IN FOCUS** Question **1** is similar to the **Discover** task, practising the skills of rounding a number given in a place value grid to the nearest 100. Children may do this by drawing a number line or by considering the number of 100s and then the number of 10s.

In question **2**, children have been given specific digits which they have to manipulate and put in order to make two different numbers that round to 4,100 to the nearest 100. Children should first realise that there must be 4 thousands in the number. Next, they should recognise that the next number cannot be a 5 or 8 because this would not round to 4,100. In this way, they are reducing the number of possibilities and using a structured approach to working out which numbers could have been made.

Question **3** requires children to find numbers that round to different degrees of accuracy. This is an increasingly complicated task. Ask children to start by considering the first piece of information given and then work from there. Some children may use trial and error; others may look at the smallest place value first.

**STRENGTHEN** Allow children to use a number line as they work through this section. In question **3**, children can use a number line or counters and a place value grid to make the numbers. Every time they make a number, encourage them to round it and check that it rounds to the required degree of accuracy.

**DEEPEN** To extend thinking in this lesson, ask children to make numbers that round to different degrees of accuracy. For example, can they write down three numbers that round to 3,400 to the nearest 100? Then give them two conditions, and then three conditions that they must work to. Can children show the range of applicable values?

**ASSESSMENT CHECKPOINT** Assess whether children can round a number to the nearest 10, 100 and 1,000 by considering the size of the digits. Can children work out numbers that round to a particular degree of accuracy?

**ANSWERS**

Question **1**: Lexi's number to the nearest 100 is 3,500.

Question **2**: 4,085 and 4,058

Question **3**: For Danny's number, accept any answer between 4,850 and 4,949. For Lexi's number, accept any answer between 5,295 and 5,304.

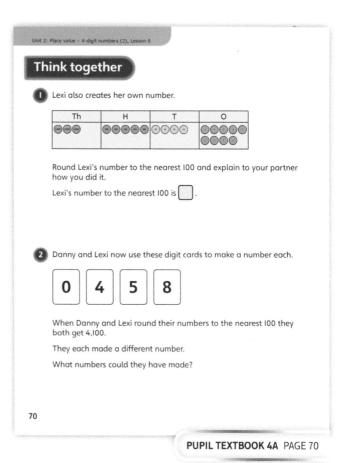

## Practice

**WAYS OF WORKING** Independent thinking

**IN FOCUS** Questions in this **Practice** section focus on practising rounding to the nearest 10, 100 and 1,000. Question ② pulls out learning about how, when you round a number to the nearest 10, 100 or 1,000, you can get the same answer. In question ⑥ children work out missing digits that will make a number round to a particular degree of accuracy. Look for children who guess the answer rather than employing a specific strategy, and check for those who have used a method. Can children reason that if 8,___7___ rounds to 9,000, the digit in the first space must be 5 or greater? In some instances, children will need to consider all of the possible outcomes.

**STRENGTHEN** Place value grids and concrete equipment such as base 10 equipment or place value counters can be used to visually represent the numbers in the word problems.

**DEEPEN** Explore thinking more deeply in question ⑥ by asking children if they have found all the possible ways that Bella can make one 4-digit number that has at least one counter in each place value column. What is their strategy for completing this exercise? Can they explain this to a partner?

**THINK DIFFERENTLY** Question ③ encourages a different way of thinking about rounding. Children can use their experience of rounding to round to the nearest 100 first.

**ASSESSMENT CHECKPOINT** Assess whether children can solve a range of problems in a variety of contexts that involve rounding. Can they demonstrate that they can round numbers to the nearest 10, 100 and 1,000 and are they able to write down numbers that round to a particular degree of accuracy?

**ANSWERS** Answers for the **Practice** part of the lesson appear in the separate **Practice and Reflect answer guide**.

## Reflect

**WAYS OF WORKING** Pair work

**IN FOCUS** This question brings together all aspects of rounding from the lesson. Children use their knowledge of rounding to the nearest 10, 100 and 1,000 to identify a number that satisfies three conditions. Children may reason that they could simply find a number that rounds to 2,000 to the nearest 10, as it would automatically round to 2,000 to the nearest 100 and to the nearest 1,000.

**ASSESSMENT CHECKPOINT** Assess whether children can identify numbers that round to a specified degree of accuracy.

**ANSWERS** Answers for the **Reflect** part of the lesson appear in the separate **Practice and Reflect answer guide**.

## After the lesson ⏸

- Can children round to the nearest 10, 100 and 1,000 using a number line?
- Can children identify numbers that round to a particular number and degree of accuracy?
- Can children solve rounding problems in a range of contexts?

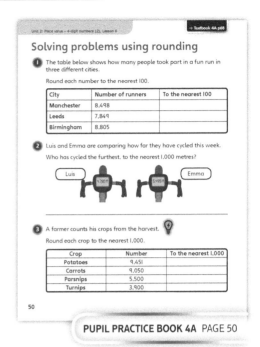

PUPIL PRACTICE BOOK 4A PAGE 50

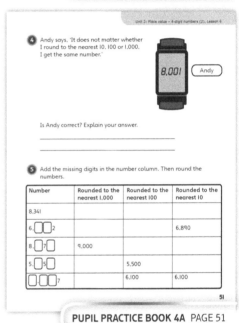

PUPIL PRACTICE BOOK 4A PAGE 51

PUPIL PRACTICE BOOK 4A PAGE 52

# Counting in 25s

## Learning focus

In this lesson children will learn about counting forwards and backwards in 25s.

## Small steps

→ Previous step: Solving problems using rounding
→ **This step: Counting in 25s**
→ Next step: Negative numbers (1)

### NATIONAL CURRICULUM LINKS

**Year 4 Number – Number and Place Value**

Count in multiples of 6, 7, 9, 25 and 1,000.

### ASSESSING MASTERY

Children can successfully count forwards and backwards in 25s, from 0 and from any multiple of 25. Children can spot patterns and recognise numbers that will be in the count (for example, they recognise that 925 will be in a count of 25s from 0 to 1,000 because it ends with 25).

### COMMON MISCONCEPTIONS

Children may count forwards or backwards incorrectly. For example, from 25, children may say 40 next as they incorrectly add on 25. Expose children to the pattern of numbers 0, 25, 50, 75, 100, 125, 150, 175, 200, encouraging them to count out loud as a class to help embed this important counting pattern. Ask:
• *In this pattern, what number comes after 25?*

### STRENGTHENING UNDERSTANDING

Provide children with clearly marked number lines from 0 to 200, which go up in increments of 25. This will help children see that 25 is half-way between 0 and 50, 75 is half-way between 50 and 100, and so on, and help them to visualise and then memorise this pattern.

### GOING DEEPER

Challenge children to think more deeply by asking them to work out where they will be after 7 counts of 25 from 0. Can they work out what number they will be at after 7 counts of 25 from 175? Extend thinking further by asking them to do this without a number line or any other concrete equipment.

### KEY LANGUAGE

**In lesson:** how many, score, more than, total, counting up, counting backwards

**Other language to be used by the teacher:** count, interval, forwards, backwards

### STRUCTURES AND REPRESENTATIONS

number line, base 10 equipment

### RESOURCES

**Mandatory:** number lines

**Optional:** blank number lines, counters, base 10 equipment

 In the eTextbook of this lesson, you will find interactive links to a selection of teaching tools.

## Before you teach

• Can children use a number line?
• Can children recognise the intervals on a number line?
• Can children count in 5s, 10s and 50s?

# Discover

**WAYS OF WORKING** Pair work

**ASK**

- Question ① a): *How many points do you get for hitting a monster? What can you use to help you count in 25s? How many times do you need to count? Why?*
- Question ① a): *What does the count in 25s look like? What do you notice about the numbers? Can you see any patterns?*
- Question ① b): *Did you start from 0 again? How can you start from the previous number?*

**IN FOCUS** Question ① a) introduces the concept of counting in 25s. Children can use number lines or base 10 equipment to help them work out how many points Amelia has scored. Encourage children to notice and describe any patterns that they see. How quickly can they continue the count? Ask them to count backwards too, to check their answer.

Question ① b) allows children to think about the idea of comparing two numbers that have been counted in 25s and come up with an efficient strategy of counting on in 25s. Look for children who go back to 0 and start the count again rather than continuing the count up from Amelia's score.

**PRACTICAL TIPS** Allow children to consolidate their counting by using concrete equipment such as coins (20p + 5p), base 10 equipment and number lines.

**ANSWERS**

Question ① a): Amelia scored 175 points.

Question ① b): Ambika scored 50 points more than Amelia.

# Share

**WAYS OF WORKING** Whole class teacher led

**ASK**

- Question ① a): *How many intervals are there between 0 and 100 when counting in 25s? How does the number line help you to count up in 25s? What equipment can you use to check that you have got this right? Do you notice a pattern in the numbers?*
- Question ① b): *When comparing Amelia and Ambika's scores, do you need to count all of Ambika's monsters, if you already know Amelia's score? Why? Why not?*

**IN FOCUS** The focus of question ① a) is to support children counting up in 25s using a number line. Reinforce this concept further by using coins or base 10 equipment underneath the number line to help children see why the answers are 25, 50, 75, and so on. Some children may have added on 25 using column addition; discuss all the methods that children have used to get the answers. Take time to spot patterns in the numbers, such as the pattern of the last two digits: 00, 25, 50, 75. This will help children work out if a given number is in the 25 count.

Question ① b) focuses on efficient methods for counting up in 25s from a starting point other than 0. Have children identified that they do not need to count from 0 again, but instead need to add two more 25s to Amelia's score?

## Counting in 25s

### Discover

① a) For each monster the children hit, they receive 25 points.
How many points did Amelia score?

b) How many more points did Ambika score than Amelia?

72

**PUPIL TEXTBOOK 4A** PAGE 72

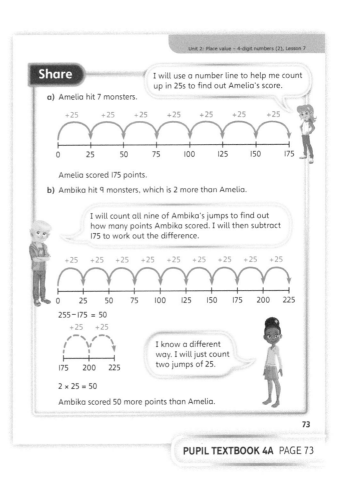

**PUPIL TEXTBOOK 4A** PAGE 73

# Think together

**WAYS OF WORKING** Whole class teacher led (I do, We do, You do)

**ASK**

- Question **1**: *How can you find Richard's score if you already know Amelia's score? Do you need to start at 0 again? How many 25s are in 100?*
- Question **2**: *What strategy could you use to help you work out the total points scored by each person? How could you work out Amelia's score by counting in 25s? How could you use doubles to help you? Can you use Amelia's score to work out Richard's new score?*
- Question **3**: *What different methods can you use to work out Richard's darts score? Which is the most efficient method?*

**IN FOCUS** Question **1** builds on the **Discover** task, asking children to count on 1 more, rather than counting from 0.

Question **2** focuses on adding scores with multiples of 25. Check how children approach this task; for example, do they count up in 25s and then use different strategies, such as doubling, to find the totals? Encourage children to count backwards to check their answers.

Question **3** requires children to count forwards and backwards in 25s according to Richard's scores. Children start from 500 and must count in 25s from this point. Children should use their knowledge of pattern spotting to help them here.

**STRENGTHEN** If children struggle with the concept of counting in 25s, allow them to build numbers using concrete materials, such as coins or base 10 equipment, to help them see what 25 + 25 physically looks like. Link this to the numbers on the number line.

**DEEPEN** Challenge children to keep track of the count in 25s without using a number line. For example, you could ask: *What number is nine counts of 25 from 0? What number is seven counts of 25 forwards from 400? What number is three counts of 25 backwards from 450?*

Question **3** offers many opportunities to extend thinking. For example, you could ask children to explore possible totals if Richard throws five darts. What scores could Richard get? Could he get back to 500? What scores could he get if he threw 6 darts?

**ASSESSMENT CHECKPOINT** Assess whether children can count forwards and backwards in 25s from any multiple of 25.

**ANSWERS**

Question **1**: Richard got a score of 200.

Question **2**: Amelia: 350, Ambika: 325, Richard: 425

Question **3**: Richard's points total is 550.

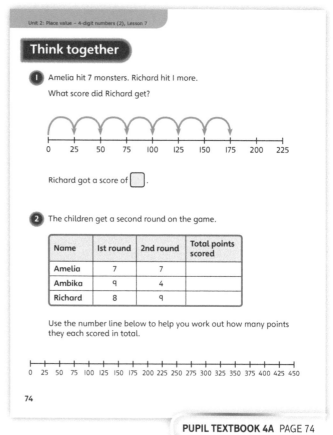

**PUPIL TEXTBOOK 4A** PAGE 74

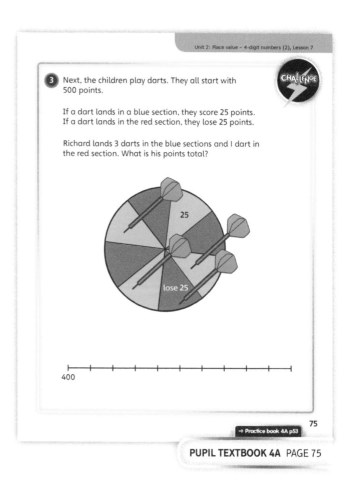

**PUPIL TEXTBOOK 4A** PAGE 75

## Practice

**WAYS OF WORKING** Independent thinking

**IN FOCUS** In questions **2** and **3**, children use number lines and number tracks to demonstrate their understanding of counting in 25s from increasingly large numbers. Encourage children to look for the pattern in the last 2 digits to check their answers. Question **4** consolidates this further, asking children to recognise and circle numbers that will appear in a count of 25s by looking at the pattern of the last 2 digits.

**STRENGTHEN** Use concrete equipment such as coins and base 10 equipment to support understanding in this section. As the numbers get bigger from question **3** onwards, children should notice a pattern. Take children back down to smaller numbers and ask them about the patterns they see. What do they notice about the last two digits? Does this pattern continue? Can they apply this pattern to the larger numbers?

**DEEPEN** In question **5**, challenge children to work out how many counts of 25 make 325 without using a number line. What strategies do they use?

Question **6** requires more creative thinking from children. Is 313 in the 25 count? How do they know? As the stickers only come in packs of 25, children will need to reason that the number of packs they need will take them over 313, so they will have to count over, rather than looking for the closest 25.

**ASSESSMENT CHECKPOINT** Check that children can count forwards and backwards in 25s from any number less than 10,000. Do they recognise the pattern in the last two digits, and can they therefore spot numbers that appear in a count of 25s?

**ANSWERS** Answers for the **Practice** part of the lesson appear in the separate **Practice and Reflect answer guide**.

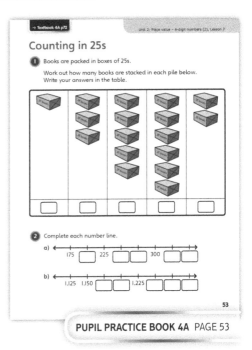

PUPIL PRACTICE BOOK 4A PAGE 53

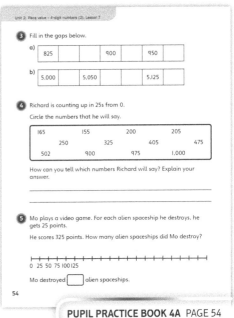

PUPIL PRACTICE BOOK 4A PAGE 54

## Reflect

**WAYS OF WORKING** Pair work

**IN FOCUS** This question focuses on recognising, justifying and reasoning which numbers will appear in the count back in 25s from 5,025 to 0. Encourage children to discuss their methods with a partner.

**ASSESSMENT CHECKPOINT** Assess which strategies children use and how they approach this question. Do they start the count from 5,025? Do they count up from 0? Do children recognise that the most efficient way to check which numbers should be circled is to look at the last two digits?

**ANSWERS** Answers for the **Reflect** part of the lesson appear in the separate **Practice and Reflect answer guide**.

### After the lesson ⏸

- Can children count forwards and backwards in 25s using a number line?
- Can children count forwards and backwards in 25s without using a number line?
- Do children recognise numbers that are in the count from 0 by looking at the last two digits?

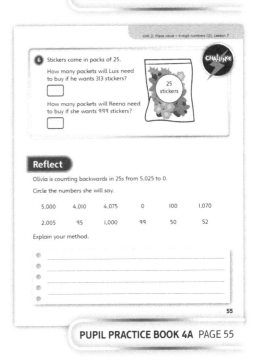

PUPIL PRACTICE BOOK 4A PAGE 55

# Negative numbers ❶

## Learning focus

In this lesson children will be introduced to negative numbers for the first time. They will count back through 0 on number lines using negative numbers.

## Small steps

→ Previous step: Counting in 25s
→ **This step: Negative numbers (1)**
→ Next step: Negative numbers (2)

### NATIONAL CURRICULUM LINKS

**Year 4 Number – Number and Place Value**

Count backwards through zero to include negative numbers.

**Year 5 Number – Number and Place Value**

Interpret negative numbers in context, count forwards and backwards with positive and negative whole numbers, including through zero.

### ASSESSING MASTERY

Children can count backwards through zero using negative numbers.

### COMMON MISCONCEPTIONS

Children may misunderstand the order of negative numbers. Ask:
- *Can you use a number line to help you count backwards through 0?*
- *Can you see the symmetry in numbers on either side of 0 to help you 'see' negative numbers?*

Children may miscount. For example, when working out how many to count back from ⁻3 to 1 they may count 5 (by counting ⁻3, ⁻2, ⁻1, 0, 1). Ask:
- *Do you count the numbers or the jumps between the numbers?*

### STRENGTHENING UNDERSTANDING

To strengthen understanding, encourage children to use a number line to support their counting. Display the number line both horizontally and vertically to physically represent negative numbers, and encourage children to count aloud through 0, forwards and backwards, to reinforce the counting pattern.

### GOING DEEPER

Prompt children to count through 0 in different multiples and to count through 0 both forwards and backwards.

### KEY LANGUAGE

**In lesson:** down, jumps, negative, horizontal, sequences, forwards, backwards

**Other language to be used by the teacher:** multiples, vertical, less than zero (< 0), greater than zero (> 0), positive

### STRUCTURES AND REPRESENTATIONS

vertical and horizontal number lines

### RESOURCES

**Mandatory:** number lines

 In the eTextbook of this lesson, you will find interactive links to a selection of teaching tools.

## Before you teach

- Can children count backwards to 0?
- Can children count in different multiples?
- Can children locate positive numbers on a number line?

## Discover

**WAYS OF WORKING** Pair work

**ASK**

- Question ❶ a) *Which floor is the restaurant on? What do you think a negative floor number means? (below ground) Do you know what to call numbers with a negative sign in front of them?*
- Question ❶ b) *Which floor is the penthouse on? Which floor is Car Park A on? Which direction are you going to count in?*

**IN FOCUS** Question ❶ a) focuses children on the end point after counting backwards through 0. Look for children counting aloud with their partner and counting each step. Children should not simply jump straight to floor ⁻3.

Question ❶ b) requires children to find the difference between two numbers, counting back through 0. Some children may miscount because they count the numbers, rather than the jumps.

**PRACTICAL TIPS** Children could make a human number track where each child represents a number. They could also contribute to making, and then counting back on, a large number line in the classroom or playground. This will reinforce their understanding of the number lines they use in class. Number lines in class should be horizontal and vertical, as vertical number lines can be especially helpful when representing negative numbers and backwards counting. Children could move counters forwards and backwards on the number lines to represent each question.

**ANSWERS**

Question ❶ a): The waiter is in the kitchens on floor ⁻3.

Question ❶ b): Reena travels down 5 floors.

## Share

**WAYS OF WORKING** Whole class teacher led

**ASK**

- Question ❶: *Can a number line help you to count back through 0?*
- Question ❶: *Does it matter if the number line is horizontal or vertical? Do you get the same answer on a horizontal number line and on a vertical number line?*
- Question ❶: *Which number do you start counting on when you are counting backwards?*

**IN FOCUS** Question ❶ a) focuses on how to effectively use a number line to count backwards through 0.

It introduces the idea of negative and positive numbers. Show children a variety of different number lines and explain how they can be vertical and horizontal. Compare them. Ask children if their answers are dependent on which number lines they use.

Question ❶ b) requires children to find the number of jumps between two numbers by counting through 0 on a number line. Model for children how to count the jumps rather than the numbers. Encourage children to count aloud as they work their way through this lesson, taking every opportunity to embed this important counting skill.

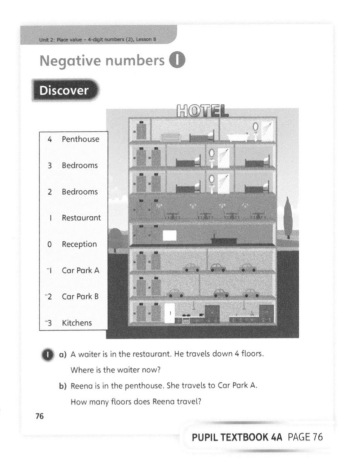

### Negative numbers ❶

**Discover**

❶ a) A waiter is in the restaurant. He travels down 4 floors.
Where is the waiter now?

   b) Reena is in the penthouse. She travels to Car Park A.
How many floors does Reena travel?

76

**PUPIL TEXTBOOK 4A** PAGE 76

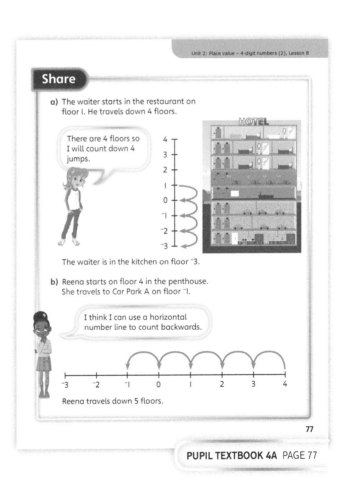

**Share**

a) The waiter starts in the restaurant on floor 1. He travels down 4 floors.

There are 4 floors so I will count down 4 jumps.

The waiter is in the kitchen on floor ⁻3.

b) Reena starts on floor 4 in the penthouse. She travels to Car Park A on floor ⁻1.

I think I can use a horizontal number line to count backwards.

Reena travels down 5 floors.

77

**PUPIL TEXTBOOK 4A** PAGE 77

109

# Think together

Unit 2: Place value – 4-digit numbers (2), Lesson 8

**WAYS OF WORKING** Whole class teacher led (I do, We do, You do)

**ASK**

- Question **1**: *Which numbers do you start counting from? Do you count forwards or backwards?*
- Question **2**: *Can you use a number line to help you find the next two numbers in the sequences?*
- Question **3**: *Can you see a pattern when counting back in fives into negative numbers?*

**IN FOCUS** In question **1** children practise the skills they have focused on in the **Discover** section, counting on a number line. Count aloud with children to strengthen counting skills here.

In question **2** children must use their counting skills and knowledge of number patterns to help them complete number sequences, using a number line to support them.

Question **3** requires children to count in different multiples. What different methods do children use here? Some children may remember number patterns, or be able to jump straight back to the numbers, and immediately be able to confirm if the sentence is true or false. Others may need to count each number back to check.

**STRENGTHEN** Continue to use a number line to support counting into negative numbers. For children who are struggling to count back in certain multiples, ask them to count back in 1s and pause after each count of 2, 5 or 4, depending on which multiple they are counting back in.

**DEEPEN** Questions **2** and **3** challenge children to count in multiples with negative numbers. Extend thinking further by expanding question **3** and asking children to count back in more challenging multiples, such as 3 or 6. Do children use their knowledge of number patterns, times-tables and counting backwards in negative numbers to make informed decisions about whether they will say ⁻20?

**ASSESSMENT CHECKPOINT** In question **1** check whether children can count effectively using a number line to support them. In questions **2** and **3**, can children accurately count backwards in multiples into negative numbers?

**ANSWERS**

Question **1** a): I am now on floor 2

Question **1** b): I am now on floor ⁻3

Question **2** a): ⁻2, ⁻3

Question **2** b): ⁻5, ⁻6

Question **2** c): ⁻4, ⁻6

Question **3**   Lee is correct.

Zac is incorrect.

Emma is correct.

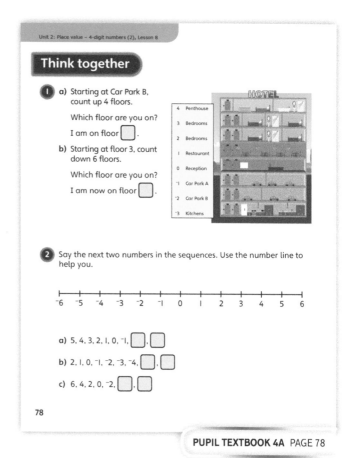

**PUPIL TEXTBOOK 4A** PAGE 78

**PUPIL TEXTBOOK 4A** PAGE 79

## Practice

**WAYS OF WORKING** Independent thinking

**IN FOCUS** Questions in this **Practice** section use a mixture of horizontal and vertical number lines to support children and to help them practise counting forwards and backwards through 0. Questions ❶ and ❹ practise using negative numbers in context: it is important to highlight to children how counting in negative numbers is a useful and practical skill. Question ❻ is an extension of the skills practised in the Challenge question of the **Textbook**.

**STRENGTHEN** Continue to encourage children to use a number line to support counting forwards and backwards through 0. Model and prompt counting aloud, both forwards and backwards, in singles and multiples, until children can securely demonstrate this important skill.

**DEEPEN** Can children count backwards in steps of 2, 5, 10, 4 and so on from any given number? Challenge children to practise this skill by asking them to count backwards in steps of 10 from 42. What is the first negative number that they meet?

**ASSESSMENT CHECKPOINT** Assess whether children can count forwards and backwards through 0 in both single numbers and multiples of 2, 5 and 10.

**ANSWERS** Answers for the **Practice** part of the lesson appear in the separate **Practice and Reflect answer guide**.

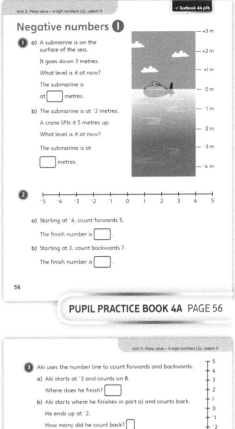

PUPIL PRACTICE BOOK 4A PAGE 56

PUPIL PRACTICE BOOK 4A PAGE 57

## Reflect

**WAYS OF WORKING** Independent thinking or pair work

**IN FOCUS** Children play a game using their knowledge of counting forwards and backwards through negative numbers.

**ASSESSMENT CHECKPOINT** Assess whether children can confidently count forwards and backwards on the number track. Can children predict where they will land without counting?

**ANSWERS** Answers for the **Reflect** part of the lesson appear in the separate **Practice and Reflect answer guide**.

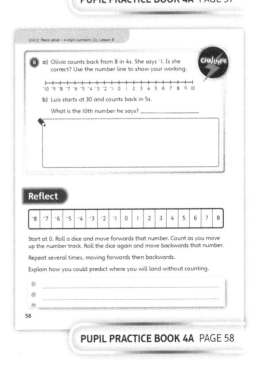

PUPIL PRACTICE BOOK 4A PAGE 58

## After the lesson ⏸

- Do children rely on the number line to count backwards through 0?
- Can children spot patterns when counting backwards and forwards in multiples?
- Can children explain what happens when you count backwards into negative numbers?

# Negative numbers ②

## Learning focus

In this lesson children will look at negative numbers in context. They will count back through 0 on number lines using negative numbers.

## Small steps

→ Previous step: Negative numbers (1)
→ **This step: Negative numbers (2)**
→ Next step: Adding and subtracting 1s, 10s, 100s, 1,000s

## NATIONAL CURRICULUM LINKS

**Year 4 Number – Number and Place Value**

Count backwards through zero to include negative numbers.

**Year 5 Number – Number and Place Value**

Interpret negative numbers in context, count forwards and backwards with positive and negative whole numbers, including through zero.

## ASSESSING MASTERY

Children can count backwards through zero in context, using negative numbers. They read negative numbers on a number line and can find the difference between a positive and a negative number.

## COMMON MISCONCEPTIONS

If children misunderstand the order of negative numbers, ask:
• *Can you use a number line to help you count back through 0?*
• *Can you see the symmetry in numbers on either side of 0 to check your counting?*

Children may continue to miscount by counting the numbers rather than the number of jumps back. Ask:
• *What strategies did you use for counting backwards in the last lesson?*

When using number lines, children may not realise that some number lines do not go up and down in intervals of 1. Remind children to check the intervals on number lines before using them by asking questions that prompt this thinking. For example, if there are five increments between 0 and 10, ask:
• *Does this number line count up in 1s? What about in 2s? How can you tell?*

## STRENGTHENING UNDERSTANDING

To strengthen understanding, encourage children to use a number line to support their counting. Show the number line both horizontally and vertically and ask children to slowly count aloud with you, to help embed the rhythm and pattern of the numbers.

## GOING DEEPER

To deepen thinking and give further opportunities to practise working in negative numbers, ask children to complete the start and end numbers on a variety of number lines using the position of the other numbers on the line to help them.

## KEY LANGUAGE

**In lesson:** difference, intervals, degrees Celsius, estimate

**Other language to be used by the teacher:** negative, positive, forwards, backwards, position

## STRUCTURES AND REPRESENTATIONS

vertical and horizontal number lines

## RESOURCES

**Mandatory:** number lines

 In the eTextbook of this lesson, you will find interactive links to a selection of teaching tools.

## Before you teach

• Can children count backwards through 0?
• Can children count in different multiples?
• Can children estimate numbers on a positive number line?

## Discover

**WAYS OF WORKING** Pair work

**ASK**

- Question **1** a) *How do you read the temperature on a thermometer? How is it similar to a number line? What unit do you measure temperature in?*
- Question **1** b) *Can you count backwards to find the difference between the two temperatures? Can you check your answer by counting forwards?*

**IN FOCUS** In question **1** a) children begin to see where number lines are used in context. Explore the connection between number lines and thermometers. Children may sometimes read the negative temperatures as positive. Prompt children to check the intervals on the thermometer before they try to answer the question – this is good practice.

Children develop their skills from previous lessons in question **1** b), using them to find the difference between the temperatures in the two worlds. Some children may focus on subtracting the two numbers; prompt them to instead count the number of steps from the positive temperature to the negative temperature. Ask children how they think they might be able to check their answers.

**PRACTICAL TIPS** Children could use real thermometers to look at how to read temperature.

**ANSWERS**

Question **1** a): Arctic World is ⁻8 degrees Celsius.
Nocturnal World is ⁻2 degrees Celsius.
Oceanic World is 13 degrees Celsius.

Question **1** b): The difference in temperature between Oceanic World and Nocturnal World is 15 degrees Celsius.

## Share

**WAYS OF WORKING** Whole class teacher led

**ASK**

- Question **1** a): *What do thermometers help us to do? How do you read a thermometer? What intervals does this thermometer go up in? How can you check?*
- Question **1** b): *Can a number line help you to find the difference? Does it matter if your number line is horizontal or vertical? Which number do you start counting on when you are finding the difference?*

**IN FOCUS** Question **1** a) focuses on reading a scale and finding missing numbers on a scale, including negative numbers. Children may think that the thermometer goes up in 1s: encourage them to check this by counting aloud and realising that this does not work. Ask if the intervals go up in 2s and encourage children to check this for themselves.

Question **1** b) looks at finding the difference between two numbers by counting through 0 on a number line. Stress the importance of counting backwards through 0. Assist children if necessary with working out the starting point and end point for their counting.

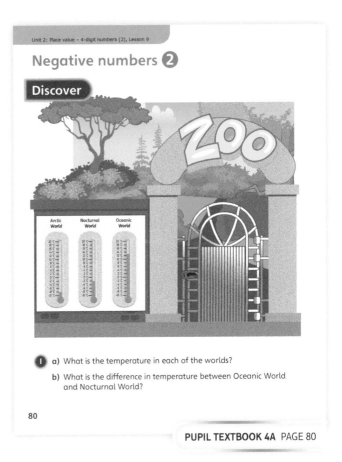

**PUPIL TEXTBOOK 4A** PAGE 80

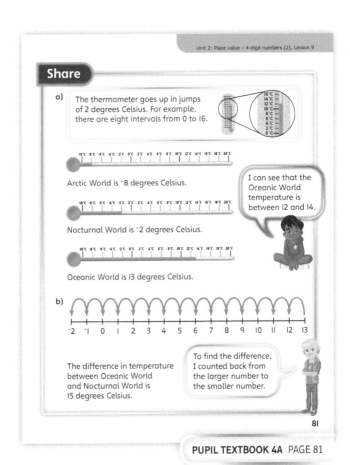

**PUPIL TEXTBOOK 4A** PAGE 81

# Think together

Whole class teacher led (I do, We do, You do)

**ASK**

- Question **1** a) and **1** b): *Does each of the thermometers go up in the same intervals? How can you check? What do they go up in?*
- Question **2**: *What are the number lines counting up in?*
- Question **3** a): *Are the increments on the number lines equally spaced? How does this help you work out the missing numbers?*
- Question **3** b): *What could the start and end numbers be? Can you complete the scale on the number line?*

**IN FOCUS** In questions **1** and **2**, children complete missing numbers on scales and number lines to read numbers and estimate the positions of numbers. Look out for children who split the intervals up when estimating the values of the arrows.

**STRENGTHEN** Continue to use a number line to support counting into negative numbers. Remind children that scales may be different sizes so it is essential that they count aloud to check if the interval they have chosen works. In question **3**, refer children to what Astrid and Flo are saying to help them structure their thinking.

**DEEPEN** Question **3** requires children to think carefully about the start and end numbers and the scale that could be used on a number line. Can children reason what the start numbers could be rather than using trial and error?

**ASSESSMENT CHECKPOINT** Assess whether children can complete missing numbers on a number line. Can they successfully estimate numbers when using different scales on a number line?

**ANSWERS**

Question **1** a): The temperature is 5 degrees Celsius.

Question **1** b): The temperature is ⁻5 degrees Celsius.

Question **2** a): ⁻2

Question **2** b): ⁻7

Question **2** c): ⁻16

Question **3** a): ⁻10

⁻4

Question **3** b): Many answers are possible; the difference between the start number and ⁻5, and the difference between ⁻5 and the end number should be the same. Examples include ⁻6 and ⁻4 (counting in 1s) and ⁻10 and 0 (counting in 5s).

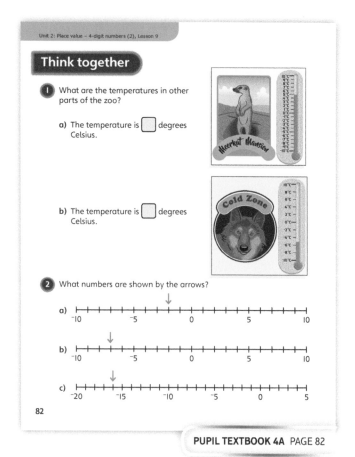

## Think together

**1** What are the temperatures in other parts of the zoo?

a) The temperature is ☐ degrees Celsius.

b) The temperature is ☐ degrees Celsius.

**2** What numbers are shown by the arrows?

82

**PUPIL TEXTBOOK 4A** PAGE 82

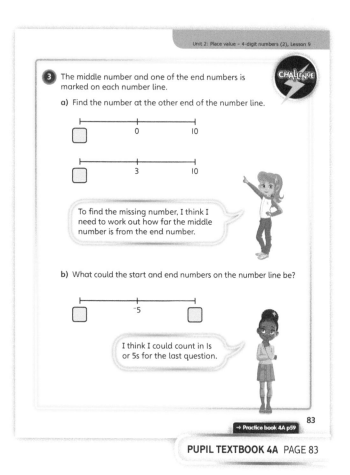

**3** The middle number and one of the end numbers is marked on each number line. CHALLENGE

a) Find the number at the other end of the number line.

To find the missing number, I think I need to work out how far the middle number is from the end number.

b) What could the start and end numbers on the number line be?

I think I could count in 1s or 5s for the last question.

83

→ Practice book 4A p59

**PUPIL TEXTBOOK 4A** PAGE 83

## Practice

**WAYS OF WORKING** Independent thinking

**IN FOCUS** In questions **1**, **2** and **3**, children complete missing numbers on a scale and read numbers off a scale, reinforcing what they have been learning in the **Textbook**. The scales have different interval sizes, so it is important that children check this before answering.

In question **4**, children count backwards and forwards through negative numbers to find new numbers after temperature changes. Prompt children to count in the other direction to check their answers.

**STRENGTHEN** Continue to encourage children to use a number line to support counting forwards and backwards through 0. Refer children to some of the number lines you have made in class to help support their answers in this section.

**DEEPEN** Extend children's thinking further by using the same number line as in question **7**, but replacing ¯3 with a different number as a starting point. Do children consistently complete the number line correctly? Can they add numbers in the correct sequence using a range of intervals?

**ASSESSMENT CHECKPOINT** Assess whether children count backwards and forwards through 0 to complete a variety of number lines which use different intervals. Can they reason what numbers are needed to complete number lines, with an awareness of intervals, rather than using trial and error?

**ANSWERS** Answers for the **Practice** part of the lesson appear in the separate **Practice and Reflect answer guide**.

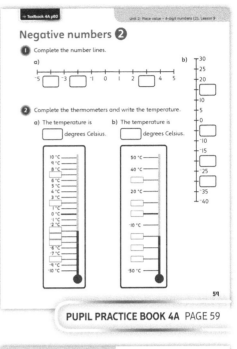

**PUPIL PRACTICE BOOK 4A** PAGE 59

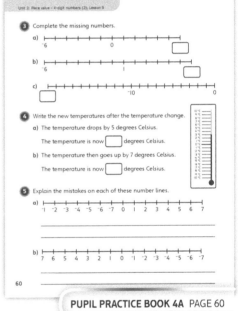

**PUPIL PRACTICE BOOK 4A** PAGE 60

## Reflect

**WAYS OF WORKING** Independent thinking

**IN FOCUS** Children focus on their understanding of the position of negative numbers in order to explain why Max is wrong. They may explain in words or they may use a number line to illustrate their thinking.

**ASSESSMENT CHECKPOINT** Assess whether children can clearly explain why Max is wrong, using accurate vocabulary or models to support their answer.

**ANSWERS** Answers for the **Reflect** part of the lesson appear in the separate **Practice and Reflect answer guide**.

### After the lesson

- Can children read a variety of number lines with differing intervals and find missing numbers on these number lines?
- Can children read positive and negative numbers on a number line?
- Can children explain what a negative number is?

**PUPIL PRACTICE BOOK 4A** PAGE 61

# End of unit check

Don't forget the *Power Maths* unit assessment grid on p26.

**WAYS OF WORKING** Group work adult led

**IN FOCUS** Children recap their understanding of 4-digit numbers shown in various different representations. Question **1** focuses on finding 1,000 more or less. Question **2** looks at rounding. Question **3** looks at counting in 25s. Question **4** focuses on negative numbers. Question **5** compares two 4-digit numbers. Question **6** is a SATS-style question.

**ANSWERS AND COMMENTARY** Children who have mastered the concepts in this unit will know that a 4-digit number is made up of 1,000s, 100s, 10s and 1s and will be able to represent numbers in multiple ways. They will be able to compare and order 4-digit numbers by looking at the digits in each place value column. Children will understand the number line to 10,000 and will be beginning to know where numbers lie on the number line. They will extend this knowledge to look at negative numbers below 0 on the number line. Children will be able to round numbers to the nearest 10, 100 and 1,000.

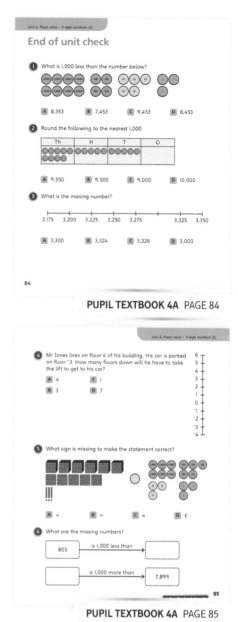

PUPIL TEXTBOOK 4A PAGE 84

PUPIL TEXTBOOK 4A PAGE 85

| Q | A | WRONG ANSWERS AND MISCONCEPTIONS | STRENGTHENING UNDERSTANDING |
|---|---|---|---|
| 1 | B | Choosing A indicates that the child has found 100 less instead of 1,000 less. C indicates that the child has found 1,000 more. D indicates that the child has found the number shown. | Secure children's understanding of 4-digit numbers by using base 10 equipment and place value counters in conjunction with a place value grid. |
| 2 | D | Choosing A indicates that the child has found the number represented. B suggests that the child has rounded down incorrectly to the nearest 100. C suggests that the child has rounded down instead of up. | When comparing 3-digit and 4-digit numbers, use the place value grid to show the importance of comparing the same place value, not the first digit of the number. |
| 3 | D | Choosing B or C indicates that the child has chosen one more or one less than 3,325. A suggests that the child has rounded the number to the nearest 1,000. | Link physical numbers to numbers on the number line to support children with counting. |
| 4 | D | Choosing A or B suggests that the child has chosen a number from within the question. C suggests that the child has mistaken ⁻3 for 3 and found the difference of 1. | Encourage children to count aloud when counting up or back on a number line to help them see the counting pattern. |
| 5 | C | Choosing A or B suggests that the child has compared incorrectly. | |
| 6 | 1,805  8,899 | Children may misinterpret the question. For example, they may try to find 1,000 less than 805 or 1,000 less than 7,899. | |

# My journal

**WAYS OF WORKING** Independent thinking

**ANSWERS AND COMMENTARY**

In the first question, children should find that the 100s, 10s and 1s will never change when the original number is at least 1,000. They may look at numbers that go from 4-digit numbers into 3-digit numbers, such as 1,345 to 345. They could also look at 1,085 to 85, for example, and comment that although no 0 is needed in 85 there are still no 100s in both numbers.

In the second question, children will find that when they round a number to the nearest 1,000 all the columns can change; for example, 7,564 to the nearest 1,000 is 8,000.

# Power check

**WAYS OF WORKING** Independent thinking

**ASK**

- How confident do you feel about ordering and comparing 4-digit numbers?
- Do you think you could explain how to find 1,000 more or less than a number?
- Would you feel confident counting in multiples of 25 without a number line?

# Power play

**WAYS OF WORKING** Pair work or small groups

**IN FOCUS** Use this Power play to check if children understand the different objectives covered in the unit. Children focus on rounding to the nearest 10, 100 and 1,000 and finding 100 more and 1,000 more or less than a number. The modification suggested by Sparks requires children to think carefully about where they place the digits and the importance of the order.

**ANSWERS AND COMMENTARY** Within this Power play, children will generate a variety of numbers and show whether they can round them correctly and find 100 more and 1,000 more or less.

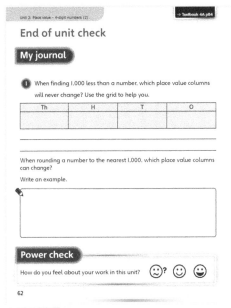

**PUPIL PRACTICE BOOK 4A** PAGE 62

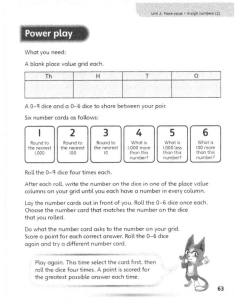

**PUPIL PRACTICE BOOK 4A** PAGE 63

## After the unit ⏸

- Can children represent 4-digit numbers in multiple ways?
- Do children display flexibility with 4-digit numbers and are they able to make numbers to fit certain criteria, and to compare and order these numbers?

**Strengthen** and **Deepen** activities for this unit can be found in the *Power Maths* online subscription.

# Unit 3
## Addition and subtraction

**Mastery Expert tip!** "The bar model is useful for representing additions and subtractions, but don't just show it to children, ask them to explain it and to draw their own!"

**Don't forget to watch the Unit 3 video!**

## WHY THIS UNIT IS IMPORTANT

This unit is important because it focuses on learning a range of addition and subtraction strategies, in particular the column method. Mastering this will lead to confidence in many other areas of mathematics, especially when children apply their strategies to word problems and puzzles.

## WHERE THIS UNIT FITS

→ Unit 2: Place value – 4-digit numbers (2)

→ **Unit 3: Addition and subtraction**

→ Unit 4: Measure – perimeter

This unit builds on children's Year 3 work on adding and subtracting with 3-digit numbers. It further develops their estimation and answer-checking strategies and their problem-solving skills. This unit provides essential preparation for beginning to add and subtract numbers with more than four digits.

Before they start this unit, it is expected that children:

• have a firm understanding of place value (up to 4-digit numbers)
• know a range of mental addition and subtraction strategies
• can apply these strategies to a range of contexts including measure.

## ASSESSING MASTERY

Children who have mastered this unit can find totals and differences using the column method of addition and subtraction. They should not, however, always rely on the column method, but should understand when there is a more efficient method. They can confidently apply their knowledge when solving word problems and explain all answers clearly, using the correct vocabulary.

| COMMON MISCONCEPTIONS | STRENGTHENING UNDERSTANDING | GOING DEEPER |
|---|---|---|
| Children may not align the columns correctly when using the column method. | Run an intervention in which children use place value grids to support aligning columns and understanding the importance of this. | Solve some addition and subtraction sentences that have missing numbers. |
| Children may not understand the place value behind the method of exchanging. | Practise exchanging using place value grids and place value counters. | Provide children with some multi-step word problems. Can they represent them with a diagram and then solve them? |
| Children may not know whether to add or subtract when solving a problem. | Ask children to represent the problem with a bar model. | Ask children to make up their own word problems to fit an addition or subtraction sentence. |

# Unit 3: Addition and subtraction

## WAYS OF WORKING

Go through the unit starter pages of the **Pupil Textbook**. Talk through the key learning points that the characters mention and the key vocabulary.

## STRUCTURES AND REPRESENTATIONS

**Place value grid:** This model uses counters to show the value of each column, which supports the column method layout.

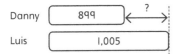

**Bar model:** This model can be used to represent the situation in some addition and subtraction word problems.

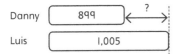

**Part-whole model:** This model is an alternative way to represent the situation in addition and subtraction word problems.

## KEY LANGUAGE

There is some key language that children will need to know as a part of the learning in this unit.

→ addition, subtraction
→ total
→ more than, less than
→ difference, exchange
→ column method
→ estimate, accurate, efficient, exact
→ strategy
→ diagram

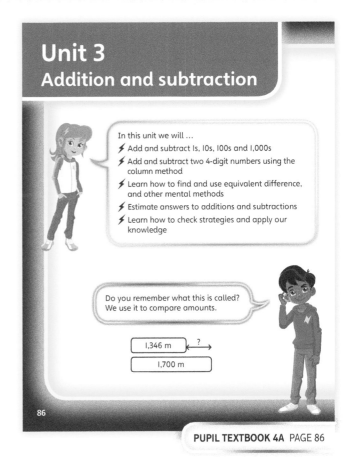

PUPIL TEXTBOOK 4A PAGE 86

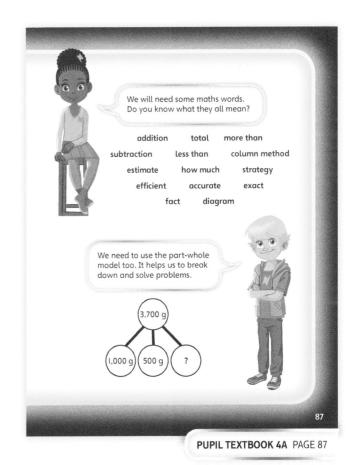

PUPIL TEXTBOOK 4A PAGE 87

# Adding and subtracting Is, I0s, I00s, I,000s

## Learning focus

In this lesson children will use their knowledge of place value to add and subtract 1, 10, 100 and 1,000 to and from 4-digit numbers.

## Small steps

→ Previous step: Negative numbers (2)
→ **This step: Adding and subtracting 1s, 10s, 100s, 1,000s**
→ Next step: Adding two 4-digit numbers (1)

### NATIONAL CURRICULUM LINKS

**Year 4 Number – Addition and Subtraction**

Add and subtract numbers with up to 4 digits using the formal written methods of columnar addition and subtraction where appropriate.

**Year 4 Number – Number and Place value**

Solve number and practical problems that involve [addition and subtraction] with increasingly large positive numbers.

### ASSESSING MASTERY

Children can quickly make mental calculations when adding and subtracting 1, 10, 100 and 1,000. Children can explain their method, demonstrating a deep understanding of place value, and can solve related problems in a range of contexts.

### COMMON MISCONCEPTIONS

Children may have place value misconceptions, i.e. they may think 3,423 + 100 = 4,423. Ask:
• *Can you put the numbers into a place value grid to help?*

### STRENGTHENING UNDERSTANDING

Give children the opportunity to practise adding 1, 10, 100, 1,000 to a range of numbers with a place value grid to help. Repeat until children can calculate place value additions and subtractions mentally.

### GOING DEEPER

Give children a variety of missing number place value problems which will require them to think more deeply about the relationship between digits and what information they can use to find the missing numbers. For example, 3,487 + 2,000 = ?, 1,298 – 70 = ?, 6,815 + ? = 6,819, 2,731 – ? = 2,131.

### KEY LANGUAGE

**In lesson:** more, fact

**Other language to be used by the teacher:** place value, thousands, hundreds, tens, ones, add, subtract, reduce, increase

### STRUCTURES AND REPRESENTATIONS

place value grid

### RESOURCES

**Mandatory:** place value counters, base 10 equipment

 In the eTextbook of this lesson, you will find interactive links to a selection of teaching tools.

## Before you teach ⏸

• Would base 10 equipment help some children with their understanding of place value in this lesson?
• Which children do you think will need support in this lesson?

## Discover

WAYS OF WORKING **WAYS OF WORKING** Pair work

**ASK**

- Question **1** a): *What is the same about 3, 30, 300 and 3,000? What is different?*
- Question **1** b): *Can you explain your answer?*

**IN FOCUS** Ask children what is similar and what is different about +3, +30, +300 and +3,000. Doing this will help them to think about the relationship and connections between these numbers.

**PRACTICAL TIPS** For this activity, some children may benefit from representing the numbers in the place value grids with concrete objects – use base 10 equipment for this.

**ANSWERS**

Question **1** a): 4,256 + 300 = 4,556

Reena's score is 4,556 points.

Question **1** b): 4,556 + 3 = 4,559

4,559 < 7,267

4,556 + 30 = 4,586

4,586 < 7,267

4,556 + 3,000 = 7,556

7,556 > 7,267

The +3,000 bonus beats the high score.

## Share

**WAYS OF WORKING** Whole class teacher led

**ASK**

- Question **1** b): *Can you tell me what the signs < and > mean?*
- Question **1** b): *Can you use the vocabulary 'more than' and 'less than' to explain your answer?*

**IN FOCUS** The place value grids support children with their understanding of place value. Count the counters in the grids aloud as a whole class – doing this will help children understand the numbers at a deeper level, and will also help them to make comparisons between numbers.

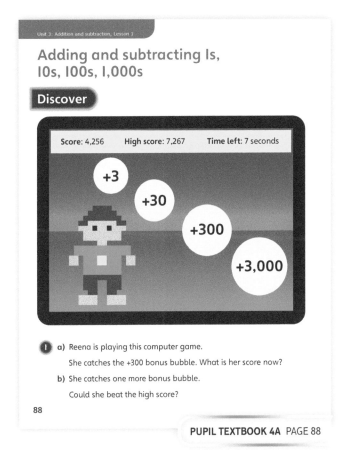

Unit 3: Addition and subtraction, Lesson 1

### Adding and subtracting Is, I0s, I00s, I,000s

**Discover**

Score: 4,256    High score: 7,267    Time left: 7 seconds

+3
+30
+300
+3,000

**1** a) Reena is playing this computer game.

She catches the +300 bonus bubble. What is her score now?

b) She catches one more bonus bubble.

Could she beat the high score?

88

**PUPIL TEXTBOOK 4A** PAGE 88

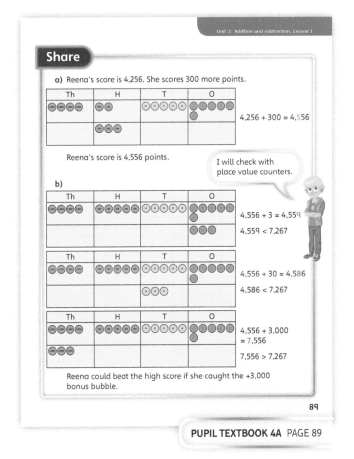

Unit 3: Addition and subtraction, Lesson 1

**Share**

a) Reena's score is 4,256. She scores 300 more points.

| Th | H | T | O |
|---|---|---|---|

4,256 + 300 = 4,556

Reena's score is 4,556 points.

I will check with place value counters.

b)

| Th | H | T | O |
|---|---|---|---|

4,556 + 3 = 4,559
4,559 < 7,267

| Th | H | T | O |
|---|---|---|---|

4,556 + 30 = 4,586
4,586 < 7,267

| Th | H | T | O |
|---|---|---|---|

4,556 + 3,000 = 7,556
7,556 > 7,267

Reena could beat the high score if she caught the +3,000 bonus bubble.

89

**PUPIL TEXTBOOK 4A** PAGE 89

# Think together

Whole class teacher led (I do, We do, You do)

**ASK**

- Question **1**: *Which is changing in each calculation – the 1s, 10s, 100s or 1,000s?*
- Question **1**: *Why do you need 0s in numbers like 1,001?*
- Question **2**: *How can you work out calculations with missing numbers?*

**IN FOCUS** In question **1**, you may need to highlight that in the second example there are no tens left, and so you need to include 0 as a placeholder, i.e. 7,646 – 40 = 7,606. Some children may not understand how to write this and so may give 766 as their answer.

**STRENGTHEN** For each question provide base 10 equipment to visually represent place value for children who need it.

Asking children to explain their working will strengthen learning.

**DEEPEN** Give children some calculations with mistakes, e.g. 4,576 – 30 = 4,276. Challenge them to correct the mistakes and explain where the person who made the mistake went wrong.

**ASSESSMENT CHECKPOINT** Use question **2** to assess whether children can work mentally, or whether they still rely on place value grids.

**ANSWERS**

Question **1** a): 7,646 – 4 = 7,642

b): 7,646 – 40 = 7,606

c): 7,646 – 400 = 7,246

d): 7,646 – 4,000 = 3,646

Question **2** a): 8,888 – 500 = 8,388

b): 8,888 – 5 = 8,883

c): 3,888 = 8,888 – 5,000

d): 8,838 = 8,888 – 50

Question **3** a): 6,869 points

Question **3** b): There are many solutions for this question, as long as the star and the bubble lead to a score increase of 10.

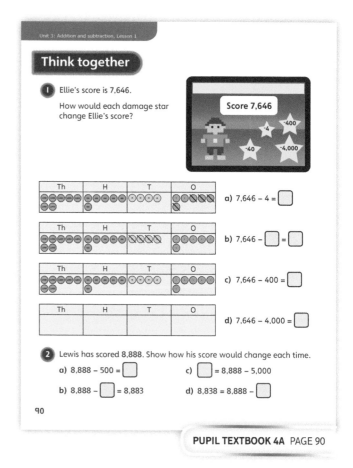

PUPIL TEXTBOOK 4A PAGE 90

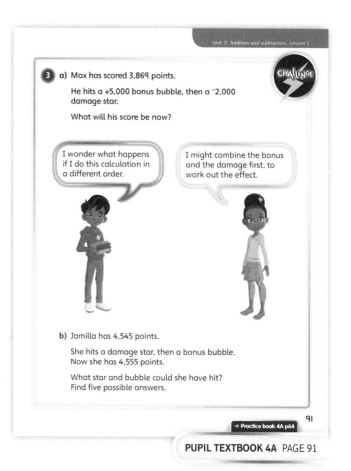

PUPIL TEXTBOOK 4A PAGE 91

## Practice

**WAYS OF WORKING** Independent thinking

**IN FOCUS** Make sure children understand the contexts in question **4**: what the prices were originally and how they have now been reduced.

**STRENGTHEN** Question **6** will strengthen learning by encouraging children to think about place value relationships across a variety of numbers. The task may seem difficult at first, but reassure children that if they think hard they can reach a solution. Build children's confidence by explaining that there are multiple answers for each question.

**DEEPEN** Deepen learning by providing two-step questions with missing numbers, for example 4,264 + ? – 200 = 4,564.

**THINK DIFFERENTLY** Question **5** challenges children to relate addition and subtraction. Listen carefully to children's reasoning for this question.

**ASSESSMENT CHECKPOINT** Question **4** will allow you to assess which children are able to apply their knowledge in context. Children should demonstrate problem-solving skills to work with what they know and complete the steps needed to find the solution.

**ANSWERS** Answers for the **Practice** part of the lesson appear in the separate **Practice and Reflect answer guide**.

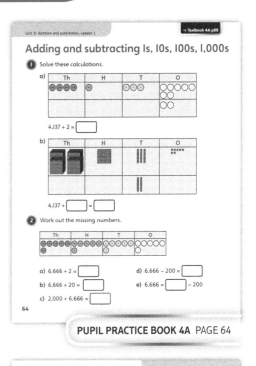

PUPIL PRACTICE BOOK 4A PAGE 64

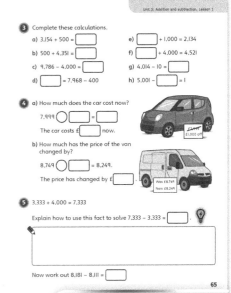

PUPIL PRACTICE BOOK 4A PAGE 65

## Reflect

**WAYS OF WORKING** Pair work

**IN FOCUS** This section will give children the opportunity to explain their understanding of the lesson. Encourage them to use a place value grid and place value counters as part of their answer.

**ASSESSMENT CHECKPOINT** Can children explain the method correctly? Do they use the correct vocabulary?

**ANSWERS** Answers for the **Reflect** part of the lesson appear in the separate **Practice and Reflect answer guide**.

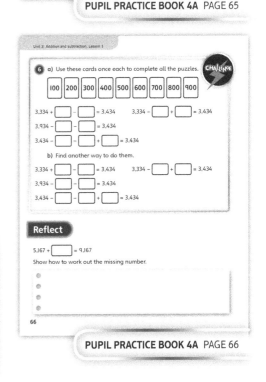

PUPIL PRACTICE BOOK 4A PAGE 66

### After the lesson ⏸

- How will you support children who found the learning difficult in this lesson? What intervention sessions would be useful?
- Which children mastered the lesson?
- Could you make a display to support children in the subsequent lessons?

# Adding two 4-digit numbers

## Learning focus

In this lesson children will add 4-digit numbers using the column method (without exchanging). This is closely paired with a place value grid to ensure children have a deeper understanding.

## Small steps

→ Previous step: Adding and subtracting 1s, 10s, 100s, 1,000s
→ **This step: Adding two 4-digit numbers (1)**
→ Next step: Adding two 4-digit numbers (2)

## NATIONAL CURRICULUM LINKS

**Year 4 Number – Addition and Subtraction**

Add and subtract numbers with up to 4 digits using the formal written methods of columnar addition and subtraction where appropriate.

## ASSESSING MASTERY

Children can use the column method to calculate. They can explain their working clearly, and understand fully what they are doing when using this method.

## COMMON MISCONCEPTIONS

Children may think that they are simply adding the digits (rather than 10s, 100s etc.). Ask:
• *In 2,323 + 7,111, what does each digit represent?*

Children may not understand the importance of layout, and so may not align the columns correctly. Ask:
• *Why is it important to lay out your work correctly?*

## STRENGTHENING UNDERSTANDING

To strengthen understanding, ask children to represent the numbers with base 10 equipment. This will give them a more concrete understanding.

## GOING DEEPER

Deepen learning by providing children with some column additions with mistakes. Can they spot the mistakes and explain why the errors may have been made?

## KEY LANGUAGE

**In lesson:** total, ones (1s), tens (10s), hundreds (100s), thousands (1,000s), add, place value, digit, altogether, addition, column

## STRUCTURES AND REPRESENTATIONS

place value grid, number line

## RESOURCES

**Mandatory:** base 10 equipment, place value counters

 In the eTextbook of this lesson, you will find interactive links to a selection of teaching tools.

## Before you teach ⏸

• How did children get on in the previous lesson?
• What is children's prior knowledge of column addition?
• How will you deal with misconceptions?

## Discover

**WAYS OF WORKING**  Pair work

**ASK**

- Question ❶ a): *What methods could you use?*
- Question ❶ a): *Do you remember how you solved a calculation like this one in Year 3?*
- Question ❶ b): *How do you know you are correct?*

**IN FOCUS**  For question ❶ a), observe the different methods that children use. Many will partition the numbers and use the expanded method (which they learnt in the previous year).

**PRACTICAL TIPS**  For this activity, leave blank place value grids on the tables for children to use if they wish.

**ANSWERS**

Question ❶ a): 4,523 + 3,431 = 7,954. The luggage weighs 7,954 g in total.

Question ❶ b): 7,954 < 9,000. They are under the weight limit.

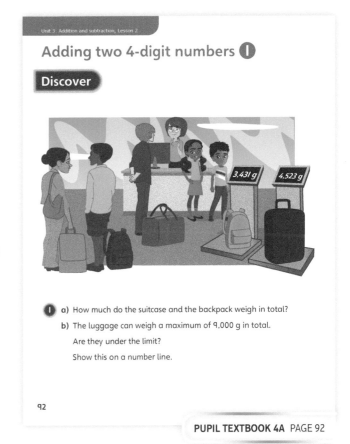

## Adding two 4-digit numbers ❶

### Discover

❶ a) How much do the suitcase and the backpack weigh in total?

b) The luggage can weigh a maximum of 9,000 g in total.

Are they under the limit?

Show this on a number line.

92

**PUPIL TEXTBOOK 4A** PAGE 92

## Share

**WAYS OF WORKING**  Whole class teacher led

**ASK**

- Question ❶ a): *Do you know what to call this method of addition?*
- Question ❶ b): *What sign has been used in the answer? Why?*

**IN FOCUS**  For question ❶ a), the column addition is broken down into steps, which is very important for children to see. Discuss the steps and explain them. You may want to ask children if they can think why they do not start with the thousands.

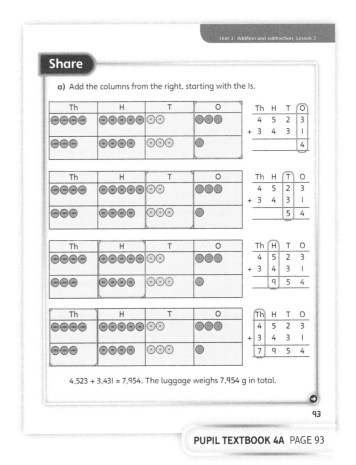

### Share

a) Add the columns from the right, starting with the 1s.

4,523 + 3,431 = 7,954. The luggage weighs 7,954 g in total.

93

**PUPIL TEXTBOOK 4A** PAGE 93

# Think together

Unit 3: Addition and subtraction, Lesson 2

**WAYS OF WORKING** Whole class teacher led (I do, We do, You do)

**ASK**
- Question ③: *How can you work out the missing numbers?*
- Question ④: *Why is it important to lay out your work correctly?*
- Question ④: *What can you use to explain your answer?*

**IN FOCUS** Question ③ has a column addition with missing numbers. Talk to children about how they might solve it. They will soon realise that they must do a subtraction to find the correct answer.

**STRENGTHEN** Provide base 10 equipment for children who need it. Children progressing from place value grids to written columns may need support with labelling the columns.

**DEEPEN** Deepen learning by challenging children to become the teacher. Show them a list of additions, some of which have mistakes, for example 4,556 + 2,002 = 6,008. Challenge them to mark the additions, correct the mistakes and explain where the person who made the error may have gone wrong.

**ASSESSMENT CHECKPOINT** Use question ④ to see if children understand the importance of laying out their work correctly. This will also give you an insight into their understanding of place value.

**ANSWERS**

Question ①: 3,142 + 2,306 = 5,448

The two bags weigh 5,448 g in total.

Question ②:

| Th | H | T | O |
|---|---|---|---|
| 2 | 5 | 2 | 5 |
| + 1 | 2 | 3 | 4 |
| 3 | 7 | 5 | 9 |

| Th | H | T | O |
|---|---|---|---|
| 1 | 5 | 3 | 5 |
| + 2 | 2 | 2 | 4 |
| 3 | 7 | 5 | 9 |

Each pair weighs the same, because the digits in the additions are the same, but in a different order.

Question ③:

| 3 | 4 | 5 | 2 |
|---|---|---|---|
| + **4** | **3** | **2** | **5** |
| 7 | 7 | 7 | 7 |

3,452 + 4,325 = 7,777

Question ④:

| 4 | 5 | 2 | 1 |
|---|---|---|---|
| + | 3 | 4 | 6 |
| 4 | 8 | 6 | 7 |

4,521 + 346 = 4,867

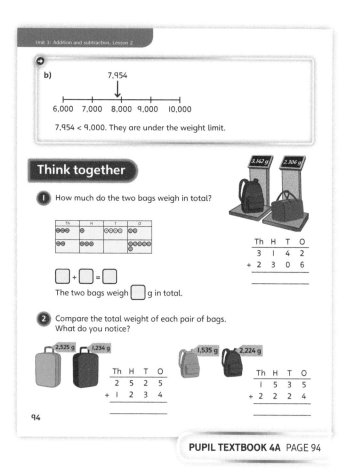

b)

7,954

6,000  7,000  8,000  9,000  10,000

7,954 < 9,000. They are under the weight limit.

## Think together

① How much do the two bags weigh in total?

☐ + ☐ = ☐

The two bags weigh ☐ g in total.

| Th | H | T | O |
|---|---|---|---|
| 3 | 1 | 4 | 2 |
| + 2 | 3 | 0 | 6 |

② Compare the total weight of each pair of bags. What do you notice?

| Th | H | T | O |
|---|---|---|---|
| 2 | 5 | 2 | 5 |
| + 1 | 2 | 3 | 4 |

| Th | H | T | O |
|---|---|---|---|
| 1 | 5 | 3 | 5 |
| + 2 | 2 | 2 | 4 |

94

**PUPIL TEXTBOOK 4A** PAGE 94

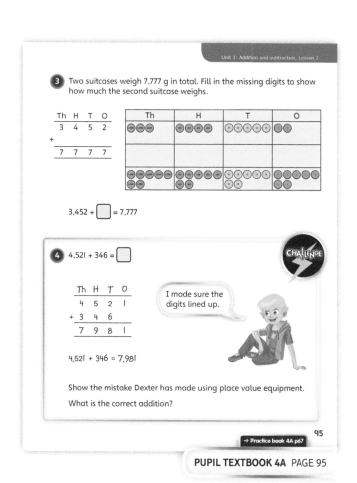

Unit 3: Addition and subtraction, Lesson 2

③ Two suitcases weigh 7,777 g in total. Fill in the missing digits to show how much the second suitcase weighs.

| Th | H | T | O |
|---|---|---|---|
| 3 | 4 | 5 | 2 |
| + | | | |
| 7 | 7 | 7 | 7 |

3,452 + ☐ = 7,777

④ 4,521 + 346 = ☐

| Th | H | T | O |
|---|---|---|---|
| 4 | 5 | 2 | 1 |
| + 3 | 4 | 6 | |
| 7 | 9 | 8 | 1 |

*I made sure the digits lined up.*

4,521 + 346 = 7,981

Show the mistake Dexter has made using place value equipment. What is the correct addition?

→ Practice book 4A p67

95

**PUPIL TEXTBOOK 4A** PAGE 95

## Practice

**WAYS OF WORKING** Independent thinking

**IN FOCUS** Question ❶ uses column addition in the context of money. Explain to children that this is still the same method, but ensure they understand the importance of the units.

**STRENGTHEN** If children are struggling with the method, work through some more additions with them, linking the column method to place value grids, base 10 equipment or both.

**DEEPEN** Give children some word problems in which they need to add 4-digit numbers.

**THINK DIFFERENTLY** In question ❹ children have to spot the mistakes. If they are struggling, prompt them to look carefully at the layout of the column additions and the numbers that are being used.

**ASSESSMENT CHECKPOINT** Question ❼ will allow you to assess which children have achieved mastery in this lesson. Those who have will be able to find multiple solutions using a mixture of place value knowledge and mental calculations.

**ANSWERS** Answers for the **Practice** part of the lesson appear in the separate **Practice and Reflect answer guide**.

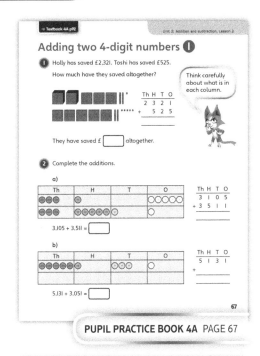

PUPIL PRACTICE BOOK 4A PAGE 67

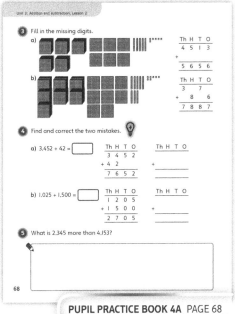

PUPIL PRACTICE BOOK 4A PAGE 68

## Reflect

**WAYS OF WORKING** Pair work

**IN FOCUS** This activity is an excellent opportunity for children to show their understanding by teaching this topic themselves. This reinforces the saying that by learning you will teach, and by teaching you will learn.

**ASSESSMENT CHECKPOINT** Assess whether children can articulate their answers in simple steps, using the correct vocabulary.

**ANSWERS** Answers for the **Reflect** part of the lesson appear in the separate **Practice and Reflect answer guide**.

## After the lesson ⏸

- Do you need to run any intervention activities to give some children a boost?
- Which children depended heavily on using apparatus or place value grids?
- Was the layout that children used in their books neat and aligned?

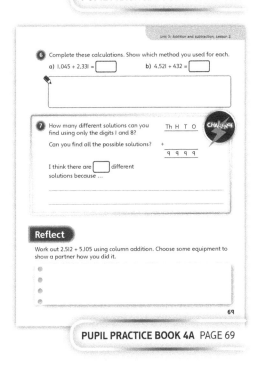

PUPIL PRACTICE BOOK 4A PAGE 69

# Adding two 4-digit numbers ②

## Learning focus

In this lesson children will add 4-digit numbers using the column method with an exchange in one column.

## Small steps

→ Previous step: Adding two 4-digit numbers (1)
→ **This step: Adding two 4-digit numbers (2)**
→ Next step: Adding two 4-digit numbers (3)

### NATIONAL CURRICULUM LINKS

**Year 4 Number – Addition and Subtraction**

Add and subtract numbers with up to 4 digits using the formal written methods of columnar addition and subtraction where appropriate.

### ASSESSING MASTERY

Children can use the column method to calculate with one exchange. They can explain their working clearly and understand what the exchange means, and they can use their methods in context to solve problems.

### COMMON MISCONCEPTIONS

Children often make mistakes with an exchange, for example if a column is 7 + 6, they just put the total as 0, or just put 3 without exchanging. Ask:
• *Can you explain your method to me?*

Children often do not understand that they are exchanging 10 or 100 etc., but instead think of it as 1. Ask:
• *Can you show me the exchange using place value counters?*

### STRENGTHENING UNDERSTANDING

Variation in the types of addition (find the total, or add on more) will strengthen learning in this lesson.

Model the exchanges with place value counters, to ensure children know what an exchange looks like.

### GOING DEEPER

Use missing digit problems to deepen learning in this lesson. Can children identify what information they have and how they can use it to find missing information? Do they understand what to do when exchanges occur with missing digits?

### KEY LANGUAGE

**In lesson: strategy**, total, addition, exchange, ones (1s), tens (10s), hundreds (100s), story problem, altogether, column method, digits

**Other language to be used by the teacher:** place value, thousands (1,000s)

### STRUCTURES AND REPRESENTATIONS

place value grid

### RESOURCES

**Mandatory:** base 10 equipment, place value counters

 In the eTextbook of this lesson, you will find interactive links to a selection of teaching tools.

## Before you teach ⏸

• How will you explain the word 'exchange'?
• Would a display showing diagrams similar to those in the **Share** section of the **Textbook** support children?

# Discover

**WAYS OF WORKING** Pair work

**ASK**

- Question ❶ a): *What are the key words in this question?*
- Question ❶ a): *What is the question asking you to do?*
- Question ❶ a): *Can you write down the number sentence?*
- Question ❶ b): *What methods could you use?*

**IN FOCUS** Some children will need support with question ❶ b). They must find the answer to question ❶ a), and then work out how to find the difference between it and 2,000. You may want to remind children of Lesson 1 in this unit (using knowledge of place value to subtract).

**PRACTICAL TIPS** For this activity, ask children to draw out and discuss the key words in the problem.

**ANSWERS**

Question ❶ a): 4,237 + 1,554 = 5,791. The aeroplane will fly 5,791 miles in total.

Question ❶ b): 5,791 – 2,000 = 3,791. It will still have 3,791 miles to fly.

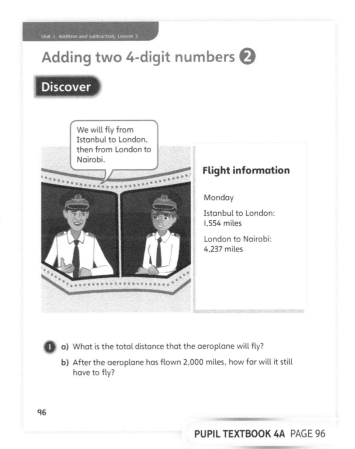

# Share

**WAYS OF WORKING** Whole class teacher led

**ASK**

- Question ❶ a): *Why can you not have 11 counters in the ones column?*
- Question ❶ a): *What does 'exchange' mean?*

**IN FOCUS** For question ❶ a), discuss why it is not possible to have 11 counters in the ones column. Show children clearly how the 10 ones are exchanged for 1 ten. In question ❶ b), the subtraction could be solved using a column method. A number line is also a helpful way of approaching this calculation, based on the number of exchanges required. Children will need to make decisions about which methods suit the calculations in terms of efficiency and accuracy.

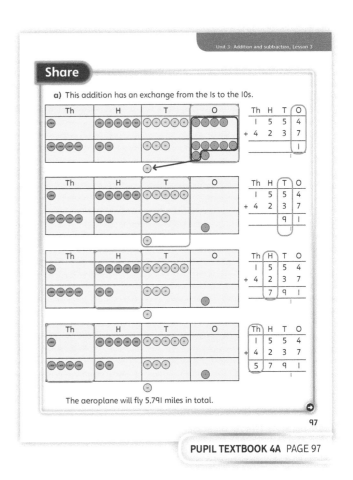

**129**

# Think together

**WAYS OF WORKING**  Whole class teacher led (I do, We do, You do)

**ASK**

- Question **3** a): *Can you solve all of the additions mentally?*
- Question **3** a): *How do you know when you need to exchange?*
- Question **3** b): *Can you check your partner's story problems?*

**IN FOCUS**  Question **3** a) gives a chance to draw out children's reasoning about when an exchange is necessary. Discuss how they can tell that an exchange is needed.

**STRENGTHEN**  Some children may need help with layout (especially when writing the '1' when exchanging). Other children may forget to count the exchange, so give plenty of practice of this.

**DEEPEN**  For question **3** b), deepen learning by asking children to add an extra line to their story problem making it a multi-step problem.

**ASSESSMENT CHECKPOINT**  Use question **3** b) to see if children can create addition problems using 4-digit numbers with an exchange.

**ANSWERS**

Question **1**: 5,791 + 1,154 = 6,945

It flies 6,945 miles on Tuesday.

Question **2**: Accept any answer with an 8 or 9 in the hundreds column.

Question **3** a): Exchange 10 tens: 2,341 + 1,593 = 3,934

No exchange needed: 1,010 + 2,549 = 3,559

Exchange 10 hundreds: 7,699 = 6,917 + 782

Exchange 10 ones: 2,010 = 2,001 + 9

Question **3** b): Check that the children's story problems are appropriate and correct.

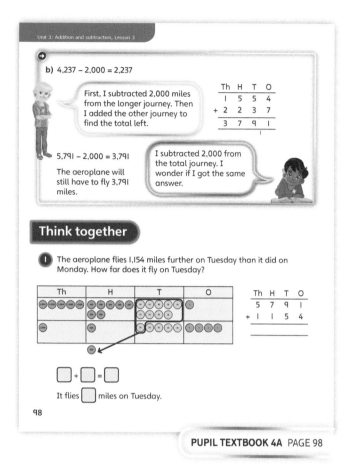

**PUPIL TEXTBOOK 4A** PAGE 98

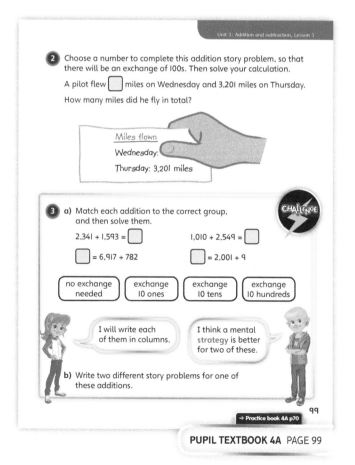

**PUPIL TEXTBOOK 4A** PAGE 99

130

# Practice

**WAYS OF WORKING** Independent thinking

**IN FOCUS** You will notice that in this section there are place value counters and grids to support at the start, but not later on. This is to gradually reduce scaffolding, encouraging children to become more independent with solving additions.

**STRENGTHEN** If children are struggling with using the vertical column method, provide more opportunities to practise additions with an exchange.

**DEEPEN** Challenge children to think of number sentences in which the ones, tens and hundreds all require an exchange, for example 1,345 + 1,886. Ask them to investigate the solutions that they will get.

Give children an answer, such as 4,533. Tell them to create a question with that answer, which involves only one exchange, for example 2,822 + 1,711.

**ASSESSMENT CHECKPOINT** Question ❹ will allow you to assess which children can complete a problem by thinking about the exchanges involved. Children who can do this confidently are likely to have mastered the lesson.

**ANSWERS** Answers for the **Practice** part of the lesson appear in the separate **Practice and Reflect answer guide**.

# Reflect

**WAYS OF WORKING** Pair work

**IN FOCUS** In this section, children will have to think carefully about the numbers they choose and the exchanges that will happen.

**ASSESSMENT CHECKPOINT** Assess whether children can reason why they chose the numbers they did. You may hear comments such as, 'I needed to create an addition with an exchange of ones, so I used 9 and 2 in this column.'

**ANSWERS** Answers for the **Reflect** part of the lesson appear in the separate **Practice and Reflect answer guide**.

## After the lesson ⏸

- Can children explain what an exchange is?
- Can children represent an exchange with place value counters?
- Did any misconceptions crop up in this lesson?

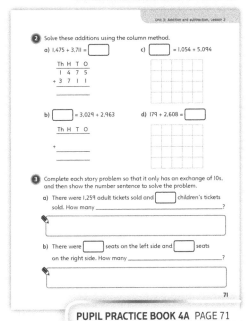

PUPIL PRACTICE BOOK 4A PAGE 70

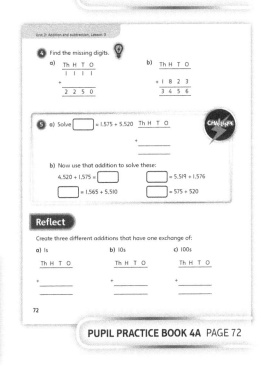

PUPIL PRACTICE BOOK 4A PAGE 71

PUPIL PRACTICE BOOK 4A PAGE 72

# Adding two 4-digit numbers ❸

## Learning focus

In this lesson children will add 4-digit numbers using the column method with exchanges across more than one column.

## Small steps

→ Previous step: Adding two 4-digit numbers (2)
→ **This step: Adding two 4-digit numbers (3)**
→ Next step: Subtracting two 4-digit numbers (1)

### NATIONAL CURRICULUM LINKS

**Year 4 Number – Addition and Subtraction**

Add and subtract numbers with up to 4 digits using the formal written methods of columnar addition and subtraction where appropriate.

### ASSESSING MASTERY

Children can use the column method to calculate with more than one exchange. Children can correctly explain the methods they use, and can identify calculations that would be more suited to mental methods.

### COMMON MISCONCEPTIONS

Children often make mistakes when there are multiple exchanges, for example forgetting to do the second exchange. Ask:
• *Did you remember to count the exchange?*

Children sometimes forget to add on the exchange (especially when there are multiple exchanges). Ask:
• *How could you check your answer?*

### STRENGTHENING UNDERSTANDING

Together use place value counters to work through and solve several calculations with multiple exchanges. Model making each exchange and discuss what effect it will have on the next column and on the total.

### GOING DEEPER

Look at examples where one exchange leads to another exchange in the next column, such as 189 + 13. Can children mentally spot calculations where this will happen?

### KEY LANGUAGE

**In lesson:** total, exchange, addition, ones (1s), tens (10s), hundreds (100s), method, digit, columns

**Other language to be used by the teacher:** place value, thousands (1,000s)

### STRUCTURES AND REPRESENTATIONS

place value grid, number line

### RESOURCES

**Mandatory:** base 10 equipment, place value counters

 In the eTextbook of this lesson, you will find interactive links to a selection of teaching tools.

## Before you teach

• How will you introduce calculations with multiple exchanges?
• Have you got place value counters to support children whose understanding needs strengthening?

## Discover

**WAYS OF WORKING** Pair work

**ASK**

- Question ① a): *What happens when there is more than one exchange in a calculation?*
- Question ① b): *Do you have to write down the calculation to see the exchanges? Can you tell by looking at the digits in each number?*

**IN FOCUS** In questions ① a) and ① b), focus on children's explanations of how to add with more than one exchange. Listen carefully to their vocabulary and reasoning skills.

**PRACTICAL TIPS** For this activity, ask children to write the calculations neatly and to highlight each of the exchanges using a different colour.

**ANSWERS**

Question ① a): 4,799 + 1,095 = 5,894. The total value of the sports car and the motorbike is £5,894.

Question ① b): Adding the prices of the sports car and the vintage car would need three exchanges.

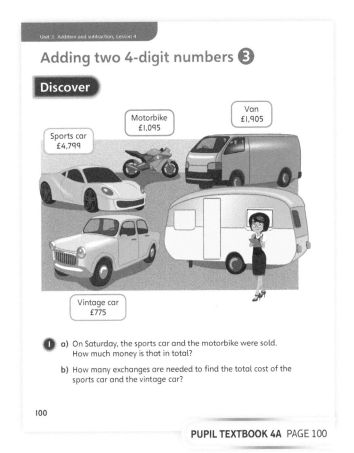

### Adding two 4-digit numbers ❸

**Discover**

Motorbike £1,095

Van £1,905

Sports car £4,799

Vintage car £775

① a) On Saturday, the sports car and the motorbike were sold. How much money is that in total?

  b) How many exchanges are needed to find the total cost of the sports car and the vintage car?

100

**PUPIL TEXTBOOK 4A** PAGE 100

## Share

**WAYS OF WORKING** Whole class teacher led

**ASK**

- Question ① a): *Can you explain this working to me?*
- Question ① b): *How can you spot where there will be an exchange?*

**IN FOCUS** Question ① b) focuses children on how they might spot where there will be an exchange. They should start to realise that their knowledge of number bonds to 10 will come in handy.

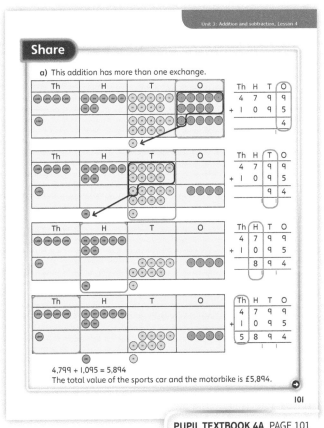

**Share**

a) This addition has more than one exchange.

4,799 + 1,095 = 5,894
The total value of the sports car and the motorbike is £5,894.

101

**PUPIL TEXTBOOK 4A** PAGE 101

# Think together

Whole class teacher led (I do, We do, You do)

**ASK**

- Question ❶ : *How will you lay out your work correctly?*
- Question ❸ a): *Which method would be best with these numbers?*
- Question ❸ b): *Can you check your partner's additions?*

**IN FOCUS** Question ❸ gives children the opportunity to discuss the merits of the column written method and the mental method, and to find that they both give the same answer. The question does not teach the mental method as a trick, instead it gives children the chance to evaluate both methods themselves. You may want to model the mental method using a number line.

**STRENGTHEN** Give children place value equipment to help them explain their workings. Children may need support in laying out calculations correctly on squared paper. If necessary you could label the ones, tens, hundreds and thousands columns for them before they start their working.

**DEEPEN** Deepen learning in this section by providing children with a range of calculations where they must decide whether a written method or a mental method would be more effective.

**ASSESSMENT CHECKPOINT** Use question ❸ to see whether children can choose between a written method and a mental method. In particular, listen to their reasoning.

**ANSWERS**

Question ❶ : 1,905 + 775 = 2,680

The van and the vintage car cost £2,680 in total.

Question ❷ : 1,095 + 1,775 = 2,870

The caravan costs £2,870.

Question ❸ a): Look for children using both the column method of addition and mental strategies, for example a number line showing a jump on of 2,000 from 575 to 2,575, and then a jump back of 1 to 2,574. Children should find that both methods give the same answer but that the mental method is more efficient because there is a near multiple of 1,000 and you can avoid the exchanges.

Question ❸ b): Answers will vary. Look for examples of additions where a mental method is more efficient.

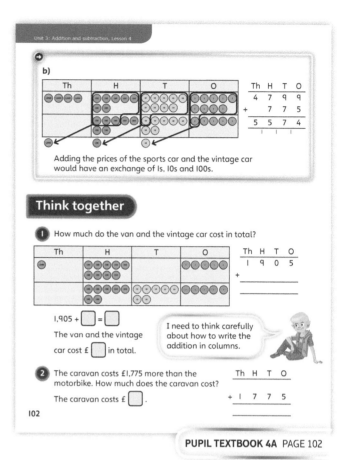

**PUPIL TEXTBOOK 4A** PAGE 102

**PUPIL TEXTBOOK 4A** PAGE 103

**134**

## Practice

**WAYS OF WORKING** Independent thinking

**IN FOCUS** Question ② will focus children's learning on finding calculations that have two exchanges, which should lead to mastery. Encourage children to explain their thinking verbally.

**STRENGTHEN** Question ③ gives the opportunity to strengthen learning through correcting mistakes. Provide children who need it with other questions like this where they address examples of common misconceptions.

**DEEPEN** Challenge children to solve an addition with exchanges in all four columns, including the thousands. Discuss how sometimes adding two 4-digit numbers can lead to a 5-digit answer, and model the need for a ten thousands column.

Ask children to give you an example of an addition where one exchange causes there to be an exchange in the next column (where the carry digit means that the column total will now be 10 or more). Can they explain why this happens? Encourage them to refer to bonds to 10 in their explanation.

**ASSESSMENT CHECKPOINT** Question ③ will allow you to assess whether children can check and correct answers, which will demonstrate a deeper understanding of the lesson.

**ANSWERS** Answers for the **Practice** part of the lesson appear in the separate **Practice and Reflect answer guide**.

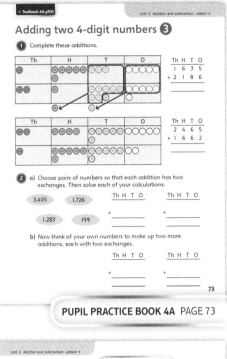

PUPIL PRACTICE BOOK 4A PAGE 73

PUPIL PRACTICE BOOK 4A PAGE 74

## Reflect

**WAYS OF WORKING** Independent thinking

**IN FOCUS** This section requires children to explain their written workings in three steps. They must be clear and concise in their answers.

**ASSESSMENT CHECKPOINT** Assess whether children have remembered all of the steps of column addition with exchanges. You may want to encourage children to provide an example alongside their answers.

**ANSWERS** Answers for the **Reflect** part of the lesson appear in the separate **Practice and Reflect answer guide**.

### After the lesson ⏸

- Can children identify exchanges without having to do the workings?
- Can children represent an exchange with place value counters?
- Which children will need intervention following this lesson?

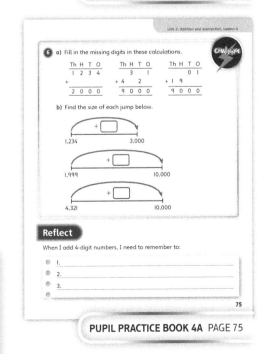

PUPIL PRACTICE BOOK 4A PAGE 75

# Subtracting two 4-digit numbers ❶

## Learning focus

In this lesson children will subtract 4-digit numbers using the column method where there are no exchanges.

## Small steps

→ Previous step: Adding two 4-digit numbers (3)
→ **This step: Subtracting two 4-digit numbers (1)**
→ Next step: Subtracting two 4-digit numbers (2)

### NATIONAL CURRICULUM LINKS

**Year 4 Number – Addition and Subtraction**

Add and subtract numbers with up to 4 digits using the formal written methods of columnar addition and subtraction where appropriate.

### ASSESSING MASTERY

Children can use the column method to subtract. They can explain their method clearly and demonstrate a clear understanding of place value, i.e. they know that they are not just subtracting separate digits, but recognise the ones, tens, hundreds and thousands.

### COMMON MISCONCEPTIONS

Children may not correctly align the columns to show 1s, 10s, 100s and 1,000s. Ask:
• *What happens if the columns are not lined up neatly?*

Some children may just subtract the digits without showing an understanding of the place value of each column. Ask:
• *Does that column show 3 – 1 or 30 – 10?*

### STRENGTHENING UNDERSTANDING

As well as using place value counters to make learning more concrete, model for children how to work with bar models to represent subtractions.

### GOING DEEPER

Give children a column subtraction with some digits missing and discuss what strategies they can use to complete it. Explore how to check a subtraction by finding the inverse, i.e. doing an addition.

### KEY LANGUAGE

**In lesson:** bar model, subtraction, fewer, more than, column, digits, odd, even, story problem

**Other language to be used by the teacher:** place value, thousands (1,000s), hundreds (100s), tens (10s), ones (1s).

### STRUCTURES AND REPRESENTATIONS

place value grid, bar model, number line

### RESOURCES

**Mandatory:** base 10 equipment, place value counters

**Optional:** strips of paper to make bar models

 In the eTextbook of this lesson, you will find interactive links to a selection of teaching tools.

## Before you teach ❚❚

• How will you explain the key vocabulary?
• Which children are likely to struggle with the concept of place value?

# Discover

**WAYS OF WORKING** Pair work

**ASK**

- Question ① a): *How can you draw the bar model?*
- Question ① b): *How can you use the bar model to help you work out the answer?*

**IN FOCUS** The bar model is a powerful tool for representing subtraction. Children can clearly see the largest amount and the amount that is taken away to leave the answer. It also helps them relate subtraction to addition.

**PRACTICAL TIPS** Provide children with strips of paper to create their bar models.

**ANSWERS**

Question ① a):

Total votes
5,432

| ? | 1,312 |
|---|---|

Decimal Pointer Sisters    Make That

Question ① b): 5,432 – 1,312 = 4,120

The Decimal Pointers got 4,120 votes.

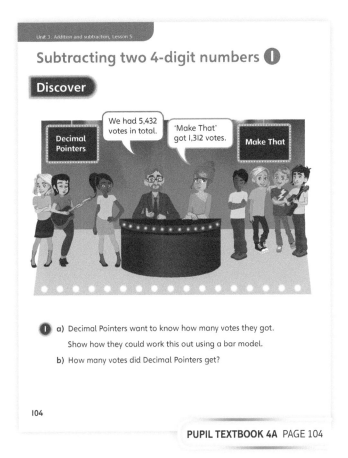

## Subtracting two 4-digit numbers ①

### Discover

We had 5,432 votes in total.

Decimal Pointers

'Make That' got 1,312 votes.

Make That

① a) Decimal Pointers want to know how many votes they got. Show how they could work this out using a bar model.

b) How many votes did Decimal Pointers get?

104

**PUPIL TEXTBOOK 4A** PAGE 104

# Share

**WAYS OF WORKING** Whole class teacher led

**ASK**

- Question ① b): *How does the column method of subtraction work?*
- Question ① b): *What do the place value counters tell you about the digits in the calculation?*

**IN FOCUS** In question ① b), it is worth discussing that when we use equipment to show a subtraction, we don't need to make both numbers. We can just represent the whole, and then remove the parts that are being taken away.

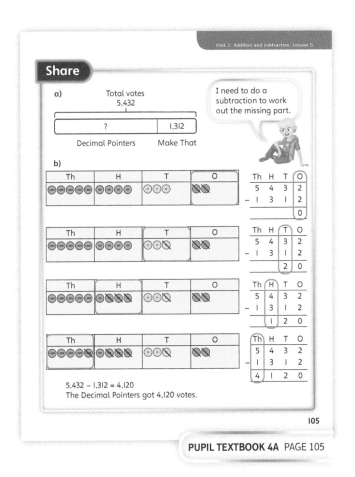

### Share

a)    Total votes
5,432

| ? | 1,312 |
|---|---|

Decimal Pointers    Make That

I need to do a subtraction to work out the missing part.

b)

5,432 – 1,312 = 4,120
The Decimal Pointers got 4,120 votes.

105

**PUPIL TEXTBOOK 4A** PAGE 105

# Think together

**WAYS OF WORKING** Whole class teacher led (I do, We do, You do)

**ASK**

- Question **1**: *What is the question asking you to do?*
- Question **3**: *How do you work out a subtraction with a missing number?*
- Question **4** b): *How do the models you have drawn help you to understand the subtraction?*

**IN FOCUS** Some children may need support with interpreting the word problems in questions **1** and **2**. Use bar models to support your explanations.

**STRENGTHEN** The language 'more than' is usually associated with addition. Explain that in question **2** it is actually a subtraction. You could represent it on a bar model for clarity.

**DEEPEN** Look closely at question **3** and discuss how to solve missing number subtractions. Draw out that a calculation like 9 – ? = 5 is solved with a subtraction, i.e. 9 – 5 = 4, and a calculation like ? – 4 = 5 is solved with an addition, i.e. 4 + 5 = 9.

**ASSESSMENT CHECKPOINT** Use question **4** to see if children can recognise and use different representations of subtractions, which shows a deeper understanding of what a subtraction actually means.

**ANSWERS**

Question **1**: 4,324 – 2,120 = 2,204

Scissor Squares got 2,204 votes.

Question **2**: 4,436 – 3,425 = 1,011

Division Express got 1,011 more votes than Measure Minds.

Question **3**: 5,465 – 264 = 5,201

Question **4** a): 9,876 – 5,432 = 4,444

9,999 – 7,654 = 2,345

7,890 – 450 = 7,440

Question **4** b): Expect children to show
7,654 – 4,321 = 3,333 using a bar model, number line and comparison bar model.

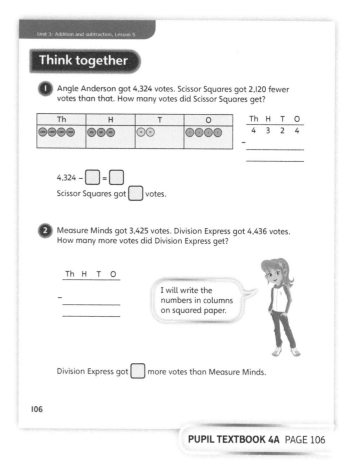

**PUPIL TEXTBOOK 4A** PAGE 106

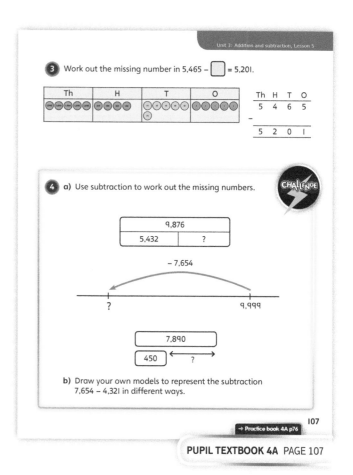

**PUPIL TEXTBOOK 4A** PAGE 107

## Practice

**WAYS OF WORKING** Independent thinking

**IN FOCUS** The reasoning in question **5** will give you a good insight into which children are thinking in a deeper manner. Look for children who spot the pattern, i.e. odd – odd = even. Ask them to show you why this is.

**STRENGTHEN** Children may need help forming the odd and even numbers in question **5**. Make sure they understand the place value of each digit in their numbers and can see which digit is significant in making the whole number odd or even. Support them in laying their numbers out correctly for column subtraction.

**DEEPEN** Deepen learning in this section by giving children the answer to an unspecified subtraction. Challenge them to write down as many subtractions as they can to make that answer.

**THINK DIFFERENTLY** In question **4**, children have to explain why a child has made a mistake. Listen carefully to their reasoning, and prompt them to think about layout if they are finding it hard to spot the error.

**ASSESSMENT CHECKPOINT** Question **2** gives children the opportunity to demonstrate their application of learning in a number of different ways. Children who show that they can match subtractions to different equipment and representations have likely mastered the lesson.

**ANSWERS** Answers for the **Practice** part of the lesson appear in the separate **Practice and Reflect answer guide**.

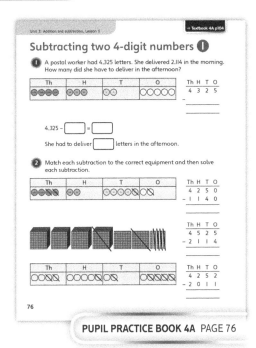

**PUPIL PRACTICE BOOK 4A** PAGE 76

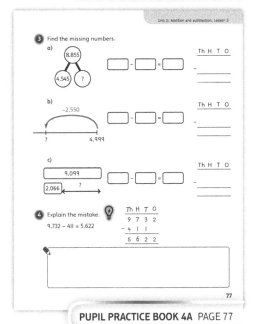

**PUPIL PRACTICE BOOK 4A** PAGE 77

## Reflect

**WAYS OF WORKING** Independent thinking

**IN FOCUS** This activity requires children to write a story problem for a subtraction. If necessary, guide them to stay within the context of the lesson (talent show votes).

**ASSESSMENT CHECKPOINT** Children are likely to have mastered the lesson if they can create a problem independently and then solve it. Ask them to explain their question and solution to you.

**ANSWERS** Answers for the **Reflect** part of the lesson appear in the separate **Practice and Reflect answer guide**.

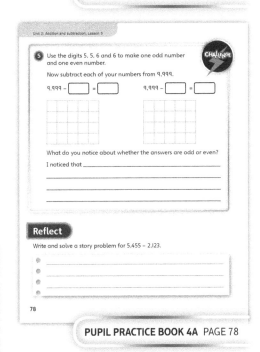

**PUPIL PRACTICE BOOK 4A** PAGE 78

### After the lesson ⏸

- Which children have mastered the lesson?
- Are all children ready to go on to subtractions with exchanges?
- In the next lesson what support will you provide for those children whose understanding still needs strengthening?

# Subtracting two 4-digit numbers ②

## Learning focus

In this lesson children will subtract 4-digit numbers using the column method where an exchange is required.

## Small steps

→ Previous step: Subtracting two 4-digit numbers (1)
→ **This step: Subtracting two 4-digit numbers (2)**
→ Next step: Subtracting two 4-digit numbers (3)

### NATIONAL CURRICULUM LINKS

**Year 4 Number – Addition and Subtraction**

Add and subtract numbers with up to 4 digits using the formal written methods of columnar addition and subtraction where appropriate.

### ASSESSING MASTERY

Children can use the column method to subtract. They can explain the method that they have used and can describe what happens when an exchange takes place (using a firm knowledge of place value).

### COMMON MISCONCEPTIONS

Children may not understand how to exchange and so may say, for example, that $4 - 5 = 0$ or may subtract the smaller digit from the larger.

$$
\begin{array}{r} 3\ \ 4 \\ -\ 2\ \ 5 \\ \hline 1\ \ 0 \end{array}
\qquad
\begin{array}{r} 3\ \ 4 \\ -\ 2\ \ 5 \\ \hline 1\ \ 1 \end{array}
$$

Ask:

• *Can you show the subtraction using equipment?*

### STRENGTHENING UNDERSTANDING

Use place value counters and equipment to model every exchange. Make the learning visual so that the process of exchanging is clear to understand. Run some more intervention enabling children to practise subtractions with exchanges.

### GOING DEEPER

Deepen learning in this lesson by giving children a range of subtractions and asking them to work the subtractions out using more than one method. Ask them to reason which method is more effective.

### KEY LANGUAGE

**In lesson:** tens (10s), hundreds (100s), thousands (1,000s), whole, part, exchange, more, difference, method, column subtraction, number line

**Other language to be used by the teacher:** place value, digits, ones

### STRUCTURES AND REPRESENTATIONS

place value grid, bar model

### RESOURCES

**Mandatory:** base 10 equipment, place value counters

**Optional:** string

 In the eTextbook of this lesson, you will find interactive links to a selection of teaching tools.

## Before you teach

• How will you explain what an exchange is?
• How will you visually represent an exchange?
• Could you put something on your working wall to support children with exchanging when subtracting?

## Discover

WAYS OF WORKING Pair work

**ASK**

- Question ❶ a): *Look carefully at the hundreds column. Can you see the mistake now?*
- Question ❶ b): *How should you lay out the subtraction?*

**IN FOCUS** Children are required to work out a 4-digit number minus a 3-digit number. Draw attention to the H column. Why has Aki ended up with a 2 in his answer? (He has subtracted the wrong digit.)

**PRACTICAL TIPS** Make a visual display in your classroom to support learning. A subtraction with an accompanying place value grid (with place value counters) is a good example to use.

**ANSWERS**

Question ❶ a): In the hundreds column, Aki has subtracted the whole from the part, but he needed to exchange from the thousands column.

Question ❶ b): 1,250 – 420 = 830. Aki has 830 ml of orange juice left.

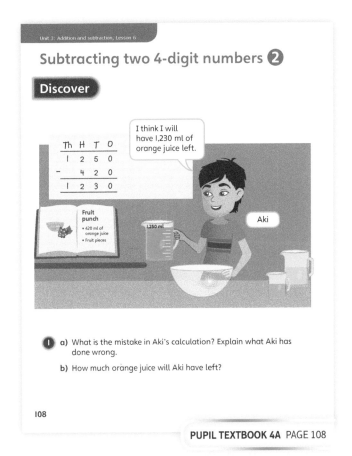

PUPIL TEXTBOOK 4A PAGE 108

## Share

WAYS OF WORKING Whole class teacher led

**ASK**

- Question ❶ a): *How can you tell when an exchange is needed?*
- Question ❶ b): *Can you explain the method in steps?*

**IN FOCUS** As a class, talk through the steps of the method. In particular, highlight the importance of place value. Ensure children understand that 1 thousand is being exchanged for 10 hundreds, so that you can do the subtraction in the H column.

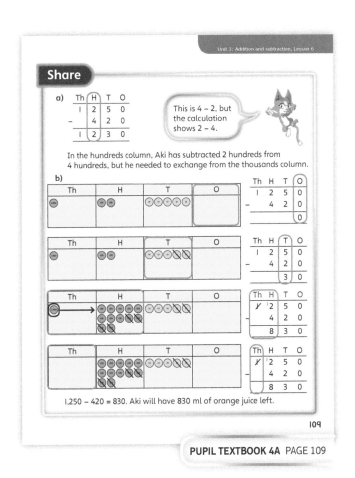

PUPIL TEXTBOOK 4A PAGE 109

# Think together

**WAYS OF WORKING** Whole class teacher led (I do, We do, You do)

**ASK**

• Question ❶: *Can you tell me what the number sentence is?*
• Question ❸: *Why is the column method not the best method for these questions?*
• Question ❸: *Can you draw a representation to help you picture your mental strategies?*

**IN FOCUS** Questions ❶ and ❷ are word problems. Use a bar model to represent them, in order to help children see that they are subtractions.

**STRENGTHEN** For question ❸, children may need some support with mental strategies. Give suggestions such as: *9 is close to 10* and *999 is how many away from 1,001?* Practise laying out subtractions without column headings for those children who need help with that.

**DEEPEN** Deepen learning in this section by asking children to solve a subtraction using two different strategies. They must then reason which is the more efficient.

**ASSESSMENT CHECKPOINT** Use question ❸ to assess whether children have a strong understanding of the column method of subtraction. Do they realise that it is not always the most efficient method?

**ANSWERS**

Question ❶: 1,750 − 625 = 1,125

Aki spilled 1,125 ml of mango juice.

Question ❷: 1,725 − 1,175 = 550

Aki has 550 more ml of pineapple juice.

Question ❸ a): 3,455 − 9 = 3,446

Strategies may include taking 10, then adding 1; taking 5, then taking 4; counting back 9. There's only one digit to subtract, so a method like a number line or using number bonds to 10 is quite easy to do mentally.

Question ❸ b): 2,991 − 2 = 2,989; strategies may include taking 1, then taking 1; or counting back 2.

2,001 − 9 = 1,992; strategies may include taking 1, then taking 8; or counting back 9; or taking 10, then adding 1.

1,001 − 999 = 2; strategies may include counting on from 999 to 1,001; or counting back from 1,001 to 999; or taking 1,000, then adding 1.

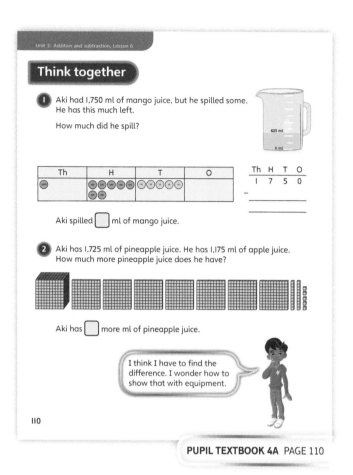

**PUPIL TEXTBOOK 4A** PAGE 110

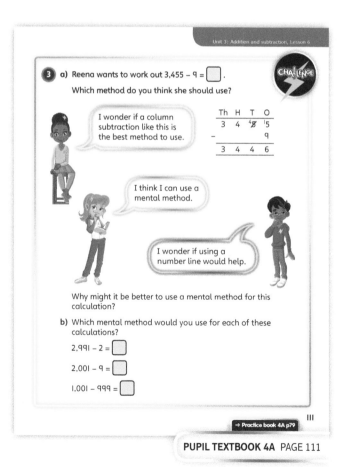

**PUPIL TEXTBOOK 4A** PAGE 111

## Practice

**WAYS OF WORKING** Independent thinking

**IN FOCUS** Question ❶ provides a lot of structured support in the first subtraction but less and less in the following subtractions, to scaffold learning. Encourage children to look back to the first example when tackling later questions.

**STRENGTHEN** Children may need some support in question ❺. Provide 'big' number lines (for example, string) and place value counters, so that they can physically represent the problems.

**DEEPEN** Deepen learning by asking children to reason about how they could spot where there will be an exchange without doing a calculation. They could write a rule for this.

**THINK DIFFERENTLY** Question ❹ promotes mastery of the lesson. Children will need to find the missing numbers, which is particularly challenging when there is an exchange needed. Encourage children to reason what each number must be (use place value apparatus for those who require it).

**ASSESSMENT CHECKPOINT** Question ❹ will give you an indication of which children have mastered the lesson. To assess further, ask children to talk you through their answers.

**ANSWERS** Answers for the **Practice** part of the lesson appear in the separate **Practice and Reflect answer guide**.

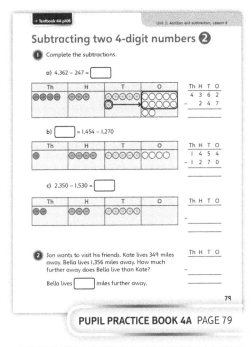

**PUPIL PRACTICE BOOK 4A** PAGE 79

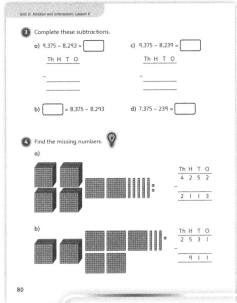

**PUPIL PRACTICE BOOK 4A** PAGE 80

## Reflect

**WAYS OF WORKING** Independent thinking

**IN FOCUS** For this exercise, put some key vocabulary on the board to support reasoning: subtraction, subtract, exchange, tens, hundreds.

**ASSESSMENT CHECKPOINT** Listen carefully to children's explanations. Have they identified the correct columns where the exchange is needed? Are they using correct vocabulary? Can they explain why an exchange is needed?

**ANSWERS** Answers for the **Reflect** part of the lesson appear in the separate **Practice and Reflect answer guide**.

### After the lesson ⏸

- Are any children still making the same mistakes that they were at the start of the lesson?
- How will you tackle these misconceptions?
- Which children mastered the lesson?

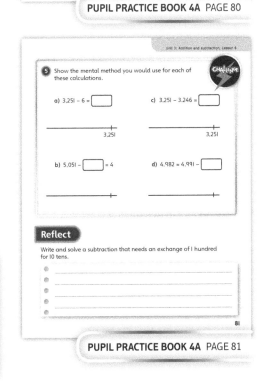

**PUPIL PRACTICE BOOK 4A** PAGE 81

## Discover

Unit 3: Addition and subtraction, Lesson 7

**WAYS OF WORKING**  Pair work

**ASK**

• Question ❶ a): *Can you tell me the number sentence you have to work out?*
• Question ❶ a): *Could you explain your method to a friend?*

**IN FOCUS**  In question ❶ a), children are asked to work out a 4-digit number minus a 3-digit number with two exchanges. Focus their learning by asking them how many exchanges there are, and how they know this. Some children will rely on jotting down the column method; others will be able to spot the exchanges from their knowledge of number bonds.

**PRACTICAL TIPS**  Ask children to make place value counters from paper or cardboard that they can physically move to represent multiple exchanges.

**ANSWERS**

Question ❶ a): 1,450 − 849 = 601

　　　　　Jen has £601 left.

Question ❶ b): 849 − 549 = 300; 601 + 300 = 901

　　　　　Alternatively, children may work out
　　　　　1,450 − 549 = 901

　　　　　Jen would have £901 left.

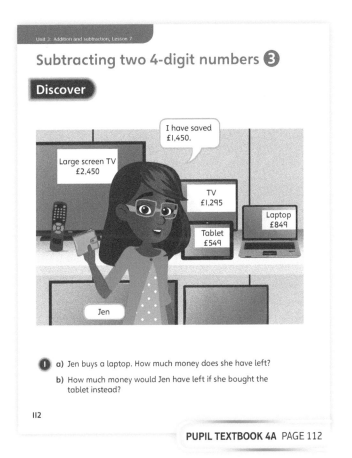

### Subtracting two 4-digit numbers ❸

**Discover**

**1** a) Jen buys a laptop. How much money does she have left?

　　b) How much money would Jen have left if she bought the tablet instead?

112

**PUPIL TEXTBOOK 4A** PAGE 112

## Share

**WAYS OF WORKING**  Whole class teacher led

**ASK**

• Question ❶ b): *How can part a) help you with this?*
• Question ❶ b): *What does the bar model show you?*

**IN FOCUS**  For question ❶ b), focus on the bar model. Show children how they can use the information from question ❶ a) to help work it out. Consider highlighting the fact that the difference between 849 and 549 is 300.

**Share**

a) 1,450 − 849

I think this needs two exchanges.

I will start with the 1s and check for exchanges as I go.

1,450 − 849 = 601

Jen has £601 left.

113

**PUPIL TEXTBOOK 4A** PAGE 113

# Think together

**WAYS OF WORKING** Whole class teacher led (I do, We do, You do)

**ASK**

- Question ①: *What does 'difference' mean?*
- Question ①: *How can you represent a difference?*
- Question ②: *How are subtraction and addition linked?*

**IN FOCUS** In question ① the word 'difference' is in the word problem. Draw out what this term means. Stand next to a child and ask what the difference in heights is. Establish that we will need a subtraction to work it out. In question ③ children may agree that only one exchange is needed as the digits in the hundreds and the tens columns of the part are not greater than the digits of the whole. Support them in seeing that once an exchange has been done from the tens to the ones, the tens whole digit will now be smaller than the tens part digit, and so a second exchange, from hundreds to tens, will be needed.

**STRENGTHEN** Question ② links subtraction and addition. Provide children with more subtractions to represent using a bar model. After this, challenge them to tell you the associated addition.

**DEEPEN** Deepen learning by asking children to think of mental strategies for the subtractions in this section. For example, in question ②, children may suggest finding the difference by counting on in jumps from 1,880 to 2,450.

**ASSESSMENT CHECKPOINT** Assess children's learning by looking at their answers to question ③. Children are likely to have mastered the lesson if they can solve the calculation and reason that one exchange caused another exchange to occur.

**ANSWERS**

Question ①: 2,450 – 1,295 = 1,155

The difference in price between the two televisions is £1,155.

Question ②: 2,450 – 1,880 = 570

Luke needs to save £570 more.

Question ③ a): 1,295 – 199 = 1,096

Astrid is not correct. The first exchange caused another exchange to occur.

Question ③ b): Answers will vary. Calculations should involve an exchange of a 10 for 1s that causes another exchange, of a 100 for 10s, to occur.

**PUPIL TEXTBOOK 4A** PAGE 114

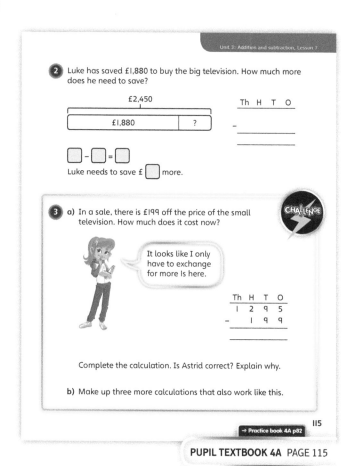

**PUPIL TEXTBOOK 4A** PAGE 115

## Practice

**WAYS OF WORKING** Independent thinking

**IN FOCUS** Question ④ provides a real challenge and will consolidate learning. Look at the third subtraction, in which some of the digits are missing. If children are struggling to get started, ask them what numbers could not go in, to focus their thinking.

**STRENGTHEN** Question ③ involves using an understanding of place value and prior knowledge of another calculation to work out a calculation. Run some quick intervention with similar problems; for example:
*If 6,785 – 238 = 6,547, what is 7,785 – 238, 5,785 – 238, 6,885 – 238, 6,685 – 238, 785 – 238?* Linking facts like this creates deep connections that strengthen learning.

**DEEPEN** Ask children to make up some of their own word problems that involve multiple exchanges.

**ASSESSMENT CHECKPOINT** Question ⑥ will allow you to assess which children have mastered the lesson. Look carefully at their reasoning. Have they linked the solution to subtraction?

**ANSWERS** Answers for the **Practice** part of the lesson appear in the separate **Practice and Reflect answer guide**.

## Reflect

**WAYS OF WORKING** Independent thinking

**IN FOCUS** This will help you to check children's understanding of the lesson. Some may mention earlier learning from question ③ of the **Think together** section, reasoning that one exchange can sometimes cause another exchange to occur.

**ASSESSMENT CHECKPOINT** Assess children on the vocabulary they use and the conciseness and clarity of their explanation.

**ANSWERS** Answers for the **Reflect** part of the lesson appear in the separate **Practice and Reflect answer guide**.

### After the lesson ⏸

- Can all children now use the column method?
- Can all children now exchange?
- Are children reasoning well?

**PUPIL PRACTICE BOOK 4A** PAGE 82

**PUPIL PRACTICE BOOK 4A** PAGE 83

**PUPIL PRACTICE BOOK 4A** PAGE 84

147

# Subtracting two 4-digit numbers ④

## Learning focus

In this lesson children will subtract 4-digit numbers using the column method with exchanges, when there is a zero in the column to be exchanged from.

## Small steps

→ Previous step: Subtracting two 4-digit numbers (3)
→ **This step: Subtracting two 4-digit numbers (4)**
→ Next step: Equivalent difference

## NATIONAL CURRICULUM LINKS

**Year 4 Number – Addition and Subtraction**

Add and subtract numbers with up to 4 digits using the formal written methods of columnar addition and subtraction where appropriate.

## ASSESSING MASTERY

Children can understand what to do when there is a zero is in the column in which an exchange is required; they can talk through their methods, demonstrating a clear understanding of place value. Children can also show their subtractions on a part-whole model.

## COMMON MISCONCEPTIONS

When children see that there is a 0 in the next column, they may not change the 0 but still exchange '1' from it anyway. Ask:
• *What should you do if there is a 0 in the column you need for an exchange?*

Children may think that 0 minus a number is either 0 or the number itself, for example, 0 – 2 = 0 or 0 – 2 = 2. Ask:
• *Can you draw 0 – 2? Is the answer 2?*

## STRENGTHENING UNDERSTANDING

Run a quick intervention in which children practise doing subtractions with a 0 in the column that is required for an exchange, for example 1,001 – 342. Encourage children to work through each step methodically.

## GOING DEEPER

Deepen learning in this lesson by providing children with subtractions that have exchange mistakes in them. Can children spot the mistakes and reason why they may have been made?

## KEY LANGUAGE

**In lesson:** subtraction, exchange, ones (1s), tens (10s), hundreds (100s), column, zero, place value, partition

**Other language to be used by the teacher:** thousands (1,000s), whole, part

## STRUCTURES AND REPRESENTATIONS

place value grid, bar model, part-whole model

## RESOURCES

**Mandatory:** base 10 equipment, place value counters

 In the eTextbook of this lesson, you will find interactive links to a selection of teaching tools.

## Before you teach ⏸

• How will you explain what to do if there is a 0 in a column required for an exchange?
• Are all children ready for this lesson? Did they master the previous lesson?
• How will you support those children who did not?

# Discover

Pair work

**ASK**

- Question ① a): *Could Bella look at the next column?*
- Question ① a): *How could the hundreds column help with the exchange?*

**IN FOCUS** Children are exploring what happens when an exchange is needed but there is a 0 in the next column. Listen carefully to what they think they should do, prompting them to look at the next column if necessary.

**PRACTICAL TIPS** Use place value counters to make numbers with 0 in some columns. Discuss what will happen if we try to subtract from a column where there are no counters, and model exchanging from the next column.

**ANSWERS**

Question ① a): Bella wants to exchange a ten for 10 ones, but she cannot because there is a zero in the tens column. First, Bella should exchange 1 hundred for 10 tens. Then she can exchange 1 ten for 10 ones.

Question ① b): 2,502 – 243 = 2,259

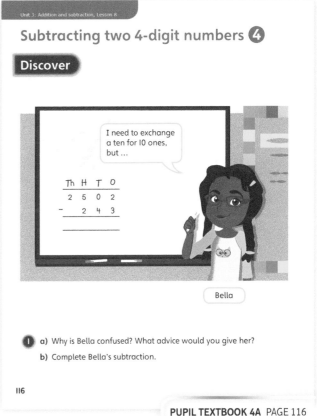

PUPIL TEXTBOOK 4A PAGE 116

# Share

**WAYS OF WORKING** Whole class teacher led

**ASK**

- Question ① b): *Do you understand how the exchange can be made with the hundreds?*
- Question ① b): *What steps do you need to take when there is a 0 in the column you need for an exchange?*

**IN FOCUS** For question ① b), model the subtraction in the column method format. Show children the importance of the layout, how to strike through the numbers being exchanged, and how to put a small 1 for the exchanged number.

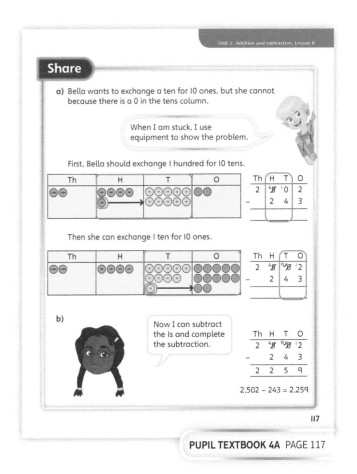

PUPIL TEXTBOOK 4A PAGE 117

149

# Think together

**WAYS OF WORKING** Whole class teacher led (I do, We do, You do)

**ASK**

- Question ③: *Can you use the words 'exchange', 'hundreds' and 'ones' in your explanation?*
- Question ④: *What do you do when there is a 0 in the tens column and the hundreds column?*
- Question ④: *How can you predict the exchange?*

**IN FOCUS** In question ④, children are faced with 5,005 – 2,929. They will see that there is a 0 in the tens column and in the hundreds column. Explain that children should follow the same method they previously learnt, working back from the thousands column. Model an example on the board.

**STRENGTHEN** Question ② requires children to exchange from the hundreds and the tens in order to subtract in the ones column. Ask them to carefully describe each step aloud as they do it, to clarify what is needed. For example, *I need to exchange 1 ten but there are none. I can take 1 hundred from the hundreds column, that is 10 tens.*

**DEEPEN** Question ④ links to previous work on subtracting by using knowledge of place value. Children should be able to spot the links between the calculations: for example, the hundreds and tens digits are switched in 5,055 – 2,929 and 5,505 – 2,929.

**ASSESSMENT CHECKPOINT** Question ③ will show you which children are confident with subtracting when there are zeros in columns that require exchanges. Listen carefully to their explanations of where Zac went wrong, and then assess their corrected answer.

**ANSWERS**

Question ①: 2,032 – 512 = 1,520

Question ②: 5,403 – 505 = 4,898

Question ③: Zac forgot to exchange 1 hundred for 10 tens, and 1 ten for 10 ones.

3,304 – 1,269 = 2,035

Question ④: 1 thousand for 10 hundreds: 2,126 = 5,055 – 2,929

1 hundred for 10 tens: 2,576 = 5,505 – 2,929

1 thousand for 10 hundreds; 1 hundred for 10 tens: 2,076 = 5,005 – 2,929

1 thousand for 10 hundreds; 1 hundred for 10 tens: 2,480 = 5,005 – 2,525

**PUPIL TEXTBOOK 4A** PAGE 118

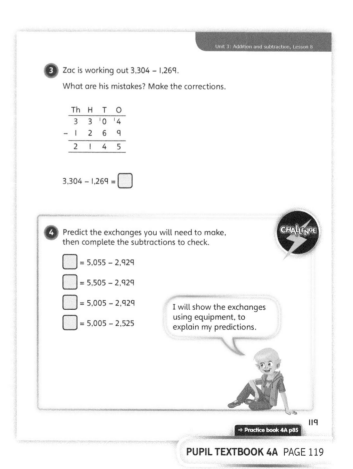

**PUPIL TEXTBOOK 4A** PAGE 119

# Subtracting two 4-digit numbers ❸

## Learning focus

In this lesson children will subtract 4-digit numbers using the column method where more than one exchange is required.

## Small steps

→ Previous step: Subtracting two 4-digit numbers (2)
→ **This step: Subtracting two 4-digit numbers (3)**
→ Next step: Subtracting two 4-digit numbers (4)

### NATIONAL CURRICULUM LINKS

**Year 4 Number – Addition and Subtraction**

Add and subtract numbers with up to 4 digits using the formal written methods of columnar addition and subtraction where appropriate.

### ASSESSING MASTERY

Children can use the column method for subtraction calculations where more than one exchange is required and can explain their answers and also check them (either with another strategy or by doing the inverse operation). Children can identify subtractions in which a mental method would be more efficient than the column method.

### COMMON MISCONCEPTIONS

Children may forget to do one of the exchanges or may subtract the whole from the part. Ask:
• *How many exchanges were in that calculation?*

### STRENGTHENING UNDERSTANDING

Keep reinforcing the place value involved in an exchange so that children learn the method and also the reasoning behind it. Continue to run quick interventions where children practice subtractions with exchanges.

### GOING DEEPER

Deepen learning in this lesson by providing children with more opportunities to solve word problems that involve subtractions with more than one exchange.

### KEY LANGUAGE

**In lesson:** difference, more, fewer, subtraction, exchange

**Other language to be used by the teacher:** place value, digits, thousands (1,000s), hundreds (100s), tens (10s), ones (1s), whole, part

### STRUCTURES AND REPRESENTATIONS

place value grid, bar model

### RESOURCES

**Mandatory:** base 10 equipment, place value counters

 In the eTextbook of this lesson, you will find interactive links to a selection of teaching tools.

## Before you teach ⏸

• How can you use the bar model to represent subtractions in this lesson?
• Would some children benefit from having place value counters that they can physically move to represent an exchange?

## Practice

**WAYS OF WORKING** Pair work

**IN FOCUS** Question ❹ a) has the numbers missing from the column subtraction. This will focus children's thinking and help them to make the link between place value, partitioning and exchanging.

**STRENGTHEN** Question ❷ requires children to show workings using place value counters. As children draw counters into the grids, encourage them to also use and move place value counters in real life, to model each step and consolidate what happens each time you make an exchange, particularly where there is a 0 in one or more columns.

**DEEPEN** Question ❶ provides a subtraction in the context of words and reading. Provide more examples of story problems with real-life contexts like this, in particular problems with multiple steps which will deepen learning even further.

**ASSESSMENT CHECKPOINT** Question ❹ b) will allow you to assess which children can solve a subtraction in which there is a 0 in one of the columns required for an exchange. It will also let you see which children can represent their workings on a part-whole model, which will show you that they have a strong knowledge of place value.

**ANSWERS** Answers for the **Practice** part of the lesson appear in the separate **Practice and Reflect answer guide**.

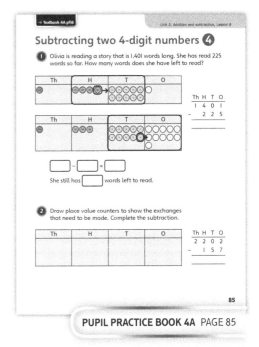

PUPIL PRACTICE BOOK 4A PAGE 85

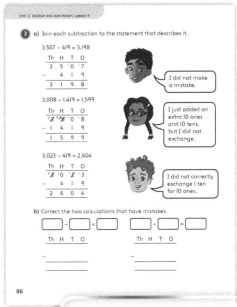

PUPIL PRACTICE BOOK 4A PAGE 86

## Reflect

**WAYS OF WORKING** Pair work

**IN FOCUS** Consider having a list of key vocabulary on the board or learning wall to support children's explanations.

**ASSESSMENT CHECKPOINT** Assess children on whether they can correctly explain their methodology, for example: *If I need to exchange 10 ones, when there is a 0 in the tens column, I must first exchange 1 hundred for 10 tens, then exchange 1 ten for 10 ones.*

**ANSWERS** Answers for the **Reflect** part of the lesson appear in the separate **Practice and Reflect answer guide**.

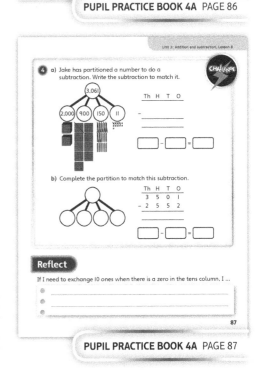

PUPIL PRACTICE BOOK 4A PAGE 87

## After the lesson ⏸

- Can all children explain how to exchange when there is a zero in a column required for the exchange?
- Are children ready to start exploring efficient methods of subtraction?
- Should you run some intervention sessions?

# Equivalent difference

## Learning focus

In this lesson children will learn the equivalent difference method of subtraction.

## Small steps

→ Previous step: Subtracting two 4-digit numbers (4)
→ **This step: Equivalent difference**
→ Next step: Estimating answers to additions and subtractions

### NATIONAL CURRICULUM LINKS

**Year 4 Number – Addition and Subtraction**

Estimate and use inverse operations to check answers to a calculation.

**Year 4 Number – Number and place value**

Round any number to the nearest 10, 100 or 1,000.

### ASSESSING MASTERY

Children understand the equivalent difference strategy and can apply it when solving problems. Children can explain the method correctly and suggest why it is more efficient than the column method (or a mental method).

### COMMON MISCONCEPTIONS

Children often do not understand the reasoning behind equivalent difference, that you can adjust the two numbers in a subtraction so that the difference remains the same. With the subtraction 232 – 98, they may know that it is easier to subtract 100 and that they will need to adjust 232 accordingly, but they are not sure whether it should be 230 – 100 or 234 – 100. Ask:
• *Can you show the equivalent difference on a bar model?*

### STRENGTHENING UNDERSTANDING

For children who need more support, use a bar model to represent subtractions, drawing attention to equivalent differences. Ask children to draw their own bar models to represent each problem.

### GOING DEEPER

Deepen learning in this lesson by asking children to think of more than one strategy that they can use to solve a subtraction, for example equivalent difference, column method and counting on to find the difference. Ask them to reason which method is the most efficient.

### KEY LANGUAGE

**In lesson:** difference, subtraction, exchange, bar model, method, **efficient**, column, equivalent

**Other language to be used by the teacher:** place value, digits, thousands (1,000s), hundreds (100s), tens (10s), ones (1s), fewer

### STRUCTURES AND REPRESENTATIONS

bar model

 In the eTextbook of this lesson, you will find interactive links to a selection of teaching tools.

## Before you teach ▮▮

• Do children know what 'equivalent' means?
• How will you explain it?
• Are children comfortable with using the bar model to represent differences?

## Discover

**WAYS OF WORKING** Pair work

**ASK**

- Question ❶ b): *How can you work out the difference?*
- Question ❶ b): *Can you spot the related calculations that do not require an exchange?*

**IN FOCUS** In question ❶ b), children should explore an efficient method to work out the subtraction. If necessary, draw their attention to the calculations that do not require an exchange.

**PRACTICAL TIPS** Discuss the context of the question and consider comparing the age of a real person, perhaps a singer or celebrity, with children's ages. This will make the learning more real, and will spark enthusiasm for real-life applications of the topic.

**ANSWERS**

Question ❶ a): Amelia's statement is not true. The difference between Amelia's age and her great-grandad's age will always be the same. Children may use a variety of methods to show this. Accept any that show that the difference will not change.

Question ❶ b): The difference between their ages will be 88 years.

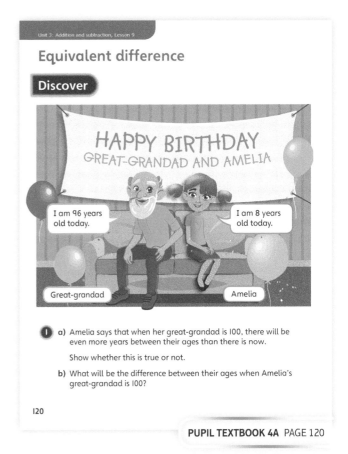

## Share

**WAYS OF WORKING** Whole class teacher led

**ASK**

- Question ❶ a): *What do you notice about the difference when both of the ages increase?*
- Question ❶ b): *Which subtractions are the easiest to calculate mentally?*

**IN FOCUS** For question ❶ a), make it clear that if we increase each number by the same amount, the difference will not change.

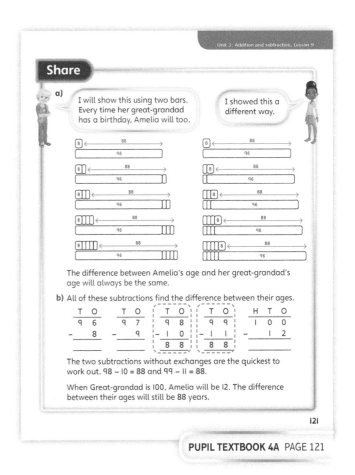

**153**

# Think together

**WAYS OF WORKING** Whole class teacher led (I do, We do, You do)

**ASK**

• Question **2**: *Why did you choose that calculation to find the difference?*
• Question **3** b): *Which methods can you remember from things you have learnt before?*
• Question **3** b): *Which methods were the most efficient?*

**IN FOCUS** In question **2**, children should realise that two subtractions do not involve an exchange (128 – 100 and 129 –101). Then they should reason that 128 – 100 is easier to work out as they are simply subtracting 100.

**STRENGTHEN** Run a quick intervention for children to practise solving more subtractions where they can use equivalent difference to get to a multiple of 100 or 10, which will be more efficient, for example 154 – 97, 222 – 198, 100 – 58.

**DEEPEN** Children can use question **3** to explore different strategies for working out subtractions. Encourage them to evaluate each subtraction and consider which would be the most efficient method each time.

**ASSESSMENT CHECKPOINT** Question **3** b) will give you an insight into which children have mastered the equivalent difference method. It will also tell you if children can apply other learnt strategies to subtractions, based on which method is more efficient.

**ANSWERS**

Question **1**: 198 – 79 = 119

199 – 80 = 119

200 – 81 = 119

The difference is 119 years.

Question **2**: 125 – 97 = 28

126 – 98 = 28

127 – 99 = 28

128 – 100 = 28

129 – 101 = 28

The whale is 28 years younger than the giant tortoise.

Question **3** a): 1,000 – 245 = 755

Astrid's method is more efficient because no exchanges are needed.

Question **3** b): 1,000 – 542 = 458

2,692 – 836 = 1,856

2,001 – 265 = 1,736

1,897 – 999 = 898

Check for a range of strategies being used, for example, equivalent difference, column method, counting on to find the difference (number line), counting back (number line), expanded method.

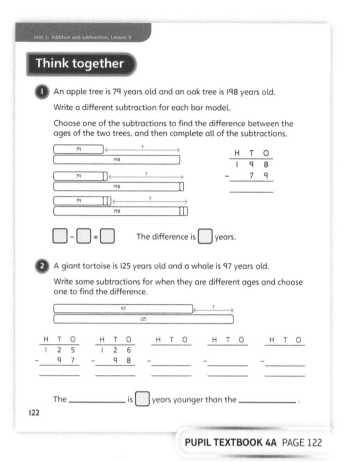

**PUPIL TEXTBOOK 4A** PAGE 122

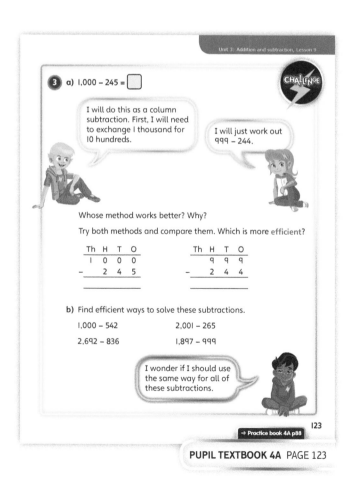

**PUPIL TEXTBOOK 4A** PAGE 123

## Practice

**WAYS OF WORKING** Independent thinking

**IN FOCUS** Question **5** is an open question in which children can choose from a range of methods that they know, identifying the most efficient. When they have finished, ask them to compare their chosen strategies with a partner. Encourage them to use correct vocabulary in their discussion.

**STRENGTHEN** Encourage children to show each of their methods using a representation such as a bar model or a number line.

**DEEPEN** Focus on question **1**. Ask children if they can think of a subtraction for which it would not be a good idea to use equivalent difference.

**ASSESSMENT CHECKPOINT** Question **1** will allow you to assess which children can find equivalent subtractions and select the most efficient one. Question **4** b) will allow you to assess children's reasoning skills around this method. If they are correct, then it is likely that they have achieved mastery of this lesson.

**ANSWERS** Answers for the **Practice** part of the lesson appear in the separate **Practice and Reflect answer guide**.

## Reflect

**WAYS OF WORKING** Pair work

**IN FOCUS** For this question, children should reason that the column method would require three exchanges, so it is not a very efficient strategy for this subtraction. Children may instead opt to use equivalent difference or counting on from 955 to 1,000 to find the difference.

**ASSESSMENT CHECKPOINT** This exercise will allow you to assess whether children understand that different methods are more suitable for different subtractions. Their reasoning will let you know if they understand why this is the case.

**ANSWERS** Answers for the **Reflect** part of the lesson appear in the separate **Practice and Reflect answer guide**.

## After the lesson ⏸

· Do all children understand equivalent difference?
· Can children visually represent equivalent difference?
· Do you need to run intervention sessions for any children?

PUPIL PRACTICE BOOK 4A PAGE 88

PUPIL PRACTICE BOOK 4A PAGE 89

PUPIL PRACTICE BOOK 4A PAGE 90

# Estimating answers to additions and subtractions

## Learning focus

In this lesson children will learn to make choices about whether to round to the nearest 10, 100 or 1,000 and how to use that to decide if a calculation is accurate.

## Small steps

→ Previous step: Equivalent difference
→ **This step: Estimating answers to additions and subtractions**
→ Next step: Checking strategies

## NATIONAL CURRICULUM LINKS

**Year 4 Number – Addition and Subtraction**

Estimate and use inverse operations to check answers to a calculation.

**Year 4 Number – Number and place value**

Round any number to the nearest 10, 100 or 1,000.

## ASSESSING MASTERY

Children can round the numbers in additions and subtractions up or down to the nearest 10, 100 or 1,000 as appropriate and can use this to make estimates and find rough answers. They can compare their estimates to the exact answers and use this to check answers.

## COMMON MISCONCEPTIONS

Children may not know whether to round a number to the nearest 10, 100 or 1,000. Ask:
• *How accurate do you need to be? Can you work that out mentally?*

## STRENGTHENING UNDERSTANDING

If children are finding rounding difficult, you may need to run some intervention for them to practise this important skill.

## GOING DEEPER

This lesson shows children that sometimes it is more accurate to round only one number, to retain better accuracy. Generate discussion around this and ask children to come up with examples that demonstrate it.

## KEY LANGUAGE

**In lesson:** accurate, estimate, round, roughly, exact, nearest, thousand, hundred, ten, one, column, subtraction, addition, check, efficient

**Other language to be used by the teacher:** approximately

## STRUCTURES AND REPRESENTATIONS

number line

## RESOURCES

Printed number lines from 1,000 to 2,000 and from 3,000 to 4,000

 In the eTextbook of this lesson, you will find interactive links to a selection of teaching tools.

## Before you teach ⏸

• Can all children round to the nearest 10, 100, 1,000?
• Could you do a mini-assessment prior to the lesson?
• Would displaying the key vocabulary support children in this lesson?

# Discover

WAYS OF WORKING  Pair work

**ASK**

• Question ➊ a): *How can you tell the ringmistress has not made a good estimate?*
• Question ➊ b): *What strategy could you use to check?*

**IN FOCUS**  The ringmistress gives an incorrect statement because she has rounded one of the amounts incorrectly. Question ➊ a) provides a good learning opportunity for children to spot this. This is a good point in the lesson at which to remind children of the rules involved in rounding.

**PRACTICAL TIPS**  Provide printed number lines from 1,000 to 2,000 and from 3,000 to 4,000 for children who need visual support with the questions.

**ANSWERS**

Question ➊ a): This is not an accurate estimate. 1,898 is closer to 2,000 than 1,000. A better estimate would be 2,000 + 3,000 = 5,000. They have sold roughly 5,000 tickets.

Question ➊ b): The exact answer is 4,914 tickets. 4,914 rounds to 5,000. 5,000 is close to the exact calculation. 4,000 is not. 5,000 is a good estimate.

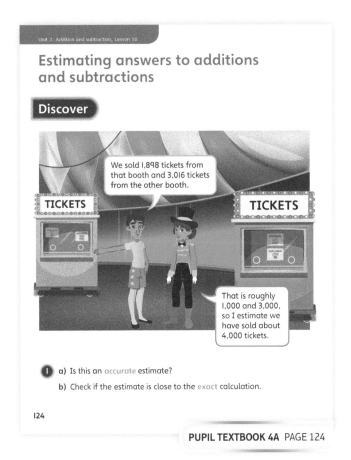

PUPIL TEXTBOOK 4A PAGE 124

# Share

WAYS OF WORKING  Whole class teacher led

**ASK**

• Question ➊ a): *How do the number lines help you round?*
• Question ➊ b): *What would the estimate be if the ringmaster had rounded to the nearest hundred?*

**IN FOCUS**  Question ➊ a) gives a good opportunity to ask children what happens if the amount is exactly in the middle of the number line, i.e. 1,500. Recap the rule that they must always round up when that is the case. Explain that the five digits that round down are 0, 1, 2, 3, 4, and the digits that round up are 5, 6, 7, 8, 9. This makes it equal.

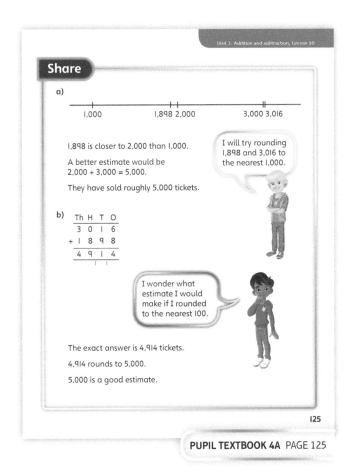

PUPIL TEXTBOOK 4A PAGE 125

# Think together

**WAYS OF WORKING** Whole class teacher led (I do, We do, You do)

**ASK**
- Question ②: *What is the next 1,000 after 9,000?*
- Question ③: *How close is Isla's estimate to Max's answer?*

**IN FOCUS** In question ②, children will need to round 9,811 to the nearest 1,000. This may confuse some children who do not see that 10,000 is the answer. Model the question on a number line to provide support, if needed.

**STRENGTHEN** Practise counting on and back in tens, hundreds and thousands. This will be particularly useful in question ②, when the tens of thousands barrier is crossed.

**DEEPEN** Question ③ deepens learning by showing that although Isla has only rounded one of the numbers, hers is the best estimate. She can subtract a thousands number which is a sensible mental method. Discuss this with children and challenge them to find other subtractions in which it would be best to round only one of the numbers.

**ASSESSMENT CHECKPOINT** Question ② will allow you to assess which children can round numbers and subtract them mentally to reach an estimate.

**ANSWERS**

Question ①: 6,149 rounds to 6,000. 912 rounds to 1,000.
6,000 – 1,000 = 5,000.

Roughly 5,000 people stayed.

Question ②: 2,794 rounds to 2,800

3,911 rounds to 3,900

2,800 + 3,900 = 6,700

9,811 rounds to 9,800

2,788 rounds to 2,800

7,000 = 9,800 - 2,800

Question ③: Children should notice that Isla's method is more accurate because it is nearer to the actual answer. Although Isla has only rounded one of the numbers, her estimate is better because when you round 5,602 to the nearest thousand, you lose quite a lot of accuracy. Doing as Isla did would have helped Max to find out whether his answer was close to the correct one.

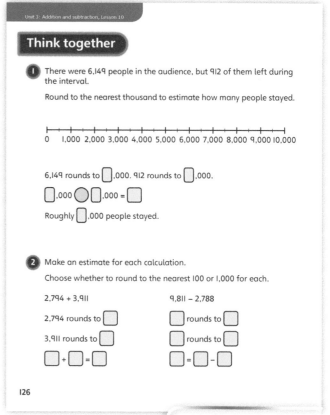

PUPIL TEXTBOOK 4A PAGE 126

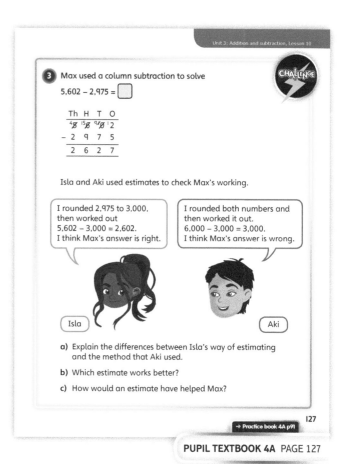

PUPIL TEXTBOOK 4A PAGE 127

## Practice

**WAYS OF WORKING** Independent thinking

**IN FOCUS** In question ❸, children calculate the exact answer and then use an estimate to check it. This will help them with their reasoning.

**STRENGTHEN** The matching exercise in question ❷ will provide support for children who need it, and will allow them to focus on developing their reasoning skills.

**DEEPEN** Focus on question ❹ and encourage discussion about rounding to different degrees of accuracy. Ask children to think of real-life situations when the degree of accuracy is important, for example estimating the rough total price of a shopping list.

**ASSESSMENT CHECKPOINT** Question ❷ will allow you to assess which children can choose a suitable estimate. They should also be able to explain why you might sometimes round a number in the 1,000s to the nearest 100.

**ANSWERS** Answers for the **Practice** part of the lesson appear in the separate **Practice and Reflect answer guide**.

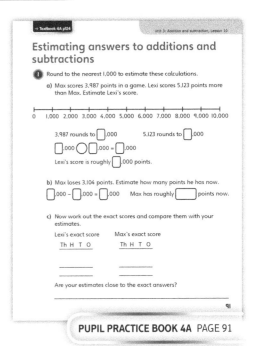

PUPIL PRACTICE BOOK 4A PAGE 91

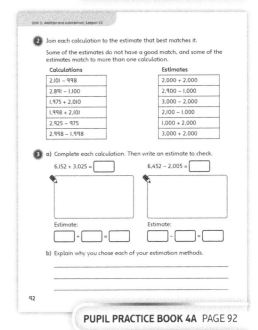

PUPIL PRACTICE BOOK 4A PAGE 92

## Reflect

**WAYS OF WORKING** Pair work

**IN FOCUS** For this question, some children may do 2,000 – 1,000. Others may do 1,915 – 1,000 and some others may do 2,000 – 1,019. Encourage children to share their solutions and debate which is the most useful.

**ASSESSMENT CHECKPOINT** This will help you to assess children's understanding of the methodology used in this lesson. Can they list the instructions in clear steps?

**ANSWERS** Answers for the **Reflect** part of the lesson appear in the separate **Practice and Reflect answer guide**.

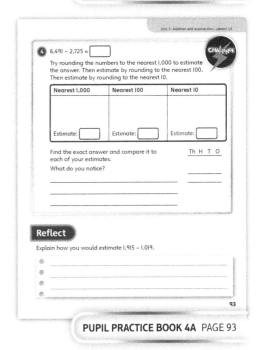

PUPIL PRACTICE BOOK 4A PAGE 93

### After the lesson ⏸

- Can all children estimate using rounding?
- How many children achieved mastery of this lesson?
- Do children understand why we estimate answers?

# Checking strategies

## Learning focus

In this lesson children will learn strategies for checking answers, using the inverse operation and estimating by rounding.

## Small steps

→ Previous step: Estimating answers to additions and subtractions
→ **This step: Checking strategies**
→ Next step: Problem solving – addition and subtraction (1)

## NATIONAL CURRICULUM LINKS

**Year 4 Number – Addition and Subtraction**

Estimate and use inverse operations to check answers to a calculation.

## ASSESSING MASTERY

Children can complete a calculation and then use the inverse operation to check their answer. They can spot mistakes and understand the importance of checking answers, and can understand that there is more than one way to check an answer (inverse, rounding, repetition).

## COMMON MISCONCEPTIONS

Children may work out the inverse, but if it is not the same as their answer, they may not know what to do. Ask:
• *Could you work out the calculation in a different way?*

## STRENGTHENING UNDERSTANDING

Some children may not be secure with inverse operations. Scaffold learning by showing simple fact families and explaining the relationship between them, for example $3 + 2 = 5$, $2 + 3 = 5$, $5 - 2 = 3$, $5 - 3 = 2$.

## GOING DEEPER

Deepen learning in this lesson by exploring different ways to check answers. Children may find the inverse, or they may use rounding or repetition. Ask them to discuss the differences between the strategies.

## KEY LANGUAGE

**In lesson:** check, estimate, addition, subtraction, inverse, accurately, fact family, **diagram**

**Other language to be used by the teacher:** round, nearest, thousand, hundred, ten, one

## STRUCTURES AND REPRESENTATIONS

bar model, part-whole model

 In the eTextbook of this lesson, you will find interactive links to a selection of teaching tools.

## Before you teach

• Do all children know what 'inverse' means?
• How will you link this lesson to the previous one?
• Do children understand the importance of checking an answer?

## Discover

**WAYS OF WORKING** Pair work

**ASK**

• Question ① a): *How many different ways can you think of to check an answer?*
• Question ① a): *What would you do if you got a different answer when checking?*

**IN FOCUS** Question ① a) focuses on the importance of checking answers. If the checked answer is different, we know there is a problem but is it the original or the checked answer that is incorrect? Discuss this with children.

**PRACTICAL TIPS** Create a display in the classroom which models different ways to check answers.

**ANSWERS**

Question ① a): A subtraction can be checked by using the inverse operation, which is addition.

799 + 574 = 1,373

The parts do not match the whole. The calculation should be done again.

Question ① b): 1225 − 799 = 426; 1226 − 800 = 426

There are 426 l of fuel left.

### Checking strategies

#### Discover

① a) How can the astronaut check her calculation?
   b) Show two ways to do the calculation.

128

**PUPIL TEXTBOOK 4A** PAGE 128

## Share

**WAYS OF WORKING** Whole class teacher led

**ASK**

• Question ① b): *Could you use equivalent difference to work out the answer?*
• Question ① b): *Why is it important to check answers?*

**IN FOCUS** For question ① b), it is a good idea to remind children of the earlier lesson in this unit about equivalent difference. Explain that there are different ways to check answers, and sometimes you may even need to use more than one to be sure. Link this to real-life examples, for example a shopkeeper totalling their takings for a day.

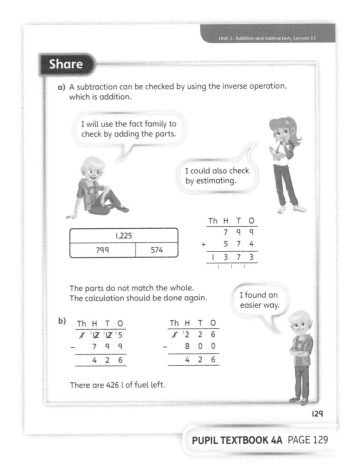

#### Share

a) A subtraction can be checked by using the inverse operation, which is addition.

There are 426 l of fuel left.

129

**PUPIL TEXTBOOK 4A** PAGE 129

## Think together

WAYS OF WORKING Whole class teacher led (I do, We do, You do)

**ASK**

• Question **2**: *What sort of calculation could you do to check the answers accurately? How could you estimate first what the answers should be?*

**IN FOCUS** Question **3** is a good way to make mathematical connections, which is an important skill for mastery. Discuss with children how fact families can help with checking answers.

**STRENGTHEN** Following on from question **2**, give children more opportunities to check answers by using the inverse operation.

**DEEPEN** Ask children to complete the calculations in question **2**, then challenge them to explain where each one went wrong. For the first one, children should be able to do 5,391 − 3,401 = 1,990 to show that a 0 was missing from the original calculation. Children should find that the second one is already correct.

**ASSESSMENT CHECKPOINT** Question **1** gives a simple way to assess children on whether they can check answers using the inverse operation. Question **4** will allow you to assess which children can check answers using visual representations such as bar models or part-whole models.

**ANSWERS**

Question **1**: 3,288 + 3,707 = 6,995

The parts do match the whole. The calculation is correct.

Question **2** a): 5,391 − 3,401 = 1,990 (Correction: either

199 + 3,401 = 3,600

or 1,990 + 3,401 = 5,391)

Question **2** b): 8,569 + 440 = 9,009

Question **3**: Model completed: 1,149.

1,999 − 850 = 1,149

1,999 − 1,149 = 850

1,149 + 850 = 1,999

850 + 1,149 = 1,999

Question **4**: Look for accurately drawn part-whole models or bar models showing:

1,090 + 1,910 = 3,000    4,000 − 2,750 = 1,250

2,550 = 700 + 1,850    2,750 − 750 = 2,000

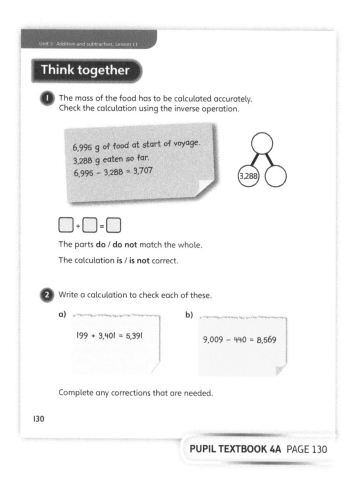

PUPIL TEXTBOOK 4A PAGE 130

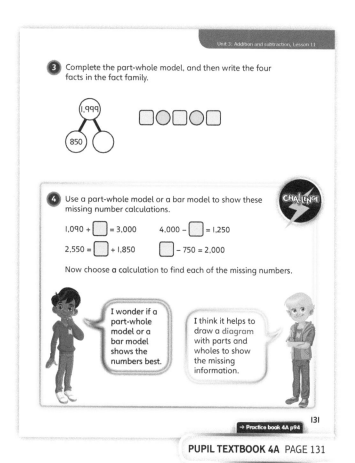

PUPIL TEXTBOOK 4A PAGE 131

## Practice

**WAYS OF WORKING** Independent thinking

**IN FOCUS** Checking answers, such as in question **1**, can empower and motivate children as they enjoy becoming like the teacher.

**STRENGTHEN** Question **3** features missing numbers in calculations. Some children's knowledge may need strengthening here. Ask them when they must do the inverse operation to find out the answer, and when they do not need to.

**DEEPEN** Deepen learning in question **1** by asking children to discuss and explain where Emma went wrong each time.

**THINK DIFFERENTLY** Question **4** shows how rounding can sometimes be flawed. First, encourage children to look at the correct answer (7,998). Then see if they can think why the rounding method used was not accurate. Children should reason that Dexter would have been more accurate if he had rounded to the nearest hundred instead of thousand.

**ASSESSMENT CHECKPOINT** Question **5** will allow you to assess whether children can solve a problem and then check their answer.

**ANSWERS** Answers for the **Practice** part of the lesson appear in the separate **Practice and Reflect answer guide**.

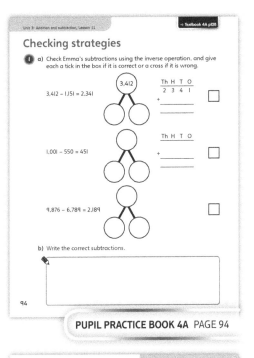

PUPIL PRACTICE BOOK 4A PAGE 94

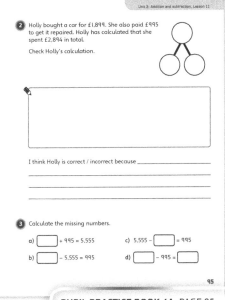

PUPIL PRACTICE BOOK 4A PAGE 95

## Reflect

**WAYS OF WORKING** Pair work

**IN FOCUS** This is a good opportunity for discussion using maths language. Ask children to work with a partner for this activity, and to work together to discuss their methods for checking.

**ASSESSMENT CHECKPOINT** This activity will let you see which children can use more than one strategy to check an answer.

**ANSWERS** Answers for the **Reflect** part of the lesson appear in the separate **Practice and Reflect answer guide**.

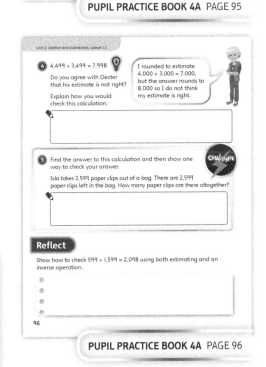

PUPIL PRACTICE BOOK 4A PAGE 96

### After the lesson ⏸

- Can children use more than one method to check answers?
- Can children reason why it is important to check answers?
- Are children ready to apply their knowledge to lessons about problem solving?

# Problem solving – addition and subtraction ❶

## Learning focus

In this lesson children will apply addition and subtraction strategies they have learnt previously to solve one-step problems.

## Small steps

→ Previous step: Checking strategies
→ **This step: Problem solving – addition and subtraction (1)**
→ Next step: Problem solving – addition and subtraction (2)

## NATIONAL CURRICULUM LINKS

**Year 4 Number – Addition and Subtraction**

Solve addition and subtraction two-step problems in contexts, deciding which operations and methods to use and why.

## ASSESSING MASTERY

Children can choose an efficient method of addition or subtraction to solve a problem. They can represent the problem on a bar model, and explain their method.

## COMMON MISCONCEPTIONS

Children may struggle to interpret the word problems and not know whether to add or subtract. Ask:
· *Can you highlight the key words that might help you?*

## STRENGTHENING UNDERSTANDING

Some children may need practice in interpreting word problems. Talk through the questions and provide bar models to visually represent them.

## GOING DEEPER

Provide more examples of problems where numbers are represented by symbols (early algebra). Discuss the best way for children to show what information they have and what they need to find out.

## KEY LANGUAGE

**In lesson:** problem solving, strategy, part, whole, bar model, story problem, altogether, left

## STRUCTURES AND REPRESENTATIONS

part-whole model, bar model

## RESOURCES

Strips of paper to make bar models

 In the eTextbook of this lesson, you will find interactive links to a selection of teaching tools.

## Before you teach ❶❶

· Are children ready to move on to problem solving?
· How will you draw out the key vocabulary in the lesson?
· How will you promote discussion of methods in this lesson?

## Discover

**WAYS OF WORKING** Pair work

**ASK**

- Question ❶ a): *Which model will you use?*
- Question ❶ a): *Would a bar model represent the problem well?*

**IN FOCUS** In question ❶ a) children have to represent a word problem visually. If children are not sure which diagram to choose, suggest the bar model or part-whole model.

**PRACTICAL TIPS** Instead of drawing bar models, children could cut strips of paper to make physical bar models.

**ANSWERS**

Question ❶ a): Look for a bar model or part-whole model showing that the whole (total votes) is 5,762, that one part (No votes) is 2,899 and that the other part (Yes votes) is not known.

Question ❶ b): You need to subtract to find the missing part and calculate the answer: 5,762 – 2,899 = 2,863.

There were 2,863 Yes votes. No got more votes because 2,899 > 2,863.

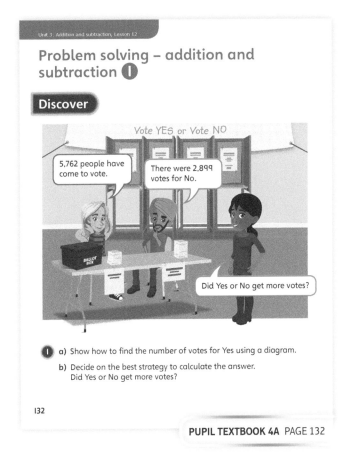

PUPIL TEXTBOOK 4A PAGE 132

## Share

**WAYS OF WORKING** Whole class teacher led

**ASK**

- Question ❶ a): *What does 'part' mean?*
- Question ❶ a): *What does 'whole' mean?*

**IN FOCUS** For question ❶ a), the bar model and the part-whole model have been used to represent the problem. Be aware that children may have used other representations, for example number lines.

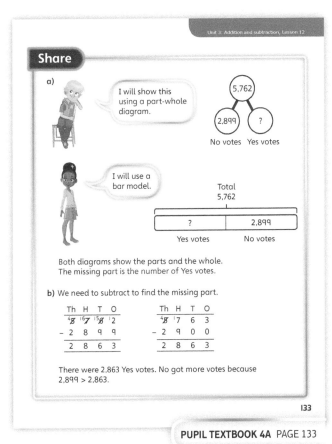

PUPIL TEXTBOOK 4A PAGE 133

# Think together

Whole class teacher led (I do, We do, You do)

**ASK**

- Question **1**: *How do you know that this is an addition problem?*
- Question **2**: *What does the bar model need to show?*
- Question **4**: *What do you need to remember when drawing a bar model?*

**IN FOCUS** Question **3** will draw out associated addition and subtraction facts. Explain to children that making connections like this is very important in maths mastery.

**STRENGTHEN** After completing question **2**, children could strengthen their learning by drawing the correct bar model once they have identified what is wrong with the two that are given.

**DEEPEN** Use question **4** to deepen learning. Children will need to represent a range of calculations using bar models, including some with missing numbers. Challenge children to find links between the calculations. They should be able to use vocabulary such as 'inverse', and explain the strategies they used to work out the correct answers. Finally, they should realise that they do not need four different bar models since the calculations are linked, and so only two models are needed. Extend learning by providing an answer, such as 3,232, and asking children to draw bar models to match it.

**ASSESSMENT CHECKPOINT** Question **2** will allow you to assess which children can accurately represent a word problem with a bar model. Look for effective reasoning and the correct use of mathematical vocabulary.

**ANSWERS**

Question **1**: 1,775 (Yes); 3,007 (No).

3,007 + 1,775 = 4,782. 4,782 people voted.

Question **2**: Jamilla has put 9,923 as a part when it should be the whole.

Max has drawn the correct bar model, but the parts should not be equally sized.

Question **3**: 6,000 − 2,999 = 3,001

6,000 − 3,001 = 2,999

2,999 + 3,001 = 6,000

3,001 + 2,999 = 6,000

Question **4**: Look for accurately drawn bar models, with parts and whole of appropriate sizes. Children should notice that only two models are needed, showing:

2,674 − 199 = 2,475 and 199 + 2,475 = 2,674

2,475 − 199 = 2,276 and 199 = 2,475 − 2,276

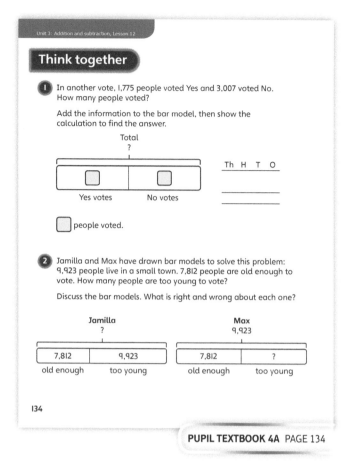

**PUPIL TEXTBOOK 4A** PAGE 134

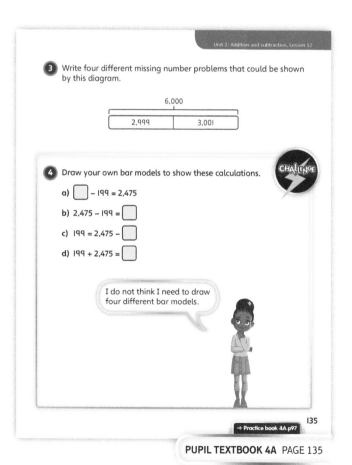

**PUPIL TEXTBOOK 4A** PAGE 135

## Practice

**WAYS OF WORKING** Independent thinking

**IN FOCUS** Question ② promotes reasoning. Ask children how they will go about solving each problem. Also ask them what their bar model will tell them, and what the size of each part should be.

**STRENGTHEN** For question ④, talk to children about how they could begin to find a solution. They may realise that starting with the triangle would be a good strategy. From the second bar model: if you add the triangle to the star you get the cloud. But also, we know that if you add 2,000 to the star you get the cloud. So the triangle must be worth 2,000. From the first model, that means that the star and the heart sum to 2,000. As the heart is worth 1,000 more than the star, the heart must be 1,500 and the star 500. This means that the cloud is 500 + 2,000 = 2,500.

**DEEPEN** In question ④, tell children that you think two hearts total less than one triangle. Challenge children to reason why this is incorrect (heart > star; star + heart = triangle).

**ASSESSMENT CHECKPOINT** Assess children's progress by looking at question ②. See if they have achieved mastery, and can interpret the question correctly and use the appropriate operation.

**ANSWERS** Answers for the **Practice** part of the lesson appear in the separate **Practice and Reflect answer guide**.

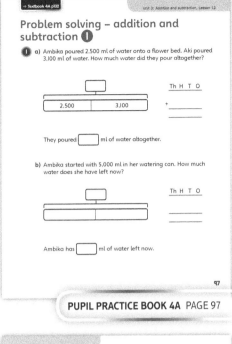

PUPIL PRACTICE BOOK 4A PAGE 97

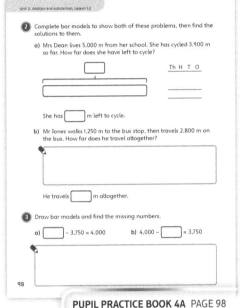

PUPIL PRACTICE BOOK 4A PAGE 98

## Reflect

**WAYS OF WORKING** Pair work

**IN FOCUS** Some children may need support with thinking of a suitable context for their problem. If needed, provide some ideas like measuring in centimetres, or counting marbles in a jar.

**ASSESSMENT CHECKPOINT** This activity will let you see which children are likely to have mastered the lesson. They will be able to create a relevant story problem and explain how it relates to the bar model.

**ANSWERS** Answers for the **Reflect** part of the lesson appear in the separate **Practice and Reflect answer guide**.

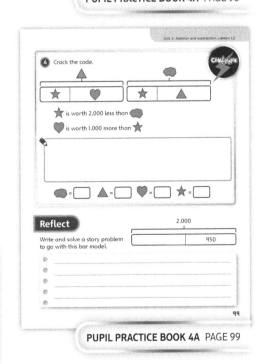

PUPIL PRACTICE BOOK 4A PAGE 99

### After the lesson ⏸

- Can all children represent addition and subtraction problems using a bar model?
- Can they explain the bar model using the words 'part' and 'whole'?
- Are children ready to move on to more complex problem solving?

# Problem solving – addition and subtraction ❷

## Learning focus

In this lesson, children will explore single bar models and comparison bar models to interpret and solve one-step problems.

## Small steps

→ Previous step: Problem solving – addition and subtraction (1)
→ **This step: Problem solving – addition and subtraction (2)**
→ Next step: Problem solving – addition and subtraction (3)

### NATIONAL CURRICULUM LINKS

**Year 4 Number – Addition and Subtraction**

Solve addition and subtraction two-step problems in contexts, deciding which operations and methods to use and why.

### ASSESSING MASTERY

Children can understand when to draw single bar models and when to draw comparison bar models to help them solve problems. They can explain the representations clearly using the correct vocabulary.

### COMMON MISCONCEPTIONS

Children may not understand when to draw single bar models and when to draw comparison bar models. Ask:
• *Can you draw both models and explain which is more useful?*

### STRENGTHENING UNDERSTANDING

If children do not know when to draw a single bar model and when to draw a comparison bar model, give them some word problems with corresponding single bar models and comparison bar models. Ask them to discuss as a group which one represents the problem more clearly.

### GOING DEEPER

Deepen learning by giving children some single bar models and comparison bar models, and ask them to write some word problems to match them.

### KEY LANGUAGE

**In lesson:** problem solving, addition, subtraction, single bar model, comparison bar model, part, whole, story problem, how much, more, fewer, left, difference

**Other language to be used by the teacher:** strategy

### STRUCTURES AND REPRESENTATIONS

single bar model, comparison bar model

 In the eTextbook of this lesson, you will find interactive links to a selection of teaching tools.

## Before you teach ⏸

• How will you explain the difference between a single bar model and a comparison bar model?
• Will you have a challenge activity for any quick finishers?
• Could you make a classroom display to support this lesson?

## Discover

**WAYS OF WORKING** Pair work

**ASK**

- Question ❶ a): *How will you show that Luis has more?*
- Question ❶ b): *Will you use column subtraction or is there another way of calculating the answer?*

**IN FOCUS** Questions ❶ a) and ❶ b) explore the difference between single bar models and comparison bar models. If necessary, suggest that the bar models may look different for each question.

**PRACTICAL TIPS** Give children visual support, by creating a classroom display featuring some word problems with single bar models and comparison bar models, to support their interpretation of them.

**ANSWERS**

Question ❶ a): A single bar model or comparison bar model where the part representing 1,005 (Luis) is noticeably longer than the part representing 899 (Danny).

Look for children who identify that the comparison bar model is a better way to represent this problem.

Question ❶ b): 1,005 – 899 = 106. Luis has 106 more points than Danny.

### Problem solving – addition and subtraction ❷

**Discover**

❶ a) Show that Luis has more using a bar model.

b) Calculate how much more Luis has than Danny.

136

**PUPIL TEXTBOOK 4A** PAGE 136

## Share

**WAYS OF WORKING** Whole class teacher led

**ASK**

- Question ❶ a): *How does the comparison bar model show who has more?*
- Question ❶ b): *Did you use the column method to calculate the answer, or a different strategy?*

**IN FOCUS** For question ❶ b), children may have used a different strategy, for example equivalent difference. Share all the strategies that children used.

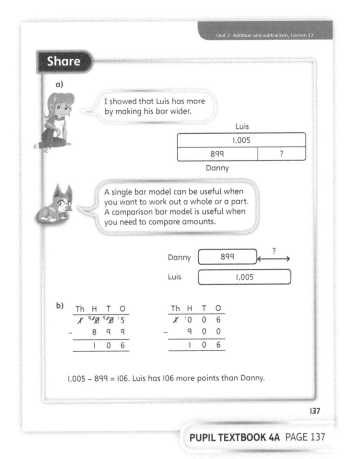

**PUPIL TEXTBOOK 4A** PAGE 137

# Think together

**WAYS OF WORKING** Whole class teacher led (I do, We do, You do)

**ASK**

- Question ❷: *Is this problem an addition or a subtraction?*
- Question ❷: *What can you fill in first on the model?*
- Question ❸: *Can you think of more than one solution for part d)?*

**IN FOCUS** Question ❷ breaks the word problem down for children. Ask them to fill in the information that they know first, then to explain what calculation they must do to find the answer.

**STRENGTHEN** Strengthen learning by talking through question ❸. Help children to identify that a comparison bar model is needed when finding a difference, and a single bar model is more useful when completing an addition.

**DEEPEN** Ask children to actually draw the different bar models for question ❸ and to reason which is more suitable for each question. For the final question, challenge children to find more than one answer.

**ASSESSMENT CHECKPOINT** Question ❸ will let you see which children have mastered the lesson and can identify the correct bar model and calculate the answers effectively.

**ANSWERS**

Question ❶: 1,050 – 678 = 372. Jack has 372 fewer points than Amelia.

Question ❷: 975 + 875 = 1,850. Isla has 1,850 points.

Question ❸ a): Single bar model showing 5,250 + 100 = 5,350

Question ❸ b): Single bar model showing 5,250 + 750 = 6,000

Question ❸ c): Comparison bar model showing 5,250 – 750 = 4,500

Question ❸ d): Comparison bar model showing any two numbers with a difference of 2000.

**PUPIL TEXTBOOK 4A** PAGE 138

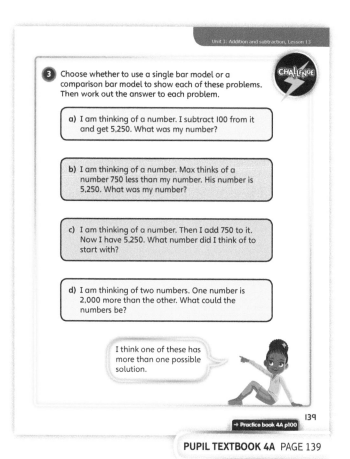

**PUPIL TEXTBOOK 4A** PAGE 139

## Practice

**WAYS OF WORKING** Independent thinking

**IN FOCUS** Questions ① a), ① b) and ① c) draw out the different ways that additions and subtractions can be represented using bar models.

**STRENGTHEN** Some children will need scaffolding for question ④. Work alongside them, or as a group, and talk through the problem. You could provide some of the bars for them.

**DEEPEN** In question ③, challenge children to find more than one way to work out the correct answer.

**THINK DIFFERENTLY** This question ② may prove challenging for some children. Usually the word 'more' is associated with addition. However, in this question you have to find how many 'more than'. Explain the difference to children to help them identify that this is a subtraction. Use a bar model to support this.

**ASSESSMENT CHECKPOINT** Question ④ will tell you which children have mastered the lesson. Check that they can break down the problem and represent it using bar models. Ask them to explain their workings to make sure they are confident with their learning.

**ANSWERS** Answers for the **Practice** part of the lesson appear in the separate **Practice and Reflect answer guide**.

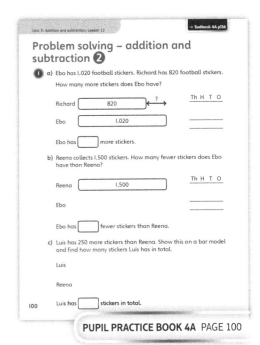

PUPIL PRACTICE BOOK 4A PAGE 100

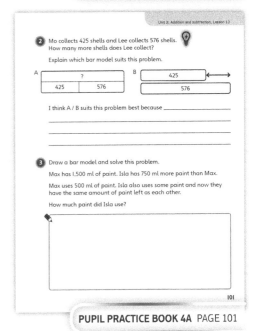

PUPIL PRACTICE BOOK 4A PAGE 101

## Reflect

**WAYS OF WORKING** Pair work

**IN FOCUS** Display the words 'compare', 'comparison', 'addition', 'subtraction' and 'difference' to help children explain their answers. Encourage children to use examples of number sentences and bar models in their explanations.

**ASSESSMENT CHECKPOINT** Assess children on the accuracy of their explanations, and the vocabulary they use.

**ANSWERS** Answers for the **Reflect** part of the lesson appear in the separate **Practice and Reflect answer guide**.

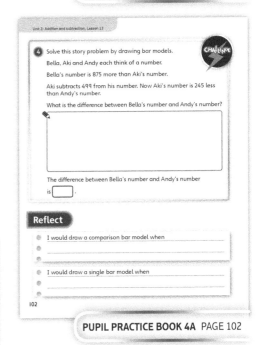

PUPIL PRACTICE BOOK 4A PAGE 102

## After the lesson ⏸

- Do all children know the difference between a single bar model and a comparison bar model?
- Which children struggled with **Practice** question ④?
- Could you do some more problems like this to strengthen learning?

# Problem solving – addition and subtraction ③

## Learning focus

In this lesson children will apply addition and subtraction strategies that they have learnt previously, to solve multi-step problems.

## Small steps

→ Previous step: Problem solving – addition and subtraction (2)

→ **This step: Problem solving – addition and subtraction (3)**

→ Next step: Problem solving – addition and subtraction (4)

### NATIONAL CURRICULUM LINKS

**Year 4 Number – Addition and Subtraction**

Solve addition and subtraction two-step problems in contexts, deciding which operations and methods to use and why.

### ASSESSING MASTERY

Children can understand how to solve a problem, and which operations they must use. They can confidently represent a word problem using a model or representation and explain this clearly.

### COMMON MISCONCEPTIONS

Children may not realise that a question is a multi-step problem, and so may only complete one of the steps. Ask:
• *Is that your final answer?*

### STRENGTHENING UNDERSTANDING

Encourage children to break each problem down into simple steps. Each step should be supported with a model or representation, helping children to interpret the mathematics.

### GOING DEEPER

Give children two completed bar models and challenge them to think of a multi-step word problem to match.

### KEY LANGUAGE

**In lesson:** problem solving, addition, subtraction, step, check, part, whole, bar model, story problem, total, difference, how much

**Other language to be used by the teacher:** multi-step, strategy

### STRUCTURES AND REPRESENTATIONS

bar model

 In the eTextbook of this lesson, you will find interactive links to a selection of teaching tools.

## Before you teach

• How will you scaffold learning in this lesson?
• Could you pair children who struggle with reading with a more capable reader?
• How can you promote maths vocabulary in this lesson?

## Discover

**WAYS OF WORKING** Pair work

**ASK**

- Question ❶ a): *Is there only one way to work this out?*
- Question ❶ a): *What number sentences will help you work out the correct answer?*

**IN FOCUS** Question ❶ a) involves children working out a multi-step problem. Focus children's learning by asking them to break the question down into two steps. They should write two number sentences and then do the calculations. There is more than one way to work out the answer. Encourage children to explore all of the options.

**PRACTICAL TIPS** Promote lots of discussion in this section, using appropriate maths vocabulary. Talking through questions in pairs can help to ensure that children gain a secure understanding of the problem.

**ANSWERS**

Question ❶ a): 2,500 − 1,200 − 750 = 550

or 1,200 + 750 = 1,950 and 2,500 − 1,950 = 550

Olivia will need to run 550 m to complete the race.

Question ❶ b): Check by adding.

1,200 + 750 = 1950 and 1,950 + 550 = 2,500

or 1,200 + 750 + 550 = 2,500

### Problem solving – addition and subtraction ❸

**Discover**

❶ a) How far will Olivia need to run to complete the race?

  b) Choose a way to check your calculation.

140

**PUPIL TEXTBOOK 4A** PAGE 140

## Share

**WAYS OF WORKING** Whole class teacher led

**ASK**

- Question ❶ b): *How can you check your answer?*
- Question ❶ b): *Can you think of more than one way to check?*

**IN FOCUS** For question ❶ b), children should check by using the inverse operation (addition). However, some children may choose to check by using a different strategy, for example a number line or rounding.

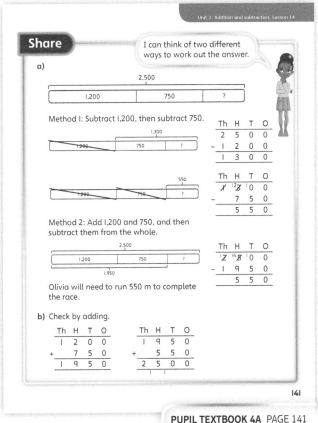

**PUPIL TEXTBOOK 4A** PAGE 141

# Think together

WAYS OF WORKING Whole class teacher led (I do, We do, You do)

**ASK**
- Question **1**: *Have you seen a similar question before?*
- Question **2**: *What is different about the bar model here?*
- Question **4**: *How can you show two numbers with a total of 1,500 but a difference of 1,000?*

**IN FOCUS** In question **2**, children will see that the whole is at the side of the bars, which is new. Explain that this is just a different way of looking at a bar model. Ask children to draw what this would usually look like, i.e. a single bar model with the whole as 2,475 and three parts of 475, 800 and 1,200.

**STRENGTHEN** Question **1** is similar to the **Discover** section. This will support children, so prompt them to think back to this if necessary. Ask children to find both ways of working out the problem.

**DEEPEN** Question **2** is a good chance to show children that you do not always have to use a written method when calculating. Some children will realise that a good strategy would be to add 1,200 and 800 to reach 2,000, then add on the 475.

**ASSESSMENT CHECKPOINT** Question **3** will allow you to assess which children can use a comparison bar model to represent a multi-step problem. Children may break it down into a number of steps, first adding 1,250 and 300 to get 1,550, then adding 1,250 and 1,550 to get 2,800, and finally subtracting 2,800 from 3,000 to get 200.

**ANSWERS**

Question **1**: 5,000 – 1,250 – 1,750 = 2,000. Toshi ran 2,000 m.

Question **2**: 475 + 800 + 1,200 = 2,475. Bella, Lexi and Mo ran 2,475 m in total.

Question **3**: For example:

1,250 + 300 = 1,550

1,550 + 1,250 = 2,800

3,000 – 2,800 = 200

200 people watched the long jump.

Question **4**: Look for comparison bar models showing the first bar as 1,500 and the second bar as 1,000 plus two equal blank boxes; then a deduction that the blanks are half of 500, or 250. So Emma ran 1,250 m and Alex ran 250 m.

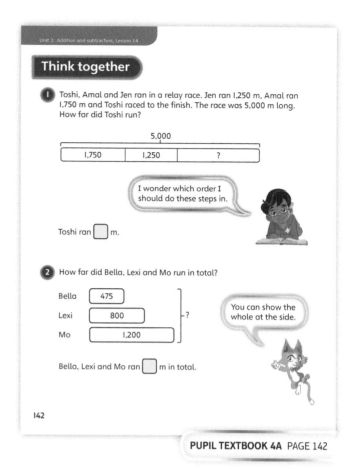

**PUPIL TEXTBOOK 4A** PAGE 142

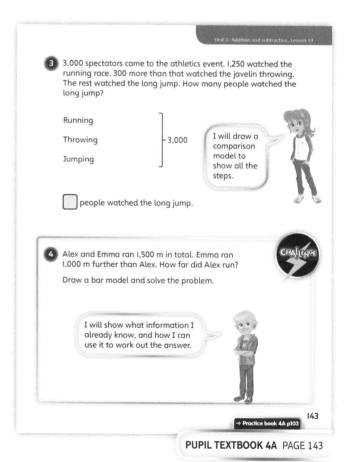

**PUPIL TEXTBOOK 4A** PAGE 143

## Practice

**WAYS OF WORKING** Independent thinking

**IN FOCUS** Question **4** a) is tricky because we are not told how much money Amy or Ben actually have. Scaffold learning by asking children to draw a bar model, or to write down the number sentences. You could start to introduce some simple algebra by representing Amy and Ben with the letters A and B. For example:

A has £1,275 less than B.

B spends £550.

£1,275 – £550 = £725

A now has £725 less than B.

A gets £750.

£750 – £725 = £25

A now has £25 more than B.

**STRENGTHEN** For question **1** b), it may be necessary to explain what a triathlon is (a race with three parts: a swim, a cycle and a run). Question **4** b) can be linked to knowledge of number bonds. Support learning by asking: *What is left if you take 800 from 2,800? Could you partition this number to help you?* They could represent this with bar models.

**DEEPEN** Question **2** displays a use of the bar model in a real-life context. Discuss this and see if children can think of other similar applications, for instance, perimeter.

**ASSESSMENT CHECKPOINT** Question **4** will allow you to assess which children have a firm understanding of interpreting multi-step word problems. Look in particular at how they have shown their workings.

**ANSWERS** Answers for the **Practice** part of the lesson appear in the separate **Practice and Reflect answer guide**.

## Reflect

**WAYS OF WORKING** Pair work

**IN FOCUS** Challenge children to think of as many solutions as they can. You could extend learning by asking them to think of a subtraction with three numbers that equal 2,050, or even an addition and subtraction with three numbers, such as 1,000 + 2,000 – 950.

**ASSESSMENT CHECKPOINT** Assess children on using the correct sizes for the bars in their models and for demonstrating depth of thinking, for example not choosing a very simple example like 2,048 + 1 + 1.

**ANSWERS** Answers for the **Reflect** part of the lesson appear in the separate **Practice and Reflect answer guide**.

### After the lesson ⏸

- How did children approach **Practice** question **4**?
- Do some children need more support with visualising problems like this?
- Are children ready to move on to the final lesson of the unit?

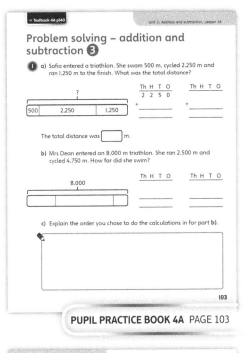

PUPIL PRACTICE BOOK 4A PAGE 103

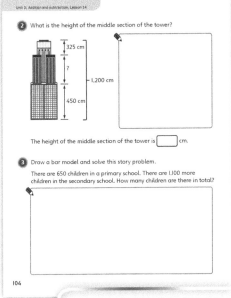

PUPIL PRACTICE BOOK 4A PAGE 104

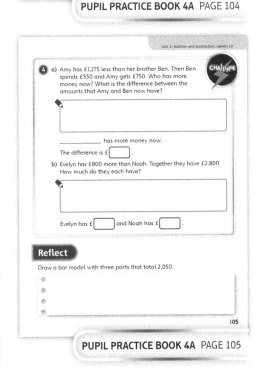

PUPIL PRACTICE BOOK 4A PAGE 105

# Problem solving – addition and subtraction ④

## Learning focus

In this lesson children will continue to apply the addition and subtraction strategies that they have previously learnt to solve multi-step problems.

## Small steps

→ Previous step: Problem solving – addition and subtraction (3)
→ **This step: Problem solving – addition and subtraction (4)**
→ Next step: Kilometres

### NATIONAL CURRICULUM LINKS

**Year 4 Number – Addition and Subtraction**

Solve addition and subtraction two-step problems in contexts, deciding which operations and methods to use and why.

### ASSESSING MASTERY

Children can understand how to solve a problem, and can identify which operations they must use. They can confidently represent a multi-step problem using models or representations and can explain them clearly.

### COMMON MISCONCEPTIONS

Children may not correctly interpret the questions. Ask:
• *Did you use the correct operations? How can you check?*

### STRENGTHENING UNDERSTANDING

To strengthen learning in this lesson, run a quick intervention in which you talk through and explain some word problems. Support the discussion with representations to make the problems visual.

### GOING DEEPER

Deepen learning by providing some more bar models with numbers but no labels, and asking children to write a story problem to go with them. Encourage children to use real-life contexts.

### KEY LANGUAGE

**In lesson:** problem solving, addition, subtraction, diagram, bar model, greater than, less than, step, total, part, whole, story problem, how much, left

**Other language to be used by the teacher:** multi-step, strategy

### STRUCTURES AND REPRESENTATIONS

part-whole model, bar model, number line

 In the eTextbook of this lesson, you will find interactive links to a selection of teaching tools.

## Before you teach ⏸

• Will you provide any practical resources in this lesson?
• How did the previous lesson go?
• Are children ready for more complex problems?

# Discover

**WAYS OF WORKING** Pair work

**ASK**

- Question ① a): *Can you spot any information that is not needed?*
- Question ① a): *Is there more than one way to work this out?*

**IN FOCUS** In this question, some 'useless' information is also provided. Ask children if they need to know about Camp 4. They should be able to reason that the information about Camp 4 does not help to answer the question.

**PRACTICAL TIPS** Encourage children to draw the problem. Having an image of the mountain with the bases and the mountaineer in front of them will allow children to interpret the question more easily.

**ANSWERS**

Question ① a): Children may use a variety of diagrams to show this. Look for diagrams that show a total of 5,275 and three parts of 2,450, 1,500 and ?

Question ① b): To solve this, find out if the distance from Jen to Camp 2 is greater than or less than 1,500 m.

2,450 + 1,500 = 3,950

5,275 − 3,950 = 1,325

1,500 > 1,325, so Jen is closer to Camp 2.

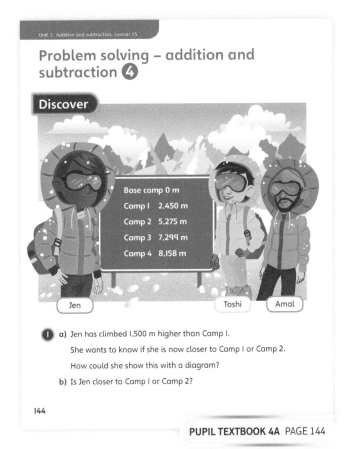

## Problem solving – addition and subtraction ④

### Discover

① a) Jen has climbed 1,500 m higher than Camp 1.

She wants to know if she is now closer to Camp 1 or Camp 2.

How could she show this with a diagram?

b) Is Jen closer to Camp 1 or Camp 2?

144

**PUPIL TEXTBOOK 4A** PAGE 144

# Share

**WAYS OF WORKING** Whole class teacher led

**ASK**

- Question ① b): *What does 'closer' mean?*
- Question ① b): *How could you use the signs < or > in your explanation?*

**IN FOCUS** Children may mistakenly think that Jen is closer to Camp 1 because 1,500 is greater than 1,325 and children often assume that the correct answer is the one that is higher. Explain what 'closer' means and then ask which is closer, something 1,500 m away or something 1,325 m away.

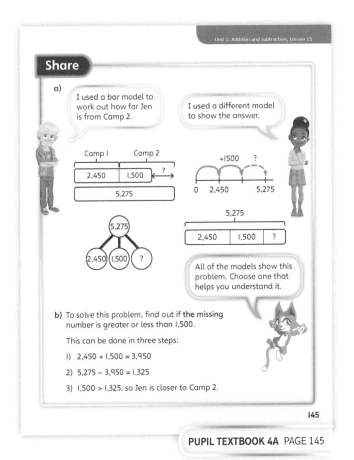

### Share

a)

I used a bar model to work out how far Jen is from Camp 2.

I used a different model to show the answer.

All of the models show this problem. Choose one that helps you understand it.

b) To solve this problem, find out if **the missing number is greater or less than 1,500.**

This can be done in three steps:

1) 2,450 + 1,500 = 3,950

2) 5,275 − 3,950 = 1,325

3) 1,500 > 1,325, so Jen is closer to Camp 2.

145

**PUPIL TEXTBOOK 4A** PAGE 145

# Think together

**WAYS OF WORKING** Whole class teacher led (I do, We do, You do)

**ASK**

- Question **1**: *Why do the other diagrams not match the problem?*
- Question **3**: *How can you solve this problem in steps?*

**IN FOCUS** You may need to break question **3** down to scaffold learning. Ask children to draw the mountains with the differences in heights marked to help them gain a visual understanding of the problem. Then ask children to convert this information into bar models, as it is more mathematical to work like this. Then ask them to calculate and mark the totals.

**STRENGTHEN** Strengthen learning in question **1** by asking children to discuss what each diagram shows, and then reason which is the correct one. Ask children why the others do not match the question. You could ask them to think of word problems that would match each diagram.

**DEEPEN** Ask children to make up their own multi-step problems based on the number sentence 453 + 234 – 101.

**ASSESSMENT CHECKPOINT** Question **3** will allow you to check which children can interpret a problem, break it down into steps, represent it with diagrams and solve it.

**ANSWERS**

Question **1**: Bar model A shows the problem.

   1,245 – 385 = 860 (shown in model B)

   1,245 + 860 = 2,105

   Amal has climbed 2,105 m in total.

Question **2**: Look for a diagram that shows:

   6,895 – 1,812 – 1,259 – 2,248 = 1,576

   Jen climbed 1,576 m on Day 3.

Question **3**: 3,466 + 1,344 = 4,810. Mont Blanc is 4,810 m high.

   4,810 – 1,030 = 3,780. Mount Fuji is 3,780 m high.

**PUPIL TEXTBOOK 4A** PAGE 146

**PUPIL TEXTBOOK 4A** PAGE 147

## Practice

**WAYS OF WORKING** Independent thinking

**IN FOCUS** In question **2**, some children may just do 3,985 – 1,700 and give 2,285 as their final answer. Discuss what 'fewer' means and also what 'total' means. This should help children to realise that they then have to add 3,985 and 2,285.

**STRENGTHEN** In question **1**, children need to add three amounts. Strengthen learning by modelling how they can do this using the column method, as they may not have come across this before. Then set other additions to practise this.

**DEEPEN** In question **4**, children are required to interpret a diagram and think of a matching story problem. Ask them to explain the diagram to you and to fill in the missing amounts for Class 1 and Class 2. Deepen learning by then asking them to replace the Class 1, 2 and 3 labels and to think of a story problem with a completely different context, to show that one diagram could represent a variety of different problems.

**ASSESSMENT CHECKPOINT** Question **4** will allow you to assess which children have a firm understanding of interpreting multi-step word problems. Look in particular at how they have shown their workings.

**ANSWERS** Answers for the **Practice** part of the lesson appear in the separate **Practice and Reflect answer guide**.

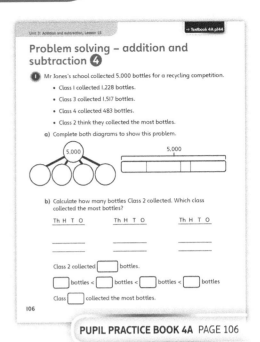

PUPIL PRACTICE BOOK 4A PAGE 106

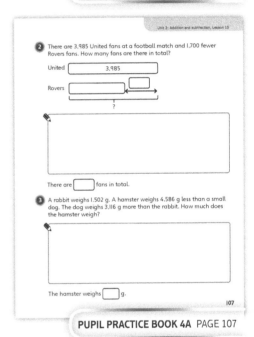

PUPIL PRACTICE BOOK 4A PAGE 107

## Reflect

**WAYS OF WORKING** Pair work

**IN FOCUS** This section asks children to reflect on how they decide what sort of bar diagram is needed to work out the answer to a problem. They should explain how they know how many bars the bar model needs to have to accurately reflect the problem and to show what the answer will be.

**ASSESSMENT CHECKPOINT** Look for children linking the pieces of information in a story problem to each bar of a bar model. It may help for children to give an example of a story problem in their explanation, and to describe how to show this on a bar model.

**ANSWERS** Answers for the **Reflect** part of the lesson appear in the separate **Practice and Reflect answer guide**.

### After the lesson ⏸

- How did children approach **Practice** question **4**?
- Could they create their own story problem?
- Will you need to run any extra intervention in which children solve more problems like these?

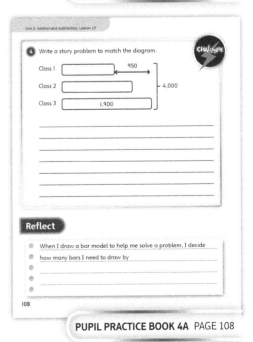

PUPIL PRACTICE BOOK 4A PAGE 108

# End of unit check

> Don't forget the *Power Maths* unit assessment grid on p26.

**WAYS OF WORKING** Group work – adult led

**IN FOCUS** This end of unit check will allow you to focus on children's understanding of addition and subtraction and whether they can apply their knowledge to solve problems.

- Look carefully at the answer that children give for question **5**. It will tell you if they understand how to visually represent and then solve a problem.
- Encourage children to think through or discuss this section before writing their answer in **My journal**.

**ANSWERS AND COMMENTARY**

Children who have mastered the concepts in this unit should be secure with adding and subtracting 1s, 10s, 100s, 1,000s and adding two 4-digit numbers using the column method. They should be confident subtracting two 4-digit numbers using the column method and be able to use a range of mental addition and subtraction strategies. Children can also find equivalent difference. Children will be able to estimate answers to additions and subtractions, check their strategies and apply knowledge to solve addition and subtraction problems.

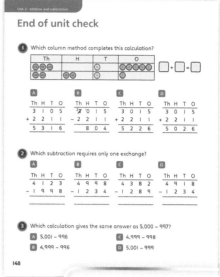

**PUPIL TEXTBOOK 4A** PAGE 148

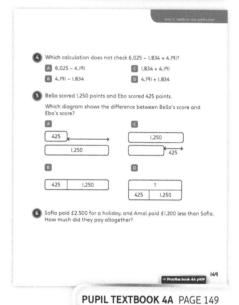

**PUPIL TEXTBOOK 4A** PAGE 149

| Q | A | WRONG ANSWERS AND MISCONCEPTIONS | STRENGTHENING UNDERSTANDING |
|---|---|---|---|
| 1 | C | A suggests that children have misread the place value grid. B is a subtraction rather than an addition. D suggests that children think that $0 + 2 = 0$. | Give practical support with place value to strengthen understanding. Using place value grids may help. |
| 2 | D | A indicates children are insecure with identifying exchanges and B that they do not understand the term. C suggests children have not noticed that the exchange from the tens will mean an exchange from the hundreds is needed. | For question 4, run an intervention in which children check answers using the inverse operation. |
| 3 | B | Any other answer suggests that children do not understand equivalent difference. | |
| 4 | B | A suggests children have misunderstood the calculation. C or D suggest that children do not know how to check an answer using the inverse operation. | Challenge children to match additions, subtractions and word problems with representations such as the bar model. |
| 5 | A | C suggests that children do not understand how to use a comparison bar model to represent the given information. B and D suggest that children do not understand what 'difference' means. | |
| 6 | 3,800 | Children might have calculated £2,500 – £1,200 and then not worked out the total. | Display the key vocabulary of the unit in your classroom. |

## My journal

WAYS OF WORKING  Independent thinking

ANSWERS AND COMMENTARY

Question **1**

Children should be able to use their knowledge of rounding to estimate an answer and find out which number is greater than 6,800. They should be able to work this out mentally, without using the column method.

To complete the first calculation, children will need to use the inverse operation to work out the missing number. 8,634 – 1,849 = 6,785.

To complete the second calculation, children will need to calculate 9,000 – 2,026. They may realise that equivalent difference is a good method here: 8,999 – 2,025 = 6,974.

Question **2**

Jamilla scores 4,875 – 3,823 = 1,052.

The difference between Aki's score and Lee's score is 8,699 – 4,875 = 3,824.

The difference between Aki's score and Jamilla's score is 4,875 – 1,052 = 3,823.

Aki's score is closer to Jamilla's score because 3,823 < 3,824.

Look for children using diagrams such as bar models to explain their answer and then using column subtraction to work out the differences.

## Power check

WAYS OF WORKING  Independent thinking

ASK

• *What visual representations and models helped you in this unit?*
• *What do you know now that you did not know at the start of the unit?*
• *What new words have you learnt and what do they mean?*

## Power puzzle

WAYS OF WORKING  Pair work or small groups

IN FOCUS  Use this **Power puzzle** to assess children's problem-solving skills. Can they explain their methods or any strategies that they used?

ANSWERS AND COMMENTARY

Puzzle A: cloud = 1,750      star = 1,250

Puzzle B: heart = 1,050      star = 150      cloud = 1,800      triangle = 600

If children can solve these puzzles, it means they can interpret problems well and use learnt strategies to find a solution. Listen to the explanations of their strategies to check that they have not just guessed a number, but have used reasoning and logic. Encourage children to deepen their understanding by creating their own similar puzzle.

## After the unit ⏸

• Which children need further support and how will you provide this support?
• Are children ready for the next unit (Measure – perimeter)? How will you link this unit to finding perimeter?

**PUPIL PRACTICE BOOK 4A** PAGE 109

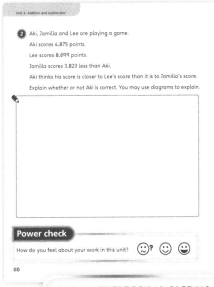

**PUPIL PRACTICE BOOK 4A** PAGE 110

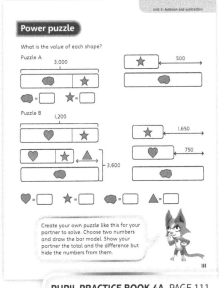

**PUPIL PRACTICE BOOK 4A** PAGE 111

**Strengthen** and **Deepen** activities for this unit can be found in the *Power Maths* online subscription.

# Unit 4
## Measure – perimeter

**Mastery Expert tip!** "When I taught this unit, I wanted to provide children with opportunities to experience the concepts outside of the classroom. For example, when considering metres and kilometres in Lesson 1, we set up a relay race where 10 children ran 100 m each, to help visualise what a kilometre looks and feels like!"

**Don't forget to watch the Unit 4 video!**

## WHY THIS UNIT IS IMPORTANT

This unit develops children's knowledge of units of measurement by introducing the kilometre and using its equivalence to express distances in kilometres and metres. Converting is a transferable skill and can be applied when moving between other units of measurement (for example, between litres and millilitres).

Children will then be introduced to the concept of perimeter as the distance around a 2D shape. They will begin by considering squares and rectangles drawn on squared paper and then progress to work with rectilinear shapes where the side measurements are labelled. The unit provides valuable opportunities for children to develop problem-solving skills, including working backwards to derive dimensions of rectangles when the perimeter is given and using reasoning to find perimeters when not all sides are labelled.

## WHERE THIS UNIT FITS

→ Unit 3: Addition and subtraction
→ **Unit 4: Measure – perimeter**
→ Unit 5: Multiplication and division (1)

This unit builds on the concept of 2D shapes, in particular children's understanding of the properties of squares and rectangles. It also applies children's prior knowledge of measurement in practical contexts.

Before they start this unit, it is expected that children:
• understand the relationship between cm and m
• understand simple properties of squares and rectangles
• can measure accurately using a ruler.

## ASSESSING MASTERY

Children who have mastered this unit will understand that 1 km equals 1,000 m and will be able to use this equivalence to convert lengths given in one unit of measurement to the other. They will understand the concept of a shape's perimeter and will be able to confidently find this for squares, rectangles and other rectilinear shapes. Children will be able to use their knowledge to find solutions involving perimeter, including where there are missing measurements.

| COMMON MISCONCEPTIONS | STRENGTHENING UNDERSTANDING | GOING DEEPER |
|---|---|---|
| Children may work out the perimeter by counting the number of squares in a border around a shape, rather than counting the edges of the squares that make up the shape. | Provide children with opportunities to use non-standard units of measurement (new pencils, counting sticks, paper clips) to make rectilinear shapes out of them. | Challenge children to prove the answers to perimeter-based problems. For example, can they prove that the perimeter of a given rectilinear L shape will be the same as that of a rectangle? |
| Children may think that every side of a rectilinear shape needs to be labelled with a measurement before they can calculate its perimeter. | Using non-standard units will embed the concept of perimeter whilst keeping its measurement simple (children just need to count the objects they have used). | Encourage children to use concrete methods of supporting their reasoning. For example, they could cut lengths of string to form the perimeter of an L shape and then rearrange them to show that they are equal to the perimeter of a rectangle. |

## WAYS OF WORKING

Use these pages to introduce the unit focus to children. You can use the characters to explore different ways of working too.

## STRUCTURES AND REPRESENTATIONS

**Number line:** Modelling with double number lines, showing kilometres and metres, helps children to see the equivalence of measurements in different units.

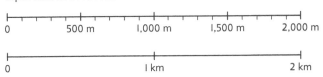

**Bar model:** This model helps children to see that the perimeter of a shape is the total of its side lengths. Children also work with bar models to represent perimeter-based problems, for example working out one dimension of a rectangle, given a perimeter and the other dimension.

| 5 m | 8 m | 5 m | 8 m |
|-----|-----|-----|-----|

5 + 8 + 5 + 8 = 26

## KEY LANGUAGE

There is some key language that children will need to know as part of the learning in this unit:

→ kilometres, metres, centimetres

→ convert, equivalent to

→ perimeter, distance, around

→ total

→ length, width

→ square, rectangle, rectilinear shape

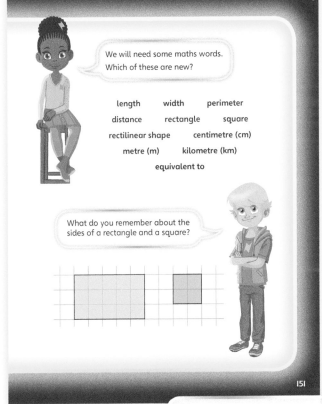

**Unit 4**
**Measure – perimeter**

In this unit we will …
⚡ Convert between kilometres and metres
⚡ Find perimeters of shapes
⚡ Work out missing lengths
⚡ Find solutions involving perimeter

Do you remember how to measure length using squares? How long is this line?

150

**PUPIL TEXTBOOK 4A** PAGE 150

We will need some maths words. Which of these are new?

length    width    perimeter

distance    rectangle    square

rectilinear shape    centimetre (cm)

metre (m)    kilometre (km)

equivalent to

What do you remember about the sides of a rectangle and a square?

151

**PUPIL TEXTBOOK 4A** PAGE 151

# Kilometres

## Learning focus

In this lesson, children will be introduced to the concept of a kilometre. They will extend their knowledge of converting between measurements to include converting between km and m.

## Small steps

→ Previous step: Problem solving – addition and subtraction (4)
→ **This step: Kilometres**
→ Next step: Perimeter of a rectangle (1)

## NATIONAL CURRICULUM LINKS

**Year 4 Measurement**

Convert between different units of measure (for example, kilometre to metre; hour to minute).

## ASSESSING MASTERY

Children can express 1 km in metres. Children can confidently convert measurements given in kilometres (including  km) into metres and vice versa.

## COMMON MISCONCEPTIONS

Children may think that the relationship between metres and kilometres follows on from centimetres and metres and that there are 100 m in 1 km. Ask:
• *How many metres are in a kilometre? Why do you think this? What does 'kilo' mean?* (1,000)

Children may identify visual links between kilometres and metres and think that conversion is about inserting or removing zeros at the end of a measurement. This may lead to incorrect answers so it is better to think about place value. Ask:
• *What method are you using to change kilometres into metres? What about changing from metres to kilometres?*

## STRENGTHENING UNDERSTANDING

To strengthen understanding, draw two parallel number lines of the same length showing just 5 km and 5,000 m, with no other marks. Ensure children understand that the number lines show the same distance but in different units. Ask them to point to 3 km on the top number line, then to move their finger straight down to the mark on the second number line. When they can confidently move between whole numbers of km and 1,000 m, move on to number lines with intermediate tick marks.

## GOING DEEPER

Ask children to investigate distance tables that show distances between cities in kilometres. Challenge them to convert part of the table so the distances are expressed in metres. Extend the activity to include world facts (such as the longest rivers) where children create conversion questions based on these distances.

## KEY LANGUAGE

**In lesson:** metre (m), kilometre (km), distance, **equivalent to**

**Other language to be used by teacher:** length, convert, equal to

## STRUCTURES AND REPRESENTATIONS

number line, bar model

## RESOURCES

**Optional:** metre sticks, distance tables

 In the eTextbook of this lesson, you will find interactive links to a selection of teaching tools.

## Before you teach

• Are there additional misconceptions that you should consider, based on children's prior work with measures?
• How might you adapt the lesson to link it to your locality and so consolidate children's understanding of 1 kilometre?

## Discover

### Kilometres

#### Discover

**WAYS OF WORKING** Pair work

**ASK**

- Question **1** a): *What units are used to measure the distances shown on the sign?*
- Question **1** b): *Where will you put the kilometres? How many metres will you need to match this amount?*

**IN FOCUS** Ensure children use the picture to identify that 1 (km) can be described as equalling 1,000 (m) because the numbers are referring to different units of measurement. Ask children to give other examples of different numbers that equal each other because one unit is smaller than the other (for example, 1 m = 100 cm).

**PRACTICAL TIPS** Use metre sticks to revise the concept of 1 metre and to help children visualise the distance they might travel if they were to measure 1,000 of them in a row.

**ANSWERS**

Question **1** a): The station is 2,000 m away.

Question **1** b): Bar model completed correctly to show
2 km = 2,000 m:

| 2 km | | |
|---|---|---|
| 1 km | 1 km | 1 km |
| 1,000 m | 1,000 m | 1,000 m |

**1** a) How many metres away is the station?

   b) Complete a bar model to show your answer.

152

**PUPIL TEXTBOOK 4A** PAGE 152

## Share

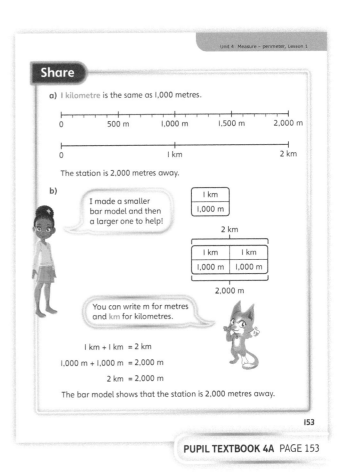

**WAYS OF WORKING** Whole class teacher led

**ASK**

- Question **1** a): *What do you notice about the two number lines? What is the same? What is different?*
- Question **1** a): *How can you use the number lines to show what 1 kilometre is worth? What about 2 kilometres?*
- Question **1** a): *How far is 500 metres, in kilometres?*

**IN FOCUS** The intervals marked on the metres line in question **1** a) help children to visualise the equivalence of 1,000 metres and 1 kilometre. The bar models in question **1** b) show the same information in a way that some children might find easier to visualise. The calculations show how you write these equivalents mathematically.

153

**PUPIL TEXTBOOK 4A** PAGE 153

## Think together

Think together

Unit 4: Measure – perimeter, Lesson 1

**WAYS OF WORKING** Whole class teacher led (I do, We do, You do)

**ASK**

- Question **1**: *How could you ask the question differently? What does each bar model show? Show how you could use the second bar model to find the answer.*
- Question **2**: *What makes this question harder than question **1**? How can you use the number lines to represent half a kilometre? Are there any other fractions you can change to metres? What needs to be done to complete the bar model?*

**IN FOCUS** The double number line in question **2** has been included as a way of modelling the various parts of a kilometre (primarily $\frac{1}{2}$, but it can also be used to find $\frac{1}{4}$ in questions **3** and **4**). Ensure children are able to combine this with their knowledge of whole kilometres to find distances that include a whole number and a fraction.

**STRENGTHEN** In question **2**, if children are finding it challenging to work out fractions of kilometres, encourage them to first draw out the double number line and label each interval. It may help to extend the lines up to $6\frac{1}{2}$ km so that children can read the answer off directly.

**DEEPEN** In question **4**, ask children how they might find the fraction part of each distance. Encourage them to use the double number line shown in question **2** to help. Ensure that they understand how to combine the whole number equivalent with the fractional equivalent to find the overall distance in metres.

**ASSESSMENT CHECKPOINT** Use questions **2**, **3** and **4** to assess whether children can convert between kilometres and metres. Look for clear explanations of how they are using number lines and bar models to represent their conversions.

**ANSWERS**

Question **1**: 4,000

The beach is 4,000 metres away.

Question **2**: $\frac{1}{2}$ km is the same as 500 m.

6 km is equivalent to 6,000 m.

So the nearest town is 6,500 m away.

Question **3**: a) 4,000 m = 4 km

b) 4,100 m = 4 km 100 m

c) 4,500 m = 4 km 500 m = $4\frac{1}{2}$ km

d) 4,250 m = 4 km 250 m = $4\frac{1}{4}$ km

Question **4**: Little Bampton 3,000 m

Battley 750 m

Kingsbridge 7,500 m

Southwell 1,250 m

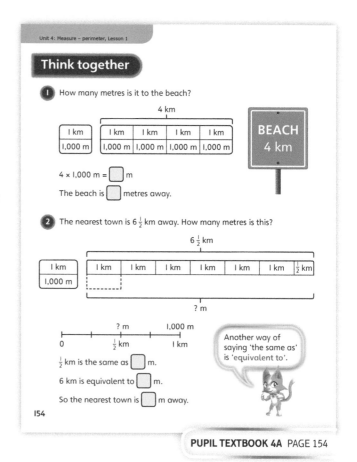

PUPIL TEXTBOOK 4A PAGE 154

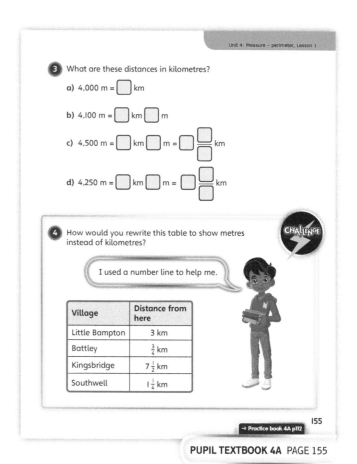

PUPIL TEXTBOOK 4A PAGE 155

## Practice

**WAYS OF WORKING** Independent thinking

**IN FOCUS** Questions **1** and **2** scaffold children's understanding of the equivalence of kilometres and metres through the use of bar models and double number lines, respectively. The number lines are particularly useful when converting between simple fractions of kilometres and metres.

**STRENGTHEN** For children finding it difficult to convert one unit into the other, get them to make their own bar models out of pieces of coloured card. They could write 1 km on the front of each piece and 1,000 m on the back. Having formed a bar model that matches their known information, they could turn all the cards over to find the answer. They could also make cards for simple fractions ($\frac{1}{2}$ and $\frac{1}{4}$) of a kilometre.

**DEEPEN** Question **6** challenges children to explore fractions of kilometres. Ask how they could use a double number line to show the fractions. Ask whether they can work out the fractions without using a number line. Encourage children to consider how they might use known fractions of distances to help find unknown fractions (for example, using $\frac{1}{10}$ to work out $\frac{2}{10}$).

**THINK DIFFERENTLY** Question **5** asks children to use their knowledge of converting between kilometres and metres when solving visual problems. Use the question to develop children's fluency when moving between the units of measurement. Ask them to trace a route that is 5 km long, or 7 km long. Challenge them to work out the longest route from A to B that doesn't use any links twice.

**ASSESSMENT CHECKPOINT** Use questions **2** and **3** to assess whether children can convert kilometres into metres and vice versa. Children should be able to directly convert between kilometres and metres without the provision of scaffolding. They should also recognise fractional equivalences of km and m ($\frac{1}{2}$ km = 500 m) and be able to apply this knowledge.

**ANSWERS** Answers for the **Practice** part of the lesson appear in the separate **Practice and Reflect answer guide**.

## Reflect

**WAYS OF WORKING** Independent thinking

**IN FOCUS** This question provides an opportunity to check children's methodology. Check that they are converting all the amounts to the same units: either km, in which case they will need to include a fraction, or m, which will mean multiplying 1 by 1,000. Check that they give their answer in the units that they have chosen to use.

**ASSESSMENT CHECKPOINT** Look for children who understand that all the amounts must be given in the same units in order to do a calculation.

**ANSWERS** Answers for the **Reflect** part of the lesson appear in the separate **Practice and Reflect answer guide**.

### After the lesson ⏸

- How many opportunities were given for children to explain their reasoning in this lesson?
- How confident are children when converting between kilometres and metres?

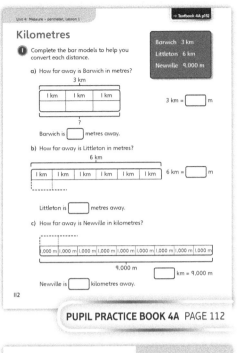

**PUPIL PRACTICE BOOK 4A** PAGE 112

**PUPIL PRACTICE BOOK 4A** PAGE 113

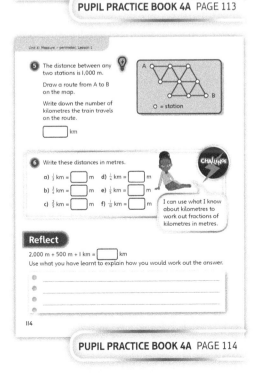

**PUPIL PRACTICE BOOK 4A** PAGE 114

# Perimeter of a rectangle ①

## Learning focus

In this lesson, children will be introduced to the concept of perimeter. They will initially find this by counting square lengths around rectangles and squares.

## Small steps

→ Previous step: Kilometres
→ **This step: Perimeter of a rectangle (1)**
→ Next step: Perimeter of a rectangle (2)

### NATIONAL CURRICULUM LINKS

**Year 4 Measurement**

Measure and calculate the perimeter of a rectilinear figure (including squares) in centimetres and metres.

### ASSESSING MASTERY

Children can identify perimeter as the distance around a shape. Children show confidence when finding perimeter by counting square lengths (i.e. the number of sides of a square along each side of a rectangle).

### COMMON MISCONCEPTIONS

Children may count the number of squares that fit around a rectangle, including around the corners, rather than the number of squares along each side. Emphasise that it is the length of a side of a square that you are using to count. Ask:
• *What do you do to find the perimeter of this rectangle? What length are we counting in?*

Children may think that they need to be given all four measurements in order to calculate the perimeter. They may not make connections between what they can see and the properties of rectilinear shapes. Ask:
• *What do you need to know to work out the perimeter of this rectangle? This side of this rectangle is 4 cm – how long is the opposite side? The side of this square is 4 cm, so what are the other sides?*

### STRENGTHENING UNDERSTANDING

To strengthen understanding, provide children with rectangles drawn on squared paper. Remind them that these shapes have right angles. Ask them to use different coloured pencils to draw along each side of the rectangle. Ensure that they understand that the perimeter is all the coloured lines added together. Ask how many squares long each coloured line is.

Mark out simple squares and rectangles on floor tiles so children can work on a large scale.

### GOING DEEPER

Extend learning by giving children parts of rectangles (for example, a rectangle cut out of squared paper with a part torn off). Ask how they can still work out what the perimeter of the rectangle was.

### KEY LANGUAGE

**In lesson:** width, length, around, square, distance, **perimeter**, represents, rectangle, metres, centimetres

**Other language to be used by teacher:** square length

### STRUCTURES AND REPRESENTATIONS

bar model

### RESOURCES

**Optional:** coloured pencils, squared paper, floor/carpet tiles, string

 In the eTextbook of this lesson, you will find interactive links to a selection of teaching tools.

## Before you teach

• Are there areas of your school or classroom already split into squares (for example, floor tiles) that you could use for a practical exploration of perimeter?
• How will you ensure children understand the concept of perimeter as being the distance around a shape? What will you use as examples?

## Discover

**WAYS OF WORKING** Pair work

**ASK**

- Question ❶ a): *How would you know you've gone once around a swimming pool?*
- Question ❶ a): *In the picture, who do you think is going to swim the furthest? How do you know? Who will swim the shortest distance?*

**IN FOCUS** Question ❶ a) introduces the concept of the distance around the outside of a shape. When looking at the picture, ask children to use a finger to trace the swimming routes of all three children. Ensure that children understand that three distances are being represented: the length, the width and the distance around the outside. Check that they recognise this final distance as being the distance around the outside until they arrive back at the starting point.

**PRACTICAL TIPS** Use non-standard units of measurement (thin objects with a consistent length, like paper clips) for children to model the rectangle being shown (10 units by 4 units). Children can then organise the objects to form one long distance to represent the total distance around the shape.

**ANSWERS**

Question ❶ a): Amelia will swim 28 m.

Question ❶ b): The distance around the square swimming pool is 16 m.

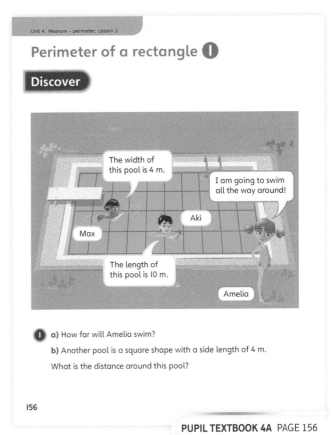

**PUPIL TEXTBOOK 4A** PAGE 156

## Share

**WAYS OF WORKING** Whole class teacher led

**ASK**

- Question ❶ a): *Where is the length of this shape? Where is its width? Where is its perimeter?*
- Question ❶ a): *How have the sticks been used to show the distance around the rectangle? Why do you think the sticks have been placed in a line to make a bar model? What does this show?*
- Question ❶ a): *What do you notice about the different methods that are shown? How are they the same? How are they different?*

**IN FOCUS** Question ❶ a) rearranges sticks from around the rectangle to match a bar model. Give children opportunities to model both the initial rectangle and the bar model using non-standard units. In particular, ensure they can see that by taking the units from around the shape and lining them up they are finding the whole distance around the shape. This is an important conceptual step.

Work through Astrid's alternative way of working out the perimeter. Ensure that children understand why they need to double the length and the width.

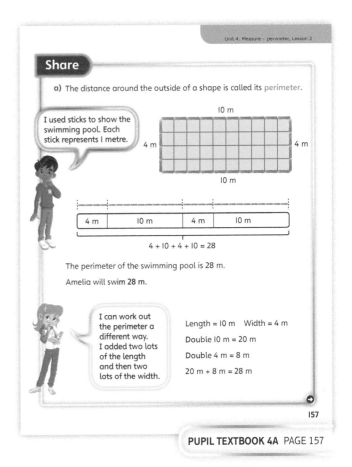

**PUPIL TEXTBOOK 4A** PAGE 157

# Think together

Whole class teacher led (I do, We do, You do)

**ASK**

- Question **1**: *How can you find the perimeter of this shape? What are you using to help?*
- Question **2**: *What do you know about the side lengths of a rectangle?*
- Question **2**: *Do you need to count along every side of the shape? Why not?*

**IN FOCUS** Question **2** leads children from counting non-standard units (sticks) around the outside of a shape to looking at the square lengths that surround the shape. As the shape has each side length labelled, ask children whether they need to count the number of square lengths along each side or whether there is another way to find the perimeter.

**STRENGTHEN** If children are finding it difficult to make the connection between the dimensions of a shape and its perimeter, give them opportunities to create their own bar models. For example, get them to use string or cut narrow strips from squared paper to represent the side lengths of a rectangle. These could then be lined up end to end, to show the total distance around the shape. Ask children what they notice about the numbers involved. Ensure they understand that a rectangle will have two sides of one length and two sides of another.

**DEEPEN** Question **3** deepens children's understanding of perimeter, encouraging them to use reasoning to consider the least amount of information they need to work out the perimeter of a rectangle or square. Give children examples of rectangles where they are only given two measurements, to put their answer into practice.

**ASSESSMENT CHECKPOINT** In questions **1** and **2**, assess whether children can use given visual information (units of measurement placed around a shape, or square lengths) to calculate perimeter. Check that children can describe or point out the perimeter of a shape.

**ANSWERS**

Question **1**: $5 + 8 + 5 + 8 = 26$

The perimeter is 26 m.

Question **2**: $5 + 3 + 5 + 3 = 16$

The perimeter is 16 cm.

Question **3** a): Only two measurements are needed to find the perimeter of a rectangle: the length and the width. The perimeter can be found by doubling the length and doubling the width and adding them together.

Question **3** b): Double the length and double the width. Then add them together.

Only one measurement is needed to find the perimeter of a square because all the sides are the same length.

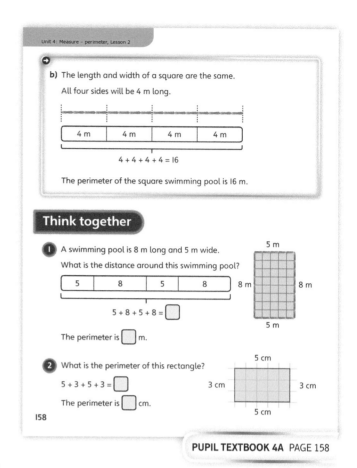

**PUPIL TEXTBOOK 4A** PAGE 158

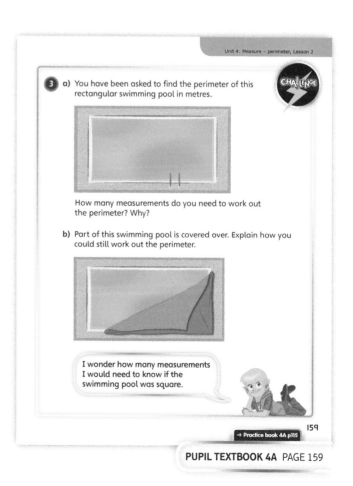

**PUPIL TEXTBOOK 4A** PAGE 159

## Practice

**WAYS OF WORKING** Independent thinking

**IN FOCUS** Question **2** provides a structured removal of scaffolding, from a rectangle on squared paper where four sides are labelled through to a rectangle with only two sides labelled and no square grid. It may be useful to observe which, if any, of the four representations children need to practise further.

**STRENGTHEN** In question **3** children are presented with different scenarios and asked which depict the concept of perimeter. For children who are less confident in identifying perimeter, provide additional scenarios and ask them to consider whether or not they show the distance around a shape. Provide equipment for children to model each scenario for themselves and show the perimeter being portrayed.

**DEEPEN** Question **4** explores the possibility of squares that have a side length of more than 1. Ask children how this will affect their answer. Support children's understanding by getting them to consider what the perimeter would be if each square had a length of 1 m, then ask what it would be if each one had a length of 5 m. What do they notice about their results?

Question **6** encourages children to explore how the perimeter of a square varies according to its side length. Children should notice that the perimeter goes up by 4 each time you add 1 to the side. Ask them to predict what the perimeter of a square rug with an 11 m side would be.

**THINK DIFFERENTLY** Question **5** is a comparison question. Encourage children to sketch and label a rectangle and trace both boys' routes with a finger. Ask children to say each measurement as they travel along the rectangle's length or width and then use this information to help calculate the answers and compare them.

**ASSESSMENT CHECKPOINT** Use question **2** to assess whether children can find the perimeters of rectangles and squares. Check whether they recognise the minimum number of side lengths they need. Children should be able to use the vocabulary of perimeter, length and width in the correct contexts.

**ANSWERS** Answers for the **Practice** part of the lesson appear in the separate **Practice and Reflect answer guide**.

## Reflect

**WAYS OF WORKING** Pair work

**IN FOCUS** Give children time to discuss in pairs how they might find the perimeter of the classroom, using the given dimensions. Encourage them to give their answer in clearly defined steps.

**ASSESSMENT CHECKPOINT** Look for children who are able to describe how to calculate perimeter using the two dimensions provided. Observe the different methods that children suggest – whether they add all four sides or whether they double the two sides they are given before adding.

**ANSWERS** Answers for the **Reflect** part of the lesson appear in the separate **Practice and Reflect answer guide**.

### After the lesson

- What concepts do you think children found most difficult to understand in this lesson?
- How will you address these concepts in the next lesson to consolidate children's understanding?

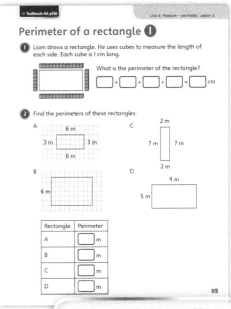

**PUPIL PRACTICE BOOK 4A** PAGE 115

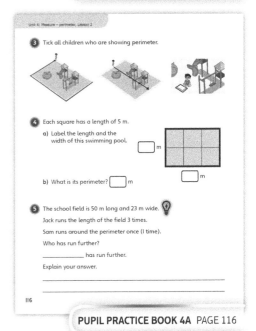

**PUPIL PRACTICE BOOK 4A** PAGE 116

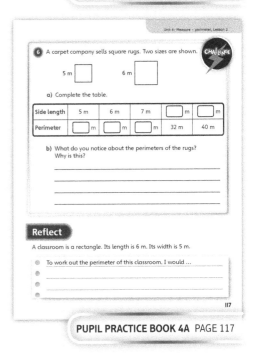

**PUPIL PRACTICE BOOK 4A** PAGE 117

# Perimeter of a rectangle ❷

## Learning focus

In this lesson, children will develop their understanding of the perimeter of rectangles and squares through problem solving. They will find the width of a rectangle given the perimeter and the length.

## Small steps

→ Previous step: Perimeter of a rectangle (1)
→ **This step: Perimeter of a rectangle (2)**
→ Next step: Perimeter of rectilinear shapes (1)

### NATIONAL CURRICULUM LINKS

**Year 4 Measurement**

Measure and calculate the perimeter of a rectilinear figure (including squares) in centimetres and metres.

### ASSESSING MASTERY

Children can build links between perimeter and the dimensions of a rectangle or square. They can use their knowledge of perimeter to find solutions, for example finding the width given the perimeter and length.

### COMMON MISCONCEPTIONS

Children may think that the perimeter of a shape is simply the total of its length and width. So, when working backwards from a given perimeter, they simply think of two measurements that equal this amount. Ask:
• *Can you trace the perimeter of this shape with your finger? How many sides of a rectangle or square make up its perimeter?*
• *How many measurements do you add together to find a rectangle's perimeter?*

### STRENGTHENING UNDERSTANDING

To strengthen understanding, tell children a perimeter length in whole centimetres. Explain that they must design a rectangular race track that is this long. Compare children's answers. If space allows, use metres instead of centimetres and get them to mark out their rectangles in chalk on the playground.

### GOING DEEPER

Extend understanding by giving groups of children different lengths of string (multiples of 4 cm, e.g. 48 cm). Ask what the perimeter would be if they cut the string into four pieces (two pairs with equal lengths) to make a rectangle. Challenge children to predict the longest rectangle they could make , and the shortest (a square). Encourage children to anticipate the outcome before they model it.

### KEY LANGUAGE

**In lesson:** perimeter, length, width, distance, around, rectangle, square, centimetres, metres, represents

### STRUCTURES AND REPRESENTATIONS

bar model

### RESOURCES

**Optional:** string, rulers, paper clips, strips of paper, chalk, art straws, new pencils

In the eTextbook of this lesson, you will find interactive links to a selection of teaching tools.

## Before you teach

• Is there an open area in your school, ideally paving, where children can measure large rectangles on the ground?
• What different question types will you use to encourage children to apply their knowledge of perimeter when finding solutions?

# Discover

**WAYS OF WORKING**  Pair work

**ASK**

- Question ❶ a): *Where is the perimeter in this picture? How do you find it? Explain a quick way to add to find the perimeter.*
- Question ❶ a): *How do you think you will be able to tell from your answer if the lights are too short? How might you be able to tell if they are just the right length?*
- Question ❶ b): *What information do you know? How do you use this to find the width?*

**IN FOCUS**  Question ❶ a) makes a link between a perimeter and a length that goes around it. When looking at this picture, ensure that children understand how a length of lights can be altered to fit around a mirror, by bending it into two lengths and two widths. At this point, it will be useful to check that children make the connection between two lots of length plus two lots of width equalling the perimeter.

**PRACTICAL TIPS**  Ask children to use thin objects with a consistent length, like art straws or new pencils, to model the mirror being described. Ask what distance each straw or pencil represents. Children can then organise the objects to form one continuous length to represent the total distance around the mirror.

**ANSWERS**

Question ❶ a): The perimeter is 140 cm. The coloured lights are 120 cm long, so they will not fit around the mirror.

Question ❶ b): The width of the mirror is 20 cm.

# Share

**WAYS OF WORKING**  Whole class teacher led

**ASK**

- Question ❶ a): *Why has Flo decided to use each pencil to represent 10 cm?*
- Question ❶ a): *Why do you think only one length and one width have been labelled?*
- Question ❶ a): *Why do you think the pencils have been placed in a line to make a bar model? What does this show? Explain a quick way of adding the numbers to find the perimeter.*
- Question ❶ b): *Why do you need to use a subtraction? Why do you need to divide by 2?*

**IN FOCUS**  Question ❶ a) reinforces the use of bar modelling to represent perimeter. Ask children what they notice about the numbers on the different bars. Address the misconception that perimeter is found just by adding length and width (the two shown measurements). Give different dimensions for different mirrors and ask children to suggest what the bar models might look like in those cases.

**PUPIL TEXTBOOK 4A** PAGE 160

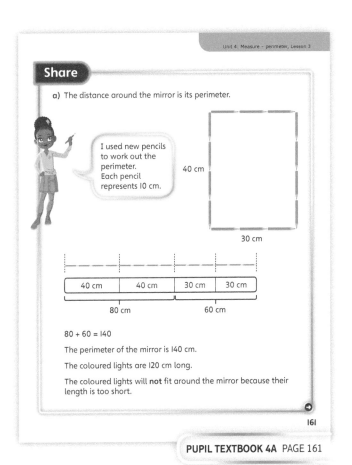

**PUPIL TEXTBOOK 4A** PAGE 161

## Think together

**WAYS OF WORKING** Whole class teacher led (I do, We do, You do)

**ASK**

- Question **1**: *How do you find the perimeter of the garden? What does the bar model show? Explain a quick method to find the total perimeter.*
- Question **2**: *What information do you know about the mirror? What do you not know? Draw a picture to show this. How do you use what you know about the perimeter to find the width?*

**IN FOCUS** Question **1** helps children to build conceptual connections between the dimensions of a rectangle and its perimeter. Children should recognise that the adding of two lengths and two widths equals the perimeter. This foundation will assist them in question **2**, when they are given the total (the perimeter) and one of the dimensions, and asked for the second dimension.

**STRENGTHEN** If children are unsure how to work backwards from the perimeter to find one of the dimensions in question **2**, make a bar model from strips of paper, to scale. Children could then subtract two lengths of 45 cm and recognise that the remainder needs to be split into two to get two widths. To check their answer, children could form the rectangle from the four strips.

**DEEPEN** To deepen children's understanding of the relationship between perimeter, length and width, ask them to alter the given height in question **2** so that it describes a different rectangle with a perimeter of 160 cm. For example, a height of 50 cm would mean the width is now 30 cm. Encourage children to explain how they would find the solution.

**ASSESSMENT CHECKPOINT** Use questions **1** and **2** to assess whether children can find a perimeter and work from a perimeter to find the dimensions of a rectangle. They should be able to calculate the perimeter of a rectangle when given one labelled length and one labelled width.

**ANSWERS**

Question **1**: $7 + 7 + 4 + 4 = 22$

The perimeter is 22 m.

The lanterns are 22 m long.

Question **2**: $45 + 45 = 90$

$160 - 90 = 70$

$70 ÷ 2 = 35$

The width of the mirror is 35 cm.

Question **3**: Ash is right. All the sides of a square are the same length, so the perimeter is four times the same amount. But the method would not work with other rectangles because the sides are two different lengths.

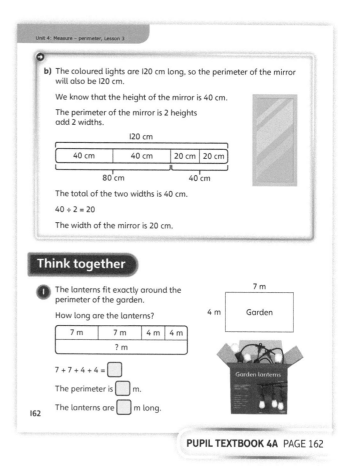

PUPIL TEXTBOOK 4A PAGE 162

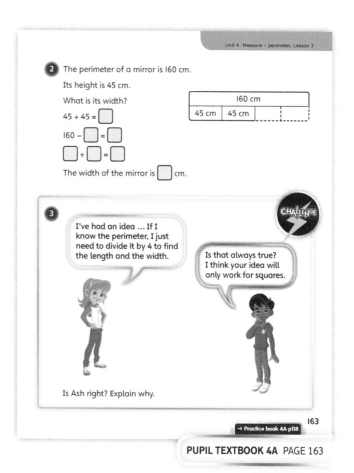

PUPIL TEXTBOOK 4A PAGE 163

194

## Practice

**WAYS OF WORKING** Independent thinking

**IN FOCUS** Question ❶ provides children with a context similar to those that they have already experienced. The problem is represented by a bar model and children should be able to complete this visual representation before using it to help find the solution.

**STRENGTHEN** Encourage children to use manipulatives to support their working, particularly in questions ❷ and ❹. They could use paper clips (or similar) to form the outline of the rectangles described in the questions.

**DEEPEN** In question ❹, children explore the different possibilities for rectangles that have a perimeter of 16 cm. Although they should identify a numerical pattern in the different lengths, ask children what they also notice about the length and width together (the length plus the width always equals 8, or half of the perimeter). Challenge children to see whether this pattern holds when they include fractions (for example, making the width $1\frac{1}{2}$ cm).

In question ❺, children look at the perimeter of two squares put together. Encourage children to work out how they could find the perimeter of the rectangle from the perimeters of the two squares and the length of the common side. Extend this to three or more squares put together. (If there are $n$ squares with side length $a$, this would be: $2an + 2a$.)

**ASSESSMENT CHECKPOINT** In questions ❶ to ❹, assess whether children can confidently find solutions related to the perimeters of squares and rectangles. In questions ❸ and ❹, they should be able to work backwards from a shape's perimeter and one of its dimensions to derive the other. They should confidently use efficient strategies to calculate perimeter.

**ANSWERS** Answers for the **Practice** part of the lesson appear in the separate **Practice and Reflect answer guide**.

## Reflect

**WAYS OF WORKING** Independent thinking

**IN FOCUS** The question asks children to explain their method for finding the length of a rectangle given its perimeter and width. Give children opportunities to share their answers with a partner. Ask them whether their methods were the same and, if not, what the differences are. Ensure that the focus is on children's strategies, rather than solely on the answer.

**ASSESSMENT CHECKPOINT** Check that children understand that, in order to find the length of the rectangle, they should first subtract two lots of 1 cm (or double 1 cm and subtract 2 cm), then divide the remainder by 2. Look for children who can do this without needing the support of a bar model.

**ANSWERS** Answers for the **Reflect** part of the lesson appear in the separate **Practice and Reflect answer guide**.

## After the lesson ⏸

- Can children find a side of a rectangle, given the perimeter and another side?
- How will you build on this skill in the following lessons when working with more complex rectilinear shapes?

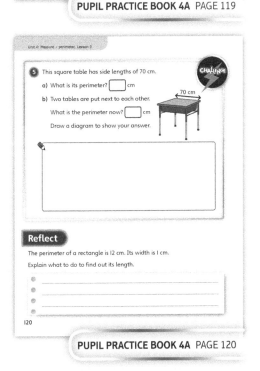

PUPIL PRACTICE BOOK 4A PAGE 118

PUPIL PRACTICE BOOK 4A PAGE 119

PUPIL PRACTICE BOOK 4A PAGE 120

# Perimeter of rectilinear shapes ❶

## Learning focus

In this lesson, children will extend their understanding of perimeter to include rectilinear shapes that are not rectangles or squares.

## Small steps

→ Previous step: Perimeter of a rectangle (2)
→ **This step: Perimeter of rectilinear shapes (1)**
→ Next step: Perimeter of rectilinear shapes (2)

## NATIONAL CURRICULUM LINKS

**Year 4 Measurement**

Measure and calculate the perimeter of a rectilinear figure (including squares) in centimetres and metres.

## ASSESSING MASTERY

Children can apply their knowledge of perimeter to rectilinear shapes that are not rectangles or squares, finding the perimeter by counting square lengths or totalling sides where all side measurements are given.

## COMMON MISCONCEPTIONS

Children may think that the perimeter of a non-rectangular rectilinear shape is less than that of a rectangle with the same total length and width because it has a smaller area (making an incorrect connection between a shape's area and its perimeter). Show children an L shape and a rectangle with the same perimeter. Ask:
• *Which shape has the greater perimeter? How do you know?*

Children have previously only worked with squares and rectangles and so may try to split the rectilinear shape into squares and rectangles or may be unsure how to deal with it as it has more than four sides. Ask:
• *How many sides does this shape have? How do you work out its perimeter?*

## STRENGTHENING UNDERSTANDING

Give children time to explore the concept of rectilinear shapes before beginning the lesson. Give them squares and rectangles made out of cardboard and get them to place two or three together in order to make a composite shape. Talk about the different shapes they make and point out the straight lines and right angles.

## GOING DEEPER

Challenge children to find rectilinear shapes around the classroom and calculate their perimeter by measuring them in centimetres and then finding the total of their sides.

## KEY LANGUAGE

**In lesson:** rectilinear shape, rectangle, perimeter, square length, metres, centimetres, represents

## STRUCTURES AND REPRESENTATIONS

bar model

## RESOURCES

**Mandatory:** squared paper

**Optional:** cardboard squares and rectangles, paper strips

 In the eTextbook of this lesson, you will find interactive links to a selection of teaching tools.

## Before you teach ⏸

• How many rectilinear shapes in your school environment could be used as examples during the lesson?
• What links will you make to models that children have already used?

## Discover

**WAYS OF WORKING** Pair work

**ASK**

- Question ① a): *What shape is the flower bed? How do you know? Compare this shape with a rectangle or square. What is the same? What is different?*
- Question ① a): *Trace the perimeter of the shape with your finger. How do you find out how long it is?*

**IN FOCUS** When looking at this picture with children, encourage them to describe how it depicts perimeter. How do they know where the perimeter starts and ends? Ask them to trace the perimeter of the shape and to give the shape a name. Provide squared paper for them to explore ideas about how to find the perimeter.

**PRACTICAL TIPS** Mark out a large L shape on the ground and ask children to model the problem, for example by pushing a broom around the shape's sides or perhaps by hopping around it. Vary the number of sides in the rectilinear shape to embed several concepts:

- the variable number of sides in a rectilinear shape
- the fact that rectilinear shapes consist of straight lines and right angles
- what needs to be considered when finding the perimeter of a rectilinear shape.

**ANSWERS**

Question ① a): The perimeter of the flower bed is 24 m.

Question ① b) L shape correctly drawn on squared paper (1 square to represent 1 metre) with a total perimeter of 24 square lengths.

## Share

**WAYS OF WORKING** Whole class teacher led

**ASK**

- Question ① a): *What is a rectilinear shape? What is a right angle? List any other shapes that have some sides that meet at right angles.*
- Question ① a): *Where have all the numbers in the bar model come from?*
- Question ① a): *What is the same about the two methods that are shown? What is different?*

**IN FOCUS** Two methods are shown here and it is important that children are given hands-on opportunities to use them both. Question ① a) (modelling the shape using objects, then counting them in a bar model) gives children a concrete strategy to use. Question ① b) (counting square lengths) is pictorial.

Provide paper clips to model the shape. Ask children what they notice about the sides of the shape. Give children opportunities to experience the shape in different ways (for example, by walking around a marked-out L shape on the playground).

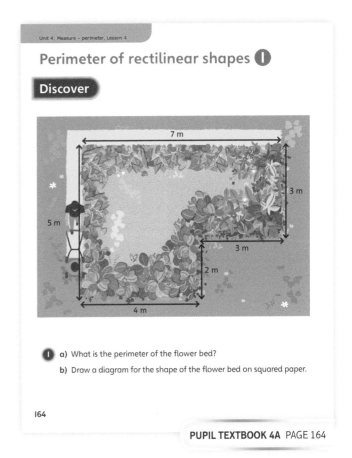

### Perimeter of rectilinear shapes ①

**Discover**

① a) What is the perimeter of the flower bed?

b) Draw a diagram for the shape of the flower bed on squared paper.

164

**PUPIL TEXTBOOK 4A** PAGE 164

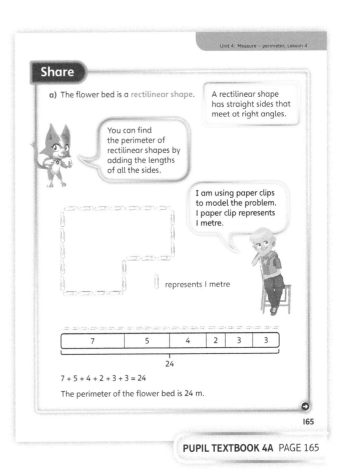

**Share**

a) The flower bed is a rectilinear shape.

A rectilinear shape has straight sides that meet at right angles.

You can find the perimeter of rectilinear shapes by adding the lengths of all the sides.

I am using paper clips to model the problem. I paper clip represents I metre.

represents I metre

| 7 | 5 | 4 | 2 | 3 | 3 |

24

7 + 5 + 4 + 2 + 3 + 3 = 24

The perimeter of the flower bed is 24 m.

165

**PUPIL TEXTBOOK 4A** PAGE 165

# Think together

**WAYS OF WORKING** Whole class teacher led (I do, We do, You do)

**ASK**

- Question **1**: *How many sides does this shape have? What would you call it? How do you know what the length of each side is? What helps you?*
- Question **2**: *Identify any quick ways to add the side lengths together.*

**IN FOCUS** It is important that, when presented with the rectilinear shape in question **1**, children look at the side lengths of the squares around it rather than considering the squares themselves. Ask them to trace the perimeter using their finger.

In question **2**, children may assume the perimeter will be the same as that of a rectangle with sides of 12 and 8 m. Make sure they understand that not all rectilinear shapes simply have the same perimeter as a rectangle with the same total length and width. While this is true in some cases, it is not true of shapes that go 'in and out again'.

**STRENGTHEN** When working on question **2**, provide children with squared paper on which to draw the shape. Children could use coloured pencils to show that they have counted each square length. Ask what 1 square length on their diagram represents.

**DEEPEN** In question **3**, after children have shown that they can see that the perimeter of both shapes is the same, challenge them to explore other rectilinear polygons that have the same perimeter as the shapes in the question (36 cm). Ask children what they notice about the side lengths of the shapes they make.

**ASSESSMENT CHECKPOINT** Use questions **1**, **2** and **3** to assess whether children can count square lengths or total given sides to find the perimeter of a rectilinear shape. Children should support their reasoning using representations used in previous lessons.

**ANSWERS**

Question **1**: 8 + 5 + 2 + 3 + 6 + 2 = 26

The perimeter of the flower bed is 26 m.

Question **2**: The perimeter of the lawn is 52 m.

Question **3**: Zac is correct. Explanations may vary. The total length and total width are the same in both rectilinear shapes. The area and number of sides do not make a difference.

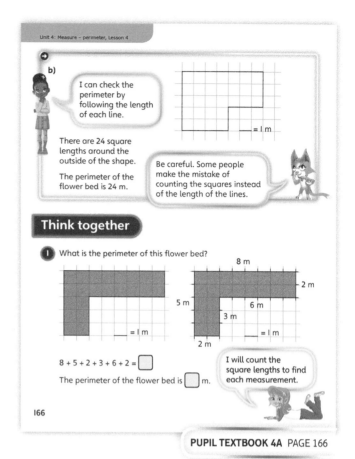

**PUPIL TEXTBOOK 4A** PAGE 166

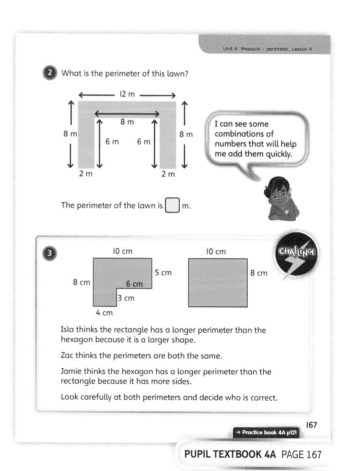

**PUPIL TEXTBOOK 4A** PAGE 167

## Practice

**WAYS OF WORKING** Independent thinking

**IN FOCUS** In question ❶, ensure children understand why the edging pieces cannot overlap at the corners. In question ❷ discuss that shapes c) and d) go 'in and then out again' so children will need to be careful with these. In question ❸, help children to see that the shape has been started bottom left and is being drawn clockwise. In question ❹ the measures start from top left. Make clear that there is no general rule about where to start measuring a shape.

**STRENGTHEN** Use question ❶ as an opportunity for children to use concrete resources to model the shape. If strips of paper are used, children could label each strip length as '1 m' before making the shape. After completing the shape, they could place the strips in a line to show the total distance of the perimeter (similar to a bar model).

**DEEPEN** Question ❺ asks children to draw a more complex rectilinear shape. Ensure they use only horizontal and vertical lines (i.e. not diagonal) and find the perimeter by carefully counting square lengths around their shape. How hard this is will depend upon where they put their chimneys. Ask: *What happens at the corners? Are there some squares you don't count? Will you use some more than once?* Remind them that what they are counting is the side lengths, not the squares themselves, so some squares will be useful two or three times, and others not at all.

**THINK DIFFERENTLY** Finding the perimeter in question ❸ a) is straightforward (adding the given dimensions). However, question ❸ b) introduces a new concept – visualising a shape purely from a list of dimensions. Children will need to consider which side each measurement relates to. Ask what they notice about the lengths of the sides and whether they can spot any links between them. This aspect will be addressed in the next lesson.

**ASSESSMENT CHECKPOINT** Question ❷ assesses whether children can confidently find perimeters of rectilinear shapes when counting square lengths. They should recognise that there are many rectilinear shapes, and be able to explain how to find the perimeter of any of them.

**ANSWERS** Answers for the **Practice** part of the lesson appear in the separate **Practice and Reflect answer guide**.

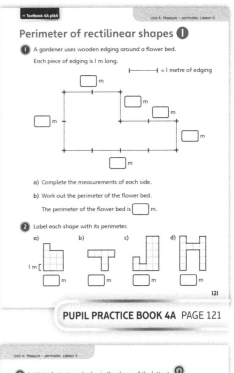

**PUPIL PRACTICE BOOK 4A** PAGE 121

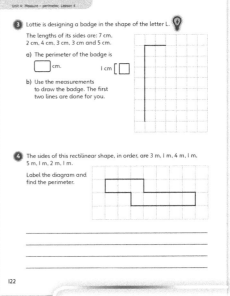

**PUPIL PRACTICE BOOK 4A** PAGE 122

## Reflect

**WAYS OF WORKING** Independent thinking

**IN FOCUS** This addresses the misconception that children need to count the number of squares around a shape (rather than the number of square lengths). Having the squares labelled in this way (to show Amy's working) may lead some children to presume that they are being shown how to find the answer. Children can talk through in pairs why this is incorrect.

**ASSESSMENT CHECKPOINT** Look for children who reason that the squares on the convex corners should not be used, because you are counting side lengths of squares around the edge of the shape.

**ANSWERS** Answers for the **Reflect** part of the lesson appear in the separate **Practice and Reflect answer guide**.

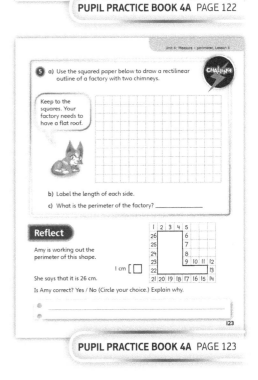

**PUPIL PRACTICE BOOK 4A** PAGE 123

## After the lesson ⏸

- Are children confident when asked to find the perimeter of a variety of rectilinear shapes?
- Have they had the chance to use a variety of methods to do this?

# Perimeter of rectilinear shapes ❷

## Learning focus

In this lesson, children will develop their understanding of perimeter by considering the perimeter of rectilinear shapes where not all the side measurements are given.

## Small steps

→ Previous step: Perimeter of rectilinear shapes (1)
→ **This step: Perimeter of rectilinear shapes (2)**
→ Next step: Multiplying by multiples of 10 and 100

### NATIONAL CURRICULUM LINKS

**Year 4 Measurement**

Measure and calculate the perimeter of a rectilinear figure (including squares) in centimetres and metres.

### ASSESSING MASTERY

Children can solve problems involving the perimeters of rectilinear shapes, particularly those where not all the side measurements are provided. Children can derive unknown measurements and then find the overall perimeter.

### COMMON MISCONCEPTIONS

Children may think that they are unable to find a shape's perimeter unless they are given every side length. Show them an unlabelled rectilinear shape and ask:

• *Which side lengths do you need to be told to work out the perimeter? What is the least number of side lengths you need to know? How do you work out the sides that you are not given?*

### STRENGTHENING UNDERSTANDING

Get children to consider who might need to work out the perimeter of rectilinear shapes, for example someone building a wall around an area. Ask children to give further examples.

Make part of an L shape with cardboard strips on the floor. Ask what is needed to complete the shape. Share suggestions about how long the missing side should be. Encourage children to consider what they would do if they had no ruler. Build connections between this simple problem and children's real-life examples.

### GOING DEEPER

Give children opportunities to explore more open-ended problems: *An L shape's longest sides are 20 m and 16 m. What could its perimeter be? Is there one shape or lots of possible shapes? Is there one perimeter or lots of possible perimeters? Why?* Children could make conceptual connections from the abstract back to the concrete/pictorial by modelling their solution(s) in different ways.

### KEY LANGUAGE

**In lesson:** rectilinear shape, perimeter, length, metres, centimetres

**Other language to be used by teacher:** rectangle, square

### STRUCTURES AND REPRESENTATIONS

rectilinear shapes (including on squared paper)

### RESOURCES

**Mandatory:** squared paper

**Optional:** cardboard strips, straws, sticks

 In the eTextbook of this lesson, you will find interactive links to a selection of teaching tools.

## Before you teach

• Are children confident with finding the perimeter of rectilinear shapes from the previous lesson?
• What models will you use to help children identify the connections between rectilinear shapes and rectangles/squares with the same perimeter?

## Discover

**WAYS OF WORKING** Pair work

**ASK**

- Question ① a): *What shape is the penguin pond? How do you know? Compare this shape with the shapes you worked with in the last lesson. What is the same? What is different?*
- Question ① a): *Which piece of fencing are you trying to find? Identify anything on the diagram that might help you.*

**IN FOCUS** These questions develop the work children did in the previous lesson on perimeter of rectilinear shapes. Encourage children to link their learning from the previous lesson to the image. Talk about the similarities and differences between this shape and those they have worked with before.

**PRACTICAL TIPS** Provide opportunities for children to see the links between rectilinear shapes and rectangles/squares. For example, make an L shape out of cardboard strips with a missing side and ask children to identify which strips they could move to create the missing side. Ensure that the conversation is always about the sides of the shapes (perimeter) rather than the size (area).

**ANSWERS**

Question ① a): Side A is 9 m long.

Question ① b): The perimeter of the pond is 32 m.

### Perimeter of rectilinear shapes ❷

**Discover**

① a) How long is side A?

b) What is the perimeter of the penguin pond?

168

**PUPIL TEXTBOOK 4A** PAGE 168

## Share

**WAYS OF WORKING** Whole class teacher led

**ASK**

- Question ① a): *The diagram does not show the measurement of side A, but what information **do** you know? How do you use it to help?*
- Question ① a): *What is the same and what is different about the two methods that are shown?*

**IN FOCUS** Both questions ① a) and b) are designed to get children to make connections between the different side lengths of a rectilinear shape. Spend time discussing the equivalences in the side lengths – in particular, the fact that the two vertical lengths of 3 m and 6 m are equal to the entire length of A. Give children opportunities to move side lengths around (for example, by representing them using straws) so that the shorter sides are placed next to the longer side and children can see that they are equal.

**Share**

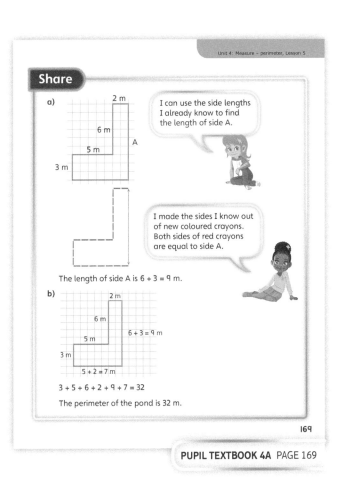

169

**PUPIL TEXTBOOK 4A** PAGE 169

# Think together

**WAYS OF WORKING** Whole class teacher led (I do, We do, You do)

**ASK**

- Question **1**: *To find the perimeter, which sides of this shape do you need to find? You have all the information you need to be able to find the missing lengths. How will you use it to help? Identify any pairs of sides that total the same length.*
- Question **3**: *What do you notice about the measurements you are given? Explain a quick way to add them together.*

**IN FOCUS** Question **1** aims to get children to use reasoning to find solutions to perimeter-related problems. Children need to consider the shape's vertical and horizontal sides separately. In order to derive each missing side length, they need to identify pairs of sides that are equal to each other and work from there.

**STRENGTHEN** For question **2**, provide children with squared paper on which to draw the shape. Check that children understand what 1 square length represents. Encourage them to find the missing side length by counting squares. Then make the link between adding sides together and counting the squares.

**DEEPEN** In question **3**, ask children to explain whether they need to know all the individual side lengths to find the perimeter. Suggest that they copy the shape and colour sides that are the same. Then ask them to colour three sides that add up to the long side. Challenge children to label the shape another way, so that the perimeter is still calculable. Ask children for the fewest number of side lengths they need to know to work out the perimeter.

**ASSESSMENT CHECKPOINT** Use questions **1** and **2** to assess whether children can use given lengths to derive unknown sides and so find the perimeter of rectilinear shapes. Children should support their reasoning using representations used in previous lessons.

**ANSWERS**

Question **1** a): 9 – 3 = 6

Side A is 6 m long.

Question **1** b): 12 – 8 = 4

Side B is 4 m long.

Question **1** c): 12 + 9 + 8 + 6 + 4 + 3 = 42

The perimeter is 42 m.

Question **2**: Side A = 9 + 8 = 17 m

Perimeter = 20 + 9 + 10 + 8 + 10 + 17 = 74

The perimeter of the pen is 74 m.

Question **3**: Perimeter = 12 + 12 + 4 + 4 + 20 + 20 = 72

The perimeter is 72 cm.

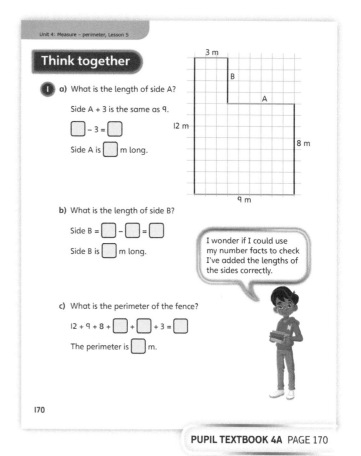

**PUPIL TEXTBOOK 4A** PAGE 170

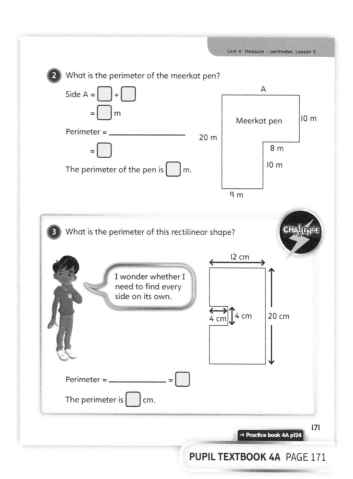

**PUPIL TEXTBOOK 4A** PAGE 171

## Practice

**WAYS OF WORKING** Independent thinking

**IN FOCUS** Question ❹ provides an opportunity for children to consider whether they are able to still find the perimeter of a rectilinear shape, even though they are only given five of the eight side lengths. Encourage them to build on the previous questions to use the given dimensions to derive the missing ones. Point to a known side length and ask which side that measurement is useful for working out. Ask whether any sides have the same length.

**STRENGTHEN** Provide children with concrete resources (such as straws or sticks) to model the partly completed shape in question ❶. Ask how they know what the missing length will be. Provide squared paper to move from the concrete to the pictorial. Ensure that children make links between the two known vertical sides and the one unknown vertical side (for example, by moving their straws or by using colours in the diagram to show the equivalence).

**DEEPEN** Question ❺ challenges children further as they need to consider units of measurement (the junctions) that are no longer worth 1 – now they are equivalent to 20 m. Ensure children are aware that the route makes a rectilinear shape. Establish how many road sections/blocks the taxi needs to drive in total. Ask children to rephrase the question in a different way. For example, *Draw two rectilinear shapes that have a perimeter of eight road sections.*

**ASSESSMENT CHECKPOINT** Use question ❸ to assess whether children can confidently find the perimeter of a rectilinear shape when not all of the side lengths are provided. They should be able to use known measurements to find unknown ones and be able to confidently explain how they derived them.

**ANSWERS** Answers for the **Practice** part of the lesson appear in the separate **Practice and Reflect answer guide**.

## Reflect

**WAYS OF WORKING** Independent thinking

**IN FOCUS** An interesting way of approaching this **Reflect** activity might be to get children to design their rectilinear shape and then erase some of the side lengths, one by one. Ensure that they can justify how the missing lengths can be worked out.

**ASSESSMENT CHECKPOINT** Look for children who understand that, to find the perimeter of a rectilinear shape, they do not need to be told all of its sides – however, they do need to be able to derive all of its sides. Observe those children who use reasoning to explain how they expect their peers to find the solutions to the task they have set.

**ANSWERS** Answers for the **Reflect** part of the lesson appear in the separate **Practice and Reflect answer guide**.

### After the lesson ⏸

- Are children confident when asked to find the perimeter of a rectilinear shape where they are not provided with all of the side lengths?
- Do you feel that children are able to confidently use the 'This is what I know and this is how I am going to use it to help' approach? What other concepts will this be useful for?

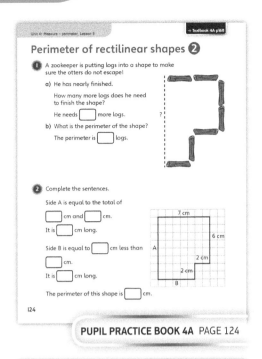

**PUPIL PRACTICE BOOK 4A** PAGE 124

**PUPIL PRACTICE BOOK 4A** PAGE 125

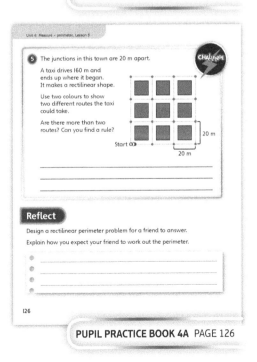

**PUPIL PRACTICE BOOK 4A** PAGE 126

# End of unit check

> Don't forget the *Power Maths* unit assessment grid on p26.

**WAYS OF WORKING** Group work – adult led

**IN FOCUS** Questions **2** to **5** assess children's ability to find perimeter, starting with length and width of a rectangle, then using properties of squares and rectangles and finally considering a non-rectangular rectilinear shape.

- Question **6** assesses children's ability to apply their knowledge of perimeter in a problem-solving context.
- Question **7** is a SATS-style perimeter question where children demonstrate their problem-solving ability.

**ANSWERS AND COMMENTARY** Children who have mastered the concepts in this unit will use their knowledge of the equivalence of 1 km and 1,000 m to convert between these units. They will be able to explain how to find a shape's perimeter and will find this for squares, rectangles and other rectilinear shapes. They will use their knowledge to find solutions involving perimeter, including where there are missing measurements.

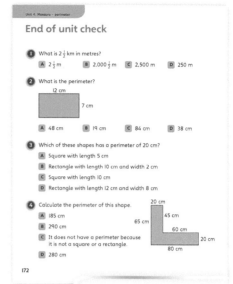

**PUPIL TEXTBOOK 4A** PAGE 172

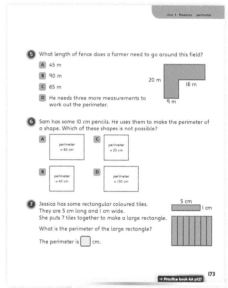

**PUPIL TEXTBOOK 4A** PAGE 173

| Q | A | WRONG ANSWERS AND MISCONCEPTIONS | STRENGTHENING UNDERSTANDING |
|---|---|---|---|
| 1 | C | D suggests children think there are 100 m in a km. A and B suggest problems with the concept of $\frac{1}{2}$ km. | Where a shape is not represented on squared paper, it may still be useful to encourage children to draw each shape in this way. This will remind them that rectilinear shapes must have right angles, and will allow them to consider how to derive any unlabelled measurements and make links between known measurements and those they do not know.

Prior to working out the perimeter, ask children to write on shapes to show measurements that are not labelled. |
| 2 | D | B means the child has not taken two of each side length. C means they have multiplied the measurements. | |
| 3 | A | B, C or D suggests that the child cannot apply the properties of squares and rectangles to find perimeter. | |
| 4 | B | A suggests that the child has only used the outside measurements of the L, not those in the cut-away part. | |
| 5 | C | A or B suggests guessing what to do with the given numbers. D indicates that the child knows how to find perimeter, but not how to derive missing measurements. | |
| 6 | C | A, B or D suggest children have not divided 20 by 4. | |
| 7 | 24 cm | Some children may multiply the perimeter of 1 tile by 7. | |

# My journal

**WAYS OF WORKING** Independent thinking

**ANSWERS AND COMMENTARY**

Each shape should be drawn on squared paper and should have a perimeter of 18 cm.

Possible shapes are:
- rectangles with lengths and widths of 7 cm and 2 cm, 6 cm and 3 cm or 5 cm and 4 cm
- other rectilinear shapes with perimeters of 18 cm.

Possible explanations include:
- The total distance around the shape is 18 cm.
- The perimeter is all the sides added together.
- Length + width + length + width = 18 cm

If children are struggling to explain how to decide on their measurements, say:
- *Draw a rectangle. Does it have a perimeter of 18 cm? If not, how could you adjust it so that it does? If it does, how could you change it so that it still has a perimeter of 18 cm?*
- *Is it possible to draw a square with a perimeter of 18 cm? How do you know?*

# Power check

**WAYS OF WORKING** Independent thinking

**ASK**

- *What did you know about perimeter before you began this unit?*
- *What do you know now?*
- *Do you think you would be able to find the perimeter of your maths book on your own?*

# Power play

**WAYS OF WORKING** Pair work or small groups

**IN FOCUS** Use this **Power play** to see whether children can work in pairs to investigate the different rectilinear shapes that are possible using given perimeters. Children should be able to explore different possibilities, especially by moving sticks themselves.

**ANSWERS AND COMMENTARY** Children should only be able to make rectilinear shapes with even perimeters (12 sticks, 10 sticks, 8 sticks and so on). This is because, where whole numbers are used, the sum of the units travelled in each dimension (including negative numbers) will always be a multiple of 2 ('there and back again').

If children can do the **Power play**, it shows that they understand the way that a shape's length and width work together to give its perimeter.

---

## After the unit ⏸

- Are there everyday opportunities for children to measure perimeter in meaningful contexts? For example, What length of paper edging is needed to go around a noticeboard? What length of fencing is needed to fence the school vegetable patch? What length of wrapping paper is needed to wrap a present?
- Can children research their own facts based on perimeter? For example, *We would need to walk the perimeter of our school x times to complete a marathon.*

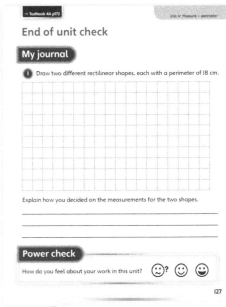

### End of unit check

**My journal**

1. Draw two different rectilinear shapes, each with a perimeter of 18 cm.

Explain how you decided on the measurements for the two shapes.

**Power check**

How do you feel about your work in this unit? 😕? 🙂 😀

127

**PUPIL PRACTICE BOOK 4A** PAGE 127

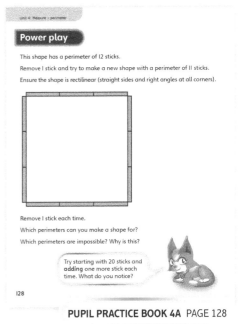

Unit 4: Measure – perimeter

**Power play**

This shape has a perimeter of 12 sticks.

Remove 1 stick and try to make a new shape with a perimeter of 11 sticks.

Ensure the shape is rectilinear (straight sides and right angles at all corners).

Remove 1 stick each time.

Which perimeters can you make a shape for?

Which perimeters are impossible? Why is this?

Try starting with 20 sticks and adding one more stick each time. What do you notice?

128

**PUPIL PRACTICE BOOK 4A** PAGE 128

**Strengthen** and **Deepen** activities for this unit can be found in the *Power Maths* online subscription.

# Unit 5
## Multiplication and division ①

**Don't forget to watch the Unit 5 video!**

**Mastery Expert tip!** "This unit is a superb opportunity to encourage all children to be able to demonstrate rapid recall of times-tables. It is important to ensure that children know the multiplication facts and related division facts, but also that they are able to explain them. Children should be encouraged to use visual representations such as arrays and number lines."

## WHY THIS UNIT IS IMPORTANT

This unit is important because it focuses on learning multiplication and division facts – a core part of maths at Key Stage 2. Children explore multiplication and division, looking first at multiplying and dividing by multiples of 10 and 100, and then at multiplying and dividing by 0 and 1, the understanding of which is key to children's mastery of this unit. This unit encourages children to use visual representations to tackle multiplication and division questions, and to understand concepts such as grouping and sharing. Mastering this unit will certainly have a positive impact on other areas of mathematics such as fractions, decimals and percentages.

## WHERE THIS UNIT FITS

→ Unit 4: Measure – perimeter
→ **Unit 5: Multiplication and division (1)**
→ Unit 6: Multiplication and division (2)

This unit builds upon the previous work children have done on multiplication and subtraction from Year 3, where children learnt how to multiply by equal grouping and to divide using sharing. This unit also builds upon previous work children have done on addition and subtraction. It also develops children's reasoning skills, which they are developing throughout the year.

Before they start this unit, it is expected that children:
• know how to multiply and divide by 2, 3, 4, 5, 8 and 10
• understand related multiplication and division facts
• know how to apply their knowledge of these facts to solve problems.

## ASSESSING MASTERY

Children who have mastered this unit will be able to rapidly recall all multiplication and division facts from the 1 to 12 times-tables. They will have learnt efficient strategies and be able to use these to apply their learning in context and to finding solutions to word problems.

| COMMON MISCONCEPTIONS | STRENGTHENING UNDERSTANDING | GOING DEEPER |
|---|---|---|
| Children may think that a number multiplied or divided by 0 equals the original number. | Run intervention sessions in which children practise multiplying by 0. Show the answer visually, such as by using empty plates. | Solve some multiplication and division sentences with missing numbers. |
| Children may confuse multiplication and addition. | Give children 2 numbers to add and multiply: forming 2 different answers. | Repeat the Strengthening Understanding activity, but also ask children to discuss how the two processes are different. |
| Children may not know whether to multiply or divide when solving a problem. | Ask children to highlight key information in the word problem and draw a representation/use concrete objects to help solve it. | Children can make up their own word problems to fit a multiplication and division sentence. |

## WAYS OF WORKING

Use these pages to introduce the unit focus to children as a whole class. You can use the different characters to explore different ways of working, and to begin to discuss and develop children's reasoning skills relating to multiplication and division. Talk through the key learning points, which the characters mention, and the key vocabulary. Do children have any misconceptions? Do they understand what the vocabulary means? A classroom display showing all of the key information, particularly the times-tables, will support children throughout this unit.

## STRUCTURES AND REPRESENTATIONS

**Number line:** The number line is an effective way to represent multiplication and division. It shows the grouping clearly and helps children practise counting on or back in groups.

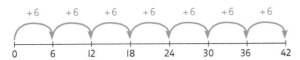

**Arrays:** Arrays visually show multiplication and division. They are particularly clear at showing commutativity, such as $2 \times 5 = 5 \times 2$.

**Ten frame:** The ten frame helps children to reinforce their knowledge of place value.

## KEY LANGUAGE

There is some key language that children will need to know as part of the learning in this unit.

→ times-table, times, times by
→ multiply (×), multiple, multiply by
→ divide (÷), divide by
→ grouping, groups of, lots of, sets of, grouped, x groups of y
→ sharing, share, equal, equally
→ number facts, number sentences, multiplication facts/sentences, division facts/sentences, fact family
→ ones (1s), tens (10s), hundreds (100s), zero (0), how many, total, method, calculation, exchange, solve, less then (<), greater than (>), added, sort, sum, recall

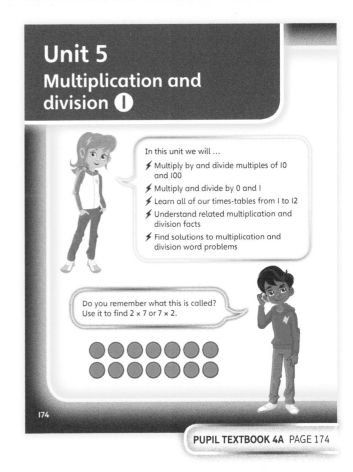

**PUPIL TEXTBOOK 4A** PAGE 174

**PUPIL TEXTBOOK 4A** PAGE 175

# Multiplying by multiples of 10 and 100

## Learning focus

In this lesson, children will learn how to multiply by multiples of 10 and 100 using known facts and place value knowledge.

## Small steps

→ Previous step: Perimeter of rectilinear shapes (2)
→ **This step: Multiplying by multiples of 10 and 100**
→ Next step: Dividing multiples of 10 and 100

### NATIONAL CURRICULUM LINKS

**Year 4 Number – Multiplication and Division**
- Recall multiplication and division facts for multiplication tables up to 12 × 12.
- Use place value, known and derived facts to multiply and divide mentally, including: multiplying by 0 and 1; dividing by 1; multiplying together three numbers.

### ASSESSING MASTERY

Children can confidently use their knowledge of place value to quickly work out the answers to multiplication questions involving multiples of 10 and 100. They have instant recall of times-table facts up to 12 × 12. Children can explain their methods clearly, spotting patterns and using reasoning to clarify why the patterns occur.

### COMMON MISCONCEPTIONS

Children may suggest that when multiplying by 10 or 100 'you just put a 0 on the end'. Ask:
- Would this work with a decimal, such as in 0.5 × 10?

Children may make place value errors. For example, 5 × 700 = 350. Ask:
- What representation might help you understand this more clearly? Could working out 5 × 70 help you?

### STRENGTHENING UNDERSTANDING

Children will need to be fluent with their times-tables to fully access this lesson. Run daily interventions to strengthen children's knowledge of these. You could use a variety of methods including chants, songs and mini-quizzes.

### GOING DEEPER

Challenge children by giving them word problems involving multiplying by multiples of 10 and 100. This will allow you to assess whether children can solve the calculations in a given context.

### KEY LANGUAGE

**In lesson:** multiply (×), multiple, multiplied, ones (1s), tens (10s), hundreds (100s), how many, total, method, calculation, number line

**Other language to be used by teacher:** times, times by, lots of, groups of

### STRUCTURES AND REPRESENTATIONS

number line

### RESOURCES

**Mandatory:** base 10 equipment

**Optional:** multiplication square, counters

 In the eTextbook of this lesson, you will find interactive links to a selection of teaching tools.

## Before you teach 🏖

- Are children secure with their times-tables?
- Can all children multiply a single digit number by 10 and 100?
- Which children will need base 10 equipment to support their understanding?

## Discover

### Multiplying by multiples of 10 and 100

**Discover**

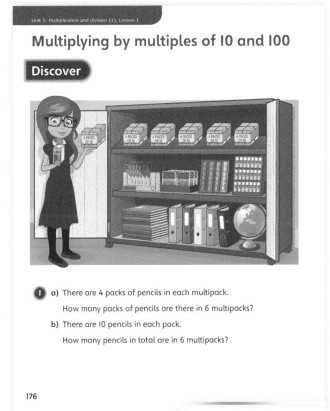

1 a) There are 4 packs of pencils in each multipack.

How many packs of pencils are there in 6 multipacks?

b) There are 10 pencils in each pack.

How many pencils in total are in 6 multipacks?

176

**WAYS OF WORKING** Pair work

**ASK**

• Question **1** a): *What method did you use?*
• Question **1** a): *Is that the only way to reach the answer?*

**IN FOCUS** Questions **1** a) and b) are great for deeper learning. Children may work out the answer and then realise that there are in fact a number of different ways to reach the answer. Children could calculate 4 × 10 = 40 then 40 × 6 = 240. Afterwards they may try 6 × 4 = 24 then 24 × 10 = 240. Promote self-discovery!

**PRACTICAL TIPS** For this activity, you may want to provide children with boxes of pencils, so they can actually see the multiplication represented in real life.

**ANSWERS**

Question **1** a): 6 × 4 = 24 packs.

There are 24 packs of pencils in 6 multipacks.

Question **1** b): 4 × 10 = 40
6 × 40 = 240

There are 240 pencils in total in 6 multipacks.

## Share

**Share**

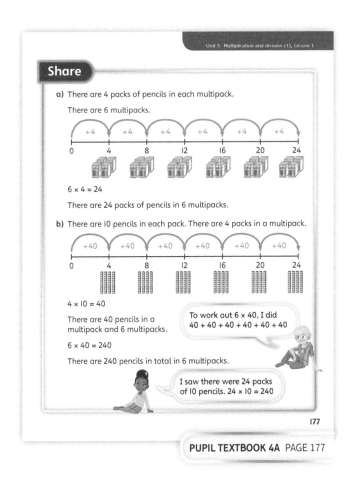

a) There are 4 packs of pencils in each multipack.

There are 6 multipacks.

6 × 4 = 24

There are 24 packs of pencils in 6 multipacks.

b) There are 10 pencils in each pack. There are 4 packs in a multipack.

4 × 10 = 40

There are 40 pencils in a multipack and 6 multipacks.

6 × 40 = 240

There are 240 pencils in total in 6 multipacks.

To work out 6 × 40, I did 40 + 40 + 40 + 40 + 40 + 40

I saw there were 24 packs of 10 pencils. 24 × 10 = 240

177

**WAYS OF WORKING** Whole class teacher led

**ASK**

• Question **1** b): *What do you notice about the 4 and 40 times-tables?*
• Question **1** b): *What other times-tables have the same pattern (6 and 60; 8 and 80)? Shall we practise these too?*

**IN FOCUS** For question **1** b) ask children to follow the number line with their finger and count in 4s (and then 40s) as a whole class. When you get to the end, count back too. This is a simple but effective way to reinforce times-tables as well as understanding of the questions.

# Think together

WAYS OF WORKING Whole class teacher led (I do, We do, You do)

**ASK**

- Question **2**: *What do we need to remember when we multiply by 100?*
- Question **3**: *Explain your methods of calculating the answers.*

**IN FOCUS** It is very important that children explain their methods in question **3**. Some children may have just spotted the pattern (0s appearing on the end of numbers), but may have not understood why this pattern exists. Use the picture to model effective reasoning: 50 is 5 tens. 7 × 5 tens = 35 tens = 350. After, children should be able to explain similar calculations, such as 6 × 30, using similar explanations.

**STRENGTHEN** Some children may need extra support with multiplying by 10 and 100. Run some intervention sessions in which they practise this. They could write down a single-digit multiplication and then find related facts, for example 3 × 4 = 12, 3 × 40 = 120, 30 × 4 = 120, 3 × 400 = 1,200, 300 × 4 = 1,200.

**DEEPEN** Provide children with some answers and ask them to think of questions that must include a multiple of 10 or 100. For instance, if 240 were the answer, children could come up with the questions 6 × 40, 60 × 4, 2 × 120, 20 × 12 and so on.

**ASSESSMENT CHECKPOINT** Question **3** will allow you to assess whether children have grasped the patterns involved with multiplying multiples of 10 and 100. Their reasoning will tell you if they have understood the mathematical thinking behind it.

**ANSWERS**

Question **1** a): 8 × 4 = 32. There are 32 packs of pencils.

Question **1** b): 8 × 40 = 320. There are 320 pencils.

Question **2** a): 3 × 5 = 15. There are 15 tubs of pins.

Question **2** b): 3 × 500 = 1,500. There are 1,500 pins.

Question **3** a): 20 is 2 tens. 6 × 2 tens = 12 tens = 120

70 is 7 tens. 4 × 7 tens = 28 tens = 280

60 is 6 tens. 4 × 6 tens = 24 tens = 240

30 is 3 tens. 9 × 3 tens = 27 tens = 270

Question **3** b): 200 is 2 hundreds. 6 × 2 hundreds = 12 hundreds = 1,200

700 is 7 hundreds. 4 × 7 hundreds = 28 hundreds = 2,800

600 is 6 hundreds. 4 × 6 hundreds = 24 hundreds = 2,400

300 is 3 hundreds. 9 × 3 hundreds = 27 hundreds = 2,700

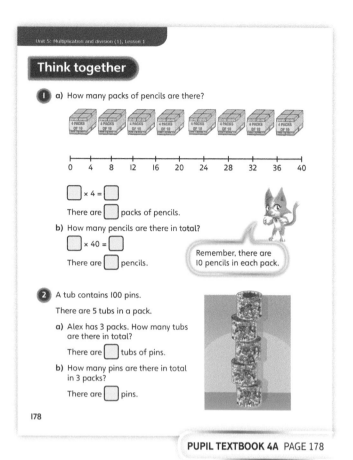

**PUPIL TEXTBOOK 4A** PAGE 178

**PUPIL TEXTBOOK 4A** PAGE 179

## Practice

**WAYS OF WORKING** Independent thinking

**IN FOCUS** Question **5** is a great exercise to reinforce understanding of place value and number patterns. Ask: *What patterns can you see?*

**STRENGTHEN** To support understanding in this lesson, ask children to look at question **4**. Ask: *Can you draw your own number lines for other calculations, for instance, 6 × 300?* You may want to run this as an intervention following the lesson.

Some children may need a multiplication square if they are not secure with their times-tables.

**DEEPEN** Question **6** will require children to think about what they have learnt in a different way. Children will have to grasp that 8 is constant in the number sentence and the 100s and 10s should be combined to find the answer: 8 × 200 + 8 × 50 + 8 × 30 + 8 × 20 = 8 × 300. You may find that you need to give similar questions for children to practise on before they have mastered this.

Set children some number sentence challenges in which calculations must be balanced. For instance, 8 × 50 = 4 × ?.

**ASSESSMENT CHECKPOINT** Can children spot patterns in the fact families? Question **6** will allow you to assess whether children have mastered the lesson.

**ANSWERS** Answers for the **Practice** part of the lesson appear in the separate **Practice and Reflect answer guide**.

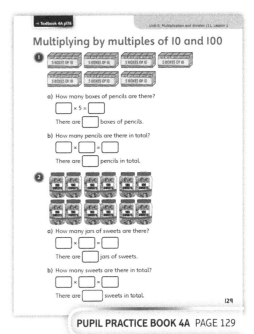

**PUPIL PRACTICE BOOK 4A** PAGE 129

**PUPIL PRACTICE BOOK 4A** PAGE 130

## Reflect

**WAYS OF WORKING** Pair work

**IN FOCUS** For this reflective exercise, remember to reinforce commutativity. Say to children that 4 × 7 also equals 28. Ask them to write the other calculations this way around as well.

**ASSESSMENT CHECKPOINT** This reflective exercise allows you to assess your class's reasoning skills. Look at the language used and whether their grasp of place value is accurate.

**ANSWERS** Answers for the **Reflect** part of the lesson appear in the separate **Practice and Reflect answer guide**.

### After the lesson ⏸

- Do any children need daily times-table practice?
- Has the key vocabulary been learnt? Would a display work well to reinforce it?

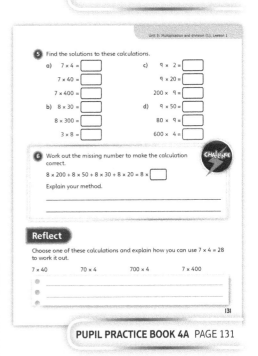

**PUPIL PRACTICE BOOK 4A** PAGE 131

# Dividing multiples of 10 and 100

## Learning focus

In this lesson, children will learn how to divide multiples of 10 and 100 using known facts and place value knowledge.

## Small steps

→ Previous step: Multiplying by multiples of 10 and 100
→ **This step: Dividing multiples of 10 and 100**
→ Next step: Multiplying by 0 and 1

## NATIONAL CURRICULUM LINKS

**Year 4 Number – Multiplication and Division**
- Recall multiplication and division facts for multiplication tables up to 12 × 12.
- Use place value, known and derived facts to multiply and divide mentally, including: multiplying by 0 and 1; dividing by 1; multiplying together three numbers.

## ASSESSING MASTERY

Children can confidently use their knowledge of times-tables and place value to quickly work out the answers to division questions involving multiples of 10 and 100. Children can spot patterns and explain their answers clearly using mathematical vocabulary.

## COMMON MISCONCEPTIONS

Children may suggest that when dividing by 10 or 100 *you just take away the 0*. Ask:
- *What would you do with a number that is not a multiple of 10, such as 44?*

Children may make place value errors. For example, 800 ÷ 4 = 2. Ask:
- *What representation might help you understand this more clearly? Can you think of a rule when working out these kinds of questions?*

## STRENGTHENING UNDERSTANDING

Children will need to be fluent with their times-tables to fully access this lesson. Run daily interventions to strengthen children's knowledge of these. You could use a variety of methods including chants, songs and mini-quizzes. Some children may need to have a multiplication square during lessons.

It is also important to ensure that all children understand the difference between grouping and sharing. Run regular interventions to strengthen children's understanding of the difference. One method would be to set children sharing and grouping exercises using resources, such as counters and base 10 equipment.

## GOING DEEPER

Challenge children by relating division to multiplication. Ask them to write the inverse of number facts. For example: the inverse of 3 × 40 = 120 is 120 ÷ 3 = 40.

You could also give children word problems involving dividing by multiples of 10 and 100. This will allow you to assess whether children can solve the calculations in a given context.

## KEY LANGUAGE

**In lesson:** divide (÷), dividing by, calculation, share, groups of, ones (1s), tens (10s), hundreds (100s), place value grid, exchange, number line, grouping, function machine

**Other language to be used by teacher:** sets of, how many, total

## STRUCTURES AND REPRESENTATIONS

number line, bar model, place value grid, function machine

## RESOURCES

**Mandatory:** base 10 equipment, place value counters

**Optional:** multiplication square, counters

In the eTextbook of this lesson, you will find interactive links to a selection of teaching tools.

## Before you teach ⏸

- Which children mastered the previous lesson?
- How can you link the previous lesson with this one?
- What links can you make between multiplication and division?

## Discover

**WAYS OF WORKING** Pair work

**ASK**

- Question ① a): *Can you explain why these cards are matched?*
- Question ① a): *How does multiplication help us with dividing?*

**IN FOCUS** In question ① b), children must think of the calculation for the missing answer. It is important to tell children that they should use the other calculations to help them find their answer, because there is a pattern.

**PRACTICAL TIPS** For this activity, it is a good idea to ask children why they have matched the cards. They may have spotted a pattern but may not be able to reason yet. Also, base 10 equipment is an effective way to represent the groups of 10 and 100.

**ANSWERS**

Question ① a): $8 ÷ 2 = 4$, $80 ÷ 2 = 40$, $800 ÷ 2 = 400$, $35 ÷ 5 = 7$, $350 ÷ 5 = 70$

Question ① b): The card with 700 does not have a calculation. The calculation could be $3,500 ÷ 5 = 700$

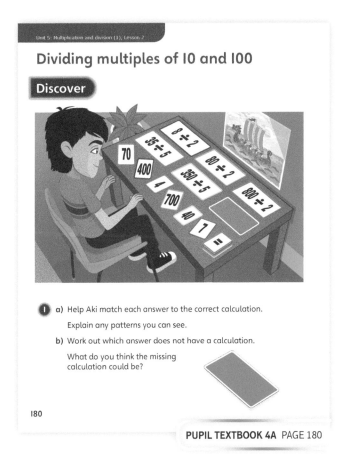

### Dividing multiples of 10 and 100

**Discover**

① a) Help Aki match each answer to the correct calculation. Explain any patterns you can see.

b) Work out which answer does not have a calculation. What do you think the missing calculation could be?

180

**PUPIL TEXTBOOK 4A** PAGE 180

## Share

**WAYS OF WORKING** Whole class teacher led

**ASK**

- Question ① a): *How do the representations help you understand the maths?*
- Question ① b): *Identify other related number facts.*

**IN FOCUS** It is important to ask children to explain the patterns they see in question ① a), as this will help them work out the missing calculation in question ① b). This is a good opportunity to revise times-tables and then make links to multiples of 10 and 100. For example, ask children to count in 5s, 50s and 500s.

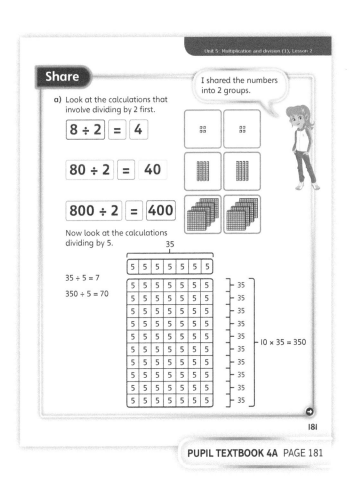

**Share**

I shared the numbers into 2 groups.

a) Look at the calculations that involve dividing by 2 first.

$8 ÷ 2 = 4$

$80 ÷ 2 = 40$

$800 ÷ 2 = 400$

Now look at the calculations dividing by 5.

$35 ÷ 5 = 7$

$350 ÷ 5 = 70$

$10 × 35 = 350$

181

**PUPIL TEXTBOOK 4A** PAGE 181

# Think together

**WAYS OF WORKING** Whole class teacher led (I do, We do, You do)

**ASK**

- Question ❷: *There are missing numbers in the calculations. How do you work these out?*
- Question ❸: *How does the place value grid help?*

**IN FOCUS** Some children may find question ❷ d) challenging as it has missing numbers in the calculations. Explain how to work them out and ask children to verbalise their thoughts when calculating.

**STRENGTHEN** Question ❶ includes a very important learning point for children to understand about dividing multiples of 10 and 100. Run some intervention with children who need it: have them completing similar problems, such as $10 \div 5$, $100 \div 5$, $1,000 \div 5$.

**DEEPEN** Question ❸ is a fantastic exercise which may need a degree of scaffolding for some children. Provide them with a part-whole model showing 50 and 35 in the parts to help with the division. Others will grasp the concept and it is a great chance to give them time to explore more fact families.

**ASSESSMENT CHECKPOINT** Question ❸ will allow you to assess whether children have grasped the patterns involved when dividing multiples of 10 and 100. Their reasoning will tell you if they have understood the mathematical thinking behind it.

Question ❷ c) is in a different order of difficulty. If children make errors, this will let you know which children have learnt the pattern, but not the understanding behind it.

**ANSWERS**

Question ❶ a): $9 \div 3 = 3$

Question ❶ b): $90 \div 3 = 30$

Question ❶ c): $900 \div 3 = 300$

Question ❷ a): $8 \div 4 = 2$     c) $320 \div 8 = 40$

          $80 \div 4 = 20$         $32 \div 8 = 4$

          $800 \div 4 = 200$      $3,200 \div 8 = 400$

Question ❷ b): $12 \div 3 = 4$     d) $60 \div 5 = 12$

          $120 \div 3 = 40$        $600 \div 5 = 120$

          $1,200 \div 3 = 400$     $6000 \div 5 = 1,200$

Question ❸ a): $85 \div 5 = 17$

Question ❸ b): $850 \div 5 = 170$

          $8,500 \div 5 = 1,700$

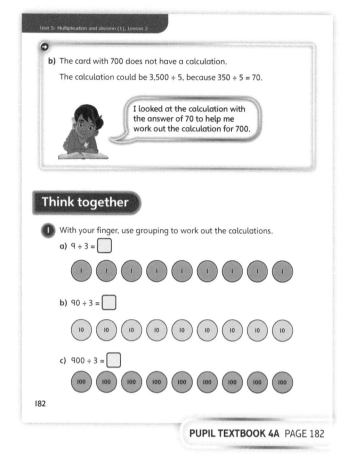

**b)** The card with 700 does not have a calculation.

The calculation could be $3,500 \div 5$, because $350 \div 5 = 70$.

> I looked at the calculation with the answer of 70 to help me work out the calculation for 700.

**Think together**

❶ With your finger, use grouping to work out the calculations.

a) $9 \div 3 = \square$

b) $90 \div 3 = \square$

c) $900 \div 3 = \square$

182

**PUPIL TEXTBOOK 4A PAGE 182**

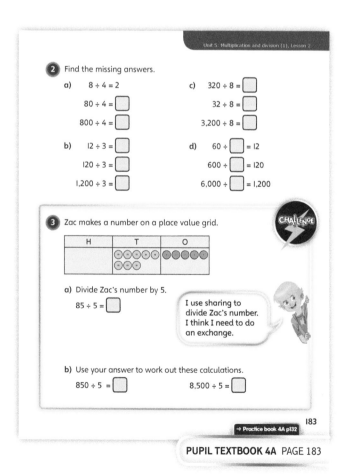

❷ Find the missing answers.

a)   $8 \div 4 = 2$      c)   $320 \div 8 = \square$

     $80 \div 4 = \square$           $32 \div 8 = \square$

     $800 \div 4 = \square$         $3,200 \div 8 = \square$

b)   $12 \div 3 = \square$     d)   $60 \div \square = 12$

     $120 \div 3 = \square$         $600 \div \square = 120$

     $1,200 \div 3 = \square$      $6,000 \div \square = 1,200$

❸ Zac makes a number on a place value grid. **CHALLENGE**

| H | T | O |
|---|---|---|

a) Divide Zac's number by 5.

$85 \div 5 = \square$

> I use sharing to divide Zac's number. I think I need to do an exchange.

b) Use your answer to work out these calculations.

$850 \div 5 = \square$      $8,500 \div 5 = \square$

183

→ Practice book 4A p132

**PUPIL TEXTBOOK 4A PAGE 183**

# Practice

**WAYS OF WORKING** Independent thinking

**IN FOCUS** Question **3** is a great activity to emphasise that an answer can have many questions. Ask children to think of other questions that would fit the answers.

**STRENGTHEN** Children's knowledge of times-tables is very important for when they are working independently during this section. Some children may need a multiplication square to complete this section. Run daily times-table practice to make sure the whole class get up to speed.

**DEEPEN** Look at question **5** and ask: *If you multiply by 8 and then divide by 2, what are you actually doing?* (What are they multiplying by?) Ask them to think of similar number machines: × 12 ÷ 4 is multiplying by 3.

**THINK DIFFERENTLY** Question **2** requires children to use a number line to show the answers. Using this representation allows children to think differently about the calculation, which will lead to mastery of the lesson. It reminds children that division is a repeated subtraction.

**ASSESSMENT CHECKPOINT** Assess children on their ability to spot patterns in numbers. Furthermore, listen to children's reasoning skills, to see if their understanding is accurate.

**ANSWERS** Answers for the **Practice** part of the lesson appear in the separate **Practice and Reflect answer guide**.

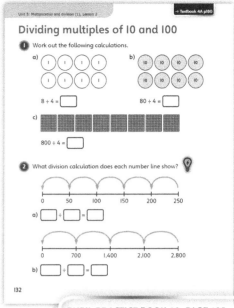

PUPIL PRACTICE BOOK 4A PAGE 132

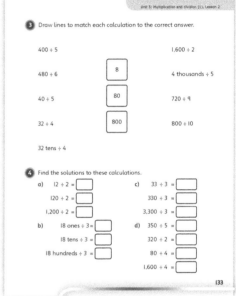

PUPIL PRACTICE BOOK 4A PAGE 133

# Reflect

**WAYS OF WORKING** Pair work

**IN FOCUS** When working with larger numbers, assure children that it does not matter how 'big' the number is; they can still follow the number patterns. Give children the number sentence '120 ÷ 4 = 30' as a support.

**ASSESSMENT CHECKPOINT** For this reflection, children should use their knowledge of times-tables and place value to work out the answer. Look for explanation such as: *I knew that 12 ÷ 4 = 3, so 1,200 ÷ 4 must be 300.*

**ANSWERS** Answers for the **Reflect** part of the lesson appear in the separate **Practice and Reflect answer guide**.

## After the lesson

- Which children need more support with division fact families?
- Do any children need daily times-table practice? How can I run this successfully?

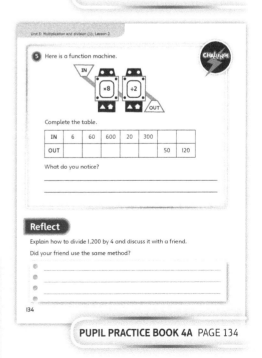

PUPIL PRACTICE BOOK 4A PAGE 134

# Multiplying by 0 and 1

## Learning focus

In this lesson, children will learn how to multiply numbers by 0 and 1, finding out the rules and using visual representations to explain answers.

## Small steps

→ Previous step: Dividing multiples of 10 and 100
→ **This step: Multiplying by 0 and 1**
→ Next step: Dividing by 1

### NATIONAL CURRICULUM LINKS

**Year 4 Number – Multiplication and Division**

Use place value, known and derived facts to multiply and divide mentally, including: multiplying by 0 and 1; dividing by 1; multiplying together three numbers.

### ASSESSING MASTERY

Children can multiply a wide range of numbers by 1 and 0; they may use visual representations effectively to support their explanations. Children can explain their answers clearly.

### COMMON MISCONCEPTIONS

Children may form the misconception that $327 \times 0 = 327$. Ask:
• If you had 327 plates of 0 biscuits, would you have any?

Children may add instead of multiply, for example they state that $327 \times 1 = 328$. Ask:
• Did you check the operation you are using?

### STRENGTHENING UNDERSTANDING

Children may need some extra practice multiplying by 0 and 1. You could run some intervention exercises in which children find solutions to real-life problems. Ask children to draw the calculations (or use counters) to strengthen their understanding.

### GOING DEEPER

Challenge children by giving them calculations with more than one missing number. For example, $240 \times ? \times ? = 240$ or $240 \times ? \times ? = 0$. Ask them if they can find more than one answer.

### KEY LANGUAGE

**In lesson:** multiply (×), zero, one, multiplication sentence, how many, groups of, grouped, in total, array, counters, function machine

**Other language to be used by teacher:** sets of, ones, (1s), tens (10s), hundreds (100s), lots of

### STRUCTURES AND REPRESENTATIONS

arrays

### RESOURCES

**Mandatory:** counters

**Optional:** base 10 equipment

 In the eTextbook of this lesson, you will find interactive links to a selection of teaching tools.

## Before you teach

• How will you explain the rules for multiplying by 1 and 0?
• Do you need to recap arrays with children at the start of the lesson?

## Discover

Unit 5: Multiplication and division (1), Lesson 3

# Multiplying by 0 and 1

## Discover

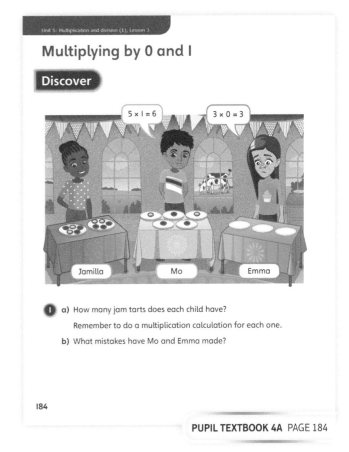

1. a) How many jam tarts does each child have?

   Remember to do a multiplication calculation for each one.

   b) What mistakes have Mo and Emma made?

184

**WAYS OF WORKING** Pair work

**ASK**

- Question 1 a): *How are the jam tarts grouped?*
- Question 1 b): *Why do you think Emma is looking a bit upset?*

**IN FOCUS** For question 1 b) children are required to think of the correct calculations in order to explain what mistakes Mo and Emma have made. It is important to tell children that they should use the calculations from question 1 a) to help them.

**PRACTICAL TIPS** It will be helpful for children to be able to represent the plates full of tarts visually. Children could use toy plates and tarts or cakes to replicate the question. Real jam tarts on plates could also be used.

**ANSWERS**

Question 1 a): There are 2 groups of 5. $2 \times 5 = 10$. Jamila has 10 tarts.

There are 5 groups of 1. $5 \times 1 = 5$. Mo has 5 tarts.

There are 3 groups of 0. $3 \times 0 = 0$. Emma has 0 tarts.

Question 1 b): Mo has added instead of multiplying. Mo says '$5 \times 1 = 6$'; but he should say '$5 \times 1 = 5$'.

Emma has made a common mistake. She thinks multiplying by 0 is the same as multiplying by 1. Any number multiplied by 0 is always 0. Emma says '$3 \times 0 = 3$'; but she should say '$3 \times 0 = 0$'.

## Share

**WAYS OF WORKING** Whole class teacher led

**ASK**

- Question 1 a): *How do the arrays help you to understand the question and answer?*
- Question 1 b): *What other mistakes could be made when multiplying by 1 or 0?*

**IN FOCUS** Question 1 b) provides a good opportunity to support children with their mathematical reasoning skills. Suggest vocabulary that children can use in their explanations, and prompt them to give the correct solution.

Unit 5: Multiplication and division (1), Lesson 3

## Share

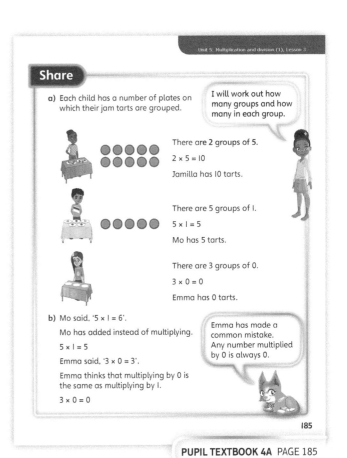

a) Each child has a number of plates on which their jam tarts are grouped.

I will work out how many groups and how many in each group.

There are 2 groups of 5.

$2 \times 5 = 10$

Jamilla has 10 tarts.

There are 5 groups of 1.

$5 \times 1 = 5$

Mo has 5 tarts.

There are 3 groups of 0.

$3 \times 0 = 0$

Emma has 0 tarts.

b) Mo said, '$5 \times 1 = 6$'.

Mo has added instead of multiplying.

$5 \times 1 = 5$

Emma said, '$3 \times 0 = 3$'.

Emma thinks that multiplying by 0 is the same as multiplying by 1.

$3 \times 0 = 0$

Emma has made a common mistake. Any number multiplied by 0 is always 0.

185

# Think together

**WAYS OF WORKING** Whole class teacher led (I do, We do, You do)

**ASK**

• Question **2** c): *Are there any counters? Why not?*
• Question **3** a): *Have you used the words 'change' and 'value' in your explanation?*

**IN FOCUS** In question **2** b) children may realise that arrays can be arranged in 2 different ways: $3 \times 1$: 3 counters vertically or 3 counters horizontally. This is a good opportunity to talk about commutativity with children, for example $3 \times 1$ is the same as $1 \times 3$.

**STRENGTHEN** Children often make mistakes when multiplying by 1 and 0. Run intervention exercises in which children can use counters and baskets to represent a range of calculations and to reinforce the fact that multiplying by 0 is always 0.

**DEEPEN** To deepen learning in this section, ask children to think of some real-life problems in which the answer to a multiplication is 0. For example: a child has just finished 3 bags of sweets, how many are left in the bags?

**ASSESSMENT CHECKPOINT** Question **2** will allow you to assess which children can represent calculations visually.

Question **3** is an excellent chance to assess children on their explanations of what happens when multiplying by 0 and 1.

**ANSWERS**

Question **1** a): $5 \times 1 = 5$

Question **1** b): $5 \times 0 = 0$

Question **2** a): ⚪⚪⚪ × ⚪⚪⚪⚪ = ⚪⚪⚪⚪
⚪⚪⚪⚪
⚪⚪⚪⚪

Question **2** b): ⚪⚪⚪ × ⚪ = ⚪⚪⚪

Question **2** c): ⚪⚪⚪ × ____ = ____

Question **2** d): ⚪⚪ × ⚪⚪⚪ = ⚪⚪⚪
⚪⚪⚪

Question **3** a): $5 \times 1 = 5$      $6 \times 1 = 6$      $10 = 10 \times 1$
$1 \times 15 = 15$      $17 \times 1 = 17$      $1 \times 183 = 183$

Mo notices that when you multiply a number by 1, it does not change in value.

Question **3** b): $5 \times 0 = 0$      $6 \times 0 = 0$      $0 = 10 \times 0$
$0 \times 15 = 0$      $17 \times 0 = 0$      $0 \times 183 = 0$

Emma notices that when you multiply a number by 0, the answer is always 0.

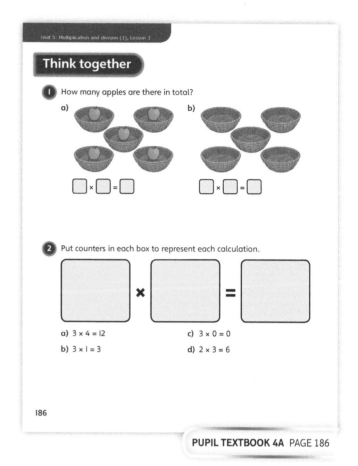

**Think together**

**1** How many apples are there in total?

a)          b)

☐ × ☐ = ☐          ☐ × ☐ = ☐

**2** Put counters in each box to represent each calculation.

☐ **×** ☐ **=** ☐

a) $3 \times 4 = 12$        c) $3 \times 0 = 0$
b) $3 \times 1 = 3$        d) $2 \times 3 = 6$

186

**PUPIL TEXTBOOK 4A** PAGE 186

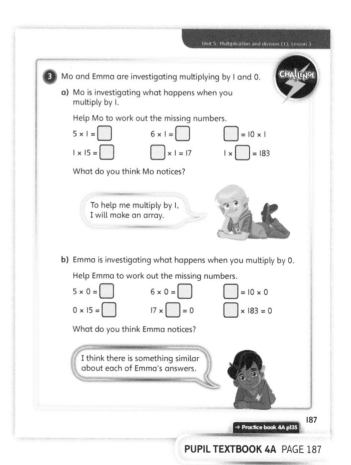

**3** Mo and Emma are investigating multiplying by 1 and 0.    **CHALLENGE**

a) Mo is investigating what happens when you multiply by 1.

Help Mo to work out the missing numbers.

$5 \times 1 = $ ☐        $6 \times 1 = $ ☐        ☐ $= 10 \times 1$

$1 \times 15 = $ ☐        ☐ $\times 1 = 17$        $1 \times$ ☐ $= 183$

What do you think Mo notices?

*To help me multiply by 1, I will make an array.*

b) Emma is investigating what happens when you multiply by 0.

Help Emma to work out the missing numbers.

$5 \times 0 = $ ☐        $6 \times 0 = $ ☐        ☐ $= 10 \times 0$

$0 \times 15 = $ ☐        $17 \times$ ☐ $= 0$        ☐ $\times 183 = 0$

What do you think Emma notices?

*I think there is something similar about each of Emma's answers.*

187

→ Practice book 4A p135

**PUPIL TEXTBOOK 4A** PAGE 187

## Practice

**WAYS OF WORKING** Independent thinking

**IN FOCUS** In question **2** c), children may put 0 × 0 = 0. It is important to explain to them that there are 4 trays with 0 cubes on, so the correct calculation is 4 × 0 = 0.

**STRENGTHEN** Sometimes children can be thrown by a larger number, like when calculating question **4** d). This is a good opportunity to show children that, even if they had 1 million multiplied by 0, the answer would still be 0.

**DEEPEN** Provide children with some more function machines, like the one in question **5**, but only provide the answers. Ask: *What number went into the machine?*

After question **5** has been completed, discuss with children what would happen if the '× 0' appeared at the start or the middle of the machine.

**ASSESSMENT CHECKPOINT** Question **5** is an excellent activity to assess for mastery. Children who have fully understood the concepts of this lesson, will not even work out the full answers. Instead, they will see that the final operation of the function machine is 0, meaning every answer will be 0.

**ANSWERS** Answers for the **Practice** part of the lesson appear in the separate **Practice and Reflect answer guide**.

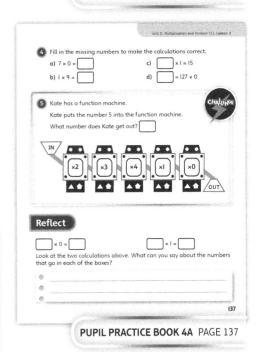

**PUPIL PRACTICE BOOK 4A** PAGE 135

**PUPIL PRACTICE BOOK 4A** PAGE 136

## Reflect

**WAYS OF WORKING** Pair work

**IN FOCUS** If children are struggling with their explanations, ask them to draw calculations or use counters. You could also put some key phrases on the board: multiply, zero, stay the same, not change in value.

**ASSESSMENT CHECKPOINT** To assess for mastery look for explanations, such as: *When you multiply any number by 0, the answer will always be 0; When you multiply a number by 1, the number will not change in value*.

**ANSWERS** Answers for the **Reflect** part of the lesson appear in the separate **Practice and Reflect answer guide**.

## After the lesson ⏸

- Would a quick recap of multiplying by 0 and 1 (at the start of the next lesson) cement understanding?
- Did all children understand that when you multiply any number by 1, it does not change in value?
- Did all children understand that any number multiplied by 0 is 0?

**PUPIL PRACTICE BOOK 4A** PAGE 137

# Dividing by 1

## Learning focus

In this lesson, children will learn how to divide numbers by 1. They will also relate their divisions to the inverse (multiplications).

## Small steps

→ Previous step: Multiplying by 0 and 1
→ **This step: Dividing by 1**
→ Next step: Multiplying and dividing by 6

### NATIONAL CURRICULUM LINKS

**Year 4 Number – Multiplication and Division**

Use place value, known and derived facts to multiply and divide mentally, including: multiplying by 0 and 1; dividing by 1; multiplying together three numbers.

### ASSESSING MASTERY

Children can confidently explain how to divide numbers by 1. Children can also link between dividing numbers by 1 and dividing a number by itself.

### COMMON MISCONCEPTIONS

Children may subtract instead of divide, for example 327 ÷ 1 = 326. Ask:
• *Did you check the operation you are using?*

Children may learn the pattern of dividing by 1, but not the understanding behind it. Ask:
• *Can you draw an array to help explain how to solve 12 ÷ 1?*

### STRENGTHENING UNDERSTANDING

Children may need some extra practice dividing by 1. Run some intervention exercises in which children find solutions to real-life problems. For example, dividing 10 toy cows between one animal pen. They could draw arrays to support their conceptual understanding.

### GOING DEEPER

Challenge children by giving them calculations which link multiplying and dividing by 1, such as 6 ÷ ? = 1 × ?

### KEY LANGUAGE

**In lesson:** divide (÷), calculation, how many, fact family, array, share, row, column, multiply (×), equal(ly), greater than,

**Other language to be used by teacher:** lots of, groups of, sets of, ones (1s), tens (10s), hundreds (100s), total, less than

### STRUCTURES AND REPRESENTATIONS

arrays

### RESOURCES

**Mandatory:** counters

**Optional:** base 10 equipment

 In the eTextbook of this lesson, you will find interactive links to a selection of teaching tools.

## Before you teach

• How will you make links between division and multiplication?
• How will you assess reasoning skills during the lesson?

## Discover

Unit 5: Multiplication and division (1), Lesson 4

**WAYS OF WORKING** Pair work

**ASK**

- Question **1** a): *What is the difference between dividing a number by 1 and dividing a number by itself?*
- Question **1** b): *How is multiplying by 1 similar to dividing by 1?*

**IN FOCUS** For question **1** a), all of the questions are dividing numbers by 1, except the final one (dividing a number by itself). Ask children what the difference is between dividing a number by 1 and a number by itself.

**PRACTICAL TIPS** Link back to the previous lesson in which children had to multiply by 1. See if children can explain similarities between multiplying and dividing by 1. Make use of counters and 1 hoop by asking children to physically put them into 1 group.

**ANSWERS**

Question **1** a): $5 \div 1 = 5$

$8 \div 1 = 8$

$3 \div 1 = 3$

$4 \div 4 = 1$

Question **1** b): $8 \times 1 = 8$

$8 \div 1 = 8$

$1 \times 8 = 8$

$8 \div 8 = 1$

## Share

**WAYS OF WORKING** Whole class teacher led

**ASK**

- Question **1** b): *How do the arrays help you to find all of the number sentences?*
- Question **1** b): *Why does this NOT show $1 \div 8$?*

**IN FOCUS** Question **1** b) provides a good opportunity to extend learning. Ask children to think of a word problem which would fit the array.

### Dividing by 1

#### Discover

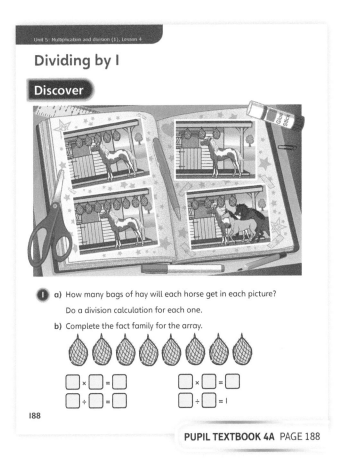

**1** a) How many bags of hay will each horse get in each picture?

Do a division calculation for each one.

b) Complete the fact family for the array.

**PUPIL TEXTBOOK 4A** PAGE 188

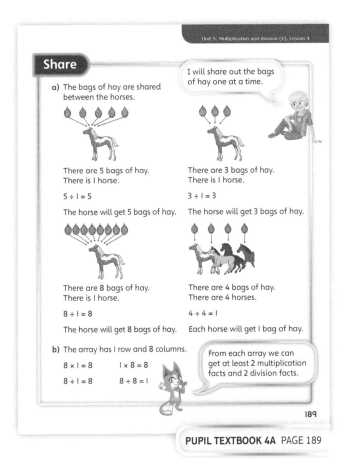

**PUPIL TEXTBOOK 4A** PAGE 189

# Think together

Whole class teacher led (I do, We do, You do)

**ASK**
- Question ❶: *Can you draw an array for this calculation?*
- Question ❶: *What is the difference between sharing and grouping?*

**IN FOCUS** Question ❸ asks children to reason why the divisions are linked. You may want to provide key words (divide, 1, itself) to support explanations.

**STRENGTHEN** Children may need extra practice with dividing by 1. Run some extra intervention sessions in which children have to sort counters into groups of 1.

**DEEPEN** Show children the difference between sharing and grouping by 1. Visual supports using counters or base 10 equipment and hoops will be helpful. For example, 4 ÷ 1 = 4: if you group it you would put 4 counters in 1 hoop, whereas if you share it out equally then you would have 4 hoops with 1 counter in each.

**ASSESSMENT CHECKPOINT** Question ❷ will allow you to assess which children can link multiplication and division facts, when multiplying and dividing by 1.

Question ❸ b) is a great opportunity to ask children if they understand why patterns occur when dividing numbers by 1 or itself.

**ANSWERS**

Question ❶: 10 × 1 = 10    10 ÷ 10 = 1

Amber gave 1 apple to 10 donkeys.

There are 10 donkeys.

Question ❷ a): 5 × 1 = 5, 1 × 5 = 5, 5 ÷ 1 = 5, 5 ÷ 5 = 1

Question ❷ b): 3 × 1 = 3, 1 × 3 = 3, 3 ÷ 1 = 3, 3 ÷ 3 = 1

Question ❸ a): 4 ÷ 1 = 4        4 ÷ 4 = 1
           5 ÷ 1 = 5        5 ÷ 5 = 1
           7 ÷ 1 = 7        7 ÷ 7 = 1
           10 ÷ 1 = 10      10 ÷ 10 = 1
           15 ÷ 1 = 15      15 ÷ 15 = 1
           32 ÷ 1 = 32      32 ÷ 32 = 1
           142 ÷ 1 = 142    142 ÷ 142 = 1

Question ❸ b): When a number is divided by 1, its value stays the same. When a number is divided by itself, the answer is always 1.

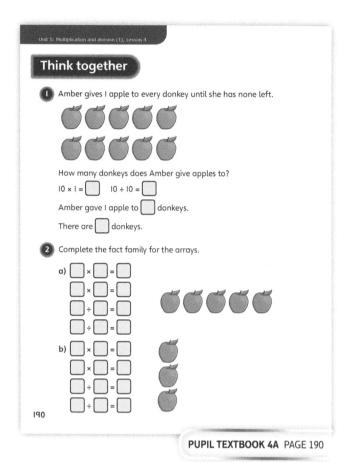

**PUPIL TEXTBOOK 4A** PAGE 190

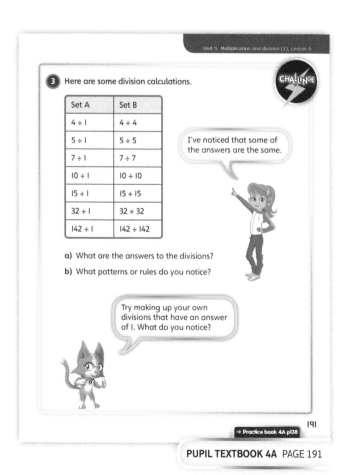

**PUPIL TEXTBOOK 4A** PAGE 191

## Practice

**WAYS OF WORKING** Independent thinking

**IN FOCUS** For question **2**, encourage children to explain their answer clearly, using an array if needed. This is also a good opportunity to explore what happens if you divide a number by 0.

**STRENGTHEN** Some children may not link dividing a number by 1 and dividing a number by itself. Support them by providing some extra intervention activities where they have to write fact families for an array.

**DEEPEN** Deepen learning by challenging children to complete number sentences with missing numbers, for example $7 \div ? = 1 \times ?$

In question **6**, challenge children to think of a range of numbers that could be represented by the shapes. Being able to complete this question correctly will show that children understand that dividing any number by 1 will give an answer of the same value because it does not need to be shared.

**ASSESSMENT CHECKPOINT** Question **5** is a great way to assess mastery of this lesson. Children will confidently complete the calculations and reason how they reached the answers when they are questioned.

**ANSWERS** Answers for the **Practice** part of the lesson appear in the separate **Practice and Reflect answer guide**.

## Reflect

**WAYS OF WORKING** Pair work

**IN FOCUS** This section is a good opportunity to link back to the previous lesson's learning. Ask children what similarities they can see between dividing by 1 and dividing by the number itself.

**ASSESSMENT CHECKPOINT** To assess for mastery, look for children giving an explanation such as: *When you divide any number by itself, the answer will always be 1; When you divide a number by 1, the number will not change in value.*

**ANSWERS** Answers for the **Reflect** part of the lesson appear in the separate **Practice and Reflect answer guide**.

### After the lesson ⏸

- Which children mastered the lesson?
- Will any children need a recap of the learning later on?
- Can children explain their calculations, backing it up with arrays?

---

**PUPIL PRACTICE BOOK 4A** PAGE 138

Unit 5: Multiplication and division (1), Lesson 4 → Textbook 4A p188

### Dividing by 1

1 Calculate the number of sweets.

a) There are 6 sweets. The sweets are shared equally between 1 person.

How many sweets does the person receive?

☐ ÷ ☐ = ☐

The person receives ☐ sweets.

b) There are 6 sweets. The sweets are shared between 6 people.

How many sweets does each person receive?

☐ ÷ ☐ = ☐

Each person receives ☐ sweet.

2 What mistake has Amelia made? ( $4 \div 4 = 0$ ) Amelia

138

---

**PUPIL PRACTICE BOOK 4A** PAGE 139

3 Circle the calculations that have an answer of 1.

$8 \div 8$    $8 \div 1$    $5 \div 5$    $16 \div 16$

$20 \div 2$    $7 \div 7$    $2 \div 1$    $150 \div 150$

4 a) Find the solutions to these calculations.

$3 \div 1 =$ ☐    $4 \div 1 =$ ☐    $5 \div 1 =$ ☐

$10 \div 1 =$ ☐    $14 \div 1 =$ ☐    $20 \div 1 =$ ☐

Use the calculations to complete the following sentence.

When you divide a number by 1 _____

b) Find the solutions to these calculations.

$3 \div 3 =$ ☐    $4 \div 4 =$ ☐    $5 \div 5 =$ ☐

$10 \div 10 =$ ☐    $14 \div 14 =$ ☐    $20 \div 20 =$ ☐

Use the calculations to complete the following sentence.

When you divide a number by itself _____

139

---

**PUPIL PRACTICE BOOK 4A** PAGE 140

Unit 5: Multiplication and division (1), Lesson 4

5 Fill in the missing numbers to make the calculations correct.

a) $11 \div 1 =$ ☐    d) $9 \div$ ☐ $= 9$    g) ☐ $\div 1 = 0$

b) $11 \div 11 =$ ☐    e) $12 \div$ ☐ $= 1$    h) $8 \div$ ☐ $= 7 \div 7$

c) ☐ $= 25 \div 25$    f) ☐ $\div 1 = 70$

6 The square and the pentagon represent numbers. Look at the number sentence then tick the correct statement. ☐ $\div 1 >$ ⬠ $\div 1$ **CHALLENGE**

The square is equal to the pentagon. ☐

The square is greater than the pentagon. ☐

The pentagon is greater than the square. ☐

Explain your answer.

**Reflect**

☐ $\div$ ☐ $= 1$      ☐ $\div 1 =$ ☐

Look at the two calculations above. What can you say about the numbers that go in each of the boxes?

○
○
○

140

---

# Multiplying and dividing by 6

## Learning focus

In this lesson, children will learn what it means to multiply and divide by 6. They will use a range of strategies to support their understanding.

## Small steps

→ Previous step: Dividing by 1
→ **This step: Multiplying and dividing by 6**
→ Next step: 6 times-table

### NATIONAL CURRICULUM LINKS

**Year 4 Number – Multiplication and Division**

Recall multiplication and division facts for multiplication tables up to 12 × 12.

### ASSESSING MASTERY

Children can confidently multiply and divide numbers by 6. They can make links, such as multiplying by 3 then doubling, or multiplying by 5 and then adding one more lot of the number they were multiplying by.

### COMMON MISCONCEPTIONS

Children may not realise that 4 × 6 is equivalent to 6 × 4. Ask:
• *Can you show these calculations on an array? What do you notice?*

When counting in 6s, children sometimes start by counting 0. Ask:
• *What number should we start on when counting in 6s?*

### STRENGTHENING UNDERSTANDING

Children may occasionally lose count, for example when working out 6 × 6 in their head, they may end up counting up too many 6s, or too few 6s. Encourage children to use a number line and follow the jumps with their fingers. Children can also use counters in groups of 6 to see the direct link between the objects and counting up in 6s on a number line.

Knowledge of times-tables is very important in this lesson: ensure that children get daily support with this. You could also ask for some home support from parents or guardians.

### GOING DEEPER

Challenge children to use multiplication facts that they know to work out other multiplication facts. For example, can they use 12 × 6 to work out 13 × 6 or 24 × 6?

### KEY LANGUAGE

**In lesson:** multiply (×), divide (÷), how many, count on, number line, grouped, total, calculation, pound (£), length, width, centimetre (cm), perimeter

**Other language to be used by teacher:** number sentence, times-table, equal, array

### STRUCTURES AND REPRESENTATIONS

number lines, arrays

### RESOURCES

**Mandatory:** counters

**Optional:** base 10 equipment

 In the eTextbook of this lesson, you will find interactive links to a selection of teaching tools.

## Before you teach ⏸

• Can children count in 3s and do they know their 3 times-table?
• Can children count in 6s and do they know their 6 times-table?

## Discover

## Multiplying and dividing by 6

### Discover

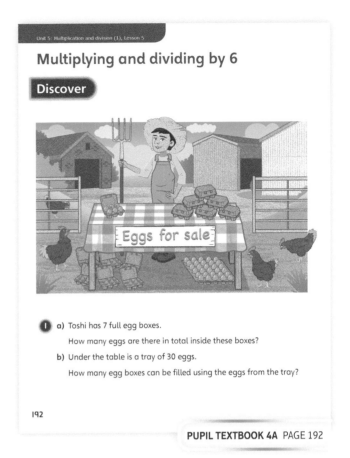

**WAYS OF WORKING** Pair work

**ASK**

- Question ① a): *What multiplication sentence would match this question?*
- Question ① b): *Could drawing an array help us?*

**IN FOCUS** For question ① a, observe carefully which children can confidently count in 6s, and which count the eggs individually. This will tell you who will need some extra support during the lesson, and following the lesson. It is an important assessment opportunity.

**PRACTICAL TIPS** For question ① b) children could draw the boxes and eggs (in arrays). This will give them more of a visual understanding of the problem.

**ANSWERS**

Question ① a): 7 × 6 = 42. There are 42 eggs in total in the boxes.

Question ① b): 30 ÷ 6 = 5. So 5 egg boxes can be filled by the tray of eggs.

① a) Toshi has 7 full egg boxes.
   How many eggs are there in total inside these boxes?

   b) Under the table is a tray of 30 eggs.
   How many egg boxes can be filled using the eggs from the tray?

192

**PUPIL TEXTBOOK 4A** PAGE 192

## Share

**WAYS OF WORKING** Whole class teacher led

**ASK**

- Question ① a): *Why do you count in 6s and not 1s? Can counting in 2s get the answer? Why can it be seen as a multiplication?*
- Question ① b): *Is it easier to count on or back in 6s?*

**IN FOCUS** Question ① a provides children with a great opportunity to practise using number lines. Ask children to put their fingers on the number line and practise counting forwards and backwards in 6s. They will see the repeated addition and link it with the problem they have been trying to find the solution for.

In question ① b), children can count backwards in 6s from 30 or count on, starting from 6. Model the counting on the number line and also on fingers, i.e. 6, 12, 18, 24, 30 (one on each finger of a hand).

### Share

a) There are 7 full egg boxes. Each box holds 6 eggs.

6 + 6 + 6 + 6 + 6 + 6 + 6 = 42
7 × 6 = 42
There are 42 eggs in the boxes.

*I counted on in 6s using a number line.*

b) There are 30 eggs in the tray. Each egg box can hold 6 eggs.

*I grouped the eggs on the tray. I can see that 5 egg boxes can be filled.*

30 ÷ 6 = 5
5 egg boxes can be filled by the tray of eggs.

193

**PUPIL TEXTBOOK 4A** PAGE 193

225

# Think together

**WAYS OF WORKING** Whole class teacher led (I do, We do, You do)

**ASK**
- Question **1**: *How did the arrays help?*
- Question **3**: *What strategies did you find worked well for you in this question?*
- Question **3**: *Can you explain your answer to a friend?*

**IN FOCUS** For question **3**, some children may draw a number line to help them work out the answer. This is fine, but also make sure they understand how the array can help them (an important learning point).

**STRENGTHEN** At each stage use concrete objects alongside a number line to help children see the link with repeated addition; counting up in 6s and then reinforcing the multiplication sentence.

**DEEPEN** Challenge children by asking them to investigate:
- How could you work out $13 \times 6$?
- How could you work out $120 \div 6$?
- How could you work out $50 \times 6$?

**ASSESSMENT CHECKPOINT** Question **2** will allow you to assess children's ability to explain what it means to multiply or divide by 6, and use their knowledge of counting in 6s to work out the answers.

**ANSWERS**

Question **1**: $6 + 6 + 6 + 6 + 6 + 6 + 6 + 6 = 48$

$8 \times 6 = 48$. There are 48 eggs altogether.

Question **2** a): $4 \times 6 = 24$

Question **2** b): $36 \div 6 = 6$

Question **3**: 3 packs of 18 bottles.

Each pack has 18 bottles arranged as a $3 \times 6$ array.

3 lots of $3 \times 6$ arrays is the same as a $9 \times 6$ arrays.

So the answer is:

$9 \times 6 = 54$

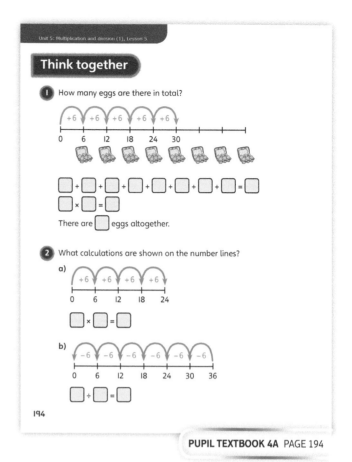

**PUPIL TEXTBOOK 4A** PAGE 194

**PUPIL TEXTBOOK 4A** PAGE 195

# Practice

**WAYS OF WORKING** Independent thinking

**IN FOCUS** The challenge (question **5**) is a fantastic way to put the learning in this lesson into a measurement context. It will involve higher-order thinking; discussion in pairs will help promote this. Let children have a go at solving it, and then, if they are struggling:

Remind them what a perimeter is. Get them to write the lengths and widths on each rectangle in the practice book. Model which rectangle sides to count.

**STRENGTHEN** Run some intervention exercises in which children practise counting in 6s, and also answer quick-fire questions, such as 4 × 6, 8 × 6 and so on.

If children are confident with their 3 times-table, you could teach them the method of multiplying by 3 and then doubling.

**DEEPEN** To deepen learning, explore how to work out 2 × 6 + 5 × 6 as one multiplication. They could show this by adding arrays together, and finding that it is the same as 7 × 6.

You could also challenge children by giving them an answer, such as 24, and asking them to think of as many questions for it as they can. They may start with simple ones, such as 4 × 6, but then may go on to think of multi-step questions, for example (8 × 6) ÷ 2.

**ASSESSMENT CHECKPOINT** Question **4** provides a good opportunity to assess whether children have understood how to multiply and divide by 6. Can children represent a question as a multiplication sentence involving × 6 and can they use counting in 6s to work out the correct answer to the multiplication? Do children know that multiplying by 3 and then doubling is the same a multiplying by 6?

**ANSWERS** Answers for the **Practice** part of the lesson appear in the separate **Practice and Reflect answer guide**.

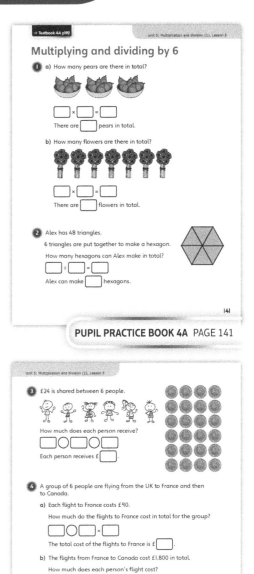

**PUPIL PRACTICE BOOK 4A** PAGE 141

**PUPIL PRACTICE BOOK 4A** PAGE 142

# Reflect

**WAYS OF WORKING** Pair work

**IN FOCUS** This question is important because children have to use their knowledge and construct their own questions. This will involve some deeper thinking.

**ASSESSMENT CHECKPOINT** Check whether children have appropriate methods and if they are reasoning effectively (they may have drawn diagrams to support their reasoning).

**ANSWERS** Answers for the **Reflect** part of the lesson appear in the separate **Practice and Reflect answer guide**.

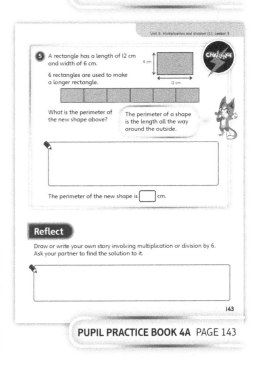

**PUPIL PRACTICE BOOK 4A** PAGE 143

# After the lesson ⏸

- Can children form number sentences involving × 6 or ÷ 6 from a word question?
- Do children know the method of multiplying by 3 and then doubling?
- How can children get extra practice – interventions, home support?

# 6 times-table

## Learning focus

In this lesson, children will focus on learning their 6 times-table. Children should be able to recite it and also learn the associated multiplication and division facts.

## Small steps

→ Previous step: Multiplying and dividing by 6
→ **This step: 6 times-table**
→ Next step: Multiplying and dividing by 9

### NATIONAL CURRICULUM LINKS

**Year 4 Number – Multiplication and Division**

Recall multiplication and division facts for multiplication tables up to 12 × 12.

### ASSESSING MASTERY

Children can demonstrate a rapid recall of multiplication and associated division facts from the 6 times-table. They can use their knowledge to find solutions and clearly explain how they worked out the answers.

### COMMON MISCONCEPTIONS

To work out whether 8 × 6 is greater than or equal to 3 × 6, children sometimes think you have to work out each multiplication fact. Ask:

• *Try reasoning why 8 groups of 6 has to be greater than 3 groups of 6 without working them out.* Children could draw arrays to help them understand this.

Children may also need to be reminded that 6 × 1 = 6 and 6 × 0 = 0. Ask:

• *What did you learn about multiplying by 0 and 1 a few lessons ago?* (Link back to Lesson 3, earlier in this unit.)

### STRENGTHENING UNDERSTANDING

Times-table facts must be constantly reinforced. Show children 6 times-table facts pictorially or by using equipment, such as counters or base 10. For example, 2 × 6 could be represented by 2 towers of 6 cubes.

Ensure that children have regular opportunities to practise rapid recall of the multiplication and division facts, but explain that they need an understanding of what they mean too.

### GOING DEEPER

Challenge children to work out missing numbers in number sentences. For example, 12 ÷ 6 < ? × 6.

### KEY LANGUAGE

**In lesson:** times-table, times-table fact, count on, number line, added, divide (÷), multiply (×), total, calculation, number sentences

**Other language to be used by teacher:** grouping, sharing, number facts

### STRUCTURES AND REPRESENTATIONS

number lines, arrays

### RESOURCES

**Mandatory:** counters

**Optional:** base 10 equipment

 In the eTextbook of this lesson, you will find interactive links to a selection of teaching tools.

## Before you teach

• How did children get on in the previous lesson?
• How will you link multiplying and dividing by 6 with the 6 times-table?
• In what ways can you encourage children to learn the 6 times-table off by heart?

## Discover

Pair work

**ASK**

- Question ① a): *Why is the 3 times-table shown here?*
- Question ① a): *What is a good method of remembering these number facts?*

**IN FOCUS** Question ① a) is important because it draws on children's knowledge of the 3 times-table to work out the 6 times-table. Look for children who realise that the 3 times-table can help them.

**PRACTICAL TIPS** Show children the 6 times-table on your maths display. Cover up different parts each day: some without answers, some with answers or all of the multiplication missing but the answer given.

**ANSWERS**

Question ① a): Full set of 6 times-table shown.

| | |
|---|---|
| $0 \times 6 = 0$ | **$7 \times 6 = 42$** |
| $1 \times 6 = 6$ | $8 \times 6 = 48$ |
| $2 \times 6 = 12$ | **$9 \times 6 = 54$** |
| **$3 \times 6 = 18$** | **$10 \times 6 = 60$** |
| **$4 \times 6 = 24$** | $11 \times 6 = 66$ |
| **$5 \times 6 = 30$** | **$12 \times 6 = 72$** |
| **$6 \times 6 = 36$** | |

Question ① b): The multiplication fact shown is $6 \times 10 = 60$ or $10 \times 6 = 60$

## Share

Whole class teacher led

**ASK**

- Question ① a): *How do the number lines help you?*
- Question ① a): *Why do you need to learn your times-tables?*
- Question ① b): *When would you need them in a real-life situation?*

**IN FOCUS** The representation in question ① b) is a really important aspect of this lesson. Children, all too often, simply learn times-tables without understanding what they mean. Visual representations are key to children's understanding.

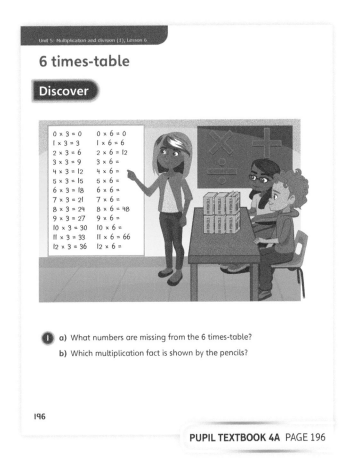

**PUPIL TEXTBOOK 4A** PAGE 196

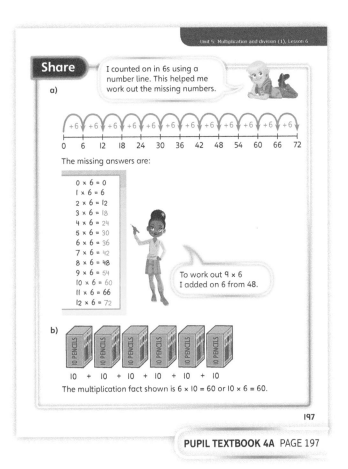

**PUPIL TEXTBOOK 4A** PAGE 197

# Think together

Unit 5: Multiplication and division (1), Lesson 6

**WAYS OF WORKING** Whole class teacher led (I do, We do, You do)

**ASK**

- Question ❸: *How does the 5 times-tables help you?*
- Question ❸: *How do you know your answers in this section are correct?*
- Question ❸: *Can you explain your methods?*

**IN FOCUS** It is important for question ❶ a) to emphasise commutativity. Explain to children that 2 × 6 = 12 and 6 × 2 = 12. Challenge children to show you the difference using a visual representation, for example 2 rows of 6 counters/cubes is the same as 6 rows of 2 counters/cubes.

**STRENGTHEN** Run some intervention sessions with children who require it. Give children a 6 times-table fact and get them to draw an array to represent it. Remind children that if they are unsure of how to work out a 6 times-table fact, they could multiply by 3 and then double it.

**DEEPEN** In question ❸, the 5 times-table is also featured. Discuss with children how this can help them work out the answers to the 6 times-table: they could multiply a number by 5 and then add on one more lot of that number. You could also challenge children to write some word problems based on the 6 times-table.

**ASSESSMENT CHECKPOINT** In question ❷, children will need to know their 6 times-table but also recall their understanding from the first lesson in this unit (multiplying by multiples of 10 and 100). This is a great point to assess which children have mastered both!

**ANSWERS**

Question ❶ a): 2 × 6 = 12, 6 × 2 = 12

Question ❶ b): 4 × 6 = 24, 6 × 4 = 24

Question ❷: a) 42 ÷ 6 = 7

b) 42 ÷ 7 = 6

c) 70 × 6 = 420

d) 700 × 6 = 4,200

e) 420 ÷ 6 = 70

f) 4,200 ÷ 6 = 700

Question ❸: You can multiply by 5 and then add on one more lot of the number you are multiplying.

**PUPIL TEXTBOOK 4A** PAGE 198

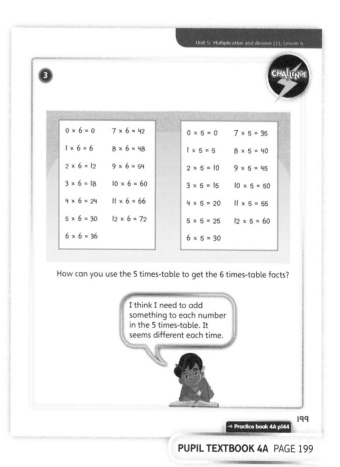

**PUPIL TEXTBOOK 4A** PAGE 199

## Practice

**WAYS OF WORKING** Independent thinking

**IN FOCUS** Question ② has some number sentences in which the answer appears first, such as ? = 6 × 10. This can often throw children. Ask them if there is another way they can write the number sentence. Showing both ? = 6 × 10 and 6 × 10 = ? is a great learning point for children.

**STRENGTHEN** Question ③ c) links the 6 times-table to the 60 times-table. This is a great opportunity to practise the 60 times-table: 0, 60, 120, 180, 240 … . Ask children what they notice when comparing the 60 and 6 times-tables.

**DEEPEN** Challenge children to complete some 6 times-table multiplication and division facts which are littered with mistakes. Ask children to become the teacher and spot the mistakes. For example, 7 × 6 = 36, 66 ÷ 6 = 1

As an extension, ask children to suggest why the mistakes were made (which would get them to reason out the misconceptions).

**THINK DIFFERENTLY** Question ⑥ asks children to say whether two 6 time-table multiplication and division facts are equal, or which is greater or less than the other. It requires children to find the solutions to the facts and compare them. It may help children to create arrays using counters for the number fact pairs they are comparing.

**ASSESSMENT CHECKPOINT** Can children recognise 6 times-table facts from arrays or number lines, like for example in questions ① and ③? Children should start to be developing a secure knowledge of their 6 times-table, both multiplication and associated division facts.

**ANSWERS** Answers for the **Practice** part of the lesson appear in the separate **Practice and Reflect answer guide**.

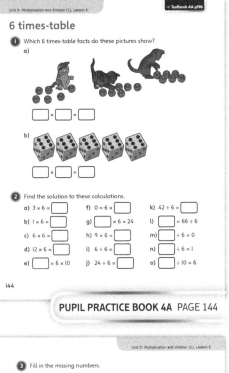

**PUPIL PRACTICE BOOK 4A** PAGE 144

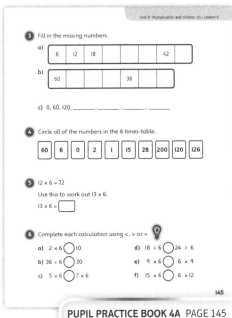

**PUPIL PRACTICE BOOK 4A** PAGE 145

## Reflect

**WAYS OF WORKING** Pair work

**IN FOCUS** Make this reflective exercise into a whole class competition. Children really enjoy times-table races, so you could make it a weekly event. This will really encourage children to learn their times-tables.

**ASSESSMENT CHECKPOINT** This is the perfect opportunity to assess which children have mastered the lesson and who needs extra times-table practice.

**ANSWERS** Answers for the **Reflect** part of the lesson appear in the separate **Practice and Reflect answer guide**.

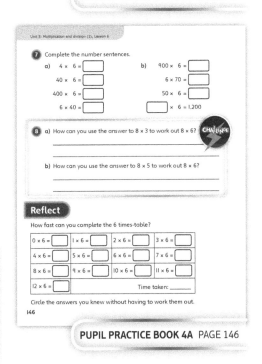

**PUPIL PRACTICE BOOK 4A** PAGE 146

### After the lesson ⏸

- Can children recall their division and multiplication facts from the 6 times-table?
- Can children think of some real-life problems associated with the 6 times-table?

# Multiplying and dividing by 9

## Learning focus

In this lesson, children will understand how they can multiply and divide a number by 9. Children will make links to the 3, 6 and 5 times-tables.

## Small steps

→ Previous step: 6 times-table
→ **This step: Multiplying and dividing by 9**
→ Next step: 9 times-table

### NATIONAL CURRICULUM LINKS

**Year 4 Number – Multiplication and Division**

Recall multiplication and division facts for multiplication tables up to 12 × 12.

### ASSESSING MASTERY

Children can use a range of strategies and representations to multiply and divide numbers by 9, making links to the 3, 6 and 5 times-tables, which will help children to work out answers quickly. Children can understand that multiplication is the inverse of division and they may use this knowledge to check answers (for example, 108 ÷ 9 = 12 can be checked by working out 12 × 9).

### COMMON MISCONCEPTIONS

When multiplying and dividing by 9, children may lose track of the count. Encourage children to learn the multiplication facts and associated division facts by heart. This may involve intervention sessions and some home learning. Ask:
• *How quickly can you recall a multiplication or division? Practise them daily to increase your recall.*

Children may get confused between sharing between 9 and grouping in 9s. Ask:
• *What is the difference between sharing and grouping? Draw the difference.*

### STRENGTHENING UNDERSTANDING

Children often learn multiplication and division facts without understanding what they mean. Work with concrete objects to show them clearly. Use a number line to visually show repeated addition and repeated subtraction by counting on and back in 9s. Times-table practice is vital throughout this unit – run daily challenges to encourage children to memorise them.

### GOING DEEPER

Linking multiplication and division facts to measures will deepen children's learning. For instance, you could set problems in which amounts of money are shared between 9 people.

### KEY LANGUAGE

**In lesson:** multiply (×), divide (÷), cube, square, length, how many, number line, array, grouping, sharing, perimeter, equally

**Other language to be used by teacher:** multiplication fact/statement, division fact/statement, equal grouping, equal sharing.

### STRUCTURES AND REPRESENTATIONS

number lines, arrays

### RESOURCES

**Mandatory:** base 10 equipment, counters

 In the eTextbook of this lesson, you will find interactive links to a selection of teaching tools.

## Before you teach ⏸

• Can children count in 3s, 6s and 9s?
• Do they understand the key vocabulary?
• Can children explain what 6 × 9 means? Can they show it using a visual representation?

# Discover

Unit 5: Multiplication and division (1), Lesson 7

## Multiplying and dividing by 9

### Discover

**WAYS OF WORKING** Pair work

**ASK**

- Question ① a): *How many sides does a cube have? Show your workings on a number line.*
- Question ① b): *How many toy people are in a box?*

**IN FOCUS** Question ① b) focuses on equal grouping. Give children 27 counters and ask them to make lines of 9 with them. You may want to highlight to children that they are grouping and not sharing here.

**PRACTICAL TIPS** Providing children with actual puzzle cubes will really help them to visualise 6 × 9.

**ANSWERS**

Question ① a): 9 + 9 + 9 + 9 + 9 + 9 = 54

6 × 9 = 54

There are 54 coloured squares.

Question ① b): 27 ÷ 9 = 3

She can make 3 rows of toy people.

① a) Reena has a puzzle cube.

Each side of a puzzle cube has 9 coloured squares.

How many coloured squares in total are on the outside of the cube?

b) Ambika buys a box of the toy people. A box has 27 toy people.

She puts the people into rows of 9.

How many rows can she make?

200

**PUPIL TEXTBOOK 4A** PAGE 200

# Share

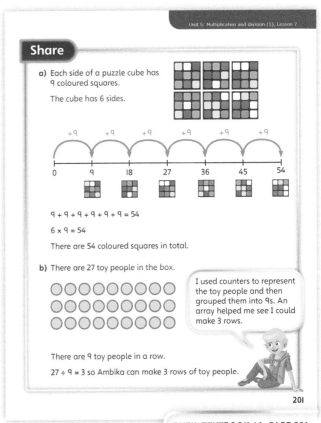

**WAYS OF WORKING** Whole class teacher led

**ASK**

- Question ① a): *Is multiplication quicker than repeated addition?*
- Question ① b): *What could you use to represent the toy people?*

**IN FOCUS** Discuss with children the different methods they use to find solutions to ① a) (9 + 9 + 9 + 9 + 9 + 9 = 54 or 6 × 9 = 54). This will encourage children's deep thinking and understanding about the differences between repeated addition and multiplication.

### Share

a) Each side of a puzzle cube has 9 coloured squares.

The cube has 6 sides.

9 + 9 + 9 + 9 + 9 + 9 = 54

6 × 9 = 54

There are 54 coloured squares in total.

b) There are 27 toy people in the box.

I used counters to represent the toy people and then grouped them into 9s. An array helped me see I could make 3 rows.

There are 9 toy people in a row.

27 ÷ 9 = 3 so Ambika can make 3 rows of toy people.

201

**PUPIL TEXTBOOK 4A** PAGE 201

# Think together

**WAYS OF WORKING** Whole class teacher led (I do, We do, You do)

**ASK**
- Question **1**: *How could you represent the multiplication and division visually?*
- Question **2**: *What is the biggest number you can think of that is a multiple of 9?*

**IN FOCUS** The challenge activity (question **2**) looks at divisibility tests. Explain the method clearly and let children work with some examples to see how it works. Ask: *Can you explain why this method works?*

**STRENGTHEN** To strengthen children's understanding of question **1**, multiply and share using counters to represent the objects (you could even ask children to draw the 5 cm carriages accurately with a ruler).

Another way to strengthen learning here is to model some incorrect answers and ask children to mark and correct them. For example, 5 × 9 = 43. Further to this, ask children to explain where the person who made the mistake may have gone wrong.

**DEEPEN** Challenge children to explore the relationship between multiplying by 9 and dividing by 9. How could they use division to work out the missing number problem such as ? × 9 = 72? Can they explain why? Can they make up their own problems similar to this?

You could also ask children to reason if the divisibility rule for 9 would also apply for 3.

**ASSESSMENT CHECKPOINT** Ask children how they know if they are doing a multiplication or division. This will show you which children understand the difference between multiplication and division and why the two processes are needed for different situations, and will show which children need more support. Ask: *What are the clues you look for?*

**ANSWERS**

Question **1** a): 9 + 9 + 9 + 9 + 9 = 45

         5 × 9 = 45

         The carriages are 45 cm long in total.

Question **1** b): 72 ÷ 9 = 8

         There are 8 carriages.

Question **2** a): 39, 521 and 752 do not divide by 9.

         144, 279 and 522 do divide by 9.

Question **2** b): The missing digit is 5: 657.

         6 + 5 + 7 = 18, which can be divided by 9; 18 ÷ 9 = 2.

Question **2** c): There are many correct answers. Look for use of the appropriate method in children's workings.

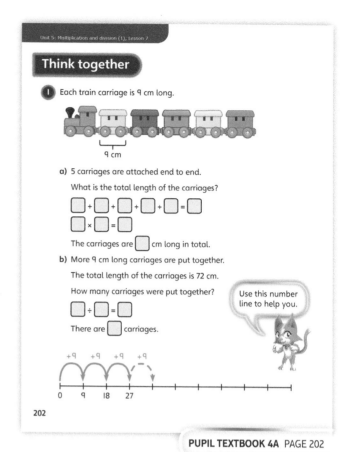

**PUPIL TEXTBOOK 4A** PAGE 202

**PUPIL TEXTBOOK 4A** PAGE 203

## Practice

**WAYS OF WORKING** Independent thinking

**IN FOCUS** Question ❹ is an excellent opportunity to make links between multiplying and dividing and problem solving with measures (in a practical, real context). Remind children of what 'perimeter' means and support them when working out which sides to multiply in part b).

**STRENGTHEN** Support children by linking the 9 times-table to other times-tables. Show them that they could work out 10 times a number and then subtract one lot of that number. This will need to be represented visually, perhaps on a number line. Also, show children that multiplying by 9 is the same as multiplying a number by 3 and then 3 again.

You may want to display the multiplication and division facts on your learning walls. This will encourage children to practise them daily.

**DEEPEN** Challenge children to make their own playing card problems (like in question ❶).

Question ❺ will also challenge children to develop deeper learning. Children will need to remember the divisibility rules and apply them.

**ASSESSMENT CHECKPOINT** Assess children's ability to link the 3 and 9 times-tables by looking at answers to question ❻. Have children managed to mentally combine 3 of the towers? Or did they have to start from scratch and draw their own towers?

**ANSWERS** Answers for the **Practice** part of the lesson appear in the separate **Practice and Reflect answer guide**.

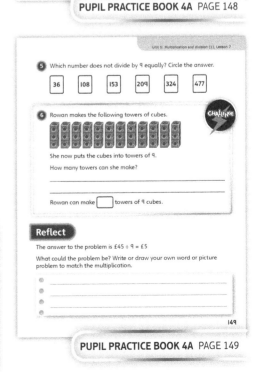

**PUPIL PRACTICE BOOK 4A** PAGE 147

**PUPIL PRACTICE BOOK 4A** PAGE 148

## Reflect

**WAYS OF WORKING** Independent thinking

**IN FOCUS** This reflective exercise requires children to create a word problem to fit a division sentence. Make sure, after the question is complete, that children swap with a partner and explain their problems, reasoning why it matches.

**ASSESSMENT CHECKPOINT** Check if children understand whether their problem involves grouping or sharing.

**ANSWERS** Answers for the **Reflect** part of the lesson appear in the separate **Practice and Reflect answer guide**.

### After the lesson

- Can children form multiplication statements involving × 9 from a word problem?
- Can children form division statements involving ÷ 9 from a word problem?
- Do children know at least one method to multiply and divide a number by 9?

**PUPIL PRACTICE BOOK 4A** PAGE 149

# 9 times-table

## Learning focus

In this lesson, children will focus on learning their 9 times-table. Children will also be able to recall associated division facts from the related multiplication facts.

## Small steps

→ Previous step: Multiplying and dividing by 9
→ **This step: 9 times-table**
→ Next step: Multiplying and dividing by 7

### NATIONAL CURRICULUM LINKS

**Year 4 Number – Multiplication and Division**

Recall multiplication and division facts for multiplication tables up to 12 × 12.

### ASSESSING MASTERY

Children can recall multiplication and associated division facts from the 9 times-table rapidly. Children can explain how the 9 times-table links to the 10 times-table and the 3 times-table.

### COMMON MISCONCEPTIONS

To work out if 6 × 9 is greater than or equal to 4 × 9, children may think you have to work out each multiplication fact separately. Ask children to reason why 6 groups of 9 has to be greater than 4 groups of 9 without working them out. Ask:
• *How can you show that 6 groups of 9 has to be greater than 4 groups of 9 using ten frames?*

### STRENGTHENING UNDERSTANDING

To strengthen children's understanding of times-table facts show them visually. For example, 3 × 9 could be represented with cubes (3 towers of 9). Once children have this understanding, it is important that they develop rapid recall of the multiplication and division facts.

Finally, remind children that if they are unsure of how to work out a 9 times-table fact they can always use their knowledge from the previous lesson. For example, to work out 3 × 9 they could do 3 × 10 = 30, then 30 − 3 = 27.

### GOING DEEPER

Challenge children to apply their 9 times-table knowledge to larger numbers. For instance, you could ask them if 945 is a multiple of 9. They should be able to reason that (100 × 9) + (5 × 9) = 945, so it is a multiple of 9. Alternatively, they could use the divisibility rule: 9 + 4 + 5 = 18, and 18 is divisible by 9, so 945 must be divisible by 9.

### KEY LANGUAGE

**In lesson:** times-table, facts, ten frames, multiply (×), less, greater, multiplication facts, division facts, number line, array, mathematical statements

**Other language to be used by teacher:** divide (÷), grouping, multiplication statement, division statement, recall, greater, number sentences

### STRUCTURES AND REPRESENTATIONS

number lines, arrays, ten frames

### RESOURCES

**Mandatory:** counters

**Optional:** base 10 equipment

 In the eTextbook of this lesson, you will find interactive links to a selection of teaching tools.

## Before you teach ⏸

• Have you got the times-table facts on display in the classroom?
• How can you promote daily practice?
• Can children multiply by 9 and divide by 9?

## Discover

**WAYS OF WORKING** Pair work

**ASK**

- Question ① a): *What can we see in the pictures? What is a good way to remember the 9 times-table?*
- Question ① b): *How do the ten frames help you with this question?*

**IN FOCUS** Question ① b) uses ten frames in an effective way to link the 9 times-table to the 10 times-table. Children should reason that the ten frames (if full) represent $6 \times 10 = 60$. However, 1 counter is missing from each, so they can subtract 6 from 60 to reach 54. Some children may need more practice: repeat this activity with other multiplications.

**PRACTICAL TIPS** Show children the 9 times-table on your maths display. Cover up different parts each day: some without answers, some with answers or all of the multiplication missing but the answer given.

**ANSWERS**

Question ① a): $4 \times 9 = 36$

$9 \times 10 = 90$

$2 \times 9 = 18$

Question ① b): $6 \times 9 = 54$

I moved counters from the last ten frame to complete the other ten frames.

The ten frames show that $6 \times 9$ is 6 less than $6 \times 10$.

## Share

**WAYS OF WORKING** Whole class teacher led

**ASK**

- Question ① a): *How will you represent the multiplication facts with arrays?*
- Question ① b): *Did it help to move the counters from the last ten frame to fill the others and see what remained on the last ten frame?*

**IN FOCUS** Undertake a whole class discussion about the methods that children have used. For question ① b), ask children which is greater, $9 \times 6$ or $10 \times 6$? Explain that they can work it out without calculating the answers (the ten frames will help with this explanation).

Listen carefully to children's reasoning. Encourage the use of correct mathematical vocabulary.

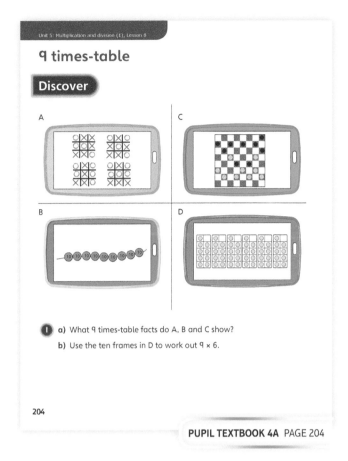

PUPIL TEXTBOOK 4A PAGE 204

PUPIL TEXTBOOK 4A PAGE 205

# Think together

**WAYS OF WORKING** Whole class teacher led (I do, We do, You do)

**ASK**

- Question **1** b): *How do you know that 7 × 9 cannot be greater than 70?*
- Question **3**: *Which method do you find useful to work out 9 times-table facts?*
- Question **3**: *Explain your method clearly.*

**IN FOCUS** Question **3** allows children to practise using different methods to learn 9 times-table facts. Ensure that children can explain out loud the process they are going through in their heads. Possibly, 13 × 9 may provide a bit of a challenge for children. Prompt them to follow Danny's method (multiply by 10 then minus 13).

**STRENGTHEN** You may want to run some intervention sessions, practising methods children could use to work out 9 times-table facts. Try repeating question **3**, with different 9 times-table facts.

**DEEPEN** Challenge children by asking if they know their 18 times-table. For instance, they will come to realise that 18 × 3 is equivalent to 9 × 6.

**ASSESSMENT CHECKPOINT** Question **2** will show whether children have learnt their 9 times-table. You could also run mini-tests with children to see if they can quickly recall 9 times-table facts.

**ANSWERS**

Question **1** a): 3 × 9 = 27 and 9 × 3 = 27

Question **1** b): 7 × 9 = 63 and 9 × 7 = 63

Question **2**: 
a) 0 × 9 = 0    e) 12 × 9 = 108    i) 8 × 9 = 72
b) 11 × 9 = 99    f) 54 ÷ 9 = 6    j) 18 ÷ 9 = 2
c) 63 ÷ 9 = 7    g) 5 × 9 = 45
d) 1 × 9 = 9    h) 36 ÷ 9 = 4

Question **3**: 4 × 9 = 36
8 × 9 = 72
11 × 9 = 99
13 × 9 = 117

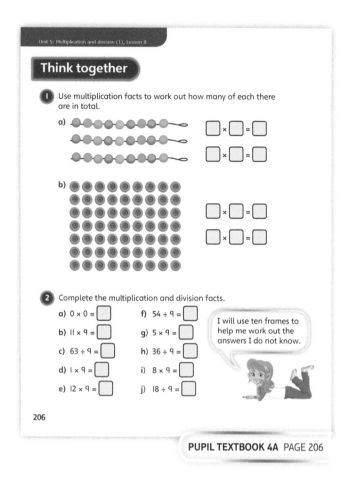

PUPIL TEXTBOOK 4A PAGE 206

PUPIL TEXTBOOK 4A PAGE 207

## Practice

**WAYS OF WORKING** Independent thinking

**IN FOCUS** Question **6** draws on learning from earlier in the unit (multiplying by multiples of 10 and 100). Recap Lesson 1. Remind children that if they know the 9 times-table, they also know the 90 and 900 times-tables.

**STRENGTHEN** Arrays are a key representation in this lesson; suggest to children that they draw them if they are unsure of a problem. This will strengthen their learning. Also, continue to encourage rapid recall of multiplication facts via daily practice of times-tables.

**DEEPEN** Challenge children to think in a different way by giving them a multiple of 9, such as 27. Ask children if they can think of all the factors of 27. This will help them make more links between times-tables.

**ASSESSMENT CHECKPOINT** When children are completing question **6**, it is a good idea to assess children's understanding by asking them: *Tell me what you know.* Reasoning is a key step to mastery of the 9 times-table. Furthermore, look for whether children can recognise 9 times-table facts from pictures.

**ANSWERS** Answers for the **Practice** part of the lesson appear in the separate **Practice and Reflect answer guide**.

## Reflect

**WAYS OF WORKING** Pair work

**IN FOCUS** This **Reflect** activity brings together their work on the 9 times-table. Peer checking of the answers is a great way of consolidating this lesson.

**ASSESSMENT CHECKPOINT** Check whether children have instant recall of their 9 times-table. You could do a thumbs assessment (thumbs up, down or in the middle) at the end of the lesson, allowing children to self-assess how they got on in the activity. Furthermore, look carefully at children's written multiplications. Are they accurate? Are there any misconceptions?

**ANSWERS** Answers for the **Reflect** part of the lesson appear in the separate **Practice and Reflect answer guide**.

## After the lesson ⏸

- Can children instantly recall their division and multiplication facts from the 9 times-table?
- Which facts are children struggling with? How can these be reinforced further?
- Do children know the connection between the 3, 9 and 10 times-tables?

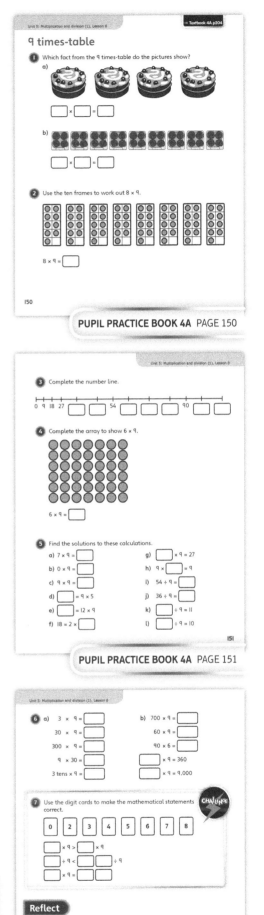

PUPIL PRACTICE BOOK 4A PAGE 150

PUPIL PRACTICE BOOK 4A PAGE 151

PUPIL PRACTICE BOOK 4A PAGE 152

# Multiplying and dividing by 7

## Learning focus

In this lesson, children will learn what it means to multiply and divide by 7. They will apply their knowledge to finding solutions involving real-life contexts.

## Small steps

→ Previous step: 9 times-table
→ **This step: Multiplying and dividing by 7**
→ Next step: 7 times-table

## NATIONAL CURRICULUM LINKS

**Year 4 Number – Multiplication and Division**

Recall multiplication and division facts for multiplication tables up to 12 × 12.

**Year 4 – Measurement**

Solve problems involving converting from hours to minutes; minutes to seconds; years to months; weeks to days.

## ASSESSING MASTERY

Children can rapidly multiply and divide numbers by 7, as well as form multiplication and division sentences. Children can fully understand links between the 7 times-table and other times-tables, such as 5 × 7 = 35 and (5 × 5) + (5 × 2) = 35.

## COMMON MISCONCEPTIONS

Children may make mistakes when counting on or back in 7s. Ask: *How do you count on or back?* Recap this.

Children may get confused with word problems – they may not understand whether they need to multiply or divide. Ask:
• *How can you use a representation to help you understand?*

Children may miscount when counting in 7s. Ask:
• *Is it helpful to count up in 7s on a number line?*

## STRENGTHENING UNDERSTANDING

To strengthen children's knowledge of the 7 times-table, run daily practice of counting in 7s. Try to get support from home.

Ensure that children know the direct link between repeated addition and multiplication (use visual representations, such as the number line).

Another way to strengthen understanding would be to show children multiplication and division sentences and ask them to represent them using counters (model how to put them into an array), for example, 2 × 7 = 14 is 2 rows of 7 counters.

## GOING DEEPER

Challenge children to use multiplication and division facts they know to work out more complicated ones, such as 13 × 7 or 140 ÷ 7. Make sure children explain how they worked out their answers.

## KEY LANGUAGE

**In lesson:** multiply (×), divide (÷), how many, groups, array, number track, ten frames

**Other language to be used by teacher:** number sentence, times-table, equal groups, *x* groups of *y*, count in 7s

## STRUCTURES AND REPRESENTATIONS

number lines, arrays

## RESOURCES

**Mandatory:** base 10 equipment, counters

 In the eTextbook of this lesson, you will find interactive links to a selection of teaching tools.

## Before you teach

• Have you got resources ready to support children?
• How did children get on in the last lesson?
• Which children do you think will need support in this lesson?

# Discover

## Multiplying and dividing by 7

### Discover

**WAYS OF WORKING** Pair work

**ASK**

- Question ① a): *What do you notice about the groups of circles in the painting? How did you know this was a multiplication? Do you have any strategies to find the answers?*
- Question ① b): *How did you know this was a division? Do you have any strategies to find the answers?*

**IN FOCUS** You may want to draw out the difference between multiplying and dividing by 7 by comparing questions ① a) and ① b). Ask children how they know question ① a) is a multiplication. Ask them how they know question ① b) is a division.

**PRACTICAL TIPS** For this activity, if children are counting the individual circles ask them if they can think of a more efficient method.

**ANSWERS**

Question ① a): The painting is called 7s because the circles are in groups of 7s. There are also 7 groups of 7 circles.

There are 35 red circles.

There are 14 blue circles.

There are 49 circles in total.

Question ① b): $28 \div 7 = 4$

There are 4 groups of 7 circles.

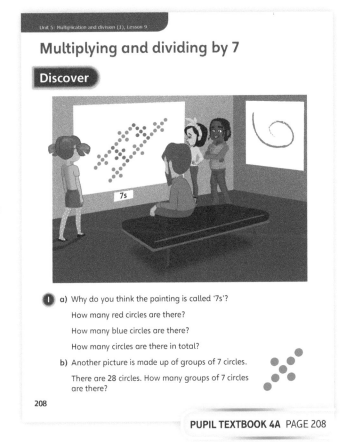

① a) Why do you think the painting is called '7s'?

How many red circles are there?

How many blue circles are there?

How many circles are there in total?

b) Another picture is made up of groups of 7 circles.

There are 28 circles. How many groups of 7 circles are there?

208

**PUPIL TEXTBOOK 4A** PAGE 208

# Share

**WAYS OF WORKING** Whole class teacher led

**ASK**

- Question ① a): *What method is more efficient than to count in groups of 7?*
- Question ① b): *How does the array help you find the solution?*

**IN FOCUS** In question ① b), encourage children to focus on the array. Discuss how it helps us understand the multiplication. It might be useful for you to model the multiplication on a number line and compare how they show multiplications and divisions in slightly different ways.

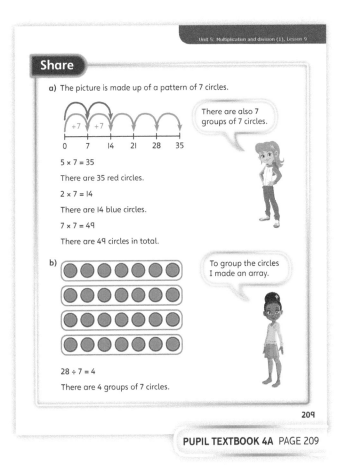

### Share

a) The picture is made up of a pattern of 7 circles.

There are also 7 groups of 7 circles.

$5 \times 7 = 35$

There are 35 red circles.

$2 \times 7 = 14$

There are 14 blue circles.

$7 \times 7 = 49$

There are 49 circles in total.

b) To group the circles I made an array.

$28 \div 7 = 4$

There are 4 groups of 7 circles.

209

**PUPIL TEXTBOOK 4A** PAGE 209

# Think together

**WAYS OF WORKING** Whole class teacher led (I do, We do, You do)

**ASK**
- Question **2**: *Why is 7 × 9 the same as 9 × 7? Is 7 – 9 the same as 9 – 7?*
- Question **3**: *Will you use multiplication or division to help Lexi and Mr Jones?*

**IN FOCUS** When discussing question **2** with children, ask them why there are 2 sets of boxes for the answer. This should lead them on to talking about commutativity: 9 × 7 = 7 × 9.

**STRENGTHEN** For each question, have concrete objects ready for children to group and share, and to help with counting on.

Children who struggle to remember the count sequence for 7s may need a multiplication square.

**DEEPEN** Challenge children to find the odd one out: 714, 7, 77, 97, 105, 140.

**ASSESSMENT CHECKPOINT** Use question **3** to assess whether children can multiply and divide by 7 when in a real-life context.

**ANSWERS**

Question **1**: 5 × 7 = 35

There are 35 circles in total.

Question **2**: 9 × 7 = 63 or 7 × 9 = 63

There are 63 counters in total.

Question **3**: Lexi: 6 × 7 = 42.

There are 42 days in 6 weeks.

6 weeks is longer than 40 days.

Mr Jones: There are 28 days in February.

28 ÷ 7 days in a week = 4 weeks in February.

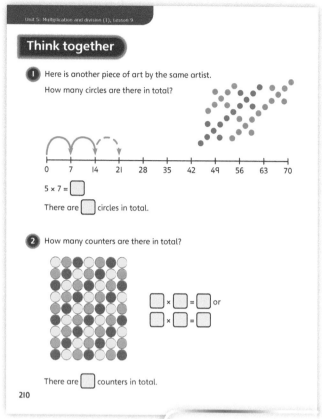

**PUPIL TEXTBOOK 4A** PAGE 210

**PUPIL TEXTBOOK 4A** PAGE 211

## Practice

**WAYS OF WORKING** Independent thinking

**IN FOCUS** Question ④ is a great way to reinforce good practice with numbers. Show children counters placed messily. Ask children to count them. Then show counters placed in neat rows. Ask children to count them again. What do they learn from this exercise?

**STRENGTHEN** Strengthen learning with question ② by running intervention sessions, in which this question is repeated but with different numbers missing. After the task is complete, practise counting out loud – forwards and back – on the number track.

**DEEPEN** Challenge children to explain why a multiple of 70 is always a multiple of 7.

You could also challenge children to answer whether the following statement is correct: 'I do not need to use a written method to know that 7,280 is divisible by 7.'

Alternatively, you may want to provide further problems similar to question ⑤.

**ASSESSMENT CHECKPOINT** Question ⑤ will allow you to assess who has mastered multiplying and dividing by 7. Children who have demonstrated excellent problem-solving skills will work with what they know and complete the steps needed to find the solution.

**ANSWERS** Answers for the **Practice** part of the lesson appear in the separate **Practice and Reflect answer guide**.

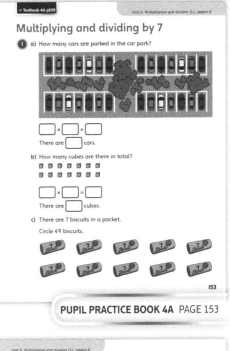

PUPIL PRACTICE BOOK 4A PAGE 153

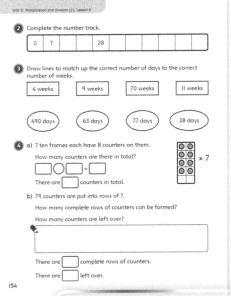

PUPIL PRACTICE BOOK 4A PAGE 154

## Reflect

**WAYS OF WORKING** Pair work

**IN FOCUS** Children should use representations and show their working out, in order to convince their partner that $5 \times 7 = 35$. Children could be given different 7 times-table multiplication facts as a further challenge.

**ASSESSMENT CHECKPOINT** Showing that they understand why $5 \times 7 = 35$ will demonstrate that children understand the 7 times-table.

**ANSWERS** Answers for the **Reflect** part of the lesson appear in the separate **Practice and Reflect answer guide**.

## After the lesson ⏸

- How will you support children who said they found the learning difficult in this lesson?
- What strategies worked well?
- Are you continuing to update your times-table display to promote daily revision?

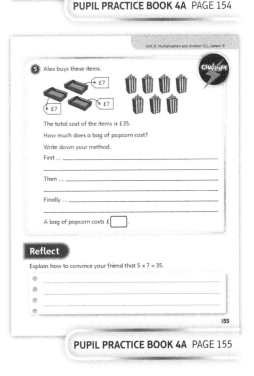

PUPIL PRACTICE BOOK 4A PAGE 155

# 7 times-table

## Learning focus

In this lesson, children will focus on learning their 7 times-table. Children should be able to recite it, and learn the associated multiplication and division facts.

## Small steps

→ Previous step: Multiplying and dividing by 7
→ **This step: 7 times-table**
→ Next step: 11 and 12 times-tables

## NATIONAL CURRICULUM LINKS

**Year 4 Number – Multiplication and Division**

Recall multiplication and division facts for multiplication tables up to 12 × 12.

## ASSESSING MASTERY

Children can demonstrate a rapid recall of multiplication and associated division facts from the 7 times-table. Children can use their knowledge to find solutions and clearly explain how they got to the answers.

## COMMON MISCONCEPTIONS

Children may make mistakes with multiplication facts, such as 7 × 6 = 43. Ask:
• *What would be a good way to revise your times-tables?*

To work out if 8 × 7 is greater or equal to 3 × 7, children may think you have to work out each multiplication fact. Ask children to reason why 8 groups of 7 has to be greater than 3 groups of 7 without calculating. Ask:
• *How could you draw an array to help you?*

Children may also need to be reminded (link back to earlier lessons in this unit) that 1 × 7 = 7 and 0 × 7 = 0. Ask:
• *What do you recall about the learning from earlier in this unit?*

## STRENGTHENING UNDERSTANDING

Times-table facts must be constantly reinforced. Try and reach out to families to support children with home practice. Another good idea is to get older children to come to practise with the class (similar to paired reading but with times-tables).

Provide children with 7 times-table facts and ask children to represent them visually (arrays or number lines work well).

## GOING DEEPER

Challenge children to create some word problems based on the 7 times-table.

## KEY LANGUAGE

**In lesson:** times-table, multiply (×), how many, groups, array, in total, related facts, solution, solving, multiplication facts, division facts, number line, multiplication wheel

**Other language to be used by teacher:** number facts, number sentences

## STRUCTURES AND REPRESENTATIONS

number lines, arrays, multiplication wheel

## RESOURCES

**Mandatory:** base 10 equipment, counters

 In the eTextbook of this lesson, you will find interactive links to a selection of teaching tools.

## Before you teach ⏸

• How will you link the previous lesson to this one?
• Is your learning wall up to date?
• Could you include some visual representations (arrays or number lines) on your learning wall?

## Discover

**WAYS OF WORKING**  Pair work

**ASK**

- Question **1** b): *How do the 5 and 2 times-tables help us?*
- Question **1** b): *How could you combine the arrays to work out the answer?*

**IN FOCUS**  Focus children on the use of arrays to visually show how the 5 and 2 times-tables combined help us with the 7 times-table. Ask children if they can think of other times-tables that could help us with the 7 times-table. (For example, the 4 and 3 times-tables, or the 6 and 1 times-tables.)

**PRACTICAL TIPS**  Show children the 7 times-table on your maths display. Cover up different parts each day: some without answers, some with answers or all of the multiplication missing but the answer given.

Also, you could ask your children to create a visual display for the 7 times-table from arrays.

**ANSWERS**

Question **1** a): 0 × 7 = 0

The 0 × 7 key opens the 0 chest.

4 × 7 = 28

The 4 × 7 key opens the 28 chest.

8 × 7 = 56

The 8 × 7 key opens the 56 chest.

Question **1** b): 14 ÷ 7 = 2

There are 2 groups of 7 in 14.

The 2 × 7 key would open the 14 chest.

## Share

**WAYS OF WORKING**  Whole class teacher led

**ASK**

- Question **1** a): *What multiplied by 7 equals 56?*
- Question **1** a): *Draw arrays for the other treasure chests.*

**IN FOCUS**  For question **1** a) explore with children how the representations help solve the multiplications.

# 7 times-table

## Discover

**1** a) Which treasure chest do you think each key opens?
Explain why.

b) What would be written on the key that opens treasure chest 14?
What about the other chests?

212

**PUPIL TEXTBOOK 4A** PAGE 212

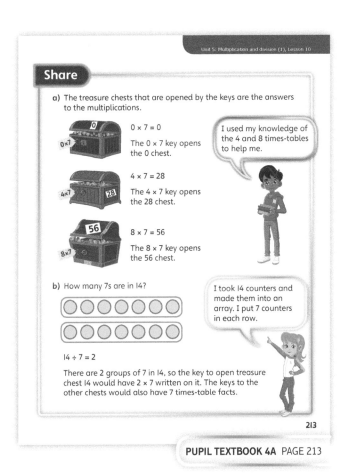

## Share

a) The treasure chests that are opened by the keys are the answers to the multiplications.

0 × 7 = 0
The 0 × 7 key opens the 0 chest.

*I used my knowledge of the 4 and 8 times-tables to help me.*

4 × 7 = 28
The 4 × 7 key opens the 28 chest.

8 × 7 = 56
The 8 × 7 key opens the 56 chest.

b) How many 7s are in 14?

*I took 14 counters and made them into an array. I put 7 counters in each row.*

14 ÷ 7 = 2

There are 2 groups of 7 in 14, so the key to open treasure chest 14 would have 2 × 7 written on it. The keys to the other chests would also have 7 times-table facts.

213

**PUPIL TEXTBOOK 4A** PAGE 213

# Think together

Think together

**WAYS OF WORKING** Whole class teacher led (I do, We do, You do)

**ASK**

- Question ❸: *How do the 2 and 5 times-tables help us?*
- Question ❸ b): *How do you know your answers in this section are correct? Explain your methods.*

**IN FOCUS** Question ❷ presents a good chance to emphasise commutativity. Explain to children that 5 × 7 = 35 and 7 × 5 = 35, so 5 × 7 = 7 × 5. Challenge them to show you the difference using a visual representation, such as by drawing two different arrays.

**STRENGTHEN** Question ❷ is also an excellent opportunity to reinforce children's knowledge of fact families. Repeat this exercise when you get a chance with children who need the reinforcement. Change the starting facts and challenge them to complete the fact family.

**DEEPEN** Challenge children to create some word problems based on the 7 times-table.

**ASSESSMENT CHECKPOINT** Question ❷ will allow you to assess whether children can link multiplication facts for the 7 times-table with related division facts. Look for the correct fact families being found – children should be able to explain them to you.

**ANSWERS**

Question ❶ a): 6 × 7 = 42

Question ❶ b): 1 × 7 = 7 or 7 × 1 = 7

Question ❷ a): 5 × 7 = 35, 7 × 5 = 35, 35 ÷ 7 = 5, 35 ÷ 5 = 7

Question ❷ b): 12 × 7 = 84, 7 × 12 = 84, 84 ÷ 7 = 12, 84 ÷ 12 = 7

Question ❸ a): 6 × 5 = 30 and 6 × 2 = 12, 30 + 12 = 42, so 6 × 7 = 42

Question ❸ b): 9 × 7 = 63

11 × 7 = 77

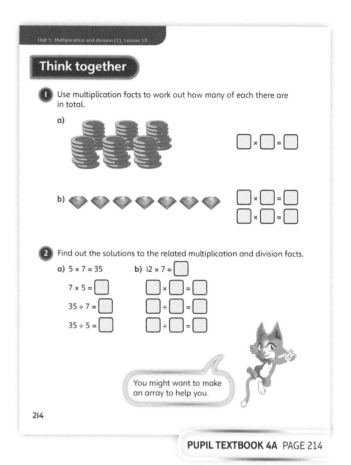

PUPIL TEXTBOOK 4A PAGE 214

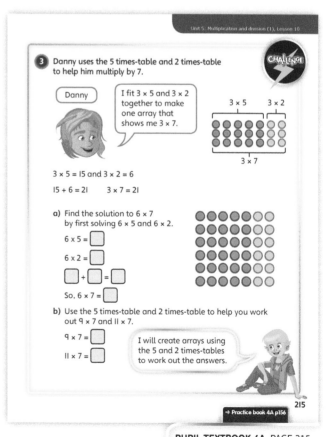

PUPIL TEXTBOOK 4A PAGE 215

## Practice

**WAYS OF WORKING** Independent thinking

**IN FOCUS** In question **4**, some children may need to be reminded what to do when:
- multiplying or dividing by 0
- multiplying or dividing by 1
- dividing a number by itself.

**STRENGTHEN** Throughout this lesson, a key learning point has been matching 7 times-table facts to representations or pictures. It is really important that children can do this. Provide more opportunities to practise for children who need it.

**DEEPEN** Challenge children by giving them some 'would you rather' statements. For example, would you rather have 6 × £7 or (6 × £3) + (6 × £4)?

**THINK DIFFERENTLY** For question **5**, children need to solve multiplications using a multiplication wheel. This different representation may throw some children, so make sure they have understood how it works.

**ASSESSMENT CHECKPOINT** Question **6** will allow you to assess which children have achieved mastery. Look for quick recall of the 7 times-table and the ability to link it to previous learning (multiplying by multiples of 10 and 100).

**ANSWERS** Answers for the **Practice** part of the lesson appear in the separate **Practice and Reflect answer guide**.

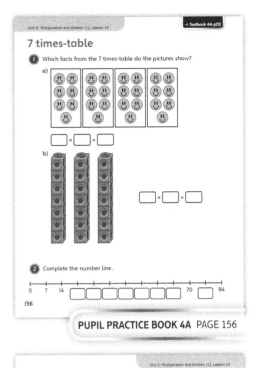

PUPIL PRACTICE BOOK 4A PAGE 156

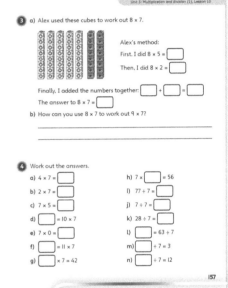

PUPIL PRACTICE BOOK 4A PAGE 157

## Reflect

**WAYS OF WORKING** Pair work

**IN FOCUS** This is a good opportunity to recap the 2, 5 and 7 times-tables and forge links between them all. Some children may still rely on arrays to work out answers – these children will need interventions to progress towards mastery.

**ASSESSMENT CHECKPOINT** Assess children on their reasoning skills – have they made links between the different times-tables?

**ANSWERS** Answers for the **Reflect** part of the lesson appear in the separate **Practice and Reflect answer guide**.

### After the lesson ⏸

- Could you set a home learning challenge?
- Would a class competition encourage children to learn their times-tables?
- Can children make links between the different times-tables?

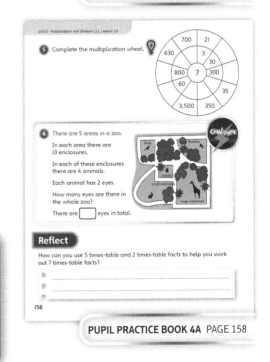

PUPIL PRACTICE BOOK 4A PAGE 158

# 11 and 12 times-tables

## Learning focus

In this lesson, children will focus on learning their 11 and 12 times-tables. Children should be able to recall them quickly, and also learn the associated multiplication and division facts.

## Small steps

→ Previous step: 7 times-table
→ **This step: 11 and 12 times-tables**
→ Next step: Problem solving – addition and multiplication

## NATIONAL CURRICULUM LINKS

**Year 4 Number – Multiplication and Division**

Recall multiplication and division facts for multiplication tables up to 12 × 12.

## ASSESSING MASTERY

Children can demonstrate rapid recall of multiplication and associated division facts from the 11 and 12 times-tables. Children can use their knowledge to find solutions and clearly explain how they got the answers – this may include combining other times-tables, such as the 10 and 2 times-tables to reach the 12 times-table.

## COMMON MISCONCEPTIONS

Children may learn the 11 times-table, but not understand why the number patterns occur, such as 11, 22, 33. Ask:
• *How could you represent the 11 times-table using ten frames?*

Children may make mistakes when counting on or back in 11s or 12s. Ask:
• *How do you count on or back? Perhaps you could use a representation in cubes to help you.*

## STRENGTHENING UNDERSTANDING

Children often struggle with the 12 times-table because of the larger numbers involved. Show them strategies to work out answers, the patterns involved and pair the facts with representations, such as arrays. Ask: *What patterns can you spot in the 12 times-table?* (12, 24, 36, 48: the second numbers are double the first.)

Times-table facts must be constantly reinforced. Run interventions until children become fluent with their recall.

## GOING DEEPER

Challenge children by linking the 11 and 12 times-tables. Ask children to find out how the 12 times-table can be worked out from the 11 times-table.

## KEY LANGUAGE

**In lesson:** times-table, base 10 equipment, number facts, groups, number line, multiply (×), how many, multiplication wheel, divide (÷)

**Other language to be used by teacher:** number sentences, common multiple

## STRUCTURES AND REPRESENTATIONS

number lines, arrays, multiplication wheels

## RESOURCES

**Mandatory:** cubes, base 10 equipment

**Optional:** counters

 In the eTextbook of this lesson, you will find interactive links to a selection of teaching tools.

## Before you teach

• How will you ensure children know all of their times-tables?
• Do children understand the links between different times-tables?
• How will you assess reasoning in this lesson?

## Discover

Unit 5: Multiplication and division (1), Lesson 11

**WAYS OF WORKING** Pair work

**ASK**

- Question **1** a): *How do you know that number is in the 11 times-table?*
- Question **1** b): *How do you know that number is in the 12 times-table?*
- Question **1** b): *Are there any numbers that appear in both the 11 and 12 times-tables?*

**IN FOCUS** Question **1** a): is important because it focuses on finding multiples of 11. In question **1** b) children need to sort the digit cards into two groups: one of numbers in the 11 times-table and one of numbers in the 12 times-table.

**PRACTICAL TIPS** Show the 11 and 12 times-table on your maths display. Cover up different parts each day. You could leave counters on a table for children to make arrays of the 11 or 12 times-tables.

**ANSWERS**

Question **1** a): $2 \times 11 = 22$

$3 \times 11 = 33$

$4 \times 11 = 44$

Question **1** b): 11 times-table: 0, 22, 66, 77, 110, 121, 132

12 times-table: 0, 12, 24, 48, 60, 96, 108, 132, 144

## Share

**WAYS OF WORKING** Whole class teacher led

**ASK**

- Question **1** a): *What patterns can you see in the image?*
- Question **1** a): *What happens when we add 11 to a number?*
- Question **1** b): *Why does 132 appear in both groups?*

**IN FOCUS** For question **1** a), ask children how they know the cubes represent numbers in the 11 times-table. Ask: *What happens every time 11 is added?* You might want to ask certain children to continue the pattern beyond $2 \times 11$, $3 \times 11$, $4 \times 11$. Ask them to create a similar representation for numbers in the 12 times-table.

For question **1** b), highlighting why 132 appears in both groups is important. Explain that it is called a common multiple.

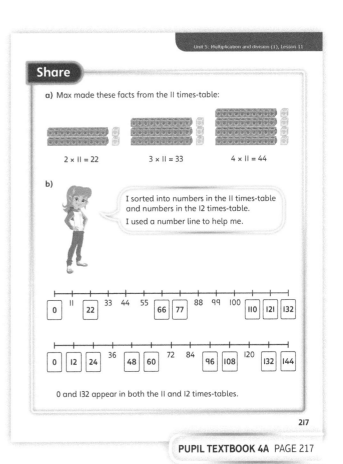

PUPIL TEXTBOOK 4A PAGE 216

PUPIL TEXTBOOK 4A PAGE 217

## Think together

**WAYS OF WORKING** Whole class teacher led (I do, We do, You do)

**ASK**

- Question **3**: *Which of your times-table facts do you remember?*
- Question **3**: *How will you check your friend's answers?*
- Question **3**: *Explain your methods.*

**IN FOCUS** Question **3** is a superb activity for bringing together all of the prior learning in the unit. Children need to remember times-table facts from a variety of times-tables.

**STRENGTHEN** For question **3**, peer-assessing answers is a great way to strengthen learning.

**DEEPEN** Challenge children to create some word problems based on the 11 or 12 times-tables. Also, you could ask children to explain why 11 × 10 isn't 111.

**ASSESSMENT CHECKPOINT** Questions **1** and **2** will allow you to assess whether children can link times-table facts to pictures or representations.

**ANSWERS**

Question **1**: 7 × 11 = 77

Question **2**: 4 × 12 = 48     12 × 4 = 48

Question **3** a): Olivia multiplied 7 × 10 = 70 and 7 × 2 = 14 and then added the two together 70 + 14 = 84. This is the same as 7 × 12 = 84.

Question **3** b): There is more than one way to solve these multiplications (but just one option below):

4 × 12 = 2 × 12 + 2 × 12 = 24 + 24 = 48

9 × 12 = 3 × 12 + 6 × 12 = 36 + 72 = 108

16 × 12 = 10 × 12 + 6 × 12 = 120 + 72 = 192

PUPIL TEXTBOOK 4A PAGE 218

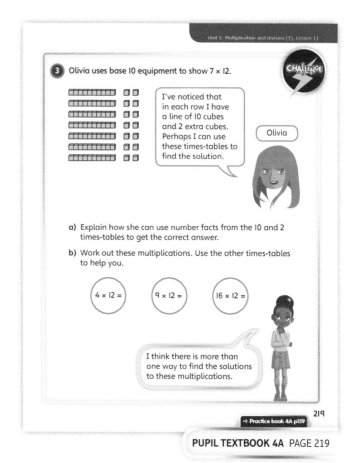

PUPIL TEXTBOOK 4A PAGE 219

# Practice

**WAYS OF WORKING** Independent thinking

**IN FOCUS** Focus on question **5** with children. Finding related facts is an important activity which promotes the application of knowledge. This can lead to mastery of the topic.

**STRENGTHEN** Question **3** has number tracks in which some times-tables are in reverse. Some children may need to be reminded of this – revision of counting on and back might help here.

**DEEPEN** Challenge children to create word problems based on the 11 or 12 times-tables.

**ASSESSMENT CHECKPOINT** Run some spot-checks of all of the times-tables. Can children quickly recall them? Do not limit this to multiplication; include division facts too. Question **5** will give you a good indication of children's confidence, and mastery can be assessed based on whether children can find the related facts.

**ANSWERS** Answers for the **Practice** part of the lesson appear in the separate **Practice and Reflect answer guide**.

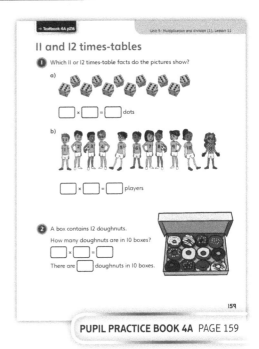

**PUPIL PRACTICE BOOK 4A** PAGE 159

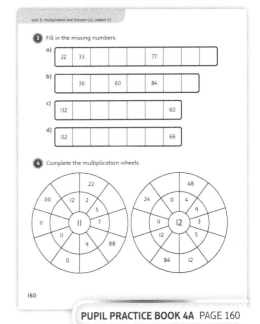

**PUPIL PRACTICE BOOK 4A** PAGE 160

# Reflect

**WAYS OF WORKING** Pair work

**IN FOCUS** Make this reflective exercise into a whole class competition. Children really enjoy times-table races – make it a weekly event – this will really encourage children to learn them.

**ASSESSMENT CHECKPOINT** Listen carefully to children's explanations of the strategies they used. Many will say: 'I just knew it'. Question them on this to encourage deeper thinking.

**ANSWERS** Answers for the **Reflect** part of the lesson appear in the separate **Practice and Reflect answer guide**.

## After the lesson

- Did children complete the times-table grid quickly?
- Which times-tables did children find quickly?
- Now the unit has finished, how can further practice be done?

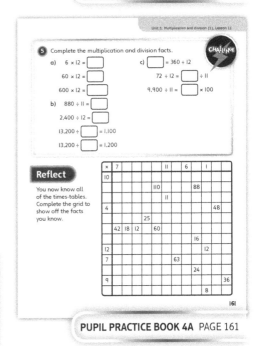

**PUPIL PRACTICE BOOK 4A** PAGE 161

# End of unit check

Don't forget the *Power Maths* unit assessment grid on p26.

**WAYS OF WORKING** Group work adult led

**IN FOCUS** This end of unit check will allow you to focus on children's understanding of times-tables and whether they can apply their knowledge to find solutions.

- Questions **1** and **2** ask children to solve multiplications and divisions where numbers are missing.
- Look carefully at the answer that is given for question **3**. It will tell you if children understand how times-tables can be visually represented.
- Question **4** asks children to solve a multiplication involving the 12 times-table in a measurement context.
- Question **5** asks children to solve a subtraction involving two multiplications. Look for children who notice that they can complete the subtraction first then one multiplication: 9 – 4 = 5, so 5 x 7 = 35.

Question **6** is a SATs-style question, which will prepare children and get them used to the format.

**ANSWERS AND COMMENTARY**

Children who have mastered this unit will be secure with multiplying by multiples of 10 and 100. They will be able to quickly recall times-tables 1 to 12 (including multiplying by 0). They will know related multiplication and division facts and be confident matching multiplication and division facts to visual representations. Also, they will be able to find solutions to multi-step problems from their times-table knowledge.

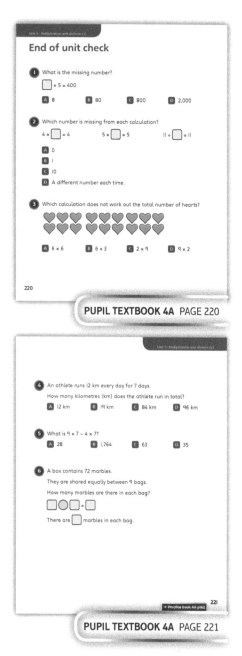

PUPIL TEXTBOOK 4A PAGE 220

PUPIL TEXTBOOK 4A PAGE 221

| Q | A | WRONG ANSWERS AND MISCONCEPTIONS | STRENGTHENING UNDERSTANDING |
|---|---|---|---|
| 1 | B | A or C suggests a misunderstanding of place value. D suggests that children thought this was a division rather than multiplication. | Practical support with place value will strengthen understanding. The use of place value grids may help here. |
| 2 | B | A suggests that children do not understand that multiplying by 0 always equals 0. | Continual practice of multiplication and division facts will lead to mastery. |
| 3 | A | C or D may suggest they do not realise that the hearts can be grouped in different ways, or that children do not understand the rules of commutativity. | Match multiplication and division facts with pictorial representations to strengthen knowledge of their meaning. |
| 4 | C | B suggests that children are adding instead of multiplying. | |
| 5 | B | A or C suggests children have given the answer for part of the multiplication. | |
| 6 | 8 marbles | Watch for children who have made errors when calculating – they may need their knowledge of times-tables strengthening. | |

# My journal

**WAYS OF WORKING** Independent thinking

**ANSWERS AND COMMENTARY**

Question **1** Children will work individually to write their response, having discussed the problem in pairs or small groups beforehand. Encourage children to think through this section before writing their answer.

45 ÷ £3 = 15, so Jamilla could buy 15 small presents. Or, for example: 2 large presents £9 × 2 = £18, 3 medium presents £6 × 3 = £18 and 3 small presents £3 × 3 = £9; £18 + £18 + £9 = £45. There are other correct answers. Children will need to use their knowledge of the 3, 6 and 9 times-tables.

Question **2** Children may know the correct answer, but may find it challenging to write the reason why. Support children with key vocabulary to use and structuring an answer for them.

A: 6 × 7 = 42
   7 books cost £42

B: 48 ÷ 6 = 8
   Each child receives 8 sweets.

C: 90 ÷ 9 = 10
   I can buy 10 board games.

D: 2 × 9 × 9 = 162
   9 bags weigh 162 kg.

# Power check

**WAYS OF WORKING** Independent thinking

**ASK**

- *What times-tables do you know that you did not at the start of the unit?*
- *What kinds of multiplication and division problems can you do now that you could not at the start of the unit?*
- *What new words have you learnt and what do they mean?*
- *How can you use visual representations to show grouping and sharing?*

# Power puzzle

**WAYS OF WORKING** Pair work

**IN FOCUS** Use this **Power puzzle** to assess children's knowledge and the speed of their times-table recall. Ask them to explain their methods or any strategies they used. Children take turns to time each other and then mark the answers.

**ANSWERS AND COMMENTARY** If children can do the puzzle successfully, then it means they can quickly recall multiplication and division facts. You will have to listen to the explanations of their strategies to assess whether they understand what they mean.

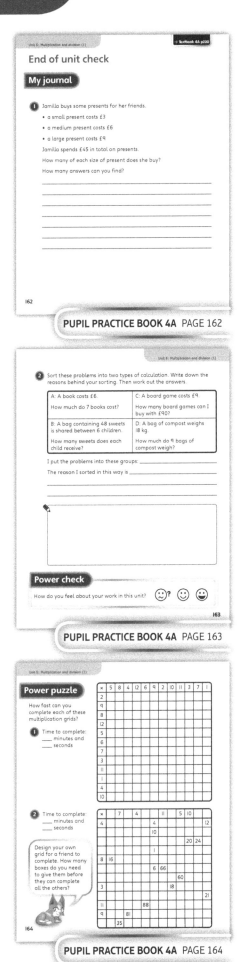

**PUPIL PRACTICE BOOK 4A** PAGE 162

**PUPIL PRACTICE BOOK 4A** PAGE 163

**PUPIL PRACTICE BOOK 4A** PAGE 164

# After the unit ⏸

- Have children got rapid recall of their multiplication facts?
- Do they know related division facts?

**Strengthen** and **Deepen** activities for this unit can be found in the *Power Maths* online subscription.

Published by Pearson Education Limited, 80 Strand, London, WC2R 0RL.

www.pearsonschools.co.uk

Text © Pearson Education Limited 2018
Edited by Pearson, Little Grey Cells Publishing Services and Haremi Ltd
Designed and typeset by Kamae Design
Original illustrations © Pearson Education Limited 2018
Illustrated by Laura Arias, John Batten, Paul Moran and Nadene Naude at Beehive Illustration; and Kamae.
Cover design by Pearson Education Ltd
Back cover illustration © Diago Diaz and Nadene Naude at Beehive Illustration.

Series Editor: Tony Staneff
Consultants: Professor Liu Jian and Professor Zhang Dan

The rights of Tony Staneff, Josh Lury, Neil Jarrett, Stephen Monaghan, Beth Smith and Paul Wrangles to be identified as authors of this work have been asserted by them in accordance with the Copyright, Designs and Patents Act 1988.

First published 2018

22 21 20 19
10 9 8 7 6 5 4 3

**British Library Cataloguing in Publication Data**
A catalogue record for this book is available from the British Library

ISBN 978 0 435 19018 7

**Copyright notice**
Pearson Education Ltd 2018

Printed in Great Britain by Ashford Colour Press Ltd.

www.activelearnprimary.co.uk

**Note from the publisher**
Pearson has robust editorial processes, including answer and fact checks, to ensure the accuracy of the content in this publication, and every effort is made to ensure this publication is free of errors. We are, however, only human, and occasionally errors do occur. Pearson is not liable for any misunderstandings that arise as a result of errors in this publication, but it is our priority to ensure that the content is accurate. If you spot an error, please do contact us at resourcescorrections@pearson.com so we can make sure it is corrected.